PORQUE ESTAMOS AQUÍ

PORQUE ESTAMOS AQUÍ

Puerto Rican Feminisms Against Empire

EDITED BY
JESSICA NYDIA PABÓN-COLÓN

Published in 2025 by the Feminist Press
at the City University of New York
The Graduate Center
365 Fifth Avenue, Suite 6200
New York, NY 10016

feministpress.org

First Feminist Press edition 2025

This book is made possible by the New York State Council on the Arts with the support of the Office of the Governor and the New York State Legislature.

First printing November 2025

Cover design by Sukruti Anah Staneley
Cover photograph by David T Diaz, Four Two Photography
Text design by Drew Stevens

Library of Congress Cataloging-in-Publication Data is available for this title.
ISBN 978-1-55861-360-7

PRINTED IN THE UNITED STATES OF AMERICA

for all who dream of and labor
for liberation from empire

Contents

PART V. OUR STRATEGIES

Reaching for Rican Feminisms: Introduction to a Rematriation Project

JESSICA N. PABÓN-COLÓN

Maria. Norma. Migdalia. Nydia. Felicita. The Boricuas who raised me did not identify themselves as feminists of color, articulate an anti-colonial consciousness, or bring me to protests or rallies. They did not educate me in the sociopolitical details that would historically situate both my paternal and maternal families' displacements—from the mountains in Borikén (colonial name: Puerto Rico) to the housing projects built on the traditional lands of the Massachusett peoples (colonial name: Boston, Massachusetts). They did not position our embodied and spiritual cultural practices—bomba, plena, santería—as assertions of Puerto Ricanness protecting us from complete USian assimilation or as part of a radical Afro-Indigenous Puerto Rican tradition. They did not identify with the term *feminista* or lay claim to feminist movement. And yet, there is no doubt that they planted the seeds to my Rican feminist political consciousness each time they shared their memories of living as Brown, poor, Spanish-speaking children of a single, undereducated mother trying to survive the racist, sexist violences they routinely experienced after migrating to 1960s South Boston.

Maria, my mother, taught me how sometimes survival means manipulating the systems built to subjugate people like us, how to be unapologetic about desire and sexuality, and how to begin anew after fleeing gender-based violence. Her eldest sister, tití Norma, taught me how to dance my way through the drudgeries of a double day as a working mother, how to release anxiety, stress, and trauma by moving my body to a beat—preferably with a group willing to sing along. Their younger sister, tití Migdalia, taught me how to bravely leave home to blaze my own educational path, to find my own community in which to thrive; she continues to model these lessons through her activism and leadership as part of the deaf, deafblind, and hard of hearing community in Minnesota. Their mamí, abuela Nydia, taught me how to harden myself so as to not be taken advantage of, how to express my love and care by cooking and feeding others, and how to proudly be of service to family and community. Abuela Felicita—my paternal grandmother—taught me how to meet pain with love, how to cultivate joy and softness under repressive and depressive conditions. Each lesson lives in my bodymind, arising and taking shape in anticipation of, or in response to, the shifting conditions of my everyday life as a queer diasporic Puerto Rican feminist hermana, mamí, y tití.

Reaching for Ricanness in Feminist Studies

I came to know and claim feminism as an eighteen-year-old first-generation college student within a women's studies classroom. There, I learned about structural racism. I came to understand how my and my families' experiences with poverty and public assistance, drug and alcohol addiction, and police brutality and incarceration were not simply the personal failings of individuals who made bad choices, but rather "choices" made under duress in a white supremacist system built to predetermine the life chances of minoritized communities. I learned the value of examining those life experiences through the lens of "the personal is political."

My understanding of the power of feminist thought deepened as a graduate student wrestling post-structuralist theory—a fancy, often jargon-laden way of doing critical analysis that underlines how every facet of our subjectivities is contingent and constructed, disciplined and punished, stylized and rehearsed to the point of naturalization. I learned that the identities we cling to are not a matter of essence but constituted through language, social conventions, and institutions like school and church. Further, that those same institutions are *deeply* invested in Enlightenment-era values of ordering the "chaos" of difference through creating, legislating, and enforcing categories and hierarchies of value. And though the language of this critical theory can be wildly inaccessible, I came to understand how naming theoretical frameworks and political strategies can activate and galvanize the collective awakening needed for social justice movement.

Between 1997 and 2004, I was not just studying academic feminism but also participating in campaigns led by liberal feminist organizations (e.g., Feminist Majority Foundation and NARAL Pro-Choice America[1]) and consuming the capitalist "girl power feminism" that was taking over popular culture—all largely defined by and deferential to an unnamed *imperial* white feminism. Though the Feminist Majority Foundation's Stop Gender Apartheid campaign launched in 1997, for example, aspects of their liberal feminist project moved into the mainstream after the events of September 11, 2001. Indian American scholar and activist Deepa Kumar points to mainstream feminist support for the war on Afghanistan as a point of "resurgence" for colonial and imperial feminisms via liberal feminism.[2] The call to action rested on the idea that (white) feminists in the Global North had a more robust analysis of Afghani women's situation than Afghani women themselves and therefore had a moral responsibility to "liberate" them. Kumar writes, "Liberals and feminists in the US, going against the wishes of Afghan feminist organizations such as RAWA (Revolutionary Association of the Women of Afghanistan) who opposed US intervention, linked arms with the Bush administration and supported the Afghan war."[3] Some of the same feminists who had voiced their staunch opposition to the Bush administration were now celebrating US occupation. Then–First Lady Laura Bush gave a radio address in November 2001 in which she glorified the US invasion, exploiting the precarious material conditions of women and children (lack of food, healthcare, and education) to rally support.[4] There was no critique of US economic interests in the region, nor any mention of how US support of Islamic fundamentalism contributed to the very conditions in Afghanistan that the war was supposedly ameliorating. Instead, she warned listeners, "we see the world the terrorists would like to impose on the rest of us,"[5] and let Islamophobia and xenophobia take it from there.

Had the interventions of Third World and women of color feminisms then been the dominant mode for analysis and action, perhaps we would have recognized how a feminist commitment to dismantling patriarchy was being manipulated in service to a patriarchal empire. Call it the savior complex, call it manifest destiny, the logic is the same and remains deeply embedded in the minds of US citizens. Propelled by a belief in American exceptionalism, for US feminists it seems to be much more alluring to look abroad for gender- or sexuality-based injustices than it is to take stock of how the evils of white supremacist empire function domestically.

While national attention was fixed on Afghanistan, Puerto Rican protesters were once again fighting for land, sea, and the living conditions of the people in Vieques. From 1941 when the US Navy relocated residents at gunpoint to a different part of the island until 2003 when then-President Bush ended military operations there, Vieques had been abused as a training and testing ground—decimating the environment, making residents sick, and in some cases killing them.[6] Standing alongside grassroots organizations like the Alianza de Mujeres Viequenses[7] on the front lines of the ecological struggle for land back in the early aughts was nationalist Dolores "Lolita" Lebrón Sotomayor—the woman US news media deemed "the terror that wore [red] lipstick" after her participation in the 1954 armed action for Puerto Rican independence at the United States Capitol. In 2001, eighty-two-year-old Lebrón, "easily the best-known Puerto Rican woman of the twentieth century,"[8] was arrested with fellow protesters for acts of civil disobedience. We might be tempted to wonder why mainstream feminist organizations weren't (at minimum) publicly supportive of these actions. But if we consider that many of the critiques missing from the Stop Gender Apartheid campaign were at the very root of the Vieques mass mobilizations against occupation and militarization, it's plain to see why the feminist activists in and of Vieques received no such solidarity from the non-Rican mainstream feminist community. I offer Lebrón as an example not to tokenize her further but to emphasize that this was not a quiet struggle led by unknown individuals and groups; Lebrón's historical notoriety belies any excuses on those terms. Taking her as an example for Rican feminist activism, we learn at least two things: (1) when you fight systems as an anti-colonial feminist, you run the risk of being labeled a terrorist by the colonial government, and (2) the US government will continue calling *us* the terrorists—even though they are the ones buying, selling, and dropping bombs that scorch the earth and murder civilians—as long as we are fighting for liberation from empire. And perhaps the third lesson we learn is: Que se joda! We're doing it anyway. Pa' Puerto Rico.

Puerto Rico has been a colony of the United States since Spain (our first colonizer) ceded the territory in 1898. For 127 years and counting, the Puerto Rican archipelago has been systematically treated like a commodity ever-available for wealth extraction, and our people treated like disposable, insubordinate children unable to self-govern. The stories, struggles, and contributions of Puerto Rican feminists are forgotten in curriculums, conversations, and narratives about liberation praxis across the Americas, partially due to the archipelago's sociopolitical status as a "territory" and the people's ambiguous status as sorta-citizens: with some rights, depending on location. From the vantage point of an imperial white feminist ideology operating in the Global North, Puerto Rican feminists have been and are too "of color" no matter our pigmentation, too loud to be civil, too much to be included, too different to be the same, and too distracted by race, ethnicity, and nation to be proper subjects of feminist movement. In the story they tell by *not* telling it, Puerto Rican feminists have no leaders worth mentioning. No warriors. No legacy. No specific struggles that would characterize Puerto Rican feminisms as, well, Puerto Rican.

We have so many anti-colonial, anti-sexist, anti-racist heroes to learn from, and yet, when we look to feminist movement narratives as taught in gender studies curriculums across the contiguous United States, Puerto Rican feminisms and feminists appear—if we do at all—as tokens or victims in a far too simple story about forced sterilization that negates the family planning advocacy of Puerto Rican feminists themselves.[9] Puerto Rican feminists disappear from feminist thinking and doing in the US because we are misbehaving colonial subjects who reveal the hypocrisy of US claims to progress, freedom, and democracy—the bedrock of liberal feminist practice.

Instead of uncritically celebrating Margaret Sanger, for example, as the founder of Planned Parenthood and a champion of the birth control movement,[10] we might situate her "feminist" advocacy in relation to her belief in the ableist and white supremacist logic of eugenics. To make oral contraceptives a reality for women like her, she collaborated with white men who happily sacrificed the health of Puerto Rican women who were the unknowing subjects of their medical trials. To hold white feminist favorites such as Sanger (and Stanton) accountable, we have to proceed with the knowledge that settler colonialism and racial slavery form the rotten roots of US liberal feminism.

Liberal feminism continues the work of imperial white feminism under a "new," less obvious name. We can think of the rebranding as a kind of echo to that 1914 choice to move away from describing Puerto Rico (along with Guam, the Philippines, American Samoa, Hawai'i, and Wake) as a colony and instead a territory. Citing a government official writing that "the word colony must not be used to express the relationship which exists between our government and its dependent peoples," historian Daniel Immerwahr breaks it down: "Better to stick with a gentler term, used for them all: territories."[11] There is a common misunderstanding that white feminism refers only to the phenotype of the feminist when in fact it refers to a way of imagining and doing feminism through and for white supremacy.[12] *You do not have to be racially white or ethnically European to enact and reinforce an imperial white feminism on and in the world.* It is far too easy, especially in the absence of focused study on feminist of color interventions, to get pulled into an imperial white feminist agenda that masquerades as *the* feminist agenda. The ongoing work for feminists in the Global North is to recognize when imperial white feminism hails us, and refuse the call. If you're down for it, Rican feminisms will lead the way.

Reaching for a Kind of *Un*definition for Rican Feminisms

In *Feminism Is for Everybody: Passionate Politics*,[13] Black feminist bell hooks wrote about her frustration every time someone described feminism as a man-hating project of angry white women. Her greatest desire in those moments was to have an accessible book that she could simply hand to someone needing a more expansive and accurate accounting of feminist politics. To alleviate her frustration and satisfy that desire, she wrote the book she needed. *Porque Estamos Aquí: Puerto Rican Feminisms Against Empire* is the result of me reaching for the book on Rican feminisms that I needed and the contributors to the anthology reaching back.

What are Puerto Rican feminisms? Boricua feminisms? What makes a feminist act a *Puerto Rican* feminist act? As a performance studies scholar who thinks of feminism as a verb (something we do, something defined by the actions we take),[14] I struggle with the rigid expectation that a "definition" reinforces. If what hooks needed was an easy-to-understand book that provided a stable definition of feminism as ending "sexism, sexist exploitation, and oppression,"[15] for me what is needed to illuminate the contours of Puerto Rican feminisms is multiplicity, fluidity, and elasticity, a kind of *un*definition we feel our way toward. Not all Puerto Rican feminists experience our feminism or our Ricanness[16] in the same way, and so I engaged my inquiry into Rican feminisms as something we embody, something we generate, something that is at once individual and collective, something that looks to the past while driving a collective decolonized future.

Spoken word poet Mariposa (María Teresa Fernández) was the first to lure me into something that felt like Rican feminist comradery with her 2007 poem "Diasporican," where she rejects rigid notions of authentic Puerto Rican identity based on place of birth and instead invites us to feel into her process of identification as a New York Puerto Rican.[17] Nuyorican poet and playwright Caridad De La Luz, aka La Bruja, brings Puerto Rican multiplicity into focus while grounding us in a shared relation to our cultura, our comunidad, and our comida with her 2005 Spanglish album *Brujalicious*. Writing about how some folks run their meat under water before cooking it, others use vinegar, and still others simply rinse and pat down with a paper towel, California-based chef and journalist Illyanna Maisonet reassures us that fluidity in practice (rather than rigidity) allows us to come closer to ourselves and each other: "If you feel like washing your meat is keeping you closer to your ancestors, wash on, Sis."[18] Just as there is not one way to look like a Puerto Rican, speak like a Puerto Rican, or cook like a Puerto Rican, there is not one rigid way to enact a Puerto Rican feminism. That said, there are of course experiences, perspectives, and ancestral connections that make us Puerto Ricans, Puerto Rican.

Revisiting the work of Black feminist Patricia Hill Collins helped me find the balance between wanting to offer a definition as a starting place for generating a politic based on our identities and actions, and knowing the dangers of essentializing ourselves as people of color too often reduced to racist stereotypes. In her work "Defining Black Feminist Thought,"[19] she models how to trace common ground, arguing that we can access the potential in a collective consciousness developed from those shared or similar experiences. From what I've embodied, experienced, observed, and studied, Puerto Rican feminisms:

— move from the understanding that Puerto Rico is a colony of the United States, that Puerto Ricans—regardless of where we live—are colonial subjects uniquely positioned in relation to our empirical rulers in the north and to our comrades in the Caribbean and to the south in Latin America;

— bridge the natural (land, sea) and manmade (geopolitical borders, language barriers, religious beliefs) divides separating our people;
— reject liberal cries for individual equality over systemic equity, do not prioritize a fight for rights conferred by systems built to oppress, and instead labor toward sovereignty;
— value the accountability enabled by direct communication and transparency;
— confront the ongoing displacement of our people and dispossession of our land;
— build familia beyond white cisgender heterosexual nationalist patriarchal norms;
— revel in sound and movement, take joy and pleasure in creative unconventional resistance practices; and
— are in reciprocal relation to other feminisms of difference, such as Palestinian feminism, Black feminism, Crip feminism, Chicana feminism, Indigenous feminism, queer feminism, and Pacific Islander feminism.

Before the work of curating a collective voice in service to identifying a Rican feminist consciousness, however, came the work of community building.

Reaching for Rican Feminisms in Practice

Motherhood opened a portal to claiming a specific Rican feminism that I had let go of years before.[20] Suddenly, I was solely responsible for imparting the Ricanness, what Rican feminist scholar Sandra Ruiz defines as "a continual performance of bodily endurance against US colonialism,"[21] that I learned in community, surrounded by family, to my child. I knew that because I was working at a predominantly white institution in a predominantly white area of the Hudson Valley, learning in community with other Ricans would not be his experience. A DiaspoRican born of a DiaspoRican, I wanted him to have a frame of reference, a deep awareness that we exist, that we come from a land rich in history and culture that is both a part of and apart from the United States. Trying to narrate my experiences as a bisexual feminist Boricua mother (now married to a cis white man), I published an essay about my struggles instilling a sense of Brownness[22] and gender fluidity in my child within a society that wanted them to claim whiteness and embody cissexist gender norms, a society that teaches binaries, opposites, and ultimatums instead of spectrums, horizons, or spirals. The work of claiming my Rican feminism was slow, cautious, vulnerable, and mostly relegated to publicly inaccessible spaces like scholarly journals and academic conferences.

In late August of 2017, my friend Anita Sarkeesian[23] asked if I would "leave a message" on the *Feminist Answering Machine*—her latest *Feminist Frequency* vlog-style miniseries, where feminists simulate a kind of visual voicemail to offer their opinion on a topic of their choice. Initially, I planned on using my sixty seconds to talk about fortifying our feminist selves in the (first) Tr*mp era with care practices not tied to capitalist consumption. But before I could record and send that message, two hurricanes hit Borikén: a Category 5 (Irma) on September 6 and a Category 4 (Maria) on September 20. These back-to-back storms, and the earthquakes that followed, have become cultural touchpoints to mark what we've collectively and increasingly felt: the need to wake up to our colonial conditions, to the violence of austerity measures, to the ways the colonial government wants to turn the archipelago into a Puerto Rico without Puerto Ricans. Bad Bunny's 2025 album *DeBÍ TiRAR MáS FOToS* is a contemporary example amplifying this point. Topping world music charts with the song "DeBÍ TiRAR MáS FOToS"—a traditional Puerto Rican plena—his anti-colonial artistry calls out: Despierta Boricua!

Visiting the archipelago weeks after Irma and Maria made landfall, then-President Tr*mp complained about how much money the destruction in PR was costing the US government, insinuated that the people were the problem, and then tossed paper towels at the crowd waiting for supplies at a disaster relief station in San Juan like some kind of "benevolent" overlord.[24] There was no fortification practice that could have braced me for the rage I felt in that moment. Moved to action by the cries for help coming from the archipelago, my slow, cautious work became urgent, assertive, visceral.

At the beginning of that same year, feminists had shattered records by taking to the streets for the Women's Marches—events that will forever be remembered by the controversial pink "pussy hats" worn as a sartorial performance of resistance to Tr*mp's predatorial assertion that men can just "grab [women] by the pussy."[25] But by the end of the year, in the wake of the highly visible conditions following the hurricanes, those same feminist leaders had nothing to say about FEMA's failures, structural abandonment, or the legislative cruelty (e.g., not pausing the Jones Act) that made those conditions worse, causing the unnecessary deaths of nearly five thousand Puerto Ricans.

Still tasked with recording a selfie-style video for Anita's podcast, I felt the best message I could send to other feminists in that moment was a call to action: "Where Are the Pussy Hats for Puerto Rico?!" (fig. 1). The video went live on her YouTube channel on November 3, 2017:

> I've got a *serious* question for my fellow feminists: where *are* you? Hurricane Maria hit Puerto Rico on September 20—devastating an already crumbling infrastructure. Since then, the island has been without power, adequate communication, potable water, and food—my people are dying

Figure 1. Screengrab from "Where Are the Pussy Hats for Puerto Rico?" on *Feminist Answering Machine* vlog.

> preventable deaths while Forty-Five turns a blind eye to what's essentially a genocide shaped and enabled by the colonial condition.
>
> As a Boricua in the diaspora, active in feminist movement for twenty years and counting, I want to know: where's the feminist rage? Where're the *3 to 5 million* feminists who marched in January? Even if their feminism only emerges in relation to sexual assault, abortion, or domestic violence, they have to know that those concerns are exacerbated under these conditions. The disaster in Puerto Rico IS a feminist issue.
>
> So for those that fancy themselves feminists: It's time to perform that feminism on behalf of the people of Puerto Rico. Do it in your pussy hat decorated with a Puerto Rican flag pin if you must, but *do something* or you're no better than the man you say you're resisting.[26]

Any hesitancy to claim my Rican feminism was replaced by empowerment, and my effort here was meant to hold complicit and apathetic feminists accountable for their collective failure to come together and respond to the conditions of their Rican "sisters" in that moment.

The following week, I spent my thirty-eighth birthday devising an imperfect action plan for the next National Women's Studies Association (NWSA) conference, which was only five days away. I wanted to offer tangible items to raise awareness and relief funds; I made T-shirts and designed an infographic. To put together the infographic, I drew on two information and advocacy projects led by Rican feminists: Puerto Rico Syllabus[27] and PR on the Map.[28] The Puerto Rico Syllabus is an online resource that had the initial goal of placing the debt crisis "within the larger political, social, and economic history of

Figure 2. Feminists for Puerto Rico logo.

this US territory"; now the syllabus has grown to include background material to put Hurricane Maria and El Verano Boricua in context.[29] Assembled by Yarimar Bonilla, Marisol LeBrón, Sarah Molinari, Isabel Guzzardo Tomago, and Kimberly Roa, the resources made available there figured prominently in my self-education in Puerto Rican studies. And through referencing the PR on the Map media project assembled by Rosa Clemente—who's been on my radar since her 2016 vice presidential run on the Green Party ticket—I was able to recommend outlets for people looking to help, including a list of vetted organizations that would ensure donations would *actually* reach the people who needed them in Borikén.[30]

I named the action Feminists for Puerto Rico (FPR) and designed a logo that combined the black-and-white Puerto Rican flag used since 2016 to visually signify the debt crisis and resistance to US colonial power over the archipelago's financial affairs (thanks, Obama), the "women's symbol" fist popularized by the women's movement in the 1970s and still widely used in feminist protest, and the shape of the archipelago's mainland (fig. 2). I printed the logo on black-and-white baseball T-shirts and set off for the conference.

On the night of the conference keynote—a conversation between Angela Davis and Alicia Garza moderated by then-NWSA President Barbara Ransby—seven friends helped me hand out 1,250 fliers; we placed them on chairs and handed them to folks as they entered the auditorium. On Saturday night, feeling vulnerable but determined to reach for solidarity among other feminists of color, I read a poem called "Micropoems Para Mi Gente" at the Women of Color Caucus's Open Mic event. Originally a series of tweets, I wrote the poem as a love letter to the children forced to leave the archipelago in the aftermath of Hurricane Maria.

On the last day of the conference, I drove to the Unity March for Puerto Rico in DC with four strangers in tow: three white allies and one fellow Boricua. I was sharing my anxieties about leading FPR and engaging Rican Studies when one of the passengers, H. Rakes, remarked: "Do you know Aurora Levins Morales? You would love her work!" I scanned my memory banks and came up empty. Back home, I did what I imagine any scholar would do in this situation, and I combed my bookshelf. Certainly, I thought, I do know, I am just forgetting. I pulled my favorite anthologies from my shelf: *This Bridge Called My Back*[31] and *Telling to Live*.[32] And there they were. The feminists living in and fighting against empire that I know now to consider ancestors and elders: Rosario Morales. Liza Fiol-Matta. Celia Alvarez. Caridad Souza. Aurora Levins Morales. Luz del Alba Acevedo. Iris Ofelia López.

As I revisited their essays, I reveled in the familiarity of their words and experiences. Caridad Souza's take on being called a crazy Rican, a loca, for both inhabiting and challenging "proper" Puerto Rican womanhood spoke directly to my sense of self. I'd had this term *loca* thrown at me entirely too often; the term is steeped in racialized sexist colloquialisms about Puerto Rican women assaulting you (with a machete or a chancla) because we are mentally unwell, fiery, and passionate, and wielded as a weapon against women by Ricans and non-Ricans alike. Coming from strangers, it is meant to sexualize and silence you. Coming from intimate relations, it is used like a term of endearment that works to tame the "wild" inside of you. Either way, and regardless of intention, the term attempts to shrink a Rican feminist presence in a world that barely recognizes our existence to begin with. We can take the power back when we identify with the term, knowing that being loca might be the only reasonable response to a white supremacist capitalist patriarchal society. When, as our radical women of color maestras Cherríe Moraga y Gloria Anzaldúa taught us, we "reflect our color loud and clear, not tone it down."[33]

Why had I forgotten about these essays that had affected me so deeply? Why had their names disappeared from my mind? What would it take for Puerto Rican feminists, wherever and whenever we are, to see each other? To remember each other? "I found most of these women in footnotes and appendices, in single lines buried in books about men."[34] In her book *Remedíos: Stories of Earth and Iron from the History of Puertorriquenas* (2001), Aurora Levins Morales writes about her struggle finding women in historical renderings of Puerto Rican resistance, endurance, and life. Levins Morales's quote takes on a different resonance when we consider that the stories of Rican feminisms that I want told are not simply buried in books about men. Perhaps more problematically, they've been buried in or excluded from books about feminism. In her 2016 TED talk, while explaining that we need an intersectional lens to understand that Black women are targets of not only gendered

Figure 3. Denise Oliver Velez speaking at Bard College, 2017. Courtesy of the author.

but also racialized violence, Kimberlé Crenshaw explains: "These women's names have slipped through our consciousness because there are no frames for us to see them, no frames for us to remember them, no frames for us to hold them."[35] (Though decades old at that point, the concept of intersectionality circulated widely on social media leading up to and especially in the aftermath of the 2017 Women's Marches.) Because complex feminist critiques and modes of analysis are taken out of context and simplified as they circulate in memes, GIFs, and viral social media videos, one of the outcomes was a reproduction of a Black feminism / white feminism binary more reliant on racial categorization than concerned with interrogating the intersections at which differently located feminists meet on the matrix of oppression. Whether we want to be or not, Rican feminisms exist in relation to contiguous-US feminisms; the relationship is difficult, but it is there—like that homophobic aunt who you still invite over for dinner. Because the frame of US feminism is so deeply intertwined with US nationalism and settler-colonial logics, there is no room for a feminism "in" the US that works against the interests of US empire.

In the spring of 2018, I took a day trip to the Lesbian Herstory Archives in Brooklyn with a group of my LGBTQIA+ students. Casually looking through the archival boxes, I found one containing material from Black lesbian activist scholar Barbara Smith—a founding member of the Combahee River Collective. In that box, I found a yellow legal pad full of writings from her reproductive justice organizing work in 1977, including drafts of speeches that she wrote advocating for the liberation of women in Borikén.

The year prior, my Black feminist colleague, former Young Lord Denise

Oliver-Velez, graciously accepted my invitation to speak at a fundraiser for hurricane relief organized by Ariana Gonzalez-Stokas at Bard College. I knew Denise would model feminist solidarity and remind folks that though she herself was not Boricua, she would always have Puerto Rico en su corazón (fig. 3):

> Most Americans don't even know that Puerto Ricans are American citizens. Most Americans don't know how we made Puerto Rico a colony in the first place! Most of us are not taught about one-third of the women on the island of Puerto Rico being sterilized by our government. We are not taught about the island of Vieques, which our US navy bombed year after year after year. 'Cause it isn't in the textbooks.[36]

Building a frame strong enough to hold the development of Puerto Rican feminisms across generations and geographies requires—at minimum—that we think Rican feminisms in a way that identifies our kinship to the Black and Indigenous feminisms of the United States and beyond.[37]

After exhausting (as far as they knew) the availability of indigenous Taíno stolen labor (*not* to the point of extinction, contrary to popular narratives), Spaniards of the late 1500s and early 1600s increasingly enslaved Africans to work their sugar plantations.[38] Not all Puerto Ricans can trace an African lineage or Indigenous ancestral belonging, but we collectively share a history of displacement, enslavement, exploitation, racialization, and sexualization. Our strength lies in appreciating our co-constitution while acknowledging how we've been repeatedly pitted against one another in service to the ruling class. Perhaps because we are always already in relation, queer and feminist of color herstories are more likely to include Puerto Ricans in the development and articulation of feminism. And though things seem to be getting "better" in terms of the way feminisms of color are valued in mainstream feminist movement and institutionalized feminism in the academy since I entered in 1997, Puerto Rican feminisms and feminists have yet to emerge from the herstorical margins in a significant way.

Reaching for Rican Feminist Communities

In the fall of 2018, one year after Hurricane Maria, I went to my first Puerto Rican Studies Association (PRSA) conference. My Rican feminist comrades Ariana Gonzalez Stokas and Claudia Sofía Garriga-López and I proposed a workshop titled "Diasporicans Decolonizing Academia / Decolonizing Diasporicans in Academia," with the rationale that, put simply, we needed each other. The decolonial urge to repair bonds broken by colonization led us to imagine a session where we would use somatic exercises to connect

DiaspoRicans in the academy who are too often isolated as the only Ricans in their programs, departments, schools. Our session was the last one of the last day, which usually means an empty session—but our session was standing room only. There was no physical space for embodied practices, but we had a very spirited conversation about the role of the DiaspoRican in Puerto Rican studies. Many of the emerging DiaspoRican scholars in the room shared their hesitancy to take on ethnographic work "at home" for fear of unintentionally participating in the extraction of knowledge with no reciprocation that is all too common in academic research (referred to as "academic tourism" or "helicopter research"). All these years later, the moment that sticks with me most is when feminist scholar of Black Puerto Rican studies Isar Godreau interrupted our navel-gazing: "Coño! If you don't do the research, who will?!"[39] Her exasperation held us accountable, and I hold her words close whenever DiaspoRican imposter syndrome comes calling.

In July 2019—now known as El Verano Boricua—hundreds of thousands of Boricuas made history by protesting for the resignation of then-Governor Ricardo Roselló. When the call for a solidarity rally in NYC came from the NY Boricua Resistance ("bring your pots and pans"; fig. 4), there was no question I would participate. Arm in arm with Ariana—both wearing our FPR shirts—we sang along to "La Borinqueña," the revolutionary national anthem penned in 1868 by Lola Rodríguez de Tío. We line danced. We chanted: "Ricky Renunica y Llevate La Junta!" And when the crowd grew in numbers so large that the corner where we gathered couldn't hold us, we marched from Columbus Circle to Grand Central Station in the pouring rain. I had attached my caldero around my shoulders with a rope, and as we marched the pot filled with water. At every intersection, it felt like the police were trying to trap us between cars and tour buses. And I will never forget the women defiantly pushing their strollers right by those police cars: "Somos Más! Y No Tenemos Miedo!" Arriving at Grand Central at peak commuter hour, we filled the building with chants and brought in a river of water beneath our feet. We sang for a different future for Puerto Ricans, a future we still hope for and witness emerging through the labors of queer feminist Boricuas unafraid to tell the colonial government to go to hell. Vete pal carajo, colonizer!

In 2020 Joanna Camacho, Lisa Jahn, Marisol LeBrón, Sarah Molinari, and Aurora Santiago Ortiz resigned from their positions on the executive board of the Puerto Rican Studies Association, explaining that they could no longer work in a "climate of sexism, infantilization, gaslighting, and racism."[40] In Puerto Rican studies, a field partially formed by feminists, radical articulations of anti-racist, queer, and anti-colonial feminist resistance have come second to struggles for independence—a situation not relegated to the academy but one that can be traced back to the interventions made by the

Figure 4. Ricky Renuncia protest supplies, 2019. Photo courtesy of the author.

women of the Young Lords Party and the nationalist movements in Puerto Rico.[41] I was nominated and then elected to be the association's secretary during the 2020–2022 cycle. I had the privilege of applying an anti-racist, feminist, queer lens to the work of rebuilding the association with Joaquín Villanueva, Marisol LeBrón, Michael Staudenmaier, Karrieann Soto Vega, Yomaira Figueroa-Vásquez, Mónica Jiménez, Pedro Lebrón-Ortíz, Zorimar Rivera-Montes, and Shakti Castro. Marisol, Karrieann, Michael, and I served once more during the 2022–2024 cycle, joined by Maura Toro-Morn, Mirelsie Velázquez, Daniel Vázquez-Sanabria, and Andrea Pimentel Rivera. Laser-focused on rebuilding the organization structurally, we also spent many hours ensuring that our statements, social media activity, and events aligned with our commitment to acknowledging how "white supremacy and colonialism continue to structure who is included and excluded from our communities."[42] Being in community with these folks (especially during those pandemic lockdown years) gave me the confidence and community I needed to organize the two Rican feminisms roundtables in 2022—one at PRSA and one at NWSA—that would seed this anthology.

When the 2022 NWSA conference schedule was published, I took to Facebook.

> An 8am panel isn't awesome, but it isn't the worst. What is frustrating, and I will certainly make this a point at the roundtable, is that our submission specifically says we want . . . "to begin developing the community needed to form a brand new interest group—making Rican Feminisms a more visible and viable part of the larger NWSA community moving forward."
>
> HOW ARE WE GOING TO DO THAT AT AN 8AM PANEL?!

Crunk feminist professor and public scholar Dr. Brittney Cooper commented: "You gotta be in leadership and involved in conference planning and decision making to make it happen. That is how Black women have managed since 2009 with the election of the first Black president of the org to make it happen."[43] She was right. I couldn't complain if I wasn't willing to do the work. I ran for and was elected to a member-at-large role, but I also began the process of forming a Puerto Rican Feminisms Interest Group at NWSA that same year. Our purpose statement reads:

> Our interest group honors and amplifies the historical contributions of Puerto Rican feminists to NWSA since the first documented conference in 1979 to the way our movement elder Levins Morales's work is employed to frame the conceptualization of inclusion in the organization's mission statement. Our intention with this group is to create a space within NWSA that recognizes and responds to the liminal space boricuas occupy as second-class citizens and subjects of the US empire who have historically and consistently crossed linguistic, cultural, and spatial borders.

In reaching for Rican feminist community, I accessed a network where reciprocal care is paramount, where collective life-affirming medicine is generated and acts as a kind of remedy for the poison of empire.

Prior to Tr*mp's second inauguration, I was seeing more and more calls to "shut down colonial feminism" on social media—a phrase circulated widely by the Palestinian Feminist Collective in 2023, a phrase that I want to see at every feminist march, rally, and protest. I hear my post-Maria appeal for people to see how Puerto Rico is a feminist issue in their calls to recognize Palestine as a feminist issue: "We reaffirm that Palestine is a feminist issue and assert that feminism is incompatible with Zionism."[44] Issuing a call that goes without response (or worse, triggers backlash that shows you who the real accomplices are) is more than frustrating. It's heartbreaking. But it is also a moment to articulate stronger relations with those who *do* respond to the call. I was feeling hopeful that we were in a moment where feminists in the contiguous US were ready to critique the limits of liberal feminism, ready to interrogate their role in sustaining imperial and colonial violence at home and elsewhere. Ready to honestly assess if they can claim to be fighting for reproductive justice considering their silence on the horrors the Israeli settler state continues to inflict on Palestinian parents and their children. Alas. Just as feminists in the late '90s stood with the Bush administration to support the US occupation of Afghanistan, far too many stood alongside Biden (and now Tr*mp) in support of the federal government's continued financial support of Israel's genocidal war on Gaza and occupation of Palestine.

In her mapping of Palestinian feminism, scholar and founding member of the Palestinian Feminist Collective Dr. Sarah Ihmoud calls us to

> continue the tradition of cultivating feminist solidarities, kinships and networks of care across borders in ways that uplift Palestinian liberation as part of a broader constellation of anticolonial, anti-racist and anti-imperialist liberatory struggles across the globe rather than reinforcing the disappearance of Palestine through its scholarly or activist erasure.[45]

The time for liberal feminism has passed; we know we need more and better than a neoliberal government will provide. We can no longer ignore the need for a transnational anti-imperial feminist politics that will deliver liberation rooted in radical decolonial love and care. Boricua feminisms are and have been on the front lines of this fight, and it is time for some recognition.

Rican Feminists Reaching for Solidarities

Porque Estamos Aquí: Puerto Rican Feminisms Against Empire maps the terrain of Boricua feminisms in the past, at the present, and for the future. It is crafted in the feminist of color tradition of collective storytelling established by *This Bridge Called My Back: Writings by Radical Women of Color* in 1981. I love the collectivity in those pages—the way that stories are offered as calls to action in service to collective consciousness raising. The way that differences between feminists of color are framed as opportunities for solidarity and collective liberation; I specifically teach the short essay that opens the first section of the anthology, "Children Passing in the Streets: The Roots of Our Radicalism," to emphasize the point.

> We were born into colored homes. We grew up with the inherent contradictions in the color spectrum right inside those homes: the lighter sister, the mixed-blood cousin, being the darkest one in the family. It doesn't

> take many years to realize the privileges, or lack thereof, attached to a particular shade of skin or texture of hair. It is this experience that moves light-skinned or "passable" Third World women to put themselves on the line for their darker sisters. We are all family. From those families we were on the one hand encouraged to leave, to climb up white. And with the other hand, the reins were held tight on us, our parents understanding the danger that bordered our homes.
>
> We learned to live with these contradictions. This is the root of our radicalism.[46]

Our title, *Porque Estamos Aquí*, has a double meaning: it is at once a provocation reminding us to remember why (por que, with a space) we are here (i.e., colonization, migration, displacement) and at the same time provides a simple and sassy response to the question, Why a book on Puerto Rican feminisms? Because we are here. We've been here. We'll be here. "Here" being wherever we are in space and time.

As editor, I did my best to reach across land and water, across the divide of academy and community—well aware that my perspectives are diasporic and most of my connections and colleagues are too. The chapters vary in terms of genre: there are poems, letters, recipes, interviews, artist statements, songs, testimonios, academic essays, herstorical re-presentations, maps, manifestos, experimental prose, a syllabus, and transcribed roundtable conversations. Chapters were solicited and contributed by artists, grassroots activists, and emerging and established scholars who identify as or study Puerto Rican feminists from and in different mediums, disciplines, and locales. Most of the contributors are Puerto Rican, but not all. What draws us together is our commitment to the transnational. The decolonial. The radical. An ideological and activist commitment to the end of empire.

Questions considered throughout the anthology include the following: How do we position Puerto Rican feminisms in the larger history of liberation movements? Who or what do we imagine when we imagine Rican feminisms? How do we re-member a distinct Puerto Rican feminist movement when—as colonized subjects—we've been separated, minoritized, and expected to disappear? How can we bridge the imperial divides—due to geography, language, and constructions of race, class, and sexuality—that dispossess us of our liberation lineages and contemporary comrades? How are Puerto Rican feminisms situated in relation to other feminisms built from identities of difference (such as Black feminisms, queer feminisms, crip feminisms, etc.)? How are Rican feminisms embodied, represented, activated, imagined, and challenged?

We don't tell readers what Rican feminisms *are*, we show what they do, what effects they have in the world. We do not seek to offer a stable definition of Puerto Rican feminism but rather to open our frames of reference to the multiplicity and complexity of Puerto Rican feminisms. The plurality is important.

For Puerto Rican feminisms to emerge, we must engage in the project of reclamation and celebration together with our non–Puerto Rican accomplices. Puerto Rican feminisms are present when the herstorical frame is expansive enough to hold us and brave enough to remove those imperial white feminist heroes from their pedestals. What follows is an offering of solidarity and visibility, a recipe for making and a spell book for conjuring Puerto Rican feminisms; an object for holding what has been taken by Anglophone hegemony and US imperialism: our memory, our traditions, our struggles, our history, our connections. From singular stereotypes of difference and otherness to complex intersectional representations of togetherness and belonging, our collective work is to move Puerto Rican feminisms and Puerto Rican feminists—wherever we are—out of the realm of invisibility.

Our hope is that *Porque Estamos Aquí* speaks to the "SortaRican" feminists who may not feel Puerto Rican enough because of a mixed ethnic lineage or a distance from the culture or Spanish language due to upbringing; to the DiaspoRican feminists who may be eager to connect with our feminist comrades on the archipelago; to the homeland Boricua feminists wanting to build bridges to their DiaspoRican comrades; to QueerRican and TransRican feminists looking to see some aspect of themselves in writing, in print, in existence; to AfroRican and Indigenous Rican feminists who have been disappeared or problematically hypervisibilized by histories written, told by, and in service to white supremacy, racial capitalism, and settler colonialism. *Porque Estamos Aquí* is also for those who do not identify as any kind of Rican feminist, but are down to shut down colonial feminism in favor of igniting and illuminating the power of anti-imperial feminisms.

I hope that we—that ambiguous (impossible?) feminist *we*—are ready to remember, to amplify, to uplift the radical narratives, the peripheral names and ideas that can lead us out of the death-dealing imperialist heteropatriarchal capitalist nightmare exacerbated by the authoritarian mode of the US government. Liberation is a group project; consider this your call to action.

—Jessica N. Pabón-Colón
Kingston, New York
October 2024

Notes

1. Renamed "Reproductive Equity Now" in 2021.
2. Deepa Kumar, "Imperialist Feminism and Liberalism," *openDemocracy* (blog), November 6, 2014, https://www.opendemocracy.net/en/imperialist-feminism-and-liberalism/.

3. Kumar, "Imperialist Feminism and Liberalism."
4. You can listen to the full address here: Laura Bush, "President's Weekly Radio Address—November 17, 2001," posted November 7, 2021, by George W. Bush Presidential Center, YouTube, https://www.youtube.com/watch?v=gr6liwDJMoU.
5. Bush, "President's Weekly Radio Address."
6. See https://guides.loc.gov/latinx-civil-rights/vieques-island-protests for a brief timeline of events.
7. Katherine T. McCaffrey, "Because Vieques Is Our Home: Defend It!; Women Resisting Militarization in Vieques, Puerto Rico," in *Security Disarmed: Critical Perspectives on Gender, Race, and Militarization*, ed. Barbara Sutton, Sandra Morgen, and Julie Novkov, 157–76 (Rutgers University Press, 2008), http://www.jstor.org/stable/j.ctt5hj5b1.12.
8. Margaret Power, "'If People Had Not Been Willing to Give Their Lives for the Patria or There Had Not Been the Political Prisoners, Then We Would Be Nothing': Interview with Lolita Lebrón," *Radical History Review*, no. 128 (2017): 37–45, https://doi.org/10.1215/01636545-3857754.
9. Laura Briggs's 2002 book *Reproducing Empire: Race, Sex, Science, and U.S. Imperialism in Puerto Rico* offers much needed complexity here. She highlights the various feminist advocacy efforts in the archipelago for consensual birth control and family planning in Puerto Rico.
10. Alexis McGill Johnson, "I'm the Head of Planned Parenthood. We're Done Making Excuses for Our Founder," *New York Times*, April 17, 2021, sec. Opinion, https://www.nytimes.com/2021/04/17/opinion/planned-parenthood-margaret-sanger.html.
11. Daniel Immerwahr, *How to Hide an Empire: A History of the Greater United States* (Farrar, Straus and Giroux, 2019), 7.
12. In 2021 two books were published on the topic. See Rafia Zakaria, *Against White Feminism: Notes on Disruption* (W. W. Norton and Company, 2021); and Koa Beck, *White Feminism: From the Suffragettes to Influencers and Who They Leave Behind* (Simon and Schuster, 2021).
13. bell hooks, *Feminism Is for Everybody: Passionate Politics* (South End Press, 2000).
14. Jessica N. Pabón-Colón, *Graffiti Grrlz: Performing Feminism in the Hip Hop Diaspora* (New York University Press, 2018).
15. hooks, *Feminism Is for Everybody*, xiii.
16. Sandra Ruiz, *Ricanness: Enduring Time in Anticolonial Performance* (New York University Press, 2019).
17. "Diasporican," performance of "Diasporican" by Mariposa, posted April 9, 2007, by leninaspicetube, YouTube, https://www.youtube.com/watch?v=n802rVXC8l0.
18. Illyanna Maisonet, *Diasporican: A Puerto Rican Cookbook* (Clarkson Potter/Ten Speed, 2022), 11.
19. Patricia Hill Collins, "Defining Black Feminist Thought," in *Feminist Theory Reader: Local and Global Perspectives*, ed. Carole McCann and Seung-kyung Kim, 3rd ed. (Routledge, 2013), 379–94.

20. Jessica N. Pabón-Colón, "Yo Soy Boricua Feminista, Pa'que Tu Lo Sepas! Notes from a DiaspoRican on Performing Outsider Identity," in *Latina Outsiders Remaking Latina Identity*, ed. Grisel Y. Acosta (Routledge, 2019).
21. Ruiz, *Ricanness*, 25.
22. José Esteban Muñoz, *The Sense of Brown* (Duke University Press, 2020).
23. Both Anita and I were speakers at the 2012 TEDxWomen conference at the United States Institute for Peace in Washington, DC. See "Feminism on the Wall: Jessica Pabón at TEDxWomen 2012," posted December 4, 2012, by TEDx Talks, YouTube, https://www.youtube.com/watch?v=z_4JOexUj0M.
24. If you're okay with fury in your body, you can watch the video on YouTube: "Trump Throws Paper Towels into Crowd in Puerto Rico," posted October 4, 2017, by Guardian News, YouTube, https://www.youtube.com/watch?v=kEe7_zgZbuI.
25. See "US Election: Full Transcript of Donald Trump's Obscene Videotape," *BBC News*, October 8, 2016, sec. US Election 2016, https://www.bbc.com/news/election-us-2016-37595321.
26. "Where Are the Pussy Hats for Puerto Rico? Jessica N. Pabón-Colón on Feminist Answering Machine," posted November 2, 2017, by Feminist Frequency, YouTube, https://www.youtube.com/watch?v=GVzwlbNGOdA.
27. See https://puertoricosyllabus.com/.
28. See https://pronthemap.com/.
29. The front page for Hurricane Maria resources reads: "About the deadly Category 5 storm of 2017, its aftermath on the island, and what the storm revealed." See https://puertoricosyllabus.com/syllabus/hurricane-maria/. The front page for Verano Boricua resources reads: "The summer of 2019 brought a plurality of Puerto Ricans into the streets, demanding Ricardo Rosselló to resign." See https://puertoricosyllabus.com/syllabus/verano-boricua-ricky-renuncia/.
30. The money raised by the first round went to La Colectiva Feminista en Construcción (a feminist organization in Borikén that has modeled revolutionary feminist action since 2014), and the second went to the community-based feminist organization Taller Salud (working to improve women's access to healthcare, reduce violence, and encourage education and activism since 1979).
31. Cherríe Moraga and Gloria Anzaldúa, *This Bridge Called My Back: Writings by Radical Women of Color*, 3rd ed. (Third Woman Press, 2002).
32. Latina Feminist Group, *Telling to Live: Latina Feminist Testimonios* (Duke University Press, 2001).
33. Moraga and Anzaldúa, *This Bridge Called My Back*, liv.
34. Aurora Levins Morales, *Remedíos: Stories of Earth and Iron from the History of Puertorriquenas* (South End Press, 2001), xxvii.
35. Kimberlé Crenshaw, "The Urgency of Intersectionality," TED talk, posted December 7, 2016, by TED, YouTube, https://www.youtube.com/watch?v=akOe5-UsQ2o.
36. Denise Oliver-Velez, "Borikén Florece," talk at Bard College, October 29, 2017.

37. Directed by Drs. Yomaira C. Figueroa-Vásquez and Jessica Marie Johnson, the Diaspora Solidarities Lab is an excellent example of this kind of feminist work. See https://www.dslprojects.org.
38. We must also remember that in the process of being dispossessed from our ancestral land, Ricans have become settlers on this Native American land. la paperson calls us "colonial byproducts of empire"—those of us who are "displaced by colonization, only to arrive at a place as another participant in colonization." la paperson, *A Third University Is Possible* (University of Minnesota Press, 2017), xxiii, https://www.upress.umn.edu/book-division/books/a-third-university-is-possible.
39. I owe a great debt to her scholarship when it comes to understanding anti-Blackness in Puerto Rico. In particular, see Isar P. Godreau, *Scripts of Blackness: Race, Cultural Nationalism, and U.S. Colonialism in Puerto Rico* (University of Illinois Press, 2015), https://muse.jhu.edu/book/37017.
40. Marisol LeBrón, "Why We Are Resigning from the Puerto Rican Studies Association Executive Board," *Medium* (blog), August 10, 2020, https://medium.com/@marisollebrn/why-we-are-resigning-from-the-puerto-rican-studies-association-executive-board-9111bf836966.
41. Iris Morales, *Through the Eyes of Rebel Women: The Young Lords 1969–1976* (Red Sugarcane Press, 2016).
42. See https://www.ricanstudies.com/past-events.
43. Brittney Cooper, "You gotta be in leadership," Facebook, August 29, 2022. Read more of Cooper's work in Brittney C. Cooper, Susana M. Morris, and Robin M. Boylorn, eds., *The Crunk Feminist Collection* (The Feminist Press at CUNY, 2017).
44. You can find the full call to action on their website: https://palestinianfeministcollective.org/shut-down-colonial-feminism-2023/.
45. Sarah Ihmoud, "Palestinian Feminism: Analytics, Praxes and Decolonial Futures," *Feminist Anthropology* 3, no. 2 (2022): 294.
46. Moraga and Anzaldúa, *This Bridge Called My Back*, 3–4.

Sofrito

TAÍNA ASILI

En lo más profundo de mi memoria (In the depths of my memory)
vive un sabor de otro día (lives the flavor of another day)
Es el olor de mi fuerte ascendencia (It is the smell of my strong ancestry)
En las sabias manos de mi abuelita (In the wise hands of my grandmother)

Sofrito el corazón de abuelita (Sofrito the heart of grandma)
Sofrito el corazón de abuelita (Sofrito the heart of grandma)

Un puñado de ajo (A fistful of garlic)
machatando en el pilón (mashing in a mortar and pestle)
mezclado sabrosos secretos (mixing tasty secrets)

Representan la fuerza de mi pueblo (Represents the strength of my people)
la potente mezcla que somos (the potent mixture that we are)
el poder de la tradición (the power of tradition)

Sofrito el corazón de abuelita (Sofrito the heart of grandma)

Es el olor que me ayuda (It is the scent that helps me)
a recordar de dónde vengo (to remember where I come from)
el combustible para donde voy (the fuel for where I am going)

Donde encuentro el coraje (Where I find the courage)
para derribar los muros injustos (to tear down walls of injustice)
la base para crear el nuevo (the base to create anew)

Sofrito el corazón de abuelita (Sofrito the heart of grandma)
Sofrito el corazón de abuelita (Sofrito the heart of grandma)

representing the trinity
stirring up the strength of my ancestry
powerful boricua I will always be

Sofrito!

cause I was fed the food of my abuelita (grandma)
woman who led como una reina (like a queen)
and taught me to fight como una guerrera (like a warrior)

Sofrito!

These ingredients running through my blood
were passed down to me with an awesome love
and never let me forget the culture I am a part of

Sofrito!

where people pushed into a colony
found the strength to break the boundaries
over 500 years fighting to be free

Sofrito el corazón de abuelita (Sofrito the heart of grandma)
Sofrito el corazón de abuelita (Sofrito the heart of grandma)

Es el olor que me ayuda (It is the scent that helps me)
a recordar de dónde vengo (to remember where I come from)
el combustible para donde voy (the fuel for where I am going)

Sofrito el corazón de abuelita (Sofrito the heart of grandma)

PART I. OUR COLLECTIVITIES

EDITOR'S NOTE: In 2022, I assembled two groups of self-identified Puerto Rican feminist scholar-activists to participate in what I called a "fall conference tour" showcasing the breadth and depth of current Puerto Rican feminist thinking and doing. The first group presented at the Puerto Rican Studies Association (PRSA) at Holyoke Community College in Massachusetts; the theme was "Morivivi: Activating Puerto Rican Futures." The second group convened at the National Women's Studies Association (NWSA) in Minneapolis, Minnesota; the theme was "killing rage: resistance on the other side of freedom."

I imagined these roundtables as beginning points—as points of entry to building the relations that would be necessary to actualize this anthology in the feminist of color tradition of collective testimonio, collective writing, and collective publishing. Both experiences were electrifying for all involved—our audiences included. By sharing how we envision and embody Rican feminisms, we began the important work of network building among Puerto Rican scholars, of mapping connections between experiences, ideas, and movements across time and space.

Although these roundtables took place within the quintessential academic environment of a conference, the purpose of our presence was not to demonstrate a definitive expertise but rather to be vulnerable enough with our stories and approaches to offer some guidelines, a kind of framework for this thing we are collectively calling Rican feminisms. And though many of us work for settler institutions of higher education in the contiguous US, our deepest hope is to uplift the radical and revolutionary interventions in our Rican communities wherever they are happening. Our academic work is not possible without our communities. Our goals are rooted in a shared commitment to liberation from colonial subjugation for Puerto Rico and Puerto Ricans. For us, living as, being engaged with, and advocating for a Puerto Rican feminist praxis can be soothing balm (if not an outright remedy) for the wounds we've acquired over generations of white supremacist, capitalist, cisheterosexist, imperialist, patriarchal violence. We offer our thoughts here to share our medicine beyond the privileged spaces of the academic conference.

I asked some of the same questions to each group, but I also asked questions tied to the environment (and the theme) of each conference. These questions and some of the responses reflect the specific histories and dynamics of each space. At NWSA, we are part of a long feminist of color struggle to decenter the dominance of white imperial feminism in thought and action. At PRSA, we were part of a recent push to confront the dominance of anti-Black cisheteropatriarchy—one that erases the Rican feminist labor that founded the field. Preparing the roundtables for print in the anthology, I let go of references to the thematic frames provided by each conference and remixed the order of our discussions to bring the claims, stories, and perspectives that shape our Rican feminisms to the front.

CHAPTER 1

Where Are the Feminisms in Puerto Rican Studies? A Remixed Roundtable from the 2022 PRSA Conference

ERIKA GISELA ABAD, ARIANA GONZALEZ STOKAS, NICOLE HERNANDEZ, JADE POWER-SOTOMAYOR, AND JESSICA N. PABÓN-COLÓN

JESSICA N. PABÓN-COLÓN: We meet on the unceded lands of the Nipmuc and Pocumtuc nations of the Wabanaki Confederacy. As we explore how Puerto Rican feminism arises in response to current conditions, I encourage us to place our experiences as colonial subjects of the US empire in relation to the reality that many of us are also living as settlers on this land. Acknowledging our participation in settler colonialism is essential to any Rican feminist praxis aiming to build new and different futures.

What moved you to join this roundtable on Rican feminisms, and how does it tie into your work and life?

NICOLE HERNANDEZ: I am a second-year doctoral student at Arizona State University in the Social Cultural Anthropology department. I'm also the cofounder of Puerto Ricans in Action, a civic activist community group; we've organized protests, press conferences, speaking tours—one with Oscar López Rivera after his release in 2017—film screenings, cultural presentations, fundraisers for disaster recovery, and more. I come to this conference by way of East LA County, where I grew up as a third-generation Puerto Rican. My mother's family came from Utuado and Morovis through New York, Chicago, and eventually SoCal. My father's side is from Moca and Aguada. His family eventually returned to Puerto Rico, so he's now in San Juan. Though I'm third-generation, I feel a close connection to Puerto Rico, since my father returned when I was young and I've spent extended periods of time there over my life.

Growing up in Southern California felt culturally isolating, but in the last five or six years, through being involved in the community work, I have learned that there are a lot of misconceptions about Puerto Ricans in the region (even from myself)—about who, how, and where we are in the

Southwest, in California, Arizona, Utah, and other places. In the Greater Bay Area, there's a very big historical presence of Puerto Ricans who have integrated into the social fabrics of locales like San Jose, Merced, Oakland, Hayward, and San Francisco City. There's a lack of education about our history here, our families' contributions, our voices and roots. So, my dissertation research focuses on the shifting nature of identity, transnationalist heritage practice, tangible and intangible cultural work. I'm looking at imperial migration of Puerto Rican groups to California, which led to the formation of community hot spots; through interviews and archives, we can map those out. Next year, I will conduct additional interviews with families that have three or four generations living in California.

At this point, I have more than two hundred community surveys completed that piece together the historical timelines of community organizing across the state. One thing I myself am guilty of is this idea, this repeating narrative that we don't exist here. That California is a Puerto Rican desert. It is untrue now and also in the past; my family's been there since the '50s, but that's very recent compared to others. I think about how we can remember and get justice for ordinary families like my grandparents, who were part of the growing industrialization of South Los Angeles. In my role at the Diaspora Solidarities Lab, I work on transcriptions of Frank Espada interviews from the late 1970s and '80s in California. Aurora Levins Morales has also done interviews with various Puerto Ricans in the Bay Area. Through Frank Espada's work, Aurora's work, and my own, I've been able to hear interviews with community leaders from the '60s, '70s, '80s, '90s, and 2000s, in Los Angeles as well as in the Bay. These narratives offer insights into the life and formation of community, which is being juxtaposed with New York City even in these archives. New York always seems to be the point of reference for what the Puerto Rican diaspora is or isn't.

ARIANA GONZALEZ STOKAS: Hi, everybody. I'm currently an independent scholar. I was a faculty member in CUNY for a while. I moved into administration and higher education, working mostly in opportunity programs—so, higher education access. Most recently, I was the vice president for DEI at Barnard College. And I left that role in June of 2021, for all kinds of reasons that we could talk about today or not talk about today. And I wrote a book about it, *Reparative Universities*, published by Johns Hopkins University Press (2023). My desire to join this roundtable came from conversations with my friend and comrade Jessica, really because I didn't know the answer to that question: What are Rican feminisms? I wanted to come here just to be in the room with other people who are thinking about that question collectively—also because I struggle against isolation, which I believe the academy cultivates. Now that I'm living in Toronto, which are the traditional lands of the Huron Wendat, the Seneca, and the Mississaugas [of the Credit],

I'm very far from the island. My family is from Aibonito, Caimito, and Loiza, and I spent my childhood going back and forth—like many people—from there, New York City, and upstate New York. I joke that there are three or four Boricuas in Toronto, but truly I haven't encountered a diasporic community there—so the questions of erasure in various geographies is really interesting to me.

I come here with no answer to Jessica's question, but with the desire to investigate it together and understand what it means. I see feminism as a liberation movement that is constructivist in its orientation—as in, it's seeking to build and create a different world, and doing so through offering modes of knowing and being that cut against a world shaped by misogyny. With our lives and knowledges engineered by misogyny, I'm interested in what being a Boricua means to that existence, to living inside of that kind of framework. I work actively to be a student of the social movements that are happening on the Island and to understand how to work in solidarity with them. I look closely at the practices of world-building that are occurring in Puerto Rico right now and consider how they can be instructive as critical tactics of decolonial repair, necessary for transforming our higher education systems that were born out of colonial logics and enslavement. As a philosopher of education, that's what my doctorate is in. I've examined how early teacher education programs in Puerto Rico were built from a colonial apparatus of epistemic suppression that we're still recovering from, through not knowing our own history and how long it took to discover certain texts. As a philosopher, it took me so long to discover philosophers from Puerto Rico in the Caribbean, having faculty tell me for many years that they just didn't exist. As a corrective to this, while I was at Teachers College at Columbia University, I helped cofound the Latin American Philosophy of Education Society (LAPES), which is still active. That led to my interest in examining how educational systems of imperialist and colonial countries in particular shape our epistemologies—how we know, how we understand truth, how we formulate knowledge and set the conditions for our knowledge production. So, like I said, as a person who was working within institutions, particularly as an administrator of DEI, this led me to really study those institutions while I was working within them. My recent book, *Reparative Universities*, is an examination and a critique of diversity work and the procedures of epistemic and ontological unsettlements. I really think that is where reparative activity leads: toward unsettlement. As for the intersection of reparations and feminism—I still am trying to think that through. Intuitively, it feels like there are deep kinships there that I want to formulate more clearly.

ERIKA GISELA ABAD: I'm going to situate who I am and why I am here with my intellectual genealogy. While I decided to return to the Puerto Rican Studies Association after eight years because Jessica organized this panel, being here in Holyoke and at a Puerto Rican Studies Association conference is difficult for me. Twenty-four years ago, I started my recovery from childhood sexual assault down the street as a scholarship kid at Deerfield Academy. This is important to note because my prestigious high school education primarily consisted of me searching for mental health support for my trauma, as well as navigating classed and raced hostility, while working to maintain the GPA required to keep my scholarship.[1]

The isolation I felt at Deerfield planted the seeds for my radical and ever-evolving trauma-informed approach to my work—which was marginally received in Puerto Rican studies. Thus, I approach the question of Rican feminism as a queer AfroBoricua-Dominicana harmed by the field of Puerto Rican studies and Puerto Rican community activism—as someone who "did the work," according to my activist-scholar foremothers, and still wasn't deemed "good enough" by prestige networks and hierarchies of academia, despite the celebration of activist-scholars across our disciplines.

As an undergrad at DePaul University in Chicago, I worked with a variety of Puerto Rican women, which normalized that people like us could be college professors. One such colleague helped me get more involved in Puerto Rican community work in the Humbold Park neighborhood, specifically on Paseo Boricua, the section of Division Street between Chicago's two steel Puerto Rican flags. I was inspired to volunteer (in 2003) and then join (in early 2004) the Cafe Teatro Batey Urbano Collective. But by November 2004, I was feeling as isolated as I felt at Deerfield Academy. College-aged activist peers questioned the motivation behind my work; I didn't feel safe disclosing the relationship between the intergenerational trauma that shaped my past silence of childhood sexual assault and the connections I was making with Puerto Ricans' ongoing struggles against internalized oppression. I let one of the last poems I performed for Batey articulate this sense of isolation, after which I left for a year before returning to advocate for Puerto Ricans' access to affordable housing and agitate against Oscar López Rivera's incarceration. I didn't return to long-term community work with Paseo Boricua until 2015, when I obtained the position of part-time oral historian and archivist working on the Notable Puerto Rican Project for Hunter College's Center for Puerto Rican Studies (colloquially called "Centro"). While on the project, I endured homophobia and misogynoir within fieldwork and even during some of the interviews I conducted. While I reported the homophobia during meetings, I relied most on local mentors like Alejandro Molina, Communications Director of the National Boricua Human Rights Network at the time, and Jose López, Oscar López Rivera's brother, for encouragement, empathy, and support. Upon noticing that I was assigned to interview a list of mostly straight and cisgender notable Puerto Ricans, I added queer Ricans in Chicago to the project and urged other oral historians in other arenas to find and include queer Ricans in their lineup.

While I had initially worked for Centro because Oscar López Rivera wanted his letters in Centro's archives, in the years after I left, it would become increasingly clear that my respect for the institution was not reciprocated. Conversations had once I settled into my position at UNLV made the lack of respect clear with messaging that countered their rejection of my post-doctoral application and their perception of supporters of Oscar López Rivera's release. As a tenure-track communications professor at Nevada State University, I still choose to risk sharing these stories—because the lack of support for my "radical" commitments has allowed me to reinvent myself through communities and projects with my Southern Nevada students and colleagues.

As I sit here with what it means to be here in this coveted tenure-track job in a traditional discipline that interdisciplinary scholars like me rarely obtain, I'm wondering how to repair my relationship with Puerto Rican studies. I come here in that vein to discuss what it means to unpack questions of prestige and questions of solidarity. And I want to discuss these questions from the vantage point of someone who believed they did everything they were supposed to and yet still wasn't good enough for their fellow Puerto Ricans.

JADE POWER-SOTOMAYOR: Like many of you, I make community and life with and within our diaspora. And while I stay connected via quotidian embodiments and cultural practices, via phone calls and WhatsApp threads, IG posts, Twitter feeds, and the many visitors and family I'm fortunate to welcome to my home, my life is also largely comprised of the distinct peoples of the place I live and work: from the dozens of tribal groups in San Diego County, Chicanxs and fronterizx Mexicans, ever-dwindling communities of California's African Americans, Filipinxs and Pacific Islanders, surfers and skaters and counterculture hippies. Displaced academics. I say this because, like many of you, my vision blurs with tears when the plane's wheels lift off the tarmac at the Aeropuerto Luis Muñoz Marin and the contoured edges of our portal of riches comes into focus with distance. Leaving a big hole in my heart, one that grows larger with every deceased or emigrated loved one, every disappeared place, and the increased vulnerability of those who remain.

The truth is, however, that while I may know something about making a life in contemporary Puerto Rico and strive to bring urgent attention to the structures and violence that contain its possibilities, that is not the life I live from day to day. Though I admire, celebrate, and study with care projects such as La Cole or Revista Étnica, Con-Sentimientos, I cannot purport to speak for feminist movements in Puerto Rico, nor to the daily struggles of life on the archipelago. However, what is a part of my daily life and a generative engine of much of what I do is something I would call Rican feminism.

From my vantage point as a light-skinned, West Coast Boricua, I have spent the greater part of the last two decades witnessing and participating in a feminist movement within bomba practice across the diaspora and the archipelago, which is what I wish to offer to our conversation today. Bomba is a centuries-old drum, dance, and song tradition cultivated and maintained by enslaved Africans and their surrounding communities through oral and embodied cultures. It is the oldest still-in-existence music/dance from the archipelago, and over the last two decades has been increasingly popularly practiced following long periods of musical racism that drove it underground and a subsequent folklorization that rendered it primarily for the stage. In 2004, I began studying and practicing bomba, then mostly as a dancer. It was a moment of burgeoning cultural interest in bomba that followed the 2001 Banco Popular special *Raíces*, which both sought to articulate the specific contours of the knowledges fundamental to the practice (parsing its history from plena's, for example) while also uplifting Afro–Puerto Rican culture and heritage (at this point, still something discussed in terms of heritage and not necessarily racialized embodiment).

At the same time, in leaving the protected spaces of the Black families who have been the custodians of bomba traditions throughout decades of virulent racism that nearly extinguished it, it took on new meanings, different bodies, different locations, at times reifying the gravitational pull toward whiteness and privilege. Simultaneously, some of the heterosexist nationalism that had become ossified in the form in the guise of "preservation" and "tradition" began to crumble; for the first time, women took their place as drummers, people in the batey scrambled sartorial codes and the gendered language of the dancing, and, importantly, women increasingly stepped into leadership roles in bomba groups, where they crafted projects and politics birthed from the collectivitiy inherent to the practice. Since then, in large part due to circumstance and good fortune, I have been part of a sustained conversation in collaboration with a group of women across the diaspora of Puerto Rico who have taken up bomba as a practice of anti-colonial, Afro-feminist liberation. Mujeres I consider my maestras, my hermanas, and my comrades; mujeres like Marién Torres López, Amarilys Ríos, Ivelisse Díaz, Norka Nadal, Manuela Arciniegas, Denise Solis, Julia Cepeda, Oxil Febles, Julia Gutiérrez, Melanie Maldonado, Shefali Shah, Elia Cortés, and others. Each of them a node in a distinct community.

In my life as a practitioner and in my own scholarship, writing, and editorial projects, I have encountered not just contemporary instances of feminism and bomba, but also the archival silences around the many Afro–Puerto Rican women through whom bomba has been given life, whether as composers, singers, dancers, clothing designers, or as the conveners themselves. (Here I want to shout out Melanie Maldonado and Sarah Bruno's important research.) I have written about what it means to listen to bodies in movement outside of visual, ocular terms, and how bomba's batey cultivates a practice of listening to Black Puerto Ricans—increasingly to women and queer and trans Puerto Ricans. Bomba, I suggest, teaches us how to listen for freedom, how to listen to flesh, turning toward each other to find liberation.

JNP: Jade, when you talk about networks of belonging—creating structures through which we can embody, understand, and come to a consciousness as Rican feminists—that is precisely what I'm trying to do here. Five years ago, I don't think I would have been able to assemble this roundtable, let alone feel like I could be the chair of it or be the one putting together the first anthology specifically on the topic. But that's what we're doing here together, right now. Building networks.

The next question was inspired by my initial experience of not knowing who to reach out to or how to build what I needed and wanted. I wanted to know my ancestors, my Rican feminist elders. I'd like us to share who we imagine when we imagine Rican feminisms. What do we imagine?

JPS: As the daughter of generations of Puerto Rican women who in one way or another sought to liberate themselves—from colonialism, white supremacy, patriarchy—I clearly wouldn't be who I am or where I am if it weren't for Rican feminisms writ large. When I think of Rican feminism, I think of my aging godmother taking me to find an higüera tree in an overgrown monte of my childhood. I had taken the machete to cut the vines, but dissatisfied with my progress, she grabbed it from me and efficiently hacked our way to the tree and our harvest. Rican feminisms clear the way.

NH: Not who but what. Rican feminism is a way of life. Someone mentioned endurance, in terms of enduring multiple displacements, generational violence, isolation. In the circles I find myself in, I think of endurance in terms of longing for community to know our genealogies. I often found myself without elders in movement spaces and familial spaces, and those who were there were burnt out and good at burning bridges. We need new models of care. People need to stay in the movement and guide others. I consider my mother, grandmother, and great-grandmother embodiments of Rican feminism. Their endurance—to remain Puerto Rican without a social network, without recognition, without a path back to Puerto Rico—is itself a radical act. Rican feminism, for me, is shaped not by political or cultural foremothers but by the quiet strength of women who survived in isolation, through memory, labor, and love.

EGA: When I think of Rican feminisms, I think about how Rican studies had women among the founders. Solidarity and support between women, femmes, and queers has always been here. I think of Nelia Olivencio, who used to work at Wisconsin Whitewater. We met in 2002, and when I returned to PRSA as a presenter in 2006, she introduced me to people. I think about one of the most powerful and beautiful things I've experienced, which was in 2008 when Gladys [Jiménez-Muñoz] held space for junior scholars, for critical conversation on solidarity, for diplomatic attempts at cleaning up messes. I met Elizabeth Crespo-Kebler that year as well. I was just getting comfortable with self-identifying as queer, and Crespo-Kebler—a queer elder I was reading for my dissertation—was awesome and made herself accessible to me.[2] Olivencio's, Jiménez-Muñoz's, and Crespo-Kebler's engagement with me and my work highlights the benefits of if and when colegas de aquí y de allá encourage each other.

At the 2010 PRSA meeting, I was on a panel with Marisol Ascencio again, and I'm having a queer Rican nerd moment. Larry [La Fountain-Stokes]—another queer Rican mentor—was like, "Oh my God, I love your work!" I was like, what? Kebler and Ana Irma Rivera Lassén show up to our panel and we're talking about Lolita Lebrón's lipstick and what it meant for her to have lipstick in her purse. That moment was created because these elders, pioneras in Puerto Rican feminisms, wanted to listen to the younger generation—because there are those de allá who want to have conversations with us here because they understand that our limited access isn't our fault. They understand that the ability to speak or read Spanish is a consequence of internalized oppression that is rooted in survival.

I'm thinking about these questions, of access and intimacy and solidarity, as not just intellectual. Not just political. And this investment in taking care of one another regardless of where we are and how we show up is rooted in our displacement, our nomadism. These solidarities helped me situate my experience as a member of the Caribbean diaspora, as much as I'm also part of the complicated Latinx diaspora—my island sensibilities haven't left me even though I've never lived there. And much like our gente, much like our Indigenous ancestors, our African ancestors, I've moved a lot. Seeking resources, seeking where I can live, specifically seeking where I can live as unapologetically queer and AfroBoricua-Dominicana. And so, when I think about these questions of feminisms, I can give you the genealogy, but I also think about these moments of contact, these moments of intimacy and solidarity. Whether or not it's center stage, I think right now these solidarities are the conversation.

AGS: I think, similarly, about errantry, a kind of wandering. I think of desire, of this longing, the kind of longing of return, what that means, how that shapes how I understand and move in the world. In particular, I think a lot about mangroves lately. They're on my mind a lot. (I love Glissant.) You know the mangroves off the coast of Guanica in Borinquen? So, there's an area off the coast of Guanica in the dry forest there, where you can swim in the mangroves a little bit, which is unusual because mangrove stands don't really let you in, because of how they grow. I think a lot about being in relation to them, how they teach me something about how to live and survive in what we might think of as hostile conditions—they live in salt water. I think about the academy that way: How do I thrive in hostile conditions, what are the possibilities of that, or not? Mangroves provide critical protection from storm surges, and they're also incredibly important in cleaning the air from carbon dioxide; they're one of these entities that we're learning are critical, like peat moss, peat bogs, places that can actually really make an impact in terms of climate change. So, they, like me, have many homes and many roots. The idea that they are rhizomatic, they don't have a single root—again, Glissant. And it makes me think about how, with Boricuas, we're talking about this wanderingness, this rhizomatic kind of manifestation, so that feminism for us is in relation to these various places that we find ourselves also. And what does that all look like as collective work? And how powerful is it when you have something that has many roots? Rather than a single one. We can think with a mangrove about collectively imagining what Rican feminism is like, or what it could be in our various places, and how all that thought and being comes together to create this organism—hopefully—of actual organizing and collective work.

NH: I'm also thinking about Rican feminism not being positive, not always about solidarity, not always intersectional. Acknowledging when it's not positive is part of the work too, because activism is also toxic and gatekept and about protectionism. It could be about keeping certain spaces exclusive or being protective of tangible and intangible cultural expressions. I was thinking of what you said, Erika; the trauma within community organizing in any context is real. We need to address our internal and external feminist practices. I would add, in terms of future thinking: How do we bring more nonacademics into this conversation about Rican feminism?—which I ask as a community organizer who sees people of all types exude a Rican feminism.

JNP: [The year] 2018, I think, was the first PRSA I went to. I attended that conference because I had already experienced a fraction of what Rican feminist community offered and wanted more, specifically in academic environments. For me, it's always been a space for Rican feminist community. That said, the Puerto Rican Studies Association went through a major transition after the 2020 exodus of most of the executive council due to sexism and racism—some are calling it a revolution. I wonder if you all could speak to the role of Rican feminisms in shaping the field of Puerto Rican studies—past, present, and future.

EGA: I'm going to go first—I'm like, *this one is for me*. When Marisol [LeBrón] wrote that *Medium* piece, I was like *thanks*! Because what she wrote about with PRSA was parallel to my experience with Centro. As I've told organizers and colleagues, I'm looking forward to this shift, this turn in leadership, considering the abovementioned struggles in the field. I chose to struggle through graduate school because I wanted to see more people like us on bookshelves and across all levels of curricula.

AGS: I don't have as long a history as Erika or other people in this room with the Puerto Rican Studies Association. For me, in my experience, it was always there, just like Centro was always there. And there were frequently challenges for me in feelings related to hospitableness, or invitation, or comfort. I, personally, never felt those things from Centro. It felt as if there was an insider language that I didn't have access to. And this yearning to belong has permeated through my own life: How you are Puerto Rican? Are you Puerto Rican enough? Do you have to perform "Puerto Rican," what does it mean to be that? How do you display that? How do you inhabit those disciplines when you come from other disciplines? Coming from philosophy, I think it's always been kind of partial—there's the longing and the desire to be part of communities of scholars who are like you, or maybe share something with you, or maybe don't. I think that, like Erika said, that desire has always been here, a part of the academy, specifically a part of Puerto Rican studies and its birth as a discipline.

In addition, accountability comes up for me in this. Seeing how academic organizations and how feminism can agitate for accountability, and what accountability is needed, for academic organizations, to the people within them, to identities that have been excluded, decentered, or unrecognized. There is so much power in the academy around organizations; like Erika, you're gesturing at and talking about access to jobs, recommendations, gatekeepers, and how academic organizations and institutions open and close opportunity. A lot of times, there's a criterion set for who can access those opportunities or not. So, the kind of changes in organizations like this need to be wider, to have a sense of accountability—that is something that is important and needed.

JPS: In my experience and in my research, I've encountered many women in bomba who said, "Ay no, yo no soy feminista!" Groundbreaking women, some of whom were the first women to take on roles previously reserved for men in bomba. Reflecting on that, I have to wonder how cultural work or performance praxis can lead to a Rican feminist consciousness? What does it mean to activate a political consciousness through the doing of something? What does it mean to experience something akin to liberation across the body before it might register as a political conscience? And how that has changed—how have the inroads created by these women made these practices a different thing to identify with? How might broad-based cultural work bring women into spaces with people they might not otherwise meet? Thinking here of the Barrileras del 8M project, which brings together many women from many different walks of life and, through their love of bomba, then activates them into a feminist consciousness.[3] How does a collective practice like bomba produce networks of belonging that also creates structures for political organizing—how has it linked Puerto Rican feminists to those from the rest of Latin America? Bomba being where women come together to play, then create the structure of community (exchanges of phone numbers, addresses, social media, group chats). I'm thinking here of bomba as the kind of proto-flash mob—right?—that provides the seed. Vamos pa' allá! Yeah, let's go. Let's take the drums. Let's bring the drums to the site of the wound. Finally, how might bomba provide opportunities for dismantling and challenging patriarchy, Rican patriarchy specifically? What does it mean for people to unlearn patriarchy within a space subjected to patriarchy? What does it look like to hold together the need to protect bomba from the exploitative forces of a market economy, of the state and the nationalist discourses that still center whiteness and cast blackness as a primitive Other external to the national identity, while *also* recognizing that this need has often resulted in a privileging of patriarchal hierarchies invested in finite definitions of gender and of gendered roles in the practice?

However, bomba has taught me that the practice itself, the logics of giving and receiving necessitated by the batey, can help instruct us and route what we might call a kind of Rican feminism. The batey as a circle is a space of enclosure, of possible protection, but one that requires vulnerability, porosity, and active exchange to function. As Fanon—who incidentally distrusted the political efficacy of dance—writes in *The Wretched of the Earth*, "The circle of the dance is a permissive circle. It protects and permits." I think when we learn this across the body, via a framework and context that supports and amplifies a feminist praxis, we archive a distinct kind of knowing. Understanding how empowerment and vulnerability are equally necessary in the batey is an important feminist teaching, not just because it celebrates woman as potential protagonists but because it actually destabilizes the hierarchical logics that uphold patriarchy as a system.

JNP: My hope with this anthology is to provoke more action in terms of welcoming nonacademic people into our conversations, into our networks of belonging—especially within the diaspora, where most of us are employed. As academics, we have so much critical language to share—and not just the jargon but the ideas and interventions behind the jargon.

Take Jade's question about embodying a politic before and without knowing the ideology behind, or even the name of, the politic. Just the other day, I was talking to my grandmother, who now has great-grandchildren who are nonbinary and trans. She kept saying *el, el, el* to refer to my niece, her granddaughter, and I was like, *wela, it's ella ella ella*. And she said, "OH! Ella es *una muchacha*, oh, okay, I'm sorry. I didn't know. Love you!" She took the correction with a smile and a hug. Her answer to most difficulties is to practice love. She didn't need a conceptual or critical analysis, but I wanted to give her one, hand her something accessible. I tweeted about it, crowdsourcing the difficulty of the moment: "How do you explain trans nonbinary identity to a bisabuela who speaks mostly Spanish when you only speak English." The stakes are too high to keep these conversations at conferences or in academic books.

EGA: When you mentioned "bisabuela," I think about my own abuela. Taken out of school before she could finish, there was stuff she could understand and other stuff she couldn't. While I could never explain my research to her, she understood the effects of political shifts on me. Cuando mi abuela murió, my grandmother's burial anniversary, is the day that COVID became a pandemic. When the Pulse nightclub shooting happened, she was conscientious enough to tell me to be careful. I was like, "I hear what you're saying. You recognize you have two queer grandchildren who you hope don't get persecuted."

So, I think it's as much about listening and touching, right? Porque it's more than words, and it's more than text, because we need to think critically about the fact that in some regions—like where Nicole and I are—they don't know Puerto Ricans write or create, until they come across us. We need to keep that in mind and keep asking: What's going to be more accessible to folks who don't know where to find our books? Because algorithms are trash, and the publishing markets are ridiculous.

Erika Gisela Abad has been assistant professor of communications at Nevada State University since 2022. From 2015 to 2016, they were the second Chicago-based oral historian and archivist for Center for Puerto Rican Studies' Notable Puerto Rican Project. Their work with Centro allowed them to follow the last year of Oscar López Rivera's amnesty campaign, including but not limited to the Mujeres Por Oscar mobilizations in Chicago.

Ariana Gonzalez Stokas is currently an independent scholar and owner of an arts-based learning studio in Toronto, Canada. She was an assistant professor of interdisciplinary studies and founding faculty member of Guttman Community College of the City University of New York, a vice president for diversity, equity, and inclusion at Barnard College, and a dean at Bard College. She published *Reparative Universities: Why Diversity Alone Won't Solve Racism in Higher Education* in 2023 with Johns Hopkins University Press.

Nicole Hernandez, a PhD candidate in sociocultural anthropology at Arizona State University, is researching US Pacific Puerto Rican history, focusing on archival sources, oral history, and genealogy. Her work spans across California and San Diego, areas linked to her family's 1940s migration. She is currently leading the creation of the California Puerto Rican Archive at California State University Fullerton, supported by notable institutions like the National Endowment for the Humanities and the Mellon Foundation, the Smithsonian's National Museum of American History, and the University of Puerto Rico–Cayey Institute for Interdisciplinary Research.

Jade Power-Sotomayor is a CaliRican educator, scholar, and performer who works as assistant professor in the Department of Theatre and Dance at UC San Diego, where she engages with Latinx/e theatre, dance studies, nightlife, epistemologies of the body, feminist of color critique, bilingualism, and intercultural performance in the Caribbean diaspora.

Notes

1. EGA: In this vein, it's also important to note that, thanks to Laura Briggs's book *Reproduction of Empire*, I learned my scholarship was funded by the descendants of one of the pharmaceutical companies who tested contraceptives on Puerto Rican women.
2. EGA: After I completed my degree, Crespo-Kebler personally sent me a job ad. I didn't apply to that job, because my longest-standing committee member discouraged other members from writing me a reference. I'm aware that part of the reason that committee member felt so strongly was rooted in Island and diasporic scholar tensions of who should work where.
3. JPS: See specifically the work of Marién Torres Lopez as a leader of Barrileras del 8M in Puerto Rico and their recent projects that take on feminicide and feminist histories in Puerto Rico; their yearly March 8 performances but also their recent video of "Canción sin Miedo," a bomba adaptation of Vivir Quintana's feminist anthem. The Barrileras del 8M are featured in the photograph on the cover of this anthology.

CHAPTER 2

Where Are the Puerto Ricans in Feminist Studies? A Remixed Roundtable from the 2022 NWSA Conference

ALESSANDRA ROSA, AURORA SANTIAGO ORTIZ, KARRIEANN SOTO VEGA, ZORIMAR RIVERA-MONTES, AND JESSICA N. PABÓN-COLÓN

JESSICA N. PABÓN-COLÓN: What moved you to join this roundtable on Rican feminisms and how does it tie into your work and life?

KARRIEANN SOTO VEGA: I came to feminism *late*, like in my doctoral studies—another long story. My educational experience was grounded in writing and rhetoric, English ed, but most importantly in a political commitment to amplify Puerto Rican struggles and activism. That strand was always there in my work, which leads me to talk about DiaspoRican feminism—and I can't do that without explaining my understanding of this category as deeply embedded in the vaivén, the coming and going, that I and so many other Boricuas, I'm sure, have experienced and continue to experience. Briefly, my first encounter with the category of DiaspoRican was through the artist and activist Mariposa and her poem "Ode to the Diasporican." Unlike Mariposa's usage of the term, and how diaspora scholars try to suggest that the concept is referring to a second-generation community that is established in a place, I think of it more as an oceanic border that transcends temporal and geographic limitations. So el vaivén fluye; it's "fluid"; the water's coming and going. Therefore, even though I was born in Orlando, Florida, I was raised in San Sebastián de las Vegas del Pepino, and as a kid, I often visited my father, who lived in New Jersey.

In relation to my book manuscript on Lolita Lebrón—the radical Puerto Rican nationalist woman whose anti-colonial action has dubbed her a terrorist *and* heroine—and what I'm calling her *Rhetorics of Defiance* against US empire, I apply a DiaspoRican feminist framework both in methodology and in content. Given that Lebrón was also part of the US diaspora in the 1940s in New York, I note how significant it was for her to experience discrimination and precarious living conditions as a politicizing force, which led her to engage in an armed assault against the US Congress in 1954. More recently, I have studied remembrances of Lebrón in Puerto Rico and in cities like New York and Chicago as reverberations of her defiant rhetoric. DiaspoRican feminism thus accounts for the many movements Puerto Ricans make as an impact of colonialism and imperialism but also as a necessary survival strategy.

ZORIMAR RIVERA-MONTES: I also came to feminism, broadly, late, and I think that's a very interesting thing to think about, because there was so much sexism in my surroundings growing up that naturally I internalized some of it. It took both my education and a personal sense of growth and rage to call myself a feminist.

I was born and grew up on the Islands, in Patillas and Arroyo Puerto Rico, which is on the southern coast and an impoverished part of the Islands—the Caribbean coast, which is a different experience than San Juan and the northern coast. These experiences have shaped my upbringing and, definitely, my relationship to feminism. I'm first gen and pretty rooted even though my family has all sorts of vaivén connections. I stayed rooted to the Islands until I left for grad school in Chicago at thirty years old—the most privileged form of migration imaginable, right?

But even when I was in Puerto Rico, I was studying English-language and US-based Puerto Rican literature. So, my first encounters are with the poet Sandra María Esteves and Mariposa as well. With the likes of Pedro Pietri and others, I found a sense of political consciousness that I did not find in Spanish and island-based literature. I identify more with migrant Nuyorican poetry because it's working class, because it's better at speaking about racialization than a lot of the literary production from the Islands; it's able to articulate a decolonial drive in a very powerful, resounding way.

In my academic work, I focus on Puerto Rican literature and popular culture from the 1980s to the present, and I look specifically at colonialism and decolonial thought in relation to neoliberalism, debt, and capitalism. In a sense, what I study is the real-time collapse that we are witnessing in Puerto Rico right now plus a massive migration of Puerto Ricans over the past two decades, which I'm a part of. My dissertation is on the debt crisis in Puerto Rico because I wanted to understand this very abstract but inescapable phenomenon of economic crisis, which was a big part of my life and experience. Puerto Rico has been in an economic recession since 2005; that was the year that I entered college. Crisis was the background of most of my life. Debt was a US national news item later [following the 2008 crisis], but before 2008 it was already a big part of my personal and family life. Before the Great Recession, we experienced the foreclosure of my home and our family business—a little supermarket in Arroyo.

The question is, how does one name this oppression that one cannot even fully understand? I always feel condemned that I chose this topic to research! I have the math skills of a fourth-grader, but I think that is the site of my historic oppression, right? Financialization is easy to ignore as a site of oppression, because it is mathematical and calculated and legal—all of this makes it alienating. I use my research as a way into trying to understand the embodied experience of that financialization—how does it feel, on the body, my own and the country's? I found answers in poetry about the experience of being in a crisis, what daily life was like, the experience of being indebted. That was my entry into Puerto Rican feminism, encountering queer feminist poetry that gave language to the experience of being indebted, framing it as a feminist issue. Puerto Rico's debt was transforming life, albeit slowly, because the temporality of austerity is slow. And then later, with Hurricane Maria, it became the kind of spectacular violence that we all understood as terrible, but before that, the slow and invisible violence of austerity was also with us.

AURORA SANTIAGO ORTIZ: My arrival to academia was also late, because I started my PhD at thirty-four, but not my arrival to feminism, because that was very much instilled since I was a young child growing up between New York City and Puerto Rico. My upbringing and my view of feminism was very much informed by my mom, who was active in the Puerto Rican Socialist Party (PSP) during the 1980s. When we moved to New York City, she connected with folks around that politic, though I knew that she also struggled with a lot of sexism within those spaces. I grew up anchored in an anti-colonial feminist and anti-racist politics, partly based on seeing my mom work as a community psychologist, particularly around HIV prevention in New York City.

I went to my first march when I was around three years old with my mother, in solidarity with political prisoners. As a teenager, I crossed the barbed wire in Vieques with her to camp out in civil disobedience against the US Navy's occupation of two-thirds of the island. Seeing the ways that my mother had such a great community of other women, who helped raise me in New York, was and is very important and is present in the work that I do now.

My work looks at the shift in anti-colonial politics from a nationalist framework into more of an identitarian politics and territorial liberation struggle in Puerto Rico. During the last fifteen years, anti-racist feminist and decolonial projects and pedagogies have grown in popularity throughout Puerto Rico, particularly those that stem from the afterlives of the student movement. I focus on the period after 2006, when Section 936 (a tax incentive for foreign corporations) phased out and led to the economic-recession-turned-depression that Puerto Rico is still reeling from.

Critical of masculinized spaces in organizing and activism, queer and feminist activists in Puerto Rico created organizations such as La Colectiva Feminista en Construcción, educational projects with visible presence online like La Sombrilla Cuir, and grassroots projects like El Hangar. These spaces are either digital or in-person and have been created for folks to educate and receive training as activists, spokespeople, and fundraisers. Solidarity, such as what has been modeled by these youth activists in Puerto Rico—solidarity as a decolonial feminist praxis, relational ethic, and political orientation—is at the heart of my research, teaching, and activism.

ALESSANDRA ROSA: I was a feminist without knowing the concept of being a feminist, initially. Growing up the only girl in my family, for our gatherings I had to wear a headband or bow, a dress with tulle underneath, and the sandals, everything matching from head to toe. As I was always very active, I learned very quickly how to negotiate what was expected of me culturally with how I actually wanted to live and move through the world. I would joke that I became very diplomatic, because I would allow my mom to get the girl that she wanted to show to the family. I would be like, look, I already modeled and said hello to everyone and we took the family photo. Now I'm going to put on my pants, my sneakers, and I'm going to go and enjoy the party—okay?

Even at that age, I was navigating how to be *me* within this world that told me how I needed to act. That's why I joke that I was a feminist before knowing I was a feminist, pushing boundaries already. Aurora also mentioned some things that I remember, growing up: I was born and raised in the Island, but I moved to Florida in 1989 and lived close to Deltona in second and third grade. Right now, the fact that I am living in Tampa is a very 360-degree thing, because now I'm here with my son—even just having him speak more in English and what that means to me, it's part of the Rican feminism embedded here. Part of the story I want to tell was that I noticed my activism exceeded what my family accepted, even my mother; I remember that in 1998 there was the Puerto Rico telephone company strike and I wanted to be there, but my mom said no, you're underage, we can drive by and you can beep the horn but that's it. I remember the Vieques strike as well, and I had to wait and go with my older brother and some of his friends to be able to attend. I always had to wiggle in order to do the things that felt right to me.

That's what guided me into cultural anthropology. I knew I was going to focus on Puerto Rico or Puerto Rican issues, but I didn't know what specifically. One of my pet peeves was education and, at that moment, when I was doing my doctoral studies, I was trying to think of a comparison study between public education (certain schools in the metropolitan area) and private education, because I wanted to look at the pushout or dropout rates in the transition to ninth grade, to high school. While I was thinking about this, that's when the 2010 student movement happened in the University of Puerto Rico. Finally, I felt, *this is it!* It became my way of connecting my love for education and the activism that has always been in me, through my academic work.

We are talking about the Diasporican experience and feminism; unfortunately, I can't live in Puerto Rico because of my job. This has been hard to acknowledge; I never used to say that I lived in the States, I would always say that I was studying in the States, to help myself accept it a little bit more. Inevitably, my family and I live in the States now, and we are part of the diaspora, and I'm glad that I feel that tension. I've never experienced an "us versus them" dynamic, particularly as the concept of "Nuyoricans" has become more blurry. I have had a lot of friends tell me, oh, you're 100 percent Puerto Rican, but I'm like, what does that even mean? Just because I was born and raised there and speak Spanish? (On the flip side, I had American friends that would tell me, "You don't look or sound Puerto Rican!") I don't think that because someone was born in New York, they're not 100 percent. Again, I navigated it very differently; what those terms and divisions mean to me or what not.

A big thing that I try to bring into my work is the notion of emotions, particularly empathy. Concerning the Puerto Rican post-disaster migrants from Hurricane Maria to Tampa Bay Area, I started thinking about and centering Rican feminism by way of empathic ethnography. The research team asked if I meant that all the other ethnographies didn't have or use or center empathy. Of course not, but this was at another level, not just my feelings but the people's feelings. Seeing them not just as participants but as people sharing their stories, among whom I was sharing my story as well. They were always more than just interviews, they were moments of connection; during one interview, as the woman spoke to me, she started bawling her eyes out, and suddenly I was bawling too. Eventually I asked her, do you want a break? She was like, I need a glass of wine. So we ended up continuing the interview as a happy hour, and it just bloomed into a very unconventional way of doing research. But it felt right, it felt like we connected; it didn't feel like she was just giving me this information for our research. Thus, empathy is very much a part of my feminist practice.

JNP: When I was thinking about putting together this roundtable, I had this nagging question in my head: Do we need another frame for feminist inquiry? For feminist methodology? For feminist practice? For me, Black feminist inquiry, theory, and praxis is my intellectual root, the kind of feminism that spoke to me and gave me the frames that I needed to do my initial academic work. So, I was thinking, how do we imagine Rican feminisms in relation to, for lack of a better word, other subfields? "Subfields"

feels so reductive. How do we think of Rican feminisms in relation to other frames for feminist study that are built from identities of difference beyond the single axis of gender? I'm thinking Asian feminisms, queer feminisms, crip feminisms. Because in one sense, Rican feminism is sort of always already those things. But in another sense, maybe there's a value to delineating how it's connected and how it's different. How do we imagine Puerto Rican feminism in relation to these other feminisms?

KSV: I think of them all as approaches. But that's just to start. I wanted to try and merge this with another question: What is liberation? It is, to me, very grounded in what rhetoricians call kairos, or kairotic concerns. Liberation is in the immediacy, the urgent, the now. But also, obviously, it is always informed by a historical lineage and situation. I wanted to go back to Mariposa, because in a recent cafecito gathering at the Center for Puerto Rican Studies, she was saying how for her, "making it" meant getting some kind of recognition, some kind of acknowledgment, which to her was "a way to defy the conquistadores." By your presence, you're already challenging the notion—the settler-colonial notion—of genocide, but also the notion of extraction. I think that this can be considered in relation to a longer history of colonial displacement, cultural erasure, and slow death, which we talked a little bit about already. For me, "making it" is synonymous to, or analogous to, having a kind of sovereignty necessary to thrive.

I'm thinking back on the remarks that my fellow panelists have made in the vein of, "Well, I didn't know I was doing some kind of feminist thing." When I took my first class on feminist narratives with Minnie Bruce Pratt at Syracuse University, she pushed me on that a little bit. She asked me, "What, or how did you think toward these things when you were a child?" And I said, "Well, seeing my mom who was working in the Avon factory, as a secretary in a nonprofit organization for disabled folks, taking night classes, and still showing up to raise us; living with my grandma, my tíos, tías, and around us the village of women that raised me." In my childhood, when my mother was able to buy land and actually build a home—admittedly it was a capitalist, material condition, but it was the security we needed! And it was also her own empowerment, her being and surviving as her own self. Very rudimentary "I don't need a man" politics. But this is a kind of liberation ideology; I think of it in relation to sovereignty. When I was taking that class with Minnie Bruce Pratt, I had no idea of feminist theory, so feminist narratives [as a subject] was new to me. I wondered, how can I insert my Puerto Rican voice here? Minnie Bruce suggested I present on Gloria Anzaldúa, specifically *Borderlands: La Frontera*, and la mestiza consciousness; for me, it was empowering to have an opportunity to speak my home language in a predominantly white and Anglo classroom. This is where I first felt this bridge; and later when I was introduced to *This Bridge Called My Back*, to Aurora Levins Morales, particularly, I felt that this is where Puerto Rican feminism is located. So I feel like that's what we need, we need another iteration of *This Bridge*. Folks like Noralis [Rodriguez-Coss], who's here, are already kind of doing that work in speaking about the Puerto Rican positionality—but Noralis also does so in relation to Haiti, Palestine, Egypt. So all these feminisms are in conversation, in coalition.

ASO: I'll go off of that because we're talking about coalition and where we find those that speak to our work. I think that Black and Latina feminists in the US have been pivotal in helping us think about how to build coalitions across difference. But we also need to look to Puerto Rico and to Puerto Rican feminist work in praxis, besides and beyond the now. This work is being and has been done through cultural production, through poetry, through being out on the street. Theorizing this is important!

Puerto Rico is a borderland because of its unique positionality within Latin America and the Caribbean, while simultaneously a colonized place that experiences both circular and unidirectional migration. It's important to look to Latin America for activism and the work that's been done there, and a lot of activists [in Puerto Rico] are doing that. Theoretically, my work looks to bridge Black, Indigenous, and Latina feminist theory and activism done in the US, while also centering Puerto Rico's agency and resistance to colonialism. Puerto Rican feminisms are informed by scholarly work, activist work, and that is very much in dialogue with all these other bodies of thought, including Caribbean thinkers like Frantz Fanon, who theorized what is known as the coloniality of being, or the psychic dimensions of decolonization.[1]

Puerto Rico has always been fertile ground for anti-colonial activism and theorizing and has been influenced by other Caribbean and Global South struggles. To me, it is exciting to think what can nutrirnos, what can nourish us in looking at other transnational projects of liberation in tandem with our own.

ZRM: I agree, and I think those are very articulate ways of answering Jessica's question. My first encounter with feminist theory was US Black feminism. On the flip side, it's important to face this ugly history of anti-Blackness in our Rican lineage. If I think of my mother and my grandmother and my great-grandmother, there is racial violence embedded in their legacies; it's important to reckon with that history and center Blackness in our Rican feminism.

I also want to say something about the tension between US feminisms and coalitions with Latin American feminisms. It's interesting to hear Jess talk about where the idea of Rican feminisms and this roundtable were born and that tension with NWSA itself. I think that US mainstream feminism historically doesn't do a good job of coalition building, but Latin American feminism does.

In thinking about feminism via debt, Argentinian feminists have done amazing work on that, like Verónica Gago, which groups like La Colectiva [Feminista en Construcción] follow. I once heard Argentinian feminists speak on their fight for reproductive rights, folks who were organizing with Mexican feminists and Polish feminists and these global networks; they said they contacted the Women's March but never heard back—and look at where we are now, here. There's an imperialist shortsightedness there in the US, because it doesn't build coalition outside itself. That being said, I think about the important place of diasporic Puerto Ricans and all they do to build relation with Islands-based Puerto Ricans. So yes, we do have to look to Puerto Rico, but also internationally. I also very much believe in the sovereignty of diasporic Puerto Rican feminism that is in English and can be in communication as it builds coalitions, but ensuring that it's not centering only the Islands and leaving behind the diasporic experience.

AR: Through my son, I see my feminism play out beyond the academy. I have been thinking about how it's always more accepted for girls to push boundaries and adopt "man" things, or "boy" things, than it is for boys to push past the boundary into "girl"' things. Sometimes my son will come home from school with a line like, "Oh, pink is for girls . . ." And I have to be like, "Is pink for girls? Well, you have a pink shirt and you look very cute in the pink shirt." I push the boundaries with him to break down that generational knowledge that has been passed down culturally to us. I think that is part of the feminism that I'm learning as I am doing it, that I am also trying to instill in him as a source of confidence. He decided to wear a *Frozen* dress costume to school one day, and one boy came up and said, "Boys can't wear dresses," and he just stood there until one of his best friends said, "Yeah, they can"—and then they both said, "Yeah," and that was it. I think the more we cultivate this confidence with younger generations, the more it will impact our work and build that future that we want to see.

JNP: The last question is an opportunity to uplift and amplify liberation praxis that you've seen. What are Rican feminists doing? What are the strategies and tactics that we're using while working toward this liberation project?

ZRM: The new Villano Antillano video; she is a transgender woman rapper from Puerto Rico doing incredibly important and beautiful work. She is a great example of praxis, of someone who doesn't come from a space of theory but still centers trans and decolonial politics and aesthetics in her work; that, to me, is trans feminist Rican liberation.

KSV: When we think of feminist groups, we think of La Cole. Through and through, *colectiva feminista* is in the name! Much of the work that I've done recently is about Vueltabajo Teatro in a performance street art action. A lot of their work is not explicitly feminist, but we can see feminist principles in it. They do a free circus on Sundays in Mayagüez, so they're reclaiming the commons and molding the next generation by saying, "We don't need to pay for entertainment. We can do it ourselves. We can create props that are made from recyclable materials." There's this kind of environmentalist rhetoric there, but again, they're not necessarily explicitly part of the climate justice [movement]. In the way that they talk, in the way that they express themselves, they always express themselves in the female form in Spanish, which to me is a queer practice. They're a transdisciplinary artist collective, and they think of their space as creation of the self but also of the society that they are living in. That's just one example that I'm thinking of in terms of work that I've done recently. Going back to liberation practice, I think that we need to also think through the implication of calling them feminist without them calling themselves that explicitly. I'm thinking about that more broadly, because we do want so badly to see it. I had a recent conversation about environmental justice in Puerto Rico, where the question was: Is there a climate change [movement] or are there groups explicitly protesting about this? I said, no, they're not going to go to the UN! They're too busy trying to fight Columbus Landing [and other foreign capitalist development projects] taking over the beaches that are supposed to be public in Puerto Rico. That's the immediate concern impacting my and their backyard. As academics, we're so quick to group, classify, categorize radical action so that we can stamp it with a label.

ASO: Since the announcement that Puerto Rico's debt was unpayable in 2015 and the subsequent installation of the Junta de Control Fiscal[2]—people (young people particularly), out of necessity, have crafted the futures that they want to be living in, today. I don't want to romanticize it. It's a hustle, and some grassroots collectives are repurposing public and private space for a public good. Many of these projects have feminist angles to them. For example, Libros Libres is a street library project that began about a decade ago by young activists. One of the aims of the street library project was to make the streets safer because of its impact on pedestrian traffic. As a result, more illumination was added in that avenue, enabling women to walk more freely in an area with a high incidence of sexual assault in Puerto Rico. There are also the feminist pantries that emerged in the wake of the COVID-19 pandemic, where hygiene and menstruation products were placed in bookcases in public spaces for people that needed them. Mutual aid practices like this, collective care, and solidarity efforts are all happening and alive on the archipelago. La Cole takes on the huge job of political education, with their bulletins that they hand out, as well as clothing swaps and sales to raise money to support the organization. They occupied an abandoned building, which has intensified police repression on their organization. About 30 percent of properties are abandoned in Puerto Rico, which makes the landscape ripe for speculator cryptobros to buy these properties and sell them at a premium—and to push people out of the archipelago. A lot of practices to counteract privatization of public space have been happening for more than a decade. There are a lot of organizations engaging in this kind of consciousness-raising work, activist work, direct service work, and community-building work. These are liberatory practices of self-determination.

KSV: Because the state doesn't provide; the state takes.

AR: I just wanted to mention a couple of the groups that I think are doing amazing work to survive because the state is not providing, like Comedores Sociales, who seek to eradicate hunger in Puerto Rico. Also, Mentes Puertorriqueñas en Accion, which I was a part of as well—they take a more academic stance but they're making direct impact in communities, like in Villas del Sol and other areas as well. Ayuda Legal Puerto Rico focuses on housing, handling all that paperwork and everything! A lot of ground-up work is being done—when we talk about practice, they're doing it! That's my guilt of being in the diaspora; I'm always looking for what else can I do for over there, because it is so needed. At the same time, being divided among so many groups, causes, and needs gets exhausting.

That brings me to this notion of resilience. We're so tired, because the time for this work has been upon us since before the debt; it's more than twenty years that we've been in the same struggle and just responding to added dimensions of it. I laugh because either I do that or I cry, right? I'd rather laugh, use a little bit of humor. But shit, man, like—when is there going to be a pause?

Alessandra Rosa (she/her) is a sociocultural anthropologist, professor, researcher, activist, public speaker, and consultant. As a transnational feminist scholar, she has dedicated her teaching, research, activism, and service to fostering diversity, inclusion, equity, and justice. Her work has been published in academic journals, electronic journals, and book chapters, as well as nonacademic outlets. Her book manuscript, *Spatializing Protest: (re)Constructing Spaces of Resistance and Contention During the 2010–11 UPR Student Movement*, is soon to be published by the University of Nebraska Press.

Aurora Santiago Ortiz is assistant professor of gender and women's studies and Chicane/Latine studies at the University of Wisconsin-Madison. Her research focuses on anti-racist feminisms, decolonial perspectives, and participatory action research. Her current book manuscript, entitled *Circuits of Self-Determination: Mapping Radical Solidarities and Infrastructures of Resistance in Twenty-First Century Puerto Rico*, focuses on anti-colonial activism stemming from the student movement, particularly grassroots prefigurative political practices anchored in solidarity and spatial repurposing.

Karrieann Soto Vega is a DiaspoRican feminista and cultural rhetorician. She is assistant professor of English and faculty affiliate with women's, gender, and sexuality studies as well as Latina/o studies at The Pennsylvania State University. Her research and teaching spans Puerto Rican and Latinx studies, anti-colonial feminism, activism and social movements, performance, and sonic rhetoric. Some of her other work can be found in *Communication and Critical/Cultural Studies*, *Enculturation: A Journal of Rhetoric, Writing, and Culture*, *Journal for the History of Rhetoric*, and *CENTRO: Journal for the Center of Puerto Rican Studies*.

Zorimar Rivera-Montes is assistant professor of Latinx literatures and cultures at Tulane University. Her research focuses on contemporary Puerto Rican and diasporic literature and popular culture in relation to neoliberalism and colonialism.

Notes

1. See Frantz Fanon, *Black Skin, White Masks* (Grove Press, 2008); Nelson Maldonado-Torres, "On the Coloniality of Being: Contributions to the Development of a Concept," *Cultural Studies* 21, nos. 2–3 (2007): 240–70.
2. Puerto Rico defaulted on some of its debt obligations in 2015, leading to the imposition of the Fiscal Oversight and Management Board (FOMB). The FOMB was created by US Congress through Ley PROMESA (Puerto Rico Oversight, Management, and Economic Stability Act). PROMESA was signed into law by President Barack Obama in June 2016. The FOMB instituted draconian budget cuts and austerity measures that curtailed labor rights and mandated steep budget cuts for the University of Puerto Rico, among other actions.

CHAPTER 3

Coalición 8 de Marzo Manifiestos (2022, 2023)

MARCH 8 COALITION
TRANSLATED BY HEATHER HOUDE

A NOTE FROM VANESA CONTRERAS CAPÓ: The March 8 Coalition of Puerto Rico is a "meeting place" for feminist organizations and individual activists. It was founded in 2009 with the intention of commemorating International Women's Day in a collective way and thus having a greater impact throughout the Puerto Rican archipelago. That is why every year different activists and organizations meet not only to organize March 8 but also to think about and discuss what urgent changes are needed to achieve the life we want and deserve.

Every year we look for a slogan for the activity, for example: *Las mujeres exigimos equidad y justicia social* (2013), *Si nosotras paramos el país se detiene* (2017), and *8 M en contra de la deuda* (2019), among others. In recent years, we have decided on the slogan *Justicia de las mujeres* (2022) and *Justicia de las mujeres es justicia verde* (2023). Normally, we meet weekly for one or two months to discuss the political approaches we want to promote and to draft a document with our demands. Over time, these documents have developed into manifiestos. We write one each year.

Below are the most recent manifiestos; both were published in Spanish in the feminist magazine *Todas PR* (www.todaspr.com). These manifiestos are documents created by our collective discussions in the years 2022 and 2023.

Manifiesto of Demands
February 28, 2022

The slogan "Justicia PARA las mujeres," or "Justice FOR women," is often used as a call to recognize and denounce the many forms of historical and structural violence that prevent women and girls—in all their diversity, including trans, queer, intersex, and nonbinary people—from equally accessing the fundamental rights that every human being deserves.

The slogan is also invoked to interrupt—as a demand to abolish the violence that emerges from various institutions as well as social, economic, political, and cultural structures. Thus, "Justice FOR women" is a call to action: urging individuals, communities, institutions, and governments to take on the social responsibility of closing all gaps in access to rights and justice, and to guarantee equity across all spheres—education, health, economics, politics, culture, and the environment, among others. However, we believe that demanding justice FOR women, within current social frameworks and dynamics, may in some ways validate the very power structures that were born from exclusionary and authoritarian social practices.

In contrast, the slogan "Justicia DE las mujeres," or "Justice BY women," represents a paradigm shift rooted in the rightful demand for equity and justice. It reclaims the notion of "justice," redefined and enacted *by* women through a feminist political stance that embraces all identities: feminized bodies, people who are nonwhite, nonbinary, cis, trans, and intersex. In light of the current system's failure to create the equitable society we envision, it becomes necessary to rethink and address the issues that affect us collectively, from our own understanding of what justice means and how to achieve it. That is, rather than a justice we merely demand, it is a justice imagined and built BY us and FOR us. The demand is NOT to be included within a justice that is confined to the legal and juridical principles that have historically excluded us, but rather to embark on a political project that redefines justice through the lens of diversity, intersectionality, and plurality. In our call for a justice defined by feminism—one that acknowledges and uplifts diversity—we propose the creation of new structures that meet the needs of all living beings, who today are subject to a form of justice historically shaped by powerful forces: patriarchy, racism, capitalism, and speciesism. These forces actively destroy lives, communities, and the planet itself.

Therefore, justice by women begins by recognizing that there can be no true justice without dismantling the sexist, racist, and classist discourse upon which the current concept of justice has been built. In the face of patriarchal justice, we must construct a feminist, anti-racist, anti-capitalist, ecofeminist, and anti-colonial justice—one that is fully aware of the vast socioeconomic disparities in today's world.

What we are referring to is a justice rooted in feminisms. Violeta Assiego has pointed out that feminist justice, unlike patriarchal justice, emphasizes conflict resolution. Justice from the perspective of women advocates for the repair and recovery of victims through a human rights lens.[1] We affirm that justice by women is a nonpunitive approach that considers the power dynamics between people and how to bring them into balance. It is essential to center the victim, their needs, and the repair of any harm done. In other words, justice by women prioritizes prevention. That's why we first highlight the importance of education rooted in a gender perspective. Secondly, we highlight mediation—mechanisms to resolve conflicts before they escalate. And finally, when the aforementioned fail, restitution for the victim, always with an eye toward building a better future. Feminist justice requires analyzing situations in all their complexity, taking into account the context that allowed one person to harm another. It is also essential to think about how to intervene and, rather than focusing on punishment, what changes are needed to prevent the harmful act from being repeated.

Our demand is that justice be defined by the diverse and plural perspectives of women. Because justice is not the judicial system, nor is it confined to it, nor is it the state's definition of what is or isn't just according to the law. We want to propose the following: what needs to be redistributed, repaired, and rebuilt; what processes must be followed to guarantee the eradication of the various forms of violence and to repair the many harms that have historically and structurally impacted women's bodies and lives in all their dimensions; how this reparation should be defined, what its limits are, and how it would be implemented; how to restore those who have suffered injustices and violence; and how to define a balanced and equitable society.

From this reflection, we understand that "Justice BY women" encompasses four fundamental aspects:

- what needs to change in order to achieve true equity
- a new way of viewing justice
- an aspiration for well-being or living a dignified life
- the power to make the necessary decisions to achieve all of the above.

To achieve true equity, we must transform the political, economic, and cultural structures and dynamics that stand in our way. We must eradicate poverty, ensure wage and distributive justice, be able to live free from violence, and have access to a dignified life and the essential services that uphold it—health, education, food, housing, and security in old age. We must also develop and implement public policy from a gender perspective that allows us to control our own bodies and sexuality, that guarantees our equal participation in political life, and that ensures our freedom to express our sexuality and gender identity.

We want to transform the concept of justice so that it is rooted in restorative justice. One that operates within a system where prisons are drastically reduced or abolished entirely. One where the focus is on individuals taking responsibility and repairing the harm they cause to other human beings and all living beings through meaningful, constructive action.

We aspire to a buen vivir—"I am because you are," an Indigenous concept from the original peoples of South America that envisions life not only in community with other living beings but also in harmony with our planet and the cosmos. In that same spirit, we are committed to a dignified life through our participation in spaces of intellectual, cultural, and artistic creation; through the defense and protection of the environment; and through the building of a culture of peace and freedom.

We assert that achieving these aspirations for change will require the political power to make the decisions necessary to bring them to life. The decolonization of our country, along with the direct participation of the people who live here, is essential to building new models of governance rooted in the paradigm shift we are advancing.

The need to shift the discourse toward equity and justice is urgent and undeniable in our current context. The deep economic depression Puerto Rico has faced for the past fifteen years is being leveraged by those in political and economic power. They justify the expansion of neoliberal austerity measures placed upon the colonial state and general population while simultaneously securing greater accumulation for private interests—whether individual, corporate, or imperial. These measures have made fertile ground for the deepening and widening of the historical structural inequalities that have long shaped our society and that have systematically and disproportionately violated the rights of women and girls.

The impacts of Hurricanes Irma and Maria, the earthquakes in the south, and the ongoing pandemic have exposed not only poor planning and governmental mismanagement but also an alarming absence of a state vision that recognizes and guarantees our right to a dignified life.

Feminist Demands of March 8, 2023

For decades, women have been at the forefront of the struggle for environmental justice in Puerto Rico. From the resistance against the Navy in Vieques, to the ongoing fight against coal ash, to the protection of beaches across the forty-four coastal municipalities, to the liberation of zoo animals, among many others—all share a common denominator: women's demand for community health, free access to natural resources, and a healthy coexistence with the environment. In practice, the struggle to protect the environment has always been intimately tied to women's struggle.

Our slogan this year, "Women's justice is green justice," affirms our right to a healthy life. A life in which we have control over our bodies and that is sustainable, free, and in solidarity with all other living beings and the planet. It is feminist, racial, economic, and environmental justice because it highlights the connection and interdependence of all beings who share this planet. The domination of one race over another, one gender over another, one economic class over another, or one species over another is the primary threat to the survival of life on Earth—in other words, it is an ecological threat. Our slogan calls for a struggle grounded in an anti-racist, gender-based perspective, because it challenges the systems that privilege one racial group over another; a decolonial perspective, because it seeks to break from the logic of modernity and address Puerto Rico's issues for and by Puerto Rico; an abolitionist perspective, because it advocates for restorative justice over punitive justice; and an anti-speciesist perspective, because it recognizes that no species is superior to another. It is a form of justice that leaves no living being behind—one that promotes health, freedom, and collective justice.

Green justice is environmental, anti-racist, decolonial, and abolitionist education

Due to our geographic reality of being an island in the Caribbean, green justice must have its foundation in an environmental, anti-racist, and decolonial education and in the pursuit of social justice. When we use education as a tool, the way a society sees itself transforms. Schools are vital for raising awareness, especially among children and youth. Therefore, included in our demands is a call for school autonomy to be respected so that environmental education can be incorporated as a core pillar of every curriculum. In addition, school leadership should have access to community and municipal forests and gardens to create spaces for recreation and to teach about environmental protection. We deserve an education that invests in food sovereignty and takes action to achieve it. We also call on the government and the Department of Education of Puerto Rico to fully fund and resource the agriculture and agronomy programs so they can carry out their critical work. Education in Puerto Rico must support both teachers and students to become leaders who embrace environmental justice as a fundamental right and take action to make it a reality.

We demand that the state adopt an education system aimed at eliminating all forms of prejudice and provide the resources necessary for a quality education that is aligned with the needs of teachers and the communities they serve. Statistics show that teachers are the most economically vulnerable to and negatively affected by policies set by the very agency whose primary role it is to advocate for their success.

From this same perspective we urgently demand that the privatization of the country's public university system be avoided at all costs. We recognize that the University of Puerto Rico (UPR), our most important educational institution, has a student and workforce population largely composed of women. In addition, we demand the full reinstatement of UPR's budget, which is rightfully and legally theirs. This funding makes it possible for campuses like UPR in Utuado—home to the only bachelor's program in sustainable agriculture—to remain open; for the student body, largely made up of women, to study without being forced to take on multiple jobs to cover the cost; for critical programs like the Seismic Network, the Experimental Stations, and Agricultural Extension (among many others) to operate and contribute to the ecological development of our archipelago; and for UPR's workforce to receive fair wages and dignified working conditions.

As part of our work, we must challenge and uproot the distorted belief held by fundamentalist sectors that our student population is homogeneous. More and more we are faced with the urgent need to embrace each member of our school community from their own perspective and with respect, acknowledging the importance of the struggles of feminized and nonbinary people. This requires a shift in awareness and a transformation of language. Fundamentalist groups have argued that a gender perspective in education and the use of terms like "todes" will not solve the specific problems women face. However, we know that truly inclusive language, when grounded in gender-aware and anti-racist education, supports the full and well-rounded development of our youth.

Lastly, quality public education must be available to everyone and at all levels. It is through education that we instigate change, shift paradigms, and adopt new perspectives that allow us to dismantle the colonial, external interest–driven educational system that has kept us in a state of insolvency.

Green justice is reproductive justice

Women and pregnant people in Puerto Rico have been threatened by the attempts of fundamentalist sectors to limit our autonomy and control our bodies and our sexuality. Limiting the right to abortion means denying that women have the capacity to make free reproductive decisions. It means forcing us to carry out unwanted pregnancies; in other words, forcing us to give birth and become mothers. Forced pregnancies and births are acts of torture that deny our humanity. Forced motherhood under conditions of economic crisis limits our ability to live a dignified life, particularly for people who are poor, young, Black, immigrants, and those with differing abilities.

In addition, the lack of access to sexual and reproductive healthcare prevents us from honoring the rhythm of each body, the same way we should honor the rhythms of our environment. Our environment and our bodies alike deserve to grow and change without interventions that disrupt their natural processes—with respect for the autonomy and capacity for change that comes with every phase of preconception, pregnancy, and postpartum. We demand that laws be created and enforced that protect us from violence throughout the entire lifespan. We demand the dignity of menstruating working people be protected by requiring all workplaces to offer menstrual leave. We demand accessible, legal, and safe abortion, where legal and economic barriers do not result in forced pregnancies. In conditions of economic, health, and housing crisis, imposing pregnancies condemns people to a life of poverty, and therefore degrades their quality of life.

Green justice is an accessible and quality healthcare system

In addition to the environmental crisis, we face a lack of accessible health-care focused on holistic well-being. There is an urgent need for a universal, accessible, and high-quality healthcare plan for everyone in Puerto Rico. We must eradicate once and for all the idea of health as a business if we are to ensure access to this essential service. Each year, the mental health of people living in Puerto Rico is increasingly at risk due to socio-natural events and pandemics. These events have left our communities without the time or resources to recover—especially those most marginalized by the system. In their aftermath, the state has failed to take meaningful action to improve our living conditions; on the contrary, it has deepened existing disparities. Our most vulnerable communities are grappling with compounding structural failures—like a collapsed bridge after heavy rains, ongoing power outages, and damaged homes—that undermine people's ability to live full, dignified lives. All while the need for direct services remains urgent. This reality creates even greater vulnerability for women who care for their families, women and people affected by gender-based violence, Black women, immigrant women, poor women, older women, and women with disabilities.

We cannot forget that as we age, we will lose some of our abilities, making us even more vulnerable in a system that does not care for its elderly population. Many of us were unable to take proper care of ourselves as wage earners because we were working double shifts. When we got sick, we ignored it because our children and/or partners needed us. The years went by, and our health issues worsened. Now, in old age and with illnesses, the only health plans we can afford don't cover the medications we need. Each day, insurance companies grow richer by further stripping us of our right to a dignified old age. That's why we demand an accessible healthcare plan for all, one that guarantees all necessary services and medications for a healthy aging process.

Green justice is dignified housing and the elimination of forced displacement

When we talk about green justice, we are also referring to the right to safe and affordable housing for women who are heads of household. This right is constantly under threat for many reasons: forced displacement due to gentrification, the atmospheric disasters we've endured over the past seven years, the challenges we face in trying to obtain property titles, and economic inequality. This last one in particular forces us to take on second and third jobs on top of our household responsibilities and oftentimes full-time caregiving for our children.

Over 70 percent of women in Puerto Rico live under the constant threat of losing or being removed from their homes. These challenges become even more severe at the intersections of inequality—for those experiencing domestic violence, for racialized people, for the LGBTTQIA+ community, for those living in rural or underdeveloped areas, for people living with HIV, and so on. The more disadvantaged we are, the fewer chances we have of accessing safe and affordable housing.

Breaking the cycle of gender-based violence, healing, gaining access to opportunities to rebuild our lives, and developing economic self-sufficiency all require safe and dignified shelter. We need homes that are not threatened by Law 20-22, or more recently by Law 60, nor by the investors who profit from them. If our basic needs are not met, we cannot address the residual trauma from violence. Moreover, more than five years after Hurricane Maria, despite the programs and the resource allocation, there are still 3,646 families living in precarious conditions and under tarps.

We demand that those responsible for leading our country into the current economic situation take immediate and decisive action to address the housing crisis. Green justice means having access to buen vivir—to living with dignity, to recovering and finding stability after leaving a violent relationship. We demand reparations and dignified housing.

Green justice is labor justice for working women

Working women make up more than 50 percent of the labor force, yet we are still treated as second-class workers. That's why we demand fair wages, equal to those of other workers. It is common for men to earn more than women, even when women carry a disproportionate share of the labor. Neither pay nor working conditions are equitable for all people. We demand that domestic work be compensated and valued as an essential activity for life, and that the minimum wage be at least $15 an hour, including for servers. We also demand that all people—particularly women, members of LGBTIQAP communities, nonwhite individuals, people with differing abilities, and immigrant workers—be guaranteed respectful, safe, accessible workplaces free from harassment and violence. We demand equal treatment and respect across government, private companies, and NGOs alike. At the same time, it is urgent to continue opening space in unions and in labor movement leadership so that women can bring their demands and offer new ways of organizing. We support unions that fight for and stand in solidarity with all workers, whether or not they are unionized. All of these demands drive green justice forward because they promote healthy jobs and lives that are free from violence.

Green justice is animal and climate justice

Green justice is concerned with the well-being of all living beings. Animals are sentient, living beings who deserve a healthy life free from violence. That is why we demand that zoos be eliminated and call for the transformation of these spaces into interactive parks—spaces free from captivity and exploitation where families can enjoy nature without harming or caging any sentient being. We therefore support Senate Bill 1041, which also proposes relocating the animals currently in zoos, many of whom live alone and are unwell, to sanctuaries. We owe them all an end of life that is dignified and free from exploitation. In addition, we call for the eradication of animal use in laboratories—one of the most appalling examples of what modern science is capable of in the twenty-first century. Fighting against animal exploitation is fighting against a political and economic system that increasingly isolates us from our environment and teaches us to see ourselves as superior to other species. If feminists defend their right to make decisions about our own bodies and affirm that "my body is mine," then as part of that same struggle, we must also recognize that the bodies and lives of animals do not belong to us.

Green justice also means supporting all the people and communities who are fighting to protect and access beaches, to decontaminate the environment, to promote agriculture and food sovereignty, and to push for public policies that once and for all lead to the exclusive use of clean and sustainable energy. As a Caribbean archipelago, we are highly vulnerable to the impacts of climate change such as rising sea levels, more intense hurricanes, droughts, and other atmospheric phenomena. Thus, talking about green justice is talking about climate justice. It is women, children, and elders who suffer most from the political disasters that follow natural events. Environmental struggles are now the foundation of all struggles. It is no surprise, then, that more than half of all violent acts recorded by Global Witness are committed by police, military, or security personnel against people who were defending the environment. Now more than ever, it is crucial that governments, companies, and international entities recognize and legitimize the essential role of environmental defenders in achieving sustainable development for our societies. We demand that the safety of environmental defenders be guaranteed in the face of increasing violence at environmental protests.

Green justice is access to energy, energy security, and a dignified retirement: people before debt

The fight against the privatization of the Puerto Rico Electric Power Authority (AEE) is a fight led by working women, caregivers, retirees, and business owners, among others. We women have borne the brunt of the abuse dealt by a colonial Fiscal Control Board that imposes privatization as a way to pay for an unsustainable public debt they refuse to audit. This has been deliberately designed to increasingly strip us of our human rights and access to essential services.

We are already suffering the consequences of privatization: rate hikes, unstable service, equipment fires, house fires, fires at AEE facilities, and even deaths. There has been no compensation for damages, employees have been displaced, and the retirement system is owed around 900 million dollars.

We are on the verge of losing 68 percent of our water reservoirs in order to generate our energy. These reservoirs provide water to the Puerto Rico Aqueduct and Sewer Authority (AAA), to our farmers, and to our homes. Green justice means the right to public renewable energy for everyone because the right to water is vital to our existence.

Today we stand in total rejection of AEE's Debt Adjustment Plan. It proposes to further increase the cost of living for women and their families by raising electricity bills for decades to come in order to pay an unjustified debt that must be canceled. In Puerto Rico we already pay some of the highest energy rates, leaving many of us already unable to afford our energy bills. In order to pay this illegitimate debt, the plan also strips AEE's workers of their acquired rights and deprives them of a dignified retirement. An unsustainable debt payment by the AEE to predatory vulture funds diverts critical resources that could be used to transition us to renewable energy. Therefore, we vehemently oppose the privatization of this essential service, a privatization that has already brought more energy insecurity, higher costs, and diminished access to our human right to energy.

We firmly demand clean, safe energy and equitable access. We want energy justice that protects our agricultural lands, our natural reserves, and our ecological spaces.

Women's justice goes far beyond demanding rights—it drives a new paradigm for living together in solidarity with one another, with other living beings, and with the planet. Women's justice is rooted in the experiences of all the groups who fight every day to build new, different ways of life by way of nonmodern frameworks. The colonial-patriarchal-racist-speciesist world system has brought us to the limits of our ability to inhabit this planet. It is urgent that we think beyond the modern, Westernized rule of law and seek other ways of life. That is why, this year, we are committing to green justice—a justice that highlights the need to rethink ourselves and reimagine our existence on Earth.

It is important to highlight that this year, on March 8, 2023, we dedicate this day to women who have devoted themselves to women's justice from their respective spaces: the workers of Cadillac Uniforms, the environmental leader and founder of Casa Pueblo in Adjuntas, Tinti Deyá, and the gynecologist and passionate advocate for reproductive justice, Yari Vale.

Note

1. Ter García, "Thinking Together to Define Feminist Justice," *Crónica en Red*, January 29, 2020.

CHAPTER 4

Radical Imaginings of Feminist Solidarities Entre Puerto Rico y Richmond, Virginia

ALICIA DÍAZ AND PATRICIA HERRERA

The dance film *Entre Puerto Rico y Richmond: Women in Resistance* was commissioned as part of the 2020 exhibit *Commonwealth* at the Institute for Contemporary Art (ICA) at Virginia Commonwealth University (VCU) in Richmond, VA.[1] This exhibit was organized across three socially engaged institutions: the ICA at VCU in Richmond, VA, Beta Local in San Juan, Puerto Rico, and Philadelphia Contemporary. The exhibit explored the historical concept of Commonwealth and its legacy in each of these three locations. The forefront of the ICA curatorial approach questions whether it is possible to unleash the collective power of the notion of "common wealth" while also recognizing its connections to exploitation, racial violence, systemic inequities, and "common debt." How could we reimagine wealth and come together to use our common resources for the common good, to influence the wealth and well-being of our communities?

ICA curators Stephanie Smith and Noah Simblist approached Puerto Rican dance artist and educator Alicia Díaz to commission a project exploring these issues. As artistic director, Alicia convened a group of multidisciplinary artist-activists to cocreate the dance film *Women in Resistance*, including conceptual collaborator and dramaturg Patricia Herrera, dance artists and cultural organizers Christine (Tine Tine) Wyatt and Christina Leoni-Osion, interdisciplinary artist and research assistant Luis Vasquez La Roche, percussionist Héctor "Coco" Barez, and singer and voiceover artist Yaraní del Valle. The film was produced and edited by David Riley, with videography by Departure Point Films and color and sound correction by Digital Fruit Snax.[2]

Our project is centered around the pivotal role of the tobacco industry and the shared history of colonial capitalism in both Richmond, VA, and

Figure 1. Christina Leoni-Osion and Christine Wyatt in the dance film *Entre Puerto Rico y Richmond: Women in Resistance Shall Not Be Moved.* Film still. Image courtesy of the authors.

Puerto Rico. This exploration fosters opportunities for envisioning bridges between these locales, all the while acknowledging and honoring legacies of activism, protest, and liberation. Our aim is to move, dance, and embody archives of resistance and anti-colonial activism, weaving narratives that are often overlooked when told in isolation.

We Pay Homage: An Ancestral Invocation for Dreaming a Better Tomorrow

As multidisciplinary creative strategists, we are reaching out across temporalities, geographies, and cultures to pay homage to our ancestors with an invitation to you, our readers, to experience our dance film *Entre Puerto Rico y Richmond: Women in Resistance Shall Not Be Moved*. The cocreators of this project come from different walks of life, different ages, cultures, racial backgrounds—Puerto Rican, Black, white, Italian, Afro-diasporic. Our ancestors and our spirits traverse a multitude of locations, from Ecuador to Italy to Puerto Rico to Trinidad and Tobago to New York to Virginia to Maryland—as well as places that we are unaware of. For us, imagining and reimagining new possibilities means reaching back to hold the hands of our ancestors, standing firmly in solidarity with those who have died to remember and honor the past.

We draw upon the legacy of both past and present ancestor activists, scholars, and artists, like Luisa Capetillo (1882–1922)[3] and Dominga de la Cruz Becerril (1909–1981) as well as Louise "Mamma" Harris (1891–?) and Black tobacco stemmers who worked for the American Tobacco Company (ATC). Their leadership and resilience all played an integral role in shaping *Women in Resistance*. They were mothers, lectoras, readers in tobacco factories, stemmers, labor union activists, anarchists, nationalists, union strikers, and so much more. They are embodiers of liberation finding ways to live through, survive, and thrive amid colonial rule and patriarchy.[4] And what an honor it is to be the embodiers of these women in our dance film!

We want to uplift them here through short bio-poems that we created and integrated in our cinematic narrative for *Women in Resistance*:[5]

Figure 2. The altar cocreated by the creative team at the entrance of the warehouse in the former American Tobacco Complex. Photo by Alicia Díaz.

Soy Dominga

Soy Dominga
Dominga de la Cruz Becerril
An Afro–Puerto Rican woman
Nacionalista, activista, lectora de tabaquería
Rebelde, atrevida, luchadora

Amo mi patria
I love poetry
La batalla de resistencia vive en mi

Trabajaba hasta la medianoche a la luz de una lámpara de aceite y aún así no ganaba lo suficiente para cubrir nuestras necesidades básicas.
My daughters starved to death.

I became líder del Partido Nacionalista junto a Pedro Albizu Campos
La Masacre de Ponce
Los vi
Tendidos a mis pies a todos mis compañeros
Con sus vientres abiertos
March 21, 1937
I dodged bullets to rescue the Puerto Rican flag splattered in blood

Thank you to the twelve-year-old boy who gave me flowers many years later.
"¡Toma estas flores, Dominga, porque a tus hijos te los mataron en Ponce!"
And I was reawakened!

Soy Luisa

Soy Luisa Capetillo
Feminista
Creyente del anarco-comunismo
Labor union activist
lectora de tabaquería

Amo la madre tierra y la naturaleza eterna
Defiendo la autonomía e igualdad de las mujeres
Creo en el amor libre

The US invades Puerto Rico
July 25, 1898
I was twenty years old
A witness of colonial power

Desafío las tradiciones sociales
Me arrestaron por usar pantalones en público
No temo nada

I was one of the lead organizers of the largest worker's strike in Puerto Rico's history.

Lucho por la emancipación de las mujeres

In Dedication to Louise "Mamma" Harris and the Black Female ATC Tobacco Stemmers

We sat right there at that table
De-stemming tobacco leaves by hand

That pungent smell of tobacco leaves
Clouds of tobacco dust coated the air
And our lungs

Made us cough
Choke
Difficult to breath

Strike!

These bio-poems are remembrance-offerings meant to acknowledge that we stand on the shoulders of ancestor women who have taken enormous strides toward awareness, understanding, and justice. As Marxist feminist scholar and activist Silvia Federici reminds us, "Our solidarity is very important. Those who have died have to be with us in the present. And our solidarity is not only with the living, but with the dead. Because we cannot allow their voice to be muted, we cannot allow the injustices that they have suffered to not be addressed. We have to be their eyes, their voices, and also their presence with us is what gives a different meaning to our struggles."[6] The practice of listening to the embodied knowledge of Luisa Capetillo, Dominga de la Cruz, Louise "Mamma" Harris, and Black tobacco stemmers who worked for the American Tobacco Company creates an intimate relationship with the past and present. This temporal link allows our dancing bodies to carry the echoes of their voices, their struggles never to be forgotten. May their courage, resistance, and activism live on.

Dancing Between Puerto Rico and Richmond's Tobacco History

The US designated Puerto Rico as a commonwealth in 1952. The term *commonwealth* obscures the role of the US as an imperial power in the Caribbean archipelago.[7] Following the Spanish American War of 1898, Puerto Rico became a "possession" of the United States.[8] In the early twentieth century, the Insular Cases decided by the Supreme Court addressed the legal status of US territories acquired and justified the abolishment of local autonomy in Puerto Rico, instituting US colonial rule in its place.[9] Since then, the US's colonial grip over Puerto Rican reality has been a constant threat to the archipelago's bodies and land through tactics of domination, including labor exploitation, government-sponsored migration, destruction of natural resources, and eugenics-driven population control. Exacerbated by the aftermath of Hurricanes Irma and Maria in September 2017, the archipelago plunged into a profound economic, political, and environmental crisis. The crisis unveiled the colonial control of the United States. The extreme austerity measures imposed since 2016 by the unelected US-appointed Financial Oversight and Management Board for Puerto Rico, known locally as "La Junta," have devastated public services, housing, and education.[10] Thus, the colonial relationship between the United States and Puerto Rico continues to pose contemporary challenges rather than being a relic of the past.

Similarly, in Virginia, the term *commonwealth* continues to carry on a colonial thread. While Virginia is not a US territory, there are still colonial patterns shrouding and perpetuating the genocide, dispossession, and displacements of Indigenous peoples. Moreover, the legacies of enslavement and institutional racism are foundational to the state's history and present condition. For centuries, the economy of Richmond, the former capital of the Confederacy, was rooted in both the tobacco industry and the labor of enslaved people.

Following the US occupation of Puerto Rico, the American Tobacco Company seized control over the tobacco industry and leaf market on the island. Established in North Carolina in 1890 by J. B. Duke (founder of Duke University), ATC was the result of a merger with several other cigarette manufacturers, including Richmond entrepreneur Lewis Ginter's company. This merger reflected a consolidation of industrial power. The rapid expansion of capitalist industrialization in Puerto Rico enabled companies like ATC to supplant the traditionally independent artisan practice of cigar rolling with a standardized factory system.[11] In Virginia, Jim Crow laws were in full effect even though slavery had been abolished in the late nineteenth century. ATC operated factories where both Black and white women worked in segregated facilities and the better job opportunities were reserved for white employees. Even when ATC was officially desegregated between 1963 and 1968, promotion policies were left mostly to the discretion of the supervisors.[12]

Filmed in one of the last standing warehouses of the ATC, now developed as the Port City Apartment Complex in Richmond's Southside, our bilingual dance film *Entre Puerto Rico y Richmond: Women in Resistance Shall Not Be Moved* honors the legacies of the fierce labor activism and anti-colonial defiance of Capetillo and de la Cruz as well as "Mamma" Harris and other Black women who toiled within the ATC. Capetillo and de la Cruz, both hired as lectoras (readers) in tobacco factories in Puerto Rico, played a pivotal role in cultural consciousness-raising by carefully curating readings that mobilized laborers to fight for better living conditions. Interestingly, Capetillo worked as a lectora for ATC in Puerto Rico.[13] Although documentation of readers in tobacco factories in Richmond is lacking, it is evident that women working in the tobacco industry, like "Mamma" Harris, played prominent roles organizing workers and leading strikes in the 1930s and 1940s to demand and secure better working conditions. The film weaves together these legacies of resistance and liberation in Puerto Rico and Virginia.

We initiated this project in the summer of 2020 in the midst of the concurrent pandemics of systemic racism and COVID-19, as well as a massive labor crisis. As a collective, we grappled with how to cocreate together during a time when our bodies were perceived as a threat to others and when the proximity to other bodies meant higher risk of jeopardizing our health and possibly our lives. We didn't know how to be, how to actually rehearse together, when the recommendation was to isolate and the very act of breathing was now filled with so much anxiety. So many questions surfaced for us. Are we going to rehearse with masks? Are we going to maintain distance? We chose to resist fear and be in the presence of others, while collectively taking the necessary precautions to keep each other safe.

Against this social backdrop, Richmond emerged as a focal point for ongoing protests and community reclamation of Confederate sites transforming them into communal gathering spaces of liberation, healing, and joy. For over a century, the towering figure of Robert E. Lee, among five Confederate statues, loomed over Richmond's notorious Monument Avenue.[14] However, during the protests, Lee's statue was transformed by artists Dustin Klein and Alex Criqui. They covered the monument with projected images of George Floyd and other Black people murdered at the hands of police, as well as freedom fighters such as Harriet Tubman and Frederick Douglass.[15] The

Figure 3. Christine Wyatt dancing in July 2020 when the Elegba Folklore Society organized a gathering with dancers and drummers in the newly reclaimed Marcus-David Peters Circle. Photo by Brian Palmer for *The New York Times*.

arts became an interventionist tool for challenging racist historical symbols that have instilled terror for generations. Klein and Criqui summoned Black ancestral liberators whose fierceness inspired protestors, particularly youth, in times of rage and hopelessness. As white coconspirators of Black liberation, Klein and Criqui modeled the practice of multiracial solidarity. Their artistic intervention in Richmond parallels the strategies of liberation used by other freedom fighters including the multiracial coalition of Gabriel's Insurrection of 1800[16] and the interracial "Richmond Underground," a spy network led by Elizabeth Van Lew, a well-to-do Southern Unionist and abolitionist.[17]

The space by Lee's statue was renamed "Marcus-David Peters Circle" by community organizers in memory of a Black biology teacher killed by police during a mental health crisis. Memorials for victims of police violence, music and dance performances, basketball games, a community garden, a free library, and public art installations were organized. This unfolding of events took place very close to the ICA, where our dance film was featured. The artistic interventions and utilization of liberatory strategies in Richmond remained deeply ingrained in our consciousness during the final stages of project preparation.

Our project also drew inspiration from the massive nonviolent protests of the Verano del 2019 in Puerto Rico, which ignited a spark of hope for collective liberation. These protests served as a resounding denouncement of corruption, misogyny, and the pervasive transphobia and homophobia that plagued the post–Hurricane Maria devastation. Lasting for two uninterrupted weeks, these decentralized protests transcended political affiliations and ideological boundaries, leading to the resignation of then-Governor Ricardo Roselló. Artists became the public face of this movement, utilizing the arts as a tool to disrupt coloniality. Rocío Zambrana explains how protestors employed tactics of subversion, inversion, refusal, and rescue aimed at interrupting the "operation of coloniality in the colony."[18] Popular icons such as Residente, iLe, and Bad Bunny energized these demonstrations with their lyrical creativity partaking in the "short-circuiting of productivity here and now."[19]

Dance in particular emerged as a feature of these protests, as a gestural, physical interruption to the historic colonial repression of queerness and Blackness in Puerto Rico. Street dancing, especially in the dynamic form of perreo combativo, operated as a subversive expression of spatial logic. Protestors danced out their queer identity in front of the Catedral Basílica Menor de San Juan Bautista, challenging religious institutions that have been historically cuirphobic.[20] Bomba also played a pivotal role in these danzas combativas, where both individual and collective bodies converged to presence Africanness in Puerto Rico, demanding justice and human dignity.

The ongoing resistance in Puerto Rico and Richmond galvanized the creative process of our dance film, reminding us of how bodies are vessels of both memory and imagination. It is through this delicate interplay of past, present, and the future that we can enact change. The subsequent demolition of the warehouse in the American Tobacco Complex where we were filming was a metaphor for how history can be erased with relative ease in the name of progress. In fact, the morning after we filmed, the space that we had imbued with stories, ritual, music, and dance had itself disappeared. As a person who grew up in Richmond in the 1990s, Christina Leoni-Osion, one of the dance artists and cocreators of the film, shared how the city often preserves white-centered histories yet easily rids itself of Black histories of resistance.[21] In place of ATC, Port City Apartments, a mixed-income housing complex, was being built amid Richmond's ongoing struggle with the affordable housing crisis. While mixed-income developments are often heralded as solutions to economic segregation, their implementation raises several concerns. They often lead to the gentrification of neighborhoods, making them unaffordable for low-income residents.

Ironically, in this case the site of what appears to be a development for public good, an "affordable luxury," as Port City publicizes, is also a toxic zone for vulnerable BIPOC communities.[22] The legacy of the tobacco industry has forever left behind contaminants in the air we breathe together. As one resident of a recently converted warehouse into a housing unit shared, on rainy and humid days you can still smell the lingering toxicity from colonial tobacco enterprise. This felt experience exposed the erasure of history in real time. The intended benefits of mixed-income living are thus overshadowed by historical and environmental injustice.

This stark reality motivated us to bridge the past into the present and the present into the past.[23] If colonialism is a project of temporal looping, as Sandra Ruiz suggests, "whereby actions to redress the past lead us into the future and back again in something prior," then we counter colonial times by disrupting time itself.[24] In *Women in Resistance*, we manipulate time to create spaces of radical imagination, freeing the erasure of Puerto Rican and Black enduring bodies from the shackles of colonial time. In doing so, we amplify the ways they created anti-oppressive and anti-colonial spaces throughout history. As the physical tobacco warehouse disappears, we body forth the spirit of resistance and liberation, embodying the struggles, endurance, and power of those who labored in tobacco factories. Their legacy of defiance and strength transcends the linearity of time, inspiring us to continue the fight for justice.

Feminist Solidarities Through Radical Imagination

Our creative process throughout the development of *Women in Resistance* centered on breathing life into the archives of Puerto Rican anti-colonial strategists Luisa Capetillo and Dominga de la Cruz, along with Richmond Black women tobacco stemmers in the American Tobacco Complex and labor activist Louise "Mamma" Harris. We position these seemingly unrelated women as feminist predecessors whose subversive "performative, bodily interventions" generate intersecting political acts of self-determination and sovereignty.[25] By bringing their histories into conversation, we cultivate feminist solidarities that illuminate a more comprehensive picture of the imperial and racial capitalist machinery of the United States. In our efforts to weave their herstories, we presence these women into our artivist practices and activate affective archives through music, song, dance, and poetry. For us, building these affective archives through radical imagination was about comprehending the humanity of these historical figures in an embodied manner.[26] In doing so, we were able to feel their courage, sacrifice, and the way they risked their lives not as a singular act but as a part of the history of movements of collective resistance, survival, and liberation.[27]

As artists planting seeds for a better tomorrow, we again take heed of the words of Silvia Federici, as well as Saidiya Hartman. Federici stresses the importance of amplifying histories of resistance and oppression through a feminist, anti-capitalist, and anti-racist lens. This approach challenges and disrupts historical narratives shaped by white supremacist culture.[28] Hartman's concept of "critical fabulation" similarly urges us to work "with and against the archive," blending and bending time, "troubl[ing] the lines between history and imagination," in ways that uplift the resilience and leadership of Black women.[29]

Inspired by Federici and Hartman, we venture beyond the confines of how archives narrate history. Since the archive is often organized in separate geographic and chronological order, these women appear distant from each other. Yet we were intrigued by what possibilities might percolate when we had them dance together, especially in how Luisa Capetillo and Dominga de la Cruz straddle the personal and the political. Viewing their lives through a narrow, singular lens erases the historical connections between the US colonial empire in Puerto Rico and the judiciary system designed to uphold systemic racism and segregation in the United States. This myopic perspective obscures the interconnected struggles that they faced and the solidarities they could inspire.

In contrast, our critical fabulation radically imagines feminist solidarities by bringing racial, gender, and colonial identities from disparate geographies and divergent political ideologies into closer proximity with each other. In doing so, we uncover untold histories of activism led by Puerto Rican and Black women. We are able to recognize their "lived, bodily sovereignty" and uplift their shared struggles and triumphs against domination.[30] This shift in perspective not only honors their legacies but also reveals that in having the historical figures dance together and enfleshing their histories in our own bodies, we create pathways for future activism and solidarities in the face of systemic injustice.

In the process of researching the ATC in Richmond, we encountered a photograph of Black women tobacco stemmers, probably taken in the late nineteenth century. We remember the excitement inside our bodies when we saw the image. This black-and-white photo brought us closer to a past we were trying to enflesh in vivid color. The cadre of women's eyes drew us in, almost like a sign of ancestral permission to tell these stories. We already had photos of Puerto Rican women stemmers, and now here were the Black women showing themselves, reaffirming the connections between Puerto Rican and Black Richmond stories of tobacco. Black women tobacco workers in Richmond and in Puerto Rico toiled primarily in the most toxic form of labor, de-stemming tobacco leaves; the process exposed them to nicotine poisoning, dust, and other harmful chemicals.

We wanted to know more about who these women were. Dressed in their Sunday best, they stand with dignity in front of the ATC factory in Richmond. Looking at some of their faces, some are stern, some are smiling, and

Figure 4. Christina Leoni-Osion and Christine Wyatt in the dance film *Entre Puerto Rico y Richmond: Women in Resistance Shall Not Be Moved*. Film still. Image provided by the authors.

others perhaps are questioning the intentions of the photographer. Above the doorway, a sign reads "Richmond Stemmery," the place where weary hands stripped many tobacco leaves. Questions keep coming to mind: Who took the photo? Why? How was this photo used? By whom? White men linger behind the women on the steps, keeping track with their managerial gaze. The photographer's name remains unknown and, unsurprisingly, so do the names of the Black women tobacco workers.

The absence of information about these women in the photograph propelled us to search for information about tobacco labor organizers in Richmond. We were excited when Louise "Mamma" Harris's name came up as one of the prominent figures leading the tobacco strikes of the late 1930s and 1940s. Notably, she convened Black and white tobacco women workers from different factories throughout the region. As a result, they were a critical part of a broader labor victory, the establishment of a standard eight-hour work day and higher wages for workers in the US.[31] While there is documentation of her labor-organizing leadership, we did not find any photos of her in the archives, and her dates of birth and death are uncertain. The archival gaps in documentation of Black women in the US prevent us from understanding the entirety of their stories—highlighting how racism and colonialism pervasively obscure and erase the record of Black women's defiant spirit.

This archival erasure mirrors the scarcity of primary sources we encountered with Dominga de la Cruz. Born in the early twentieth century, de la Cruz embodied unwavering courage and unrelenting commitment to the

Figure 5. Black female tobacco workers outside of the American Tobacco Company, Richmond Stemmery, Richmond, VA, late 1900s. Albumen photographic print. Photographer unknown. Photo courtesy of *The Valentine*.

fight for Puerto Rico's independence. Through the sole biographical source of Margaret Randall's 1970 interview, we only catch a distant, twice-removed glimpse of this extraordinary woman.[32] Despite the archival gap in material on this Afro–Puerto Rican activist, de la Cruz was a force of nature: a fierce mother, nationalist, devoted Catholic, feminista, lectora, and declamadora.[33] Her own political awakening was ignited while working as a lectora when she read the news of the killing of Manuel Rafael Suárez Díaz during a 1932 nationalist protest.[34] Inspired and impassioned by the growing anti-colonial movement, she joined forces with Pedro Albizu Campos and the Puerto Rican Nationalist Party.

During this decade of heightened political tensions, marked by protests, strikes, and violent repression from US authorities, de la Cruz became a key voice in reimagining the role of women in the party, coleading the transition from Las Hijas de la Libertad (The Daughters of Freedom) to the Enfermeras del Ejército Nacionalista (Nurses of the Nationalist Army). This shift galvanized women into decision-making leadership roles within the party. They chose to call themselves "nurses" not as an occupational title, for which they had no formal training, but as a way to challenge the patriarchal framing of women as "dutiful daughters."[35] By adopting the role of nurses, they donned their own militant uniform, marching alongside male cadets as a

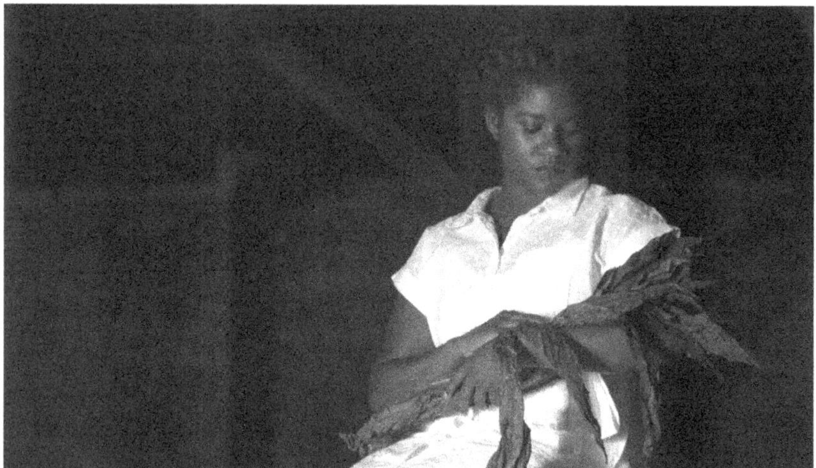

Figure 6. Christine Wyatt embodying Dominga de la Cruz Becerril, breastfeeding the tobacco in the dance film *Entre Puerto Rico y Richmond: Women in Resistance Shall Not Be Moved.* Film still. Image provided by the authors.

"performative, bodily intervention," asserting their agency as women within a predominately male movement.[36] Since the United States deemed the party dangerous, this newly formed unit, Enfermeras del Ejército Nacionalista, was also targeted by colonial surveillance and persecution. As such, de la Cruz and other women put their own bodies on the line in the struggle for Puerto Rican sovereignty.

Internationally, she is remembered as "the one who picked up the flag" during the Ponce Massacre of 1937, when bullets rained down and dozens of her comrades fell. She emerged a survivor, a symbol of her country, bearer of the beloved flag.[37] While this heroic act epitomizes de la Cruz's fierce commitment, her legacy extends far beyond this singular moment. A closer look at her life demonstrates how an Afro–Puerto Rican woman and key figure of the Nationalist Party moved from daily survival—fighting poverty, hunger, and illness—to leading in the larger national liberation struggle. De la Cruz's anti-colonial defiance subjected her to intense forms of US neocolonial repression and violence, and eventually she went into exile; first in Mexico, and then Cuba, where she resided until the end of her life.

Similar to de la Cruz, Luisa Capetillo is revered in Puerto Rican history as a lectora and feminist revolutionary figure of "indomitable bravery."[38] Unlike Harris and de la Cruz, archival records of Capetillo are more available, as she was a white Puerto Rican feminist writer who published prolifically and whose work was widely circulated. Born in the late nineteenth century, Capetillo lived through the tumultuous transition from Spanish to US domination in

Figure 7. Christina Leoni-Osion, embodying Luisa Capetillo, reveals her pants in the dance film *Entre Puerto Rico y Richmond: Women in Resistance Shall Not Be Moved.* Film still. Image provided by the authors.

Puerto Rico as a result of the Spanish–American War of 1898. While lacking access to formal education at the time, Capetillo's French Creole mother and Basque father provided her with a homeschooled liberal education shaped by the ideals of the French Revolution and the workers' rights movement in Northern Spain. Capetillo thus stands out as a self-taught writer, anarchist, spiritualist, labor organizer, abolitionist, and internationalist.

Her deep commitment to end all forms of exploitation of working peoples around the world motivated her work as an anti-colonial and anti-capitalist political organizer and agitator. In working as a tobacco lectora, she connected with leaders of the labor movement, in particular the Federación de Torcedores de Tabaco (Federation of Tobacco Rollers), and eventually became a member and leader of one of the oldest workers' unions in the island, Federación Libre de Trabajadores de Puerto Rico (Free Libertarian Federation of Puerto Rican Workers).[39] She played a crucial role in labor strikes in Puerto Rico's sugar industry as well as the tobacco industry in Puerto Rico, New York, and Florida.[40] Capetillo's work embodied a radical defiance of patriarchal institutions and gender norms. She championed women's rights, workers' rights, gender-inclusive education, sexual freedom, and universal harmony.

Beyond her writing, Capetillo put her body on the line, often facing arrest and police brutality at political rallies. Capetillo fully embodied her revolutionary vision as she used her body to advocate rights for women and workers. Notably, she was the first Puerto Rican woman to wear pants in public, a "performative, bodily intervention" for which she was arrested several times.[41] Her rhetoric went beyond theory—it was a lived practice.

Radically imagining Capetillo and de la Cruz brings their humanity and bodies to the forefront of anti-colonial struggle, allowing us to see them more fully not only as activists but also as mothers. Building on these ideas of motherhood, dance artist and cocreator of the film Christina Leoni-Osion introduced the lens of reproductive justice, emphasizing the right to choose whether or not to have children and the importance of access to conditions that enable raising children in a healthy environment:

> We don't really know if motherhood was a choice or a desire for these humans that could reproduce other humans. So, looking through that lens, we wonder about the lack of choice that both these women faced, and yet they did all of these amazing things. The resilience that arises looking at these stories through that lens is beautiful but also heartbreaking. Would they have been doing this political engagement work if they didn't have to figure out how to survive? And what kind of choices are we making today?[42]

From the archives we learned that when de la Cruz became an orphan early in her life she was sent to live with family members who were proprietors of a coffee plantation. There, she was exposed to art, theater, music, and poetry, but their livelihood was soon destroyed by American sugar corporations and economic upheavals after 1898. Sent to live with her impoverished siblings in Mayagüez, de la Cruz experienced the harsh realities of working in the needle industry. Although at the time she did not understand the notion of class struggle, she understood the "misery" of working in the needle industry and opted to marry young as a way out of poverty.[43] Her circumstances, however, did not improve. She fed her children orange peel tea when she couldn't provide enough food or breast milk, and both daughters tragically died of malnutrition. It was after losing her children that de la Cruz fully turned to political activism.

As a white working-class woman, Capetillo had a different but related experience. Drawn to anarchism for its advocacy of education and equality, she believed in freeing people from the bonds of institutions like the church, state, and marriage. Her embrace of free love, a central theme in her philosophy, was evident in her lifestyle. Shunned for having children out of wedlock with a wealthy man, whose family disapproved of her modest origins and radical beliefs, Capetillo faced societal judgment. Though she believed mothers could be agents of change and improve Puerto Rican society through education, societal expectations around relationships and women's roles weighed heavily on her. Forced to leave Puerto Rico in 1912 due to a government crackdown on anarchists, Capetillo relocated to New York

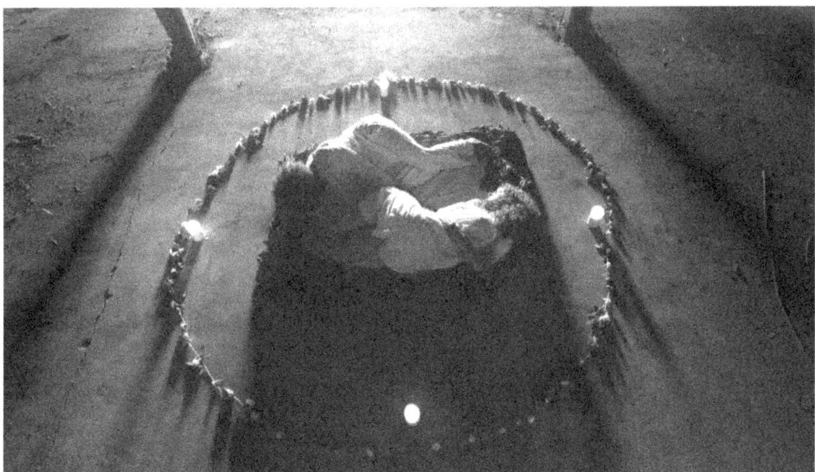

Figure 8. Christina Leoni-Osion and Christine Wyatt in the dance film *Entre Puerto Rico y Richmond: Women in Resistance Shall Not Be Moved*. Film still. Image provided by the authors.

City, where she lived as a transnational labor radical and feminist intellectual. However, this distance from her children illustrates how she, too, was constrained by the very structures she sought to dismantle.

It became clear to us that de la Cruz and Capetillo both sacrificed their own well-being and the lives of their children in the service of justice. As activists, they were often denied the label of "good mothers" within a social system rife with reproductive injustice. Even as they mothered a movement, a revolution, some believed that this came at the cost of properly mothering the children they bore.[44] How do we see their legacies reflected in the twenty-first century, particularly in relation to the bodies that reproduce and nurture future generations? In our embodiment of de la Cruz and Capetillo, we held space for the tension they navigated, reflecting on how societal pressures contributed to their emotional distress and political persecution. Federici's feminist act of transforming and politicizing our everyday reproduction resonates with us here. We, too, politicize de la Cruz and Capetillo's unease with the limitations placed on them as revolutionaries, as well as their courage in challenging societal norms. They imagined new forms of womanhood—where, as Capetillo suggests, mothers could serve as "agents of change" in Puerto Rican society.[45]

Our process is an exercise in critical fabulation—moving through the archive with a feminist, anti-racist, and class-conscious lens, carefully selecting historical fragments to construct a project that extends beyond the individuals themselves. In placing these two Puerto Rican women—one

Black, one white, separated by thirty years—into conversation, we imagine what it would mean for them to work collectively across time and experience. This is not an effort to glorify de la Cruz and Capetillo, but to engage deeply with their historical context, invoking ancestral memory and reclaiming the strategies they used to resist societal oppression. Through this, we ritualize, personalize, and collectivize the archive, sharing a constellation of critical histories that remain largely unknown.[46] We create these feminist solidarities by rendering the past, present, and future coterminous—bridging collective memory, our present moment, and our efforts to world-build a just future. By foregrounding their history of resistance, we move beyond mere biography toward the creation of imagined possibilities for collective liberation. This process enables us to dream of alternative worlds and disrupt the systems of oppression that we continue to confront today.

By weaving together the stories of these feminist predecessors and reconstructing history, we, as people in the struggle for change, regain the strength to continue in the resistance movement.[47] We center the body in motion from Puerto Rico and Richmond to unshackle a colonial history that holds the body captive even in our present time, denying Puerto Ricans, Black people, and other racialized marginalized communities the right to self-determination, autonomy, and liberation. Instead of following the linearity of the past in a singular location, we seize time and space, bringing to life de la Cruz, Capetillo, and Harris, Puerto Rican and Black women of the past, haunting the last remains of the American Tobacco Complex.[48]

As our fingertips touch computer keys to write this, our bodies summon their spirits, reverberating through the fading walls of the American Tobacco Company warehouse in Richmond. Inside this symbol of colonial capitalism, we breathe life into a sacred narrative of liberation, reshaping the ruins into realms of possibilities. Join us in this dance of defiance, as our resistance reverberates from heart to body, echoing across the universe.

Alicia Díaz is a Puerto Rican contemporary dance artist in the diaspora. Her work speaks to issues of memory, colonialism, and embodied forms of resistance and liberation. She is an award-winning artist-scholar and a community-engaged associate professor at University of Richmond, where she teaches courses on dance for social change. Her work is featured in *Inhabiting the Impossible: Dance and Experimentation in Puerto Rico*, the first book on Puerto Rican experimental dance.

Patricia Herrera is a community-engaged educator, scholar, and artist. She uses the arts to generate sanctuaries of love, hope, justice, and liberation. She is the author of *Nuyorican Feminist Performances: From the Café to Hip Hop Theater* (University of Michigan Press, 2020) and coeditor of *Sounds Acts, Part 1 & 2*. She has produced and curated digital archives, community exhibitions, films, and docudramas about segregation, gentrification, educational disparities, HIV/AIDS, and Latinos in Richmond.

Notes

1. *Commonwealth* was coorganized and cocurated by Beta-Local (Pablo Guardiola, Michael Linares, nibia pastrana santiago, and Sofía Gallisá Muriente); ICA at VCU (Stephanie Smith and Noah Simblist); and Philadelphia Contemporary (Kerry Bickford, Nicole Pollard, and Nato Thompson, Sueyun and Gene Locks).
2. The film can be viewed online at https://vimeo.com/460245304.
3. In her 1990 biography of Capetillo, Norma Valle Ferrer noted her birthdate as 1879. However, in an essay written in 2021, Teresa Peña Jordán notes her birthdate as 1882 based on a passport request she was able to track down. See Teresa Peña Jordán, "Luisa Capetillo: Una práctica del cuerpo, el pensamiento y la palabra," in *Amor y anarquía: Escritos de Luisa Capetillo* (rev. ed.), edited by Julio Ramos (Ediciones Huracán, 2021), 161–73.
4. In the Afrikana Roundtable, Christine Wyatt (Tine Tine) coins the term *embodiers of liberation* to describe our work. Alicia Díaz, Patricia Herrera, Christine Wyatt, and Christina Leoni-Osion, "Afrikana Roundtable-Entre Puerto Rico y Richmond: Women in Resistance Shall Not Be Moved," moderated by MK Abado, Afrikana Independent Film Festival, September 17, 2020, https://fb.watch/kAEo_qqDyT/.
5. Patricia Herrera wrote these bio-poems as part of her dramaturgical work. They were used as the basis for the script of the dance film.
6. Alicia Díaz, Patricia Herrera, Silvia Federici, Shariana Ferrer-Núñez, "Women in Resistance: A Panel Discussion for Commonwealth," online panel discussion, Institute for Contemporary Art, Virginia Commonwealth University, moderated by Anahí Lazarte, October 20, 2020, https://www.youtube.com/watch?v=ShK1YIzOoOY.
7. Here we are thinking of how Beatriz Llenín-Figueroa employs the concept of archipelago as a mode of relationality, emphasizing the interconnectedness, yet distinct experiences of the Caribbean. This reframing moves away from a singular perspective of Puerto Rico and challenges territorial containment, which in turn roots Puerto Rico's sovereignty in a network of Caribbean affective and archival resistance. *Affect, Archive, Archipelago: Puerto Rico's Sovereign Caribbean Lives* (Roman and Littlefield, 2022), 24–25.
8. Trumbull White, *Our New Possessions: A Graphic Account, Descriptive and Historical, of the Tropic Islands of the Sea Which Have Fallen Under Our Sway* (Philadelphia: J. H. Moore Co., 1898).
9. Charles R. Venator-Santiago and José Javier Colón Morera, eds, "Back to the Future: The Implications of Balzac One Hundred Years Later," special issue, *Centro Journal* 34, no. 1 (Spring 2022).
10. The Financial Oversight and Management Board for Puerto Rico, known by Puerto Ricans as "La Junta," was created by the Puerto Rico Oversight, Management, and Economic Stability Act (PROMESA) in 2016, under the Obama administration, to address the archipelago's more than $70 billion debt. The board has repeatedly come under fire due to conflicts of interest between board members and private businesses, along with the crippling austerity measures it has passed to satisfy Puerto Rico's creditors. Carlos Edill

Berríos Polanco, "Supreme Court: Puerto Rico's Fiscal Control Board Has 'Sovereign Immunity,'" *Latino Rebels*, May 12, 2023, https://www.latinorebels.com/2023/05/12/supremecourtjuntasovereignimmunity/.

11. For more information about movements resisting industrialization in Puerto Rico, see Kirwin R. Schaffer, *Black Flag Boricuas: Anarchism, Antiauthoritarianism, and the Left in Puerto Rico, 1897–1921* (University of Illinois Press, 2013), 27.
12. *American Tobacco Company v. John Patterson*, et al., 456 U.S. 63 (1982).
13. "Today in Labor History: Puerto Rican Labor Organizer and Feminist Luisa Capetillo Born," *People's World*, October 28, 2014, https://www.peoplesworld.org/article/today-in-labor-history-puerto-rican-labor-organizer-and-feminist-luisa-capetillo-born/.
14. Following a yearlong legal battle, the statue of Lee and his horse was removed in early September 2021, along with the other statues.
15. We incorporated the image of George Floyd projected onto the Lee statue into one of the altar installations as a tribute to George Floyd and to anchor us in the current struggle of Black liberation. The image is visible in the video at 00:02:06.
16. Douglas Egerton, in *Gabriel's Rebellion: The Virginia Slave Conspiracies of 1800 and 1802* (Chapel Hill, 1993), argues that Gabriel's conspiracy was a multiracial class revolt inspired by artisan republicanism.
17. Elizabeth Varon discusses the multiracial collaborations of the espionage work in Richmond during the Civil War in "Speaker Interview: The Unionist Espionage of Elizabeth Van Lew," Gettysburg College, https://www.gettysburg.edu/civil-war-institute/news/detail?id=9d2e9a50-b255-43de-8802-e79d454ab33b. See also her book *Southern Lady, Yankee Spy: The True Story of Elizabeth Van Lew, a Union Agent in the Heart of the Confederacy* (Oxford University Press, 2003). Lois Leveen has conducted groundbreaking research on the role of Mary Richards Bowser, a Black woman born into slavery in the Van Lew home, who collaborated closely with her in the Union spy network. See Lois Levine, "Mary Richards Bowser (fl. 1846–1867)" in *Encyclopedia of Virginia*, Virginia Humanities, last updated February 18, 2025, https://encyclopediavirginia.org/entries/bowser-mary-richards-fl-1846-1867/.
18. Rocío Zambrana, *Colonial Debts: The Case of Puerto Rico* (Duke University Press, 2021), 11.
19. Zambrana, *Colonial Debts*, 12.
20. See José M. Atiles Osoria, *Profanaciones del verano de 2019: Corrupción, frentes comunes y justicia decolonial* (Editorial Educación Emergente, 2020); Malena Rodríguez Castro, *Poéticas de la devastación y la insurgencia: María y el verano del 19* (Editorial Educación Emergente, 2022); Arnaldo M. Cruz-Malavé, *Bailando en un encierro: Duelo, danza y activismo en las manifestaciones del verano boricua de 2019* (Editorial Educación Emergente, 2023); and Christopher Powers Guimond, *4645: Crónica del verano boricua* (Editorial Educación Emergente, 2023).
21. "Afrikana Roundtable: Entre Puerto Rico y Richmond: Women in Resistance Shall Not Be Moved," Afrikana Independent Film Festival, September 17,

2020, https://www.facebook.com/afrikanafilmfestival/videos/entre-puerto-rico/359109588828083/, 00:29:49.

22. See Port City's website for a view of their advertising of "affordable luxury," https://www.portcityrva.com/gallery, accessed June 14, 2024.
23. "Women in Resistance: A Panel Discussion," Institute for Contemporary Art, October 21, 2020, https://www.youtube.com/watch?v=ShK1YIzOoOY, 00:28:21.
24. Sandra Ruiz, *Ricanness: Enduring Time in Anticolonial Performance* (New York University Press, 2019), 3.
25. We hear Beatriz Llenín-Figueroa's call to amplify embodied knowledge as a site of analysis toward understanding the political underpinnings of radical, subversive, and revolutionary figures. Beatriz Llenín-Figueroa, *Affect, Archive, Archipelago: Puerto Rico's Sovereign Caribbean Lives* (Roman and Littlefield, 2022), 75.
26. Llenín-Figueroa shows how affective archives preserve the emotional and lived experiences of colonialism, disaster, and resistance—often silenced by official histories—while reclaiming narratives of survival and collective struggle. The affective archive, in her work, becomes a tool to confront colonial and imperial forces, using embodied knowledge to resist erasure and offer alternative understandings of history and memory. As she explains: "Studying our affective archive of Caribbean relations requires deep-diving into literal and metaphorical, verbal and non-verbal, enduring and ephemeral, material and symbolic traces of Puerto Rico's commitment to decolonization and the defense of our multiple sovereignties." Llenín-Figueroa, *Affect, Archive, Archipelago*, 25.
27. Federici's words resonate here: "People risk their life because they have an understanding of the importance of it. And that importance comes when you feel that what you're doing is not an isolated singular act, but is really part of a whole history of liberation. So that you understand that anything that happens to you is not just you. Your life is not the end."
28. See Silvia Federici's renowned book *Caliban and the Witch* (Autonomedia, 2004).
29. Saidiya Hartman, "Venus in Two Acts," *Small Axe* 12, no. 2 (June 2008): 12.
30. Llenín-Figueroa, *Affect, Archive, Archipelago*, 75.
31. Alice Knox Eaton, "Harris, Louise 'Mamma,'" Oxford African American Studies Center, May 31, 2013, https://oxfordaasc.com/view/10.1093/acref/9780195301731.001.0001/acref-9780195301731-e-36468.
32. Margaret Randall, *Dominga Rescues the Flag/Dominga rescate la banderas* (Two Wings Press/Editorial Dos Alas, 2020).
33. A declamadora refers to a person, in this case a woman, who performs spoken word, recites poetry, or delivers declamations, often with a strong, dramatic presentation.
34. Learning about this pivotal moment in de la Cruz's political awakening was unexpected and exciting because Manuel Rafael Suárez Díaz was Alicia Díaz's great-uncle. He was a young sympathizer of the Puerto Rican independence movement and was killed by the colonial police in El Capitolio, the capitol

building in Old San Juan, during a protest led by Albizu Campos denouncing the co-opting of the revolutionary Puerto Rican flag as a colonial symbol. This unanticipated intersection was a beautiful and powerful reminder of the deep connections between the personal, the political, and the broader histories around us connecting us to the past and present.

35. Olga Jiménez de Wagenheim, *Nationalist Heroines: Puerto Rican Women History Forgot, 1930s–1950s* (Markus Weiner Publishers, 2016), 45–7.
36. In *Affect, Archive, Archipelago*, Beatriz Llenín Figueroa shows how bodies intervene through their collective movement and ties to land, water, and political struggle, serving not just as symbols but as acts of sovereignty, resistance, memory, and archive. *Affect, Archive, Archipelago*, 75–103.
37. For a full report of the Ponce Massacre of 1937, see Arthur Garfield Hays and the Commission of Inquiry on Civil Rights in Puerto Rico, "Report of the Commission of Inquiry on Civil Rights in Puerto Rico," New York, 1937.
38. Norma Valle Ferrer, *Luisa Capetillo, Pioneer Puerto Rican Feminist*, trans. Gloria Waldman-Schwartz (Peter Lang, 2006), 62.
39. Juan Conatz, "Capetillo, Luisa: A Biography," Libcom.org, August 17, 2010, https://libcom.org/history/biography-luisa-capetillo.
40. Julio Ramos, *Amor y anarquía: Los escritos de Luisa Capetillo* (Ediciones Huracán, 1992), 19–20.
41. For a discussion on the power of bodies-as-performative and of performance-as-struggle in the work and life of Luisa Capetillo, see Beatriz Llenín-Figueroa, "Embodying Oceanic Sovereignties: Luisa Capetillo and the Tribuna on the Street," *Affect, Archive, Archipelago*, 75–103.
42. Christina Leoni-Osion, "Afrikana Roundtable."
43. Randall, *Dominga Rescues the Flag/Dominga rescata la bandera*, 25.
44. "Women in Resistance: A Panel Discussion for Commonwealth," 00:29:38.
45. Kathleen M. de Onis, "Arguing for Free Love in an Era Free of Women's Liberation: Remembering the Life of Puerto Rican Feminist and Labor Activist Luisa Capetillo," *Women and Language* 36, no. 2 (2013): 93.
46. "Women in Resistance: A Panel Discussion for Commonwealth," 00:51:30.
47. "Women in Resistance: A Panel Discussion for Commonwealth," 00:41:20–00:42:34.
48. Bobby Seale, a cofounder of the Black Panther Party, shifted the appropriation of time from a collective effort to an intellectual endeavor with his book *Seize the Time: The Story of the Black Panther Party and Huey Newton* (Black Classic Press, 1970; reprint edition, 1997). As he states in the conclusion of his book: "We know that as a people, we must seize our time. . . . Huey P. Newton seized the time when he moved and put the bpp into motion. . . . The time is now to wage relentless revolutionary struggle against the fascist, avaricious, demagogic ruling class and their lowlife, sadistic pigs. Power to the People! Seize the Time! His call to seize the time is an exhortation to take hold of the opportunity and fight against the persistent repetitions of oppression, which he underscores in his book with a fierce militant tone through a final capitalized inscription—seize the time."

CHAPTER 5

Anti-Racist Manifesto

LA COLECTIVA FEMINISTA EN CONSTRUCCIÓN

A NOTE FROM LA COLE: We wrote this manifesto on June 2, 2020, when we organized the Black Lives Matter demonstration in solidarity with the Black Lives Matter movement and the protests in the United States following the death of George Floyd, a Black man who was murdered by the police in Minnesota. The demonstration put into context how anti-Black violence is reproduced in Puerto Rico based on the racial and colonial state of our land.

We anchor the slogan "Black Lives Matter," demanding an end to the war against Black people. A war that has been declared on us for hundreds of years and that today is reproduced through the siege of our communities, the criminalization of poverty, the illegal and abusive interventions of the police, environmental racism through the deposit of ashes and toxic chemicals in Black communities, the austerity policies designed to continue exploiting our communities, the hypersexualization of Black women and girls, and public policy designed to control our bodies.

As Black feminists, we know that anti-Black violence will only end when we manage to overthrow the colonial, capitalist, patriarchal, and racist system, which uses anti-Black violence to keep us exploited. That is why the demonstration was also a call to recognize that for this revolutionary task, our feminism and our struggle must be anti-racist. There is no community organization without the Black people who organize the communities; there is no liberation possible without the liberation of Black women, of all Black women, including Black trans women.

During the demonstration, we called for all Black people to step forward, reaffirming that Black women organized that space for Black people. This action countered how the contributions of Black people in social struggles are erased and made invisible or they are assigned a secondary role. As we said, our lives, bodies, and experiences are exploited to build narratives that exclude us in decision-making and spaces of power. We denounced the hypocrisy of figures in the media pointing out the "destruction of property" when the colonial history present in Puerto Rico continues to mark us—the Black people—as property, particularly when the demonstration was called in Old San Juan, a bastion of colonialism and the genocide of the Indigenous and Black people. In a country that owes so much to Black people, there is no "law and order" possible without reparative justice for those of us who remain subordinate to the racial state. If necessary, each paving stone on the streets of Old San Juan and La Fortaleza will be returned until the resistance is built.

There is no possible independence, no possible liberation, no possible anti-capitalism, and no possible feminism without us. There is no revolution possible without us.

> If Black women were free, it would mean that everyone else would have to be free since our freedom would necessitate the destruction of all the systems of oppression.
>
> —**COMBAHEE RIVER COLLECTIVE, 1977**

Racial states are neither ahistorical nor atemporal. They belong to a concrete political experience called modernity/coloniality and begin from the social construction of the category of race in order to establish differences and hierarchies between individuals. This experience has survived decolonization processes and has generalized the racial state everywhere as the "natural order of things," posing a near impossibility to its destruction.

Racial states are not established at the margins of capitalism. On the contrary, the centrality of race as the axis of power relations was possible thanks to the violent dispossession of the lives, work, and knowledges (saberes) of Black people and people racialized as nonwhite in the period of European imperial expansion.

Racial states are not separated from patriarchy. These, rather, are co-constitutive with the patriarchal system; it is in the domestication of feminized subjectivities, in their marginalization as the infantile, the perverse, the other, the beastly, and the savage, that racial states configure their politics of race based on racial purity or racial mixing for the purpose of "whitening" (blanquear) the progeny.

Racial states are not immovable. These are reconfigured and transformed according to the possibility of sustaining white supremacy, oppressing Black bodies and bodies racialized as nonwhite in diverse ways—always with the

Figure 1. Las Vidas Negras action, San Juan, Puerto Rico, 2020.
Photo courtesy of La Cole.

main objective of maintaining the status quo of white, capitalist, and patriarchal dominance.

Racial states are constituted under the myth of the nation-state in order to establish borders that allow them to exercise different types of dominance according to who is inside and who is outside. For this reason, racial states are also imperial states that deploy colonial violence where they prevail, in order to maintain or expand their economic and racial interests.

Racial states are as nationalist as they are internationalist. While they use the apparatus of border control or citizenship to establish life or death of one or the other, they also ally themselves with those who share, with them, white supremacy as state policy.

Racial states operate systemically. They establish an unequal system, based on race, evident in the segregation between neighborhoods, the unequal distribution of state wealth, the policies of policing Black communities, and the lack of access to state resources.

Racial states operate in collective imaginaries. These are part of the racialized identity of Black and white people, which makes each group have different experiences of existing, of being, of surviving.

Racial states permeate the individual. In the depths of being, the white subject assumes its role in the unequal relation of power, benefits from the racial state, and reproduces it with its fears, its anger, and its frustrations.

Meanwhile, in the depths of being, the Black subject survives and resists their premature death announced since their being in the world.

In the colony of Puerto Rico, the racial state operates with diverse logics. The criollo imaginary reproduces racial narratives of a mixture that does not recognize the anti-Black violence that it entails. It is hidden behind the mixture of races and the confinement of Black bodies and territories to the marginalized, the expropriable, and the criminalized. Just as hidden are the attachments of mestizo bodies and territories to white aspirations toward ascendancy in different dimensions, from the aesthetic to the economic. Likewise, within the mixture of races is hidden the devaluation of the work carried out by visibly Black people—it hides how their Black bodies are turned disposable in the face of physical, economic, and environmental violence perpetrated by the racial state. However, the racial state in the colony of Puerto Rico is not solely sustained by criollo imaginaries. In the last 122 years, United States colonialism has contributed to the linking of racial imaginaries with white social practices—namely, individualism, economic liberalism, neoliberalism, and the aspiration to belong to the racial state par excellence: the United States of America.

This is why, we insist, racial states are not atemporal. They have not always existed, and they can cease to exist. If we dismantle them, they will.

Racial states are not ahistorical. They belong to a concrete political experience that we are willing to abolish in order to build another political form that does not reproduce, ever again, the violence that has brought us here.

In Puerto Rico, anti-Black violence is manifested in "mano dura contra el crimen" (iron fist against crime) policies: the criminalization of poverty, the zoning and policing of Black communities as dangerous and insecure spaces, environmental racism, police abuse against Dominican and Haitian communities, as well as measures that impose control over the bodies of women, particularly the bodies of Black women and women racialized as nonwhite. Furthermore, the racial state operates with complete impunity, implementing austerity policies that leave Black people and people racialized as nonwhite without access to dignified housing, education, and health services.

In La Colectiva Feminista en Construcción, given these hierarchies of power that sustain the racial state, we reaffirm, together with the Black feminists who have gone before us, that the liberation of Black women will be the end of all oppressions, the end of the racial state in all its manifestations and articulations of different structures of power. The end of the racial state will be the end of the colonial state and the post-colonial criollo state; it will be the end of capitalism, it will be the end of patriarchy, and it will be the end of systemic and epistemological racism and its identitarian reproductions. That is why, as Black feminists, we assume the revolutionary task of fighting for the fall of the capitalist, racist, and patriarchal system, recognizing that its fall and the end of the racial state will be what will allow us to build other lives and other ways of being and existing, other decolonized lives—in short, other worlds.

For this reason, at the particular juncture we are living, we join the demands of the organizations that form part of the Black Lives Matter movement, demanding recognition of and accountability for the devaluation and dehumanization of Black lives. We demand radical and sustainable solutions that aim for the protection and the best quality of life for all Black people. Therefore, we demand the following:

1. **An end to the war against Black people:** This includes abolishing the death penalty as well as mass policing and abusive police intervention in our communities and violence against Black people (including trans Black people, sexual dissidents, and gender nonconforming people as well as the immigrant community); impunity for crimes against Black people, particularly those perpetuated by state agents; and environmental racism through exposing our communities to polluting agents and the imposition of austerity measures that principally affect the country's Black community and impoverished communities.

2. **Reparations:** We insist on the immediate decolonization of Puerto Rico based on the past and current harms of slavery, such as mass incarceration of Black people, the destruction of our communities and family nuclei, and the implementation of laws that impede the integral development and improvement of our quality of life; reparations for the wealth extracted from our communities; that a dignified income and free and quality higher education be guaranteed, with open admission to the University of Puerto Rico as well as community colleges, universities, and technical schools. We demand decriminalization, immediate release, elimination of records, and reparations for the derogatory effects of the "war on drugs" as well as the "criminalization of sex work" in our Black communities.

3. **Investment:** Instead of investing state and federal funds for the police to monitor and repress our communities and for the benefit of the corporations exploiting us, we demand that the state invest in long-term security strategies and in strengthening access to justice programs and gender violence prevention. In the same way, we demand that the improvement of our education system be prioritized and that an anti-racist and gender-perspective education curriculum is implemented in the public and private system. We demand investment in restorative justice programs, employment programs for marginalized and impoverished people, and universal health insurance.

4. **Economic justice:** We demand that Black communities have real collective ownership of wealth; that the necessary actions be taken so that Black people can have access to jobs with a living wage—with an increase in the minimum wage—social and labor protections, as well as access to housing and the basic food basket according to their family composition; that support be provided for the development of networks of social or economic cooperatives; and that measures and efforts that address systemic discrimination and protect the civil rights of Black people be strengthened. Additionally, we insist that the right to the restoration of land, clean air, and clean water, and the termination of the privatization and exploitation of our natural resources be guaranteed.

5. **Power to communities:** It must be ensured that our communities have active participation in decision-making on budgets and infrastructure, and that the government desist from privatizing education through charter schools.

6. **Political power:** This power must be accessed through political participation in decision-making spaces such as government agencies, the legislature, and municipalities. We demand that the protection of the right to vote be guaranteed for all Black people, and that universal and free access to the internet be provided as well as greater protection and financing for institutions that do anti-racist work.

THE LIVING WORLD (receta pal sofrito o entrando por la cocina) EL MUNDO VIVENTE

SOFÍA CÓRDOVA

The return started long before i knew it.

When i was 15

the earth started calling me back in sleep, on the bus

the animals started showing up two weeks after the accident.

I. A milky moth sleeping on the edge of the bathroom mirror when i sit down to pee first
thing in the morning foggy from a dream that doesn't end when i wake.
II. The cricket singing in the sky light for three days straight
III. The wild turkey Silvi named "Weave" (meaning "Leaf")
IV. The snails eating our butter lettuce but not the chard
V. A little green cricket brought in when i carried in the greens that grew from the earth

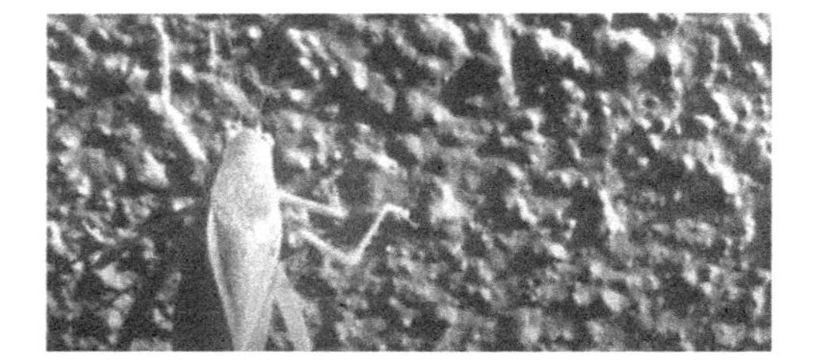

Esperanza verde luz

La tierra me apoya, una tabla de cortar inestable pero sólida
su fuerza cursa por mi espina y me hace un par de preguntas

Transiting into a feminism of the earth, vine tendrils slipping tidily into my skull.

I am in a desaturated film about a "woman in trauma," *a terrible thing has happened, she is like this now*

What if instead I could feel the grief of cricket?

What if instead I could take leave of the housemates that have moved into the tight hot cavity of my chest?
Anger and sorrow
always adorn here, how could they not?
colonial companions all
there ever but of late they have changed shape to become a giant
emerald, formed when the lava cooled
mined from the earth by those who will die
sunken by steady pincers into the alloy metal that has become my body
after so many hits.
A youth of joints, late nights, and now a set of violences.

A tragedy is a window to a political vision. You don't get it?
Maybe b/c Anger and sorrow get us there but to carry them on forever corrodes

Even in the cold and endless night of a hospital room tragedy feels like the result of empires,
they have never ended
their uneven struggle,
Arm sunk in the other's elbow
Crook
Pulled to the ground

And i and we am and are left with disaster and the
Indignity of cleaning up
Someone else's catastrophic spillage

A dozen
eggs slathering
skating
slithering
Across a floor you just mopped
In a country you hate the name of
And which you run into at every crossroads

And which runs you into the rocks

In to the ground

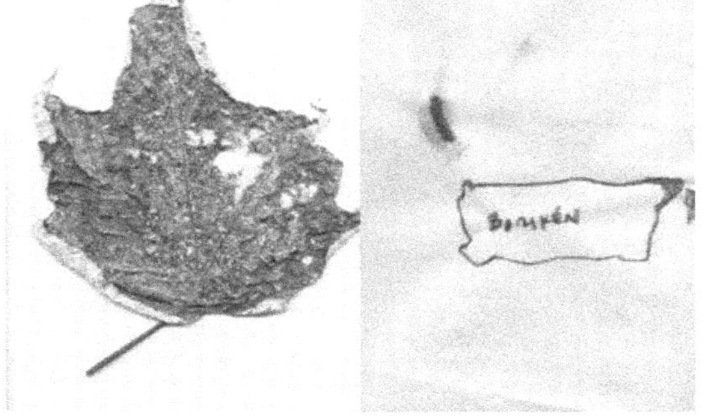

The land has been calling me

The nonhuman speaks to the subaltern too

We are
othered so our little hollowed bones
Ready for flight
End up crushed into the fine dust laying on the ground ready to be swept
Crushed into fine fine fine
Dust
FINO FINO FINO FINO FINO
NEGRO FINO
FINO FINO POLVO FINO

Polvo de las arenas del sahara

An atmospheric river of dry
That traces the route out of West Africa that our ancestors also traveled except the dust is free
and away and

Up above

Not down

Down

Down below

The bottom of a ship

Arranged in a fucked
Up puzzle

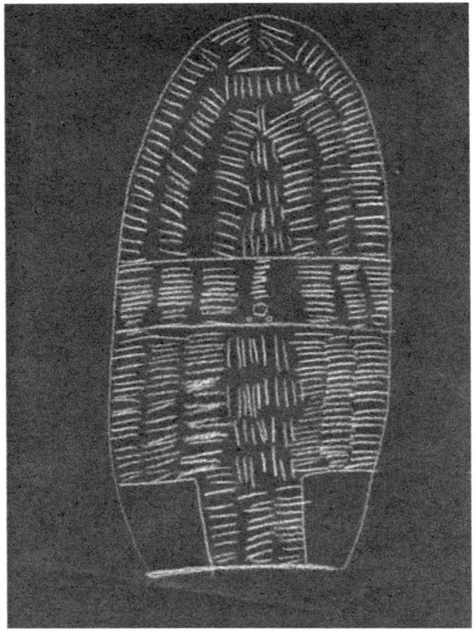

The kind of math problem that when you look at it,
it eyes you right back

Eyes tired from reading all that is printed in
icy light
Tired from gazing at the inferno men have
wrought

The body twists inside at the very sight, on its
own, just eye speaking to spine speaking
to gut

WRENCH! IN THE WORKS!

The indignity of cleaning up after some

man else

They, long gone out of the house and uncaring
That your nails crack back into the cuticle
from the angry scratching you carry out all day to get the floors
clean of

I. Melaza
II. Guarapo
III. Aceite de coco
IV. Chocolate
V. Guineo y plátano
VI. Arroz que alguien pisó, ya tu sabes como se pone, pegajoso.

Un mamposteao con el sucio de sus pies blancos

white feet smash white rice

Carmen Aboy Valldejuli

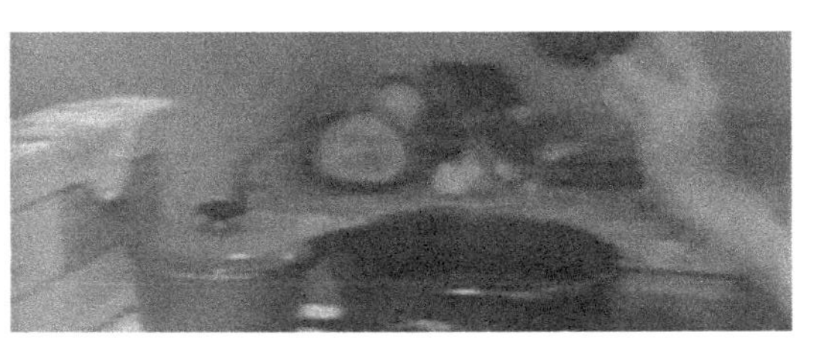

¿Conoce Carmen Aboy el trabajo de Silvia Federici?
Does she know that she asks
How our labor
Is born from our desire
Or rather
That the someones said: "look at those women

Taking care

Taking care

Taking care

Of the land of el huertillo of the little little kids

Look at them and make them take care

Take care   take care

of the half she took or who took her who with square and bullish attributes flops back into soft something and expects and demands care *in* order to leave again

do ‘what must be done’ even though that is
~~often a mystery to us all.~~

What must be done? make them take care so we can get what must be got more
moh-ney huh-ney

And when she is done taking care the
reproduction can reproduce what they see around them forever
and ever and”

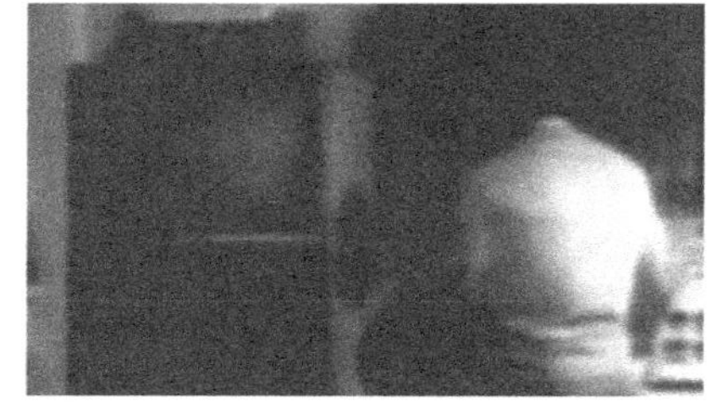

Do you think they said that or just did it?
And if they did say it
would it matter
Anyway?

Did Carmen Aboy take care because it was her desire,
an erotic impulse through her fingertips as she peeled la
yuca y el bacalao till her nails cracked back into cuticles

A little drool pooling in her mouth y en su combi completa

OR

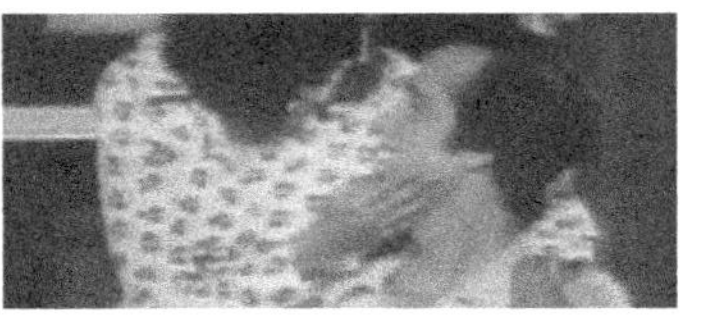

Do you think she did it because she was reproducing reproducing?
A receptacle of eggs and a clear sticky liquid spilled all over the floor

A fabuloso of the insides a perfect environment

exact temperature to take in that colono legacy and do a small miracle
That for an instant can go to work for measly wages or go to work to be
free. Taking care.

Run thru an earth that knows them that no pond or charca can catch them lacking
Carmen caught lacking

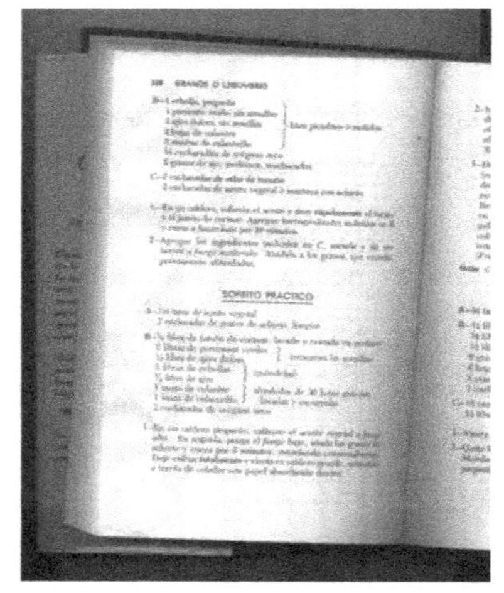

and another miracle "pa mejorar la raza," gracias pero no gracias.

A student recently awake to the disparages of labor admits to me
she likes doing the dishes

I hate doing the dishes odio lavar los trastes

I'm not into caring as a naturally occurring thing in *my* bird bones

Is it desire even ¿es deseo eso?

I think I call back
To the earth asleep

Most of all because i myself long to be cared for

Cooled down by ancient lava, deep soil
the anger of the

The one that boils in me and threatens to evaporate all that is good
i need to be set free of it

so i can cause destruction thru the entropy
of roots and rot and not the flame of fire

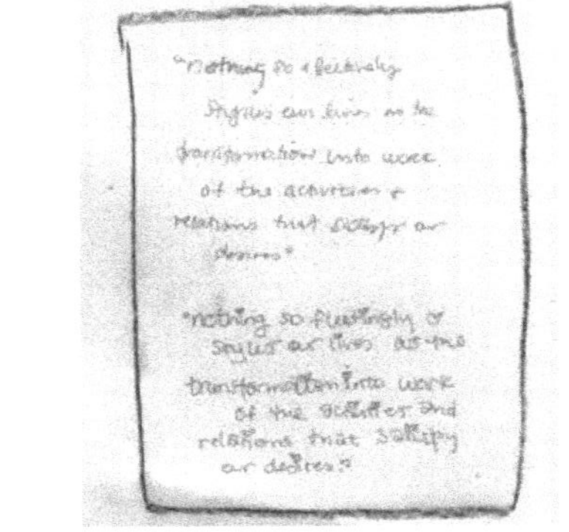

Set it to the masters' house. Cool rot vs hot rot.
La casa del patrón

Every night in my dreams, match to dead caña

I pick the snails out
of my garden
I read somewhere that people hate
rats because they hate themselves

My baby asks why i gag when i
See a large snail you know
What i've got no good answer

Is the gagging just the salivating

I. of desire?
II. To eat all the crops
III. And leave nothing?
IV. To be nasty
V. To tarnish order with the clear gel
VI. Produced [in the factory] between my legs?

The gushing waters de la charca, after the rain, after the drought?

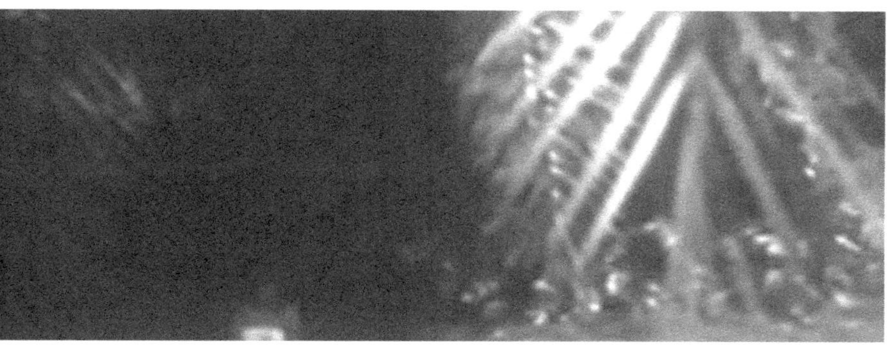

Sofía Córdova lives between Puerto Rico and Oakland and makes work that considers sci-fi as alternative history, dance music's liberatory dimensions, and revolution. She works in performance, video, sound, and installation. Her work has been exhibited at the Whitney Museum of American Art, Tufts University Galleries, and the Museo de Arte Contemporaneo, among others. She is a recent recipient of an Artadia and Creative Capital Award.

PART II. OUR REMEDIES

CHAPTER 6

Rematriate: The Rhythm of Return

MELISSA ROSARIO

Dedicated to all my kin
inhabiting the vast spectrum of existence beyond binaries
walking the red road home.

A Leap into the Void

I cannot tell you the exact moment I decided to return to my ancestral homeland, but the longing was always there. At ten years old, I was angry upon returning from my second trip to the island. My parents tell me that I exclaimed, "We should be speaking Spanish in this house!" already rejecting the assimilation trajectory being set out for me. It would be a long time before I learned to speak Spanish well enough to call myself fluent. I can still remember the frustration and sadness I felt at not being able to communicate my most authentic self in a place that I felt, in my bones, was home.

Through a series of fortuitous events, I found myself supported to regularly visit Borikén as a young scholar and began to deepen my relationship to it through the anthropology of home. Transiting between archipelago and diaspora, entering el vaivén, I began a return. After ten-plus years of this movement between, the call to return became urgent.

I always knew deciding to return against the tide of displacement was political, but even more so, the journey felt spiritual. The decision to leave all I had known became spiritual for me as I leaped into the void. In returning my body to my ancestral home, I not only relocated—I rematriated my mind, body, and spirit to the land in an act of defiance and desperation. Somewhere between naivety and bravery, I leapt into the dark possibility of being represented by the void. This insistent whisper, an impulse, followed.

Of course, one does not have to physically move from one geography to another to rematriate. Rematriation is always about repair. Returning bones, artifacts, and stories to their original stewards, as Indigenous women have long demanded, can take many forms. For those whose ancestors were colonized or enslaved, the psychic and physical territories of the self can also be voids of disconnection, places where we have little safety. It is possible to begin with the body. The first territory. The body speaks. It remembers. It knows. Do you know how to listen and interpret the signs? Do you know how to honor them?

Regardless of where you begin, rematriation is not light travel. It is a dense darkness encouraging us to emit our own brilliance and to bloom in the darkness of the cave—in Taíno mythology, also our origin—akin to the womb of the land.[1] It is in this act that we find the symbiotic truth that we are never alone in our search. Giving and receiving are always intertwined actions. What light we emit attracts in a field of resonance.

Like our bodies, all land carries stories and wisdom. Sit. Listen for the land's heartbeat. Feel the pulse beneath the surface. There is a subtlety to speech beyond words that can only be heard from the heart.

If you have learned to tune out this gift, you can still begin the return. The tools of research and the efforts of those who have come before provide a way forward. Native Land Digital's map is a great starting point (fig. 1).[2]

Still, in a reclamation journey where there has never been federal recognition and people believe in the myth of extinction, it is important to dig deeper. Simple questions may feel impossible to face at first. Whose lands am I on? What was my family's relationship to the native peoples of the lands I now inhabit? Who am I?

Here in the depths, the complexities mount. Listen beyond the myth of private property and ownership. Listen more than we speak and sit with the contradictions. As Devin Atallah, a psychologist of the Palestinian diaspora reminds me, we will inevitably be forced to contend with the "both and" nature of repair. Sitting in my living room, he tells me, "In our healing work, it is often necessary to betray some ancestors while honoring others." Hugging the duality is how we restore order. Then we must acknowledge the truth of what was. Recognize the truth of what is. Reconciliation can only come from this place of understanding and a willingness to use your influence to act.

One thing is for certain. We are all needed to turn the world inside out. Settler and native and everyone in between.

The Initiation Begins

Sometime after I made the decision to brincar el charco, challenges began to multiply.[3] Returning to ancestral lands started a kind of initiation. The

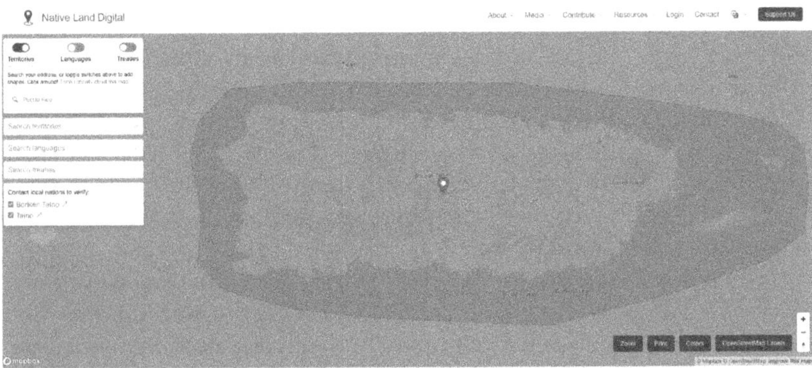

Figure 1. Native land digital map of Borikén.

longing of my childhood was replaced by the discomfort of change. The weight of everyday life in a place where buses don't come, outages are possible, and appointments take all day. The systems are designed to fail, and they do. Regularly. These are the metaphysics of colonialism en todo color. And they hit differently when they become your everyday. Even living in Borikén for a year and a half during grad school always had the promise of returning to another kind of life. Staying was a route with no clear end in sight.

This initiation period requires a deep and abiding ability to let go. Indeed, I was beginning to cross over a threshold into a new way of seeing, being, a new relationship to this place Boriké. For me, that initiation worked to destroy any lingering attachment to the comforts of privilege I worked so hard to achieve. I had no job. I had no health insurance. I had an ocean separating me from the deep networks of support I had cultivated over a lifetime. I had a vague idea of something I wanted to build, but little experience outside of academia to craft it. I did not inherit wealth, and the little savings I had was not going to help me buy land. Not that I knew how to tend land anyway. More than ever, I felt my diasporic uprootedness at its peak, and I had to reckon with the shocking truth that I did not know how to make a life in my homeland.

For a time, everything hurt. Yasmín Hernández, my rematriation sibling, said upon returning, her soul was whole but her body was broken down. Now home, I, too, felt waves of belonging that can only come from being retethered to my origin place. This is the restoration of the soul that Yas speaks of. But so, too, was the pain. I could feel and directly experience all that motivated my ancestors to leave. All the ways they were violently pushed out. Within the first two years, I had moved five times. Sometimes an agreement came to an end, other times eviction, and others, rupture with chosen kin. At this time, I felt continually challenged to hold firm in my decision to return and was surrounded by doubt.

These difficulties catalyzed illness in my body. The physical manifestation was a large chocolate cyst on my left ovary, unimaginable pelvic pain, consistent spotting, and weight loss. I knew that something deep and ancestral had moved within me to the surface for healing. My cyst appeared when I was thirty-five, the same year my mother discovered a large cyst on her left ovary and was sent into the emergency room to operate. The doctor told her that her endometriosis was so severe that he found scar tissue thick as vines within her. Although stark in its similarity, some things had changed in a generation: I was aware of the cyst before it became an emergency, and I was willing (and able) to dedicate time and energy to working with it. It unfolded the layers of embodied misogyny, disappointment, insecurity, and frustration simmering quietly below the surface of my achievements. My Indigenous elders from la tribu Yuke, and my chosen kin, welcomed me in my pain and offered me limpias, prayer, and ceremony. Surgery confirmed what I already knew: I had severe endometriosis.

I saw other versions of this embodied misogyny in the bodies of my fellow activist womb-carriers—cysts, fibroids, and painful periods in nearly all the badass feminists leading a movement to end gender violence. They knew, like me, on a deep cellular level, how difficult and dangerous it was to be alive and in one's feminine power. This wisdom is more expansive and wilder than that which is assigned female at birth. The mask of endometrium weaving like vines to protect me and imprison me at once in the chains of sexual violence, family trauma, abuse, and domination.

In the first seven years of my rematriation-initiation, I reclaimed the wisdom needed to free me from dis-ease and trust in the pulse. The pulse was so hard to hear at first, because I lived life swinging between overdoing and numbness. Slowly and in piecemeal ways, I turned toward the pain, synchronizing with the pulses and surges of energy emanating from the land. There were wells of infinite grief as I felt the hurt of the land in my bones and in my tissue. It was haunted by the legacies of sterilization, medicine provided to dry up milk and get women back to work, femicides, and domestic violence.

Peace is intermittent now. I tap into the frequency floating in the ocean, held by the mother of the fishes. I find it diving in the cold water of a river, reminding my own waters to flow again. I find it lying in the hammock under the rays of the moon, breathing in the pulse of earth connection: Slowly I saw the outline of a feminine person, and yet beyond binary, emerging from the depths of my being. The power to shed the socialization of a body assigned female at birth is here in the waters of Boriké. Slowly, Guabonito teaches me about the power of flow. Water's movement patterns—its currents and waves—are always already a reminder of the power we have to free ourselves from the expectations of others and to find our own route.

The waters teach me of the wisdom contained in the receptive realms. They teach me of ease over force. The waters teach me about shaping change and the continual act of transformation. They teach me about giving over to the cycles of life. An archipelago, held by salt water, that is filled with 5,385 miles of sweet water, provides vital medicine in the rematriation journey. Over time, rivers carve new paths for themselves. We are infinite in our multiplicity.

Feeling Undulating Connections

After some time working with the waters, the pulse became rhythm. It did not feel continuous, not to my conscious mind. My ability to tune in feels turned up at times, and at others, quiet or stagnant—a pause.

To strengthen the connection, I reach back further into my lineages. I cannot make a claim to purity as I move toward reclaiming my indigeneity. I can trace paternal and maternal lineages into the mountains of Boriké: Maricao and Orocovis—where Indigenous legacy remains palpable in the naming of place and jibaro traditions.

I am reclaiming traditions, worldview, and practice through a movement that is choppy at times, synchronous at others, but always about the remembrance that lives in the bones and my cells. I do not base my belonging on blood quantum or DNA tests, which are often used to affirm the myth of our disappearance, our reduction to percentages decreasing generation by generation. Instead, I focus on cultivating and sustaining belonging to living elders and leaders of the native community. I am ever grateful to the elders Kukuya and Makutok, who welcomed me into the ceremonies they lead in Coabey, home of the ancestors in our Taíno cosmology, and have guided me in my rematriation journey.

Each time I climb the mountain, I feel a deeper sense of integrity and understanding emerge quietly in the shadows. I look to the elders, who remind me that once you know who you are, no one can take it away. They teach me how to connect to the spiritual realm and to trust my intuition. They teach me to work with the elements, remind me of the stories and the importance of reading beyond what is told in the chronicles—one source Taíno people must look to when trying to recreate our history. The library of Agüeybaná is not the same as Father Nazario's stones. In all the ways I can, I look to the ancestors for the path forward, and I look for all the ways our ancestral Caribbean strength is recorded in our language, in our tradition, and in our myths. I find this is the only way to subvert the trap of recognition. As I move closer to my origin, I learn to trust the voice within me.

Of course, this coming-home is rife with challenges in the Caribbean, as the home of the people who met Columbus and his genocidal actions that launched a colonial war of violence and extraction in "the Americas," Abya Yala. Though in the accounts, Columbus never set foot in Borikén, he did send for the Indigenous babies to be eaten by dogs.[4] Today, there is no tribal nation recognized in this archipelago among insular or colonial government. Coming home and building those relationships requires a great deal of personal integrity and willingness to be misunderstood, judged, or excluded.

I sit in circle with other Indigenous activists and elders at least five times a year. I recognize how little this is. But each circle is an unbroken formation, without beginning or end. I draw strength from others who have spent more time on this road, who have a sense of the unity that encircles us on the rematriation path. One year at the jornada indigena taína, Pluma Barbara, a powerful Indigenous activist, explains that each of us represents a piece of shattered pottery. Colonialism purposely sought to erase, package, repress, and otherwise deny our Indigenous legacy. Today, we each hold a piece of a broken vase, and that piece is key to activating the soul intention and once again strengthening our collective wisdom.

The undulating flow of this movement is like that. With an open heart, knowledge arrives in the dream space, in sudden epiphanies and a deepening understanding of your own bodily communication. Wisdom awakens and your task becomes to protect connections. Study the pieces of language that remain, read against the grain of the chronicles, attend ceremony, and sit with the native plants. At this time, I must focus on giving offerings, listening, and waiting. I thought moving would mean I had arrived, but it was only a start. Being in place allows skills to arise to the surface of the wave, where I sit, ready to receive.

Grow Strong Roots to Fly

Today, more than seven years later, I feel rooted. I awaken to a lightness I never experienced before. A greater cycle emerges as linear time falls away. Impulse. Pulse. Flow. Pause. Begin again. Like the seasons of the earth, the phases of the moon, there is a rhythm below the surface, which continues uninterrupted by colonialism. The land is not only the gendered "mother." It is nourishment. It is source. The cosmic womb is home. A genderless place of belonging. This trans atabey contains both the receptive and the active within. They are magnetic force. Reproducing and transforming all the time. This is the queer ecology of rematriation in a post-Maria landscape—the need to read with the possibility that storms and other climate impacts could birth a future island. The possibility of living in joy.

There are depths you may never see. This truth causes me to experience a gender euphoria. Like the land, I am more than you see. This external invisibility is a key point, a touchstone. Like the directions, these elements and impulses can guide you back to your own rhythm. Now I know where to find the fruit (and it's not in the supermarkets), I can recognize the trees, and yes, I can hear another pulse. Not only wounds, now there is a sense of rootedness to the flow of the creative force. I find myself briefly touching into this flow, and yet, it's so easy to be pulled out. Me siento aclera'. I feel accelerated, often after achieving a goal or making it somewhere I only dreamed possible in the past. The push can put me back on the hamster wheel of productivity. My body feels comfortable in pushing through. My body lived here in the constant doing for a long time. I must work to slow it down with offerings, time away from devices, and feet in the mud. When I recalibrate in this way, I find the pulse of the land again. In the eternal present, I recognize that all time is now. I dance in the spiral, finding my way back to the center point. Surrendering to this place, I am rooted enough to take flight.

Melissa Rosario (she/they) is a queer cultural worker, healing justice practitioner, and artist living and working in San Juan. They imagine and cocreate cultures of liberation alongside island and diasporic Boris through writing, facilitation, and stewardship of the Center for Embodied Pedagogy and Action (CEPA).

Notes

1. Calling attention to the magic of Borikén, where three of five bioluminescent bays in the world are located, Yasmin Hernandez's own rematriation manifesto focuses on the parallels between the dinoflagellate and those returning from the diaspora to home. When the organisms are disturbed by subtle movements in the water, a protein and an enzyme—luciferin and luciferase—combine and create energy. Scientists speculate that dinoflagellates developed this trait to ward off or evade predators. But it might also be for communication. In Yasmin's inspiring work, she examines the light beings of the Puerto Rico Trench—complex beings in the family of the dinoflagellates but distinct in many ways. She imagines that shining light in the dark is a collaborative effort guiding us toward our collective liberation. See https://rematriatingBorikén.com/manifesto.
2. See https://native-land.ca/.
3. For further details on the difficult aspects of rematriation, please see the introduction to my book *Beyond Disaster: Building Collective Futures in Puerto Rico* (Northwestern University Press, 2025), 4–6.
4. Aura Bogado, "Here's the Real Story of Columbus That People Prefer to Ignore," *Grist*, October 12, 2015, https://grist.org/politics/heres-the-real-story-of-columbus-that-people-prefer-to-ignore/.

CHAPTER 7

"VAMONOS PA'L MONTE": Refuge, Radical Joy, and Transcendence

WANDA RAIMUNDI-ORTIZ

This title references the famous Puerto Rican salsa track by Eddie Palmieri, with the lyrics "Vamonos pa'l monte / al monte pa'guarachar / vamonos pa'l monte / el monte me gusta más."[1] My work has changed dramatically across my twenty-plus-year career. I've grown tired of fiery critiques and knee-jerk reactions in my work. I'm shedding that old skin and slipping into a new space of joy and wonder in my studio.

I lived through the first Trump presidency, the COVID-19 pandemic, and the murder of George Floyd in central Florida. I found myself suddenly aching to return to the trees, to become part of the landscape, seeking the kind of shelter and privacy that the forest can bring, and to hide from the pain and danger that was brewing. For a born-and-bred Bronx girl, craving a forest is radical, but the trees have always called to me. As a kid, "nature" was limited to Joyce Kilmer Park on the Grand Concourse, Orchard Beach, and the occasional family jaunts to Los Siete Lagos (the Seven Lakes) at Harriman State Park. I wasn't aware of the lack of trees in the Bronx until Mayor Michael Bloomberg announced his Million Tree initiative back in 2007, an initiative to improve the air quality of New York City.

My true love affair with the trees started when I left New York and headed to Orlando to begin my job at the university. The first sight of my new neighborhood snatched my soul and gave it back to me. It was laced with giant live oak trees dripping with Spanish moss. I wondered what joys and horrors those old sentinels had seen, quietly observing the pettiness of humanity. Over the years, I spent a lot more time meditating on the landscape and my profound attraction to the tropical forests of Florida. I realized this was the closest I had ever come to living in Puerto Rico. As an adult, all of my trips there were mainly for work purposes, and never longer than a few days. I started thinking that maybe it was time for a real visit to the Island and came up with a list of reasons why I should go:

1. I hadn't taken a proper vacation in over twenty years, and I'd become a workaholic;
2. My job as a professor afforded me a work-free summer, except that it wasn't work-free—instead, summer was the time to catch up on art-making, residencies, studio visits, and building up materials for the ever-looming academic year;
3. I felt a deep urgency to show my child the source of my identity and the epicenter of my being, and hoped that this experience would imbue him with his own sense of belonging and pride; and
4. I had never really *explored* Puerto Rico before.

While I visited almost every year as a girl and young adult, I spent much of that time on a small hillside, in the home of my maternal uncle and tía política (aunt by marriage) in a barrio on the outskirts of Guaynabo, about twenty-five minutes from the Island's capital of San Juan. I'd mostly stay with my mother and my very devout and conservative tío, tía, and grandfather, whose tiny wooden home on stilts directly behind their own home was frozen in time, encapsulating the bulk of my experience of the Island. I would perch on the ledge of the carport, eating mangoes from the huge tree that once shaded Tía's home, hoping someone might take me exploring. Out on the front porch, waiting and wishing for someone to take me to a movie, I watched young men riding Paso Fino horses bareback up and down the hill. I'd scandalously work on my teenage tan in a beach chair on my tía's front lawn, as chickens clucked nearby. I kept hoping to see a beach, a park, El Morro, or any of the treasures that were my birthright, but these trips hardly ever happened. Sure, I visited with elders, my Spanglish globbing in my throat, slapping mosquitoes while my mother chatted with Tía What'sHerName or Don ViejoWithTheThickGlasses. I would sit, muted, as my mother's friends would marvel at how much taller and lighter I was than everyone else in my family, dodging jabs at my weight and how I desperately needed to learn Spanish. The mark of La Americana was right there, etched on my skin in itchy, blotchy mosquito welts, to the horror of my family.

There was that one time when Primo SoAndSo took me off that hill to the beach out of some version of mercy; but he forgot to put sunscreen on me, so I returned looking sun-ravaged and crazy. On rare occasions, a cousin from my late father's side of the family would pop by when they heard we were in town and offer to drive us through Old San Juan (never park and walk around, just drive). There was that one time when Tío What'sHisFace offered to take me out por ahi, maybe to grab an ice cream and chicken feed,

Figure 1. Wanda Raimundi-Ortiz, "At the foot of a 400-year-old Ceiba." Sketch from the Pa'l Monte series. Image courtesy of Wanda Raimundi-Ortiz.

but first—a pit stop. "Let's stop right here for a minute," he said, pulling up to the gallera (cockfights) to place a few bets. I can still remember the smell of blood that hung in the air and the sounds . . . those god-awful sounds.

There was that one tía on my dad's side who was always fun to visit. Aside from the mosquitoes and no one speaking any English, she was quirky and had lots of daughters that were so different from my conservative cousins on the hillside with their long skirts and long hair wrapped tight in dubis to protect from humidity before heading to culto (church). These other cousins were tall, wore tight jeans and lots of makeup, dyed their hair, and were infinitely more glamorous to me. I couldn't understand them very well, but I liked to watch them move. In my tía's house, they watched TV and I saw my favorite cartoons and shows—dubbed in Spanish, of course. *The Flintstones* became *Los PicaPiedras* and *Wonder Woman* was *La Mujer Maravilla*. It was a little disorienting and exacerbated my homesickness, but it was better than nothing. Tía offered me super sweet juice, served in a repurposed bean can, with ice she made in a milk carton that she beat with a pilón to break chunks free. It was fascinating to me. She once took my mom and me a pasear, and we ended up on the grounds of a fancy hotel and casino. We didn't go inside, but we wandered the gardens, where I saw snow-white peacocks. After a few moments drinking in the grandeur, we were deposited back to the hillside.

Don't get me wrong. These trips were not terrible and served a very specific purpose. My mother was keeping me connected to her home and my dad's family. She certainly didn't have to keep taking me to see them after he died when I was eleven, but she did. While I can't say that I know them very well or have strong familial bonds, I can say with confidence that I feel more Puerto Rican because of these moments, and I have deep gratitude for that knowledge.

You may or may not know about the hierarchy of Puerto Ricanness. The ability to measure up to the expectations of cultural authenticity of one's ancestral place of origin is vital, especially when returning to one's patria. It's nothing new to anyone from the diaspora, and it is real. The better your vocabulary, pronunciation, and understanding of cultural nuance, the higher up you are on the Diasporican ladder—which helps when you nonetheless get razzed for being "de por allá" (from out there), "del otro lado del charco" (the other side of the puddle). Bonus points if you can cook the cuisine with proficiency. Authentic Ricanness is its own currency, with value both stateside and abroad; unpacking that in full would require another essay entirely.

As my particular family was raised to be Puerto Rican as opposed to Nuyorican (a term vehemently opposed by certain members of my immediate family, as for them it is a form of devaluing or negating the validity of our heritage), measuring up or impressing those on the Island with our authenticity is, as the young kids say, low-key important to me. In my work, the nature-versus-concrete-jungle tension has always flowed in the background, but now it is beginning to take center stage.

During one of my all-too-typical academic moments of grinding my gears over a grant application proposal, I thought a lot about how trees were making their way into my work. I'd started making sculptures that looked like distorted trees, drawing vine-like pictures in my sketchbooks, and spending lots of time observing the multitude of textures on different plant species. If I wasn't drawing, I was taking pictures of the species that I encountered around me. Live oaks, saw palmettos, date palms, pine trees, magnolias, cypress trees—all towering beauties that surrounded my Florida home. I never got bored of them, and riding my bike around the neighborhood in their shade was always delightful. Whenever I saw a new neighborhood development start, I felt genuine grief for the trees felled for this purpose. Seeing them stacked haphazardly, like discarded toys, shoved into a corner waiting for a woodchipper to arrive and finish the job, was (and is) gutting. I felt like I owed it to them to acknowledge them.

My upcoming trip to Puerto Rico, the first in five years, was not to be a resort and piña colada–filled Gringolandia paradise—instead, a homecoming. One other thing about going to Puerto Rico this time was to see the trees back home. I mean, *really* see the trees.

In struggling through that grant proposal, I realized that all the trees in my work were from my immediate surroundings, the contiguous United States, and not native to Puerto Rico—channeling them felt akin to channeling the Island, but it wasn't that. A fellow artist asked me to consider using Island trees, and it hit me that I couldn't authentically speak about the trees of PR, because I didn't know them. In actuality, I didn't know the Island either.

Holy shit, I don't know the ISLAND!

I decided to propose the idea of funded field research alongside scholars who specialized in the trees and plants of the Island. I would document plants and trees connected to those hillsides where my mother grew up, and learn some of the ways that those plants, fruits, seeds, and herbs were used, cross-referencing them with stateside artifacts in a national museum collection. I would have a knowledge base to authenticate my creative research. I scripted all of this with care, but ultimately the proposal got rejected. With it, momentarily, my one chance to reconnect with the land of my ancestors was rejected as well.

Yo, wait up, says who? You're kidding, right? Was I *really* telling myself that I couldn't go back to the Island unless it was research-funded? The entire thing suddenly felt stupid, and voices in my head began to chide me. "Puerto Rico is Home. Just go HOME. Home to who?" The family on the hill would absolutely welcome me, but I would just sit on the porch and *wait*. "Well, you can rent a car, can't you?" "It's expensive," I whined to myself. The truth is, I was scared. I have GPSed my way around the US with very little worry, but the thought of driving around on that crazy little island with the tiny streets, random power outages, disastrous storms, lackadaisical local culture, and my stupid Spanglish that would give me away, halted me. I wanted to know the Island, but I couldn't face how foreign it was to me. Puerto Rico is a different vibe, and I am infinitely more "American" than I care to admit—especially after nearly thirteen years away from NYC, steeped in the Gringolandia that is Florida.

I was immobilized, but I knew I needed to go. I had to get my son there while he was still young and his sense of belonging and pride was still developing. I wanted him to feel anchored to a place that will embrace him when this crazy American place won't, just as it does for me. The thought of my beloved cultura dying on the vine because I didn't invest more time sharing with my son cut into me. I wanted him to see people who look like him, in the mall, on the beach, or on the playground. I wanted the sounds, smells, tastes, and vistas of Puerto Rico to fill his senses and moor his story to a real place, instead of the Goya section at the grocery store. He will need this place as a compass as he grows into his cinnamon skin and curls as thick and stormy as the sea. He will take his place at this table, be embraced, and be filled with the stories of resistance.

I also needed to see the trees—*badly.* Going alone, I would have probably done this all wrong. I would have been daunted and squandered the time and resources that it took to get me there. I wouldn't have dared enter the rainforest or find my way to the sea. I would have succumbed to the safety of an Airbnb and local fare, cobbled together some mediocre patchwork of memories, and returned home feeling empty. Since I didn't trust myself, I needed to recruit the right tour guide. A low-maintenance partner that could gladly bypass white-linen dining and choose wax-paper street fare. Someone who would not judge me for gawking at canopies of flamboyán trees, who would let me jump out of a car to pick up mangoes on the roadside and not bat an eyelash. My travel partner had to match my dorkiness with a love of crunchy snacks, good music, and bad jokes. They couldn't flinch at driving nearly two hours of twisty roads and crossing sketchy bridges just to see a very specific four-hundred-year-old tree. I needed to experience the Island with someone whose love of the Island was as immeasurable as their love of their family; whose commitment to learning far exceeded my own, and who was infinitely braver, wiser, and more driven than me in many ways. I called my sister, Lilly.

Lilly is no joke. She's the person that you hear about in feel-good pieces at the end of the news broadcast: the retired school principal that cooks for the local soup kitchen; the one working toward a barber's license to cut hair for the elderly. To say that I am proud of her is an understatement. She's

Figure 2. Wanda Raimundi-Ortiz, "Las Hermanas (El Yunque #3—Panas)." Sketch from the Pa'l Monte series. Image courtesy of Wanda Raimundi-Ortiz.

brilliant, devoted, fiercely independent, and would move mountains just to see you smile. I can't lie, I was nervous at first, but when I asked if she would host my kid and me, I was thrilled that she agreed.

My son and I arrived in Puerto Rico without much of a plan, already down to go with the flow. I confessed my naivety of the Island to my sister and she was surprised that with all of my travel, I'd seen so little, aside from what I had read in books, on the internet, and of course—our tía on the hill. With that, our adventure began. We spent many hours in a tiny car together, winding down southern coastal throughways. I rode shotgun and white-knuckled while Lilly snaked up and down bamboo-canopied one-lane mountain roads, evading chickens and stray dogs that ambled along. I was wide-eyed and awe-stricken by the magnificence and ferocity of this place that I had always claimed but hardly knew. We ate home-grown pineapples from Cabo Rojo, got wicked lost in Jayuya, swerved around huge crabs on the streets of Islote, and danced bomba on the beach in Loiza.

More importantly, we went to see *that* tree. Tucked deep in Patillas, hugging up against the side of a small mountain road, across from a gurgling river and pana trees pregnant with ripening fruit, rose a mighty ceiba tree with enormous thorny roots like buttresses. This tree, one of the many ceibas on the Island, is storied to be the Tree of Life, the resting place of our ancestors' spirits and the bridge between heaven and earth. To stand before her is to stand at the gates of a cathedral; closing my eyes, I imagined children from centuries before playing at her feet or hiding from pale-eyed invaders. If only she would speak to me of the wonders and horrors she's seen in her four hundred years.

July 4th weekend was a transformative moment on that trip. My sister took us to her favorite place in El Yunque, called "Puente Roto," where we bathed in its ancient river. It was my first time there, dwarfed by a canopy of massive trees, dripping with cascades of ferns and vines. I wasn't prepared for what came next. Lowering myself into the water, as if being baptized, surrounded by regal witnesses, draped in lush, flowing green leaves, I was overcome with emotion. I was welcomed into the bosom of my mother's land, and for the first time, I felt a genuine sense of belonging. For once I didn't feel like an imposter or interloper. This awakened a thirst to experience her fertile bounty.

Three weeks barely scratched the surface of Puerto Rico, that beautiful, wounded place. Intermingled with the lush green foliage are the visible scars of a strangled economy. Abandoned homes with sweeping views of the ocean or high above valleys and entire communities reduced to husks of their former selves weighed on me. Observing many battery-operated lanterns resting casually within arm's reach in some homes, or stockpiles of bottled water in corners, were not-so-gentle reminders of the precariousness of the Island's power grid and the government scandals lurking beneath. My feelings of guilt and gluttony were real. To live here is to attempt a level of harmony with the restlessness of nature and the naked ambition of those who govern. It is a strange mix of gratitude, resistance, and surrender that is difficult to explain.

This is why for so long my work was so anchored in the Nuyorican story as opposed to an Island one. Again, my ethics will not allow me to attempt this complex discourse from the cushy distance of the States. I always knew deep down in my bones that I couldn't speak to something that I have not lived, because integrity is expensive. I would never proclaim something that I hadn't seen or felt with my own eyes, skin, and hands. Instead, I spent years mining my Nuyorican angst—feeling lost, unseen, misunderstood, miscategorized, and bogged down with ensuring that a place was held for us. I have built entire bodies of work in order to hold back the waters of erasure. *Your girl is tired!*

It has been a while since that enriching trip and, like the lush rainforests and nutrient-rich soil of mi isla, the seeds that were planted are growing in me and my little one. Puerto Rico is more than a resort destination, more than fried foods, beaches, and sunscreen. It is a tormented but resilient mother to a people who have had no choice but to persist and rise. She has earned a new level of respect and humbling admiration for her unbridled abundance despite how she has been treated.

My son has started to learn Spanish so he can more fully enjoy himself when we return, because we *will* return. I am back in the studio drawing, using the photos that I took as a reference of the place where I went for sanctuary and that instead grew into my family. Not just with my kin but with the giant trees in El Yunque and lining the streets on all of our journeys. I am drawing to hold fast to the place that feeds something deep and powerful inside of me. This place, with the tiny roads that course like veins through her body, and trees that sway with the same rhythm and mystery in my hips.

I must bring my son back, to adorn his mahogany skin in shimmering ocean diamonds; my partner should feel the pulse of my people's heart in his chest, to fully know that this heartbeat, like thunder, is too strong for just one body. I don't think I have ever felt such a strong pull toward Puerto Rico as I do now. I must return and grow our home there.

For the first time in my life and career, when I was on the Island I felt as if I were granted full permission to be happy and not need to explain over and over again the plight of the Latinx artist. There, deep in the mountains or on small roadside beaches, I felt an openness that is still with me. There, amid groaning towers of bamboo, at the foot of a four-hundred-year-old ceiba tree, with tears swelling in my eyes, I felt released.

Wanda Raimundi-Ortiz is a visual artist who uses multiple modes to address bias, trauma, and healing. Exhibitions include the Smithsonian National Portrait Gallery, National Museum of Women in the Arts, Museum of Arts and Design, Garage Museum Moscow, Museo de Arte de Puerto Rico, and the Manifesta and Performa biennials. Media coverage includes *Art in America*, *The New York Times*, and *The Washington Post*. Currently, she is an associate professor at George Mason University.

Note

1. Lyrics from "Vamonos Pa'l Monte," © 1971 by Eddie Palmieri, are included by generous permission of Eddie Palmieri. Visit Palmieri's website at www.eddiepalmierimusic.com or find him on social media @EddiePalmieri.

CHAPTER 8

abokehibu bia anabukuta'ni hai: A Sensory Approach to the Revitalization of the Taíno Language

ERMEN DELLICARPINI

Translated literally, "abokehibu bia anabukuta'ni hai" means "recipe for waking up." As much as arroz y gandules, resistance and reclamation are staples in Puerto Rican households. We make ourselves through our stories of survival and the survivance of our culinary and cultural heritage. Even when our survival meant hiding parts of ourselves, those parts still form a basis for our being-in-the-world, despite the social processes that make us either proud or ashamed of our heritage.

By living through and with the stories of survival told by our hebeyo'no (ancestors)—through food, language, stories—we are engaging in a resistance against a colonial system of marginalization as well as a reclamation of cultural teachings. Just like arroz y gandules, my recipe for language revitalization will be different than yours. However, also like arroz y gandules, there are things that make the dish distinct and known to many Puerto Ricans across the globe. Below you will find my recipe for revitalization, informed by my culture, community, family, and research. With this recipe, you will learn techniques for framing your self through revitalization and embracing an identity that exists in resistance to colonial intervention and rule, not subjectification by it.[1] An important step in reclaiming our narratives of self is the revitalization of our traditional Taíno language, a language that survives but is sleeping in many of those who claim it ancestrally.

What you'll need: blood memory, slipstream, survivance.

— Chef's note: A bit of courage, love, and transparency helps make this recipe something to savor.

Survivance

Gerald Vizenor defines *survivance* as "an active sense of presence over absence" and says that "survivance is the continuance of stories."[2] That is to say that stories—and the ways they influence our lives—are an embodiment of our familial and ancestral histories and that they contribute to the formation of identity. Continuing—or living—these stories establishes that sense of presence as an act of reclamation of our cultural heritages beyond a colonial narrative. According to that colonial narrative, all Taíno people died after Columbus came to the Caribbean. Curiously, Taíno women cooked our foods for settlers long after we were declared extinct as a people. African, European, and Taíno culinary cultural heritages all inform contemporary Puerto Rican cuisine. Cooking our traditional foods connects us to the history that formed that cuisine over generations.

Vizenor goes on to explain that "survivance, then, is the action . . . and sentiment of the verb *survive*."[3] To exist beyond a colonial narrative is to exist beyond just a survivable name. Acknowledging our Taíno ancestors creates a survivable name, but honoring our Taíno ancestors creates survivance. Like our varied recipes, the ways that we honor our ancestors will look different. Regardless of our approach, by engaging with ancestral and cultural memory and heritage—say, by cooking a meal that is significant culturally and within our family—we are engaging in the practice of survivance. We create an active, lived existence as people with Taíno heritage. The stories that we (re) tell become the recipe for our lives, which in turn becomes an "active sense of presence." As we cook, share, and eat the meals that represent our culinary cultural heritage, we are creating an existence beyond a survivable name.

Slipstream

Stories and oral histories do not fit statically in one place or time or even within one being's consciousness. The transcendence of these boundaries is what Grace Dillon would call "slipstream." Dillon describes slipstream as a way of experiencing reality that "replicates non-linear thinking about space-time" by "view[ing] time as pasts, presents, and futures that flow together like currents in a navigable stream."[4] Storytelling is one method of navigating the stream that Dillon describes, characterized by dipping in between times and places as narratives ebb and flow. In this way, when we cook ancestral and cultural meals, we are navigating the pasts, presents, and possible futures of ourselves and our communities in much the same way as we do when telling stories. Using the slipstream as a methodology means opening pathways between past and present by engaging with familial and cultural heritage. We use those connections and the knowledge therein to strengthen our bonds with culture and community. This is a necessary component of language revitalization efforts where there are few living speakers of the language, as is the case with Taíno. Slipstream allows us to engage with our hebeyo'no and their tekiraha'ni'no (teachings) on our own terms.

I feel especially *in* the slipstream when I cook pasteles. An important dish for many Caribbean families, this recipe marks a rite of passage and a transcendental temporal link to ancestors for womxn in my family. One holiday season when my great-grandmother Celodina was feeling homesick for Borikén, she and her cousin Carmito got together to try and reverse-engineer a pasteles recipe from memory alone. We still use that recipe in my family—our twist being that we add a bit of milk in the masa, but please don't ask me why. When my grandmother first made them on her own, she made it by memory, with a few phone calls to my bisabuela. My mother learned in a similar way, and I scouted far and wide in the pacific northwest for yautia when I was making my phone calls home for guidance. This winter, I continued the tradition by walking my sister through the arduous yet rewarding task. In this way, cooking traditional food helps me honor my ancestors in more than one way—those distant and those close. When my family cooks pasteles, relying on a memory of a memory, we are dipping into the slipstream.

Blood Memory

Monique Mojica says that as we live our stories they become "part of [our] memory, and as long as they are remembered they live on. This is *blood memory*."[5] In other words, the act of living a culture encodes the memories of those traditions in our bodies. If survivance is the action of living out our stories, then blood memory is the milieu through which we live them out and perhaps even the vessel that we occupy when navigating the slipstream. Mojica describes stories as being "passed on through blood, encoded in DNA," in a way that makes them deeply known to and a part of us.[6] Their depth can be a blessing and a curse, deeply part of us but also for many deeply unknown and foreign, as memories lay dormant within our bones. By living aspects of culture, we can locate and awaken our blood memories that have been passed to us through generations of cultural practice. Preparing and sharing a meal is a way of telling a story, something that is continually reproduced. Changing, yet foundational. The knowledges coded in and passed down through our cultural and ancestral connections, our blood memory, inform the ways we exist in the world and view ourselves. In this way, as Mojica says, "our bodies are our libraries," and the information therein informs the way we move through the world.[7]

These methodologies center understandings of self that are informed by and through cultural practice. When identity markers are informed from within cultural frameworks whose goal is survivance, rather than by colonial institutions whose goal is control, we understand ourselves and our cultural practice in terms of their own value systems rather than through the piecemeal appropriations of our own cultures that are handed back to us like merit badges in the form of an "authentic" claim on identity that is dictated by the state.

Our food and our surviving language are evidence of a connection to a history that exists beyond colonization. A sensory approach to both understanding Puerto Rican identity and engaging in language revitalization represents a possible *future* that exists beyond colonization. Grating yautia into a slimy, viscous paste for masa; pounding tough yet forgiving plantains in a mortar for mofongo; rolling grainy, clay-like corn flour into cylinders for sorullos—these are all actions that connect us to the millions of Taíno hands that have repeated those same motions since time immemorial. Blood memory shows the way to the memories that form those connections, slipstream allows us to make it across space-time to access them, and survivance helps us bring those connections forward and beyond.

As a methodology, it is revolutionary in its ability to liberate Puerto Ricans from imposed identities of subjectivation, through an active reclamation of Puerto Rican Taíno heritage and culture. Resistance by reclaiming linguistic heritage through and with our culinary cultural heritage will bring us home, because it will bring us back to ourselves.

ermen dellicarpini is an Italian, Irish, Spanish, and Puerto Rican Taíno cultural studies scholar who was born and raised in New York. ermen's work focuses in experimental and sensory auto-ethnography through a framework of endangered language revitalization of the Taíno language. Through a sensory approach to language, ermen hopes to connect linguistic and culinary cultural heritages for [diasporic] Puerto Ricans.

Notes

1. *Subjectification* is here defined as being made subject to colonial convention and rule.
2. Gerald Robert Vizenor, ed., *Survivance: Narratives of Native Presence* (University of Nebraska Press, 2008), 1.
3. Vizenor, *Survivance*, 19.
4. Grace Dillon, ed., *Walking the Clouds: An Anthology of Indigenous Science Fiction* (University of Arizona Press, 2012), 3.
5. Monique Mojica, "Stories from the Body," in *Native American Performance and Representation*, edited by S. E. Wilmer (University of Arizona Press, 2011), 109.
6. Mojica, "Stories from the Body," 97.
7. Mojica, "Stories from the Body," 97.

CHAPTER 9

The Urgency of an Anti-Racist Decolonial Feminist Pedagogy in Puerto Rico

AURORA SANTIAGO ORTIZ

EDITOR'S NOTE: An earlier version of this essay was published in Spanish as "Deconstruimos la educación patriarcal desde el lente feminista: Construyendo una educación liberadora en clave antirracista, feminista y decolonial" in *Centro Journal* 35, no. 2 (Summer 2023). This version has been translated, condensed, and edited for this volume. Many thanks to Nicole Delgado for translating this essay.

One afternoon in September 2019, while I was walking through the corridors of the Arturo Morales Carrión building at the University of Puerto Rico, Cayey Campus (UPR-C), I came across flyers with the following messages glued on the walls:

"The problem is not faith. It's your homophobia!"

"Academic freedom does not include freedom to discriminate or harass."

"When you live with male privilege, GENDER EQUALITY can feel oppressive. Deal with it!"

"WAKE UP! The University of Puerto Rico prohibits discrimination based on sex and gender in all its modalities."

The hashtag #UPRfuerafobias was written at the bottom of the flyers.[1] The campaign emerged after a professor included a note in his syllabus stating his position on the university's antidiscrimination policy. The note specified that "homosexual, lesbian, bisexual, transvestite, transgender, transexual, intersex and queer behaviors are incorrect since God forbids them."[2] Although the professor's actions prompted an investigation, nothing came of it, and he remained teaching. As a result, the students voiced their discontent through a visual campaign on campus.

The professor's statements are no exception within the broader framework of public education in Puerto Rico. The right-wing religious sector has vigorously lobbied against education with a gender perspective (EGP), leveraging its strong connections to the legislative body to thwart any initiatives aimed at incorporating such equity approaches into public schools.[3] Moreover, with the advent of the ultraconservative party Proyecto Dignidad, religious influence has intensified in the legislative sphere. Any public policy that tries to establish education with a gender perspective has been repealed, limited, or eliminated.

Despite these realities, there have been many attempts to establish EGP in Puerto Rico's public education system. For instance, on July 23, 2008, the Department of Education approved Circular Letter No. 003-2008-2009, entitled "Public Policy on the Incorporation of the Gender Perspective in Puerto Rican Public Education."[4] In the letter, the Department defined "gender perspective" as the "conceptual instrument that helps to understand that differences between genders are not due exclusively to a sexual or biological determination but rather to the social construction of human identities." Education with a gender perspective, in turn, seeks "to strip away the stereotypes that reflect these relationships and transform the content of socialization through specific educational projects that foster equality between genders, justice, peace, solidary coexistence, democratic participation, and respect for human diversity." The proposed public policy was annulled by former pro-statehood "right-wing conservative" Governor Luis G. Fortuño when he began his term in 2009.[5] Subsequent efforts by feminist organizations, legislators, and activists to implement EGP have also been vehemently opposed by conservative religious sectors. Insofar as the religious-political sector continues to exercise power in the legislature and policymaking spheres, the possibility of a gender perspective in public education remains an unfulfilled promise.

Although proposals for legislation regarding the implementation of EGP have historically been limited to primary and secondary education, the case of the UPR-C professor demonstrates the urgent need to incorporate EGP at all levels, including higher education. This means offering general education, elective, or concentration courses that adopt a gender perspective in curricula, pedagogical approaches, and research methodologies.

In this essay, I argue that an anti-racist, decolonial, feminist pedagogy and curriculum in higher education is not only necessary but urgent. Given the continuing gender violence, femicide and transfemicide[6] crises in Puerto Rico, and the lack of implementation of EGP within primary and secondary schooling, higher education becomes a crucial site for interrupting sexism, racism, colonialism, and other systems of domination. This requires questioning (our own) socialization processes that result in internalized oppression, as well as analyzing how the state's (in)actions and public policies affect racialized, gendered, queer, and working-class populations.

Research Context, Sites, and Methodology

Several programs and courses taught at the University of Puerto Rico (the archipelago's only nonspecialized public higher education institution) focus on gender and sexuality. The Río Piedras campus offers a program on Women and Gender Studies (Programa sobre Estudios de la Mujer y Género, or PEMG), and the Mayagüez campus offers a minor in Women and Gender Literary and Cultural Studies, housed in the Hispanic Studies Department. The Women's Studies Project at the UPR Cayey was founded in 1986; in 1992, said project published a report entitled *Towards a Nonsexist Curriculum*, aiming "to transform existing curricula to integrate the discussion on women and gender."[7] The UPR Cayey is currently in the process of launching an online master's degree in Gender Studies and Social Action.[8] There are also stand-alone courses taught in Social Sciences and the English Department that address gender and sexuality.

During the 2019–20 academic year, I taught an interdisciplinary research course, which also served as the central axis of my doctoral research.[9] My study examined the development of solidarity, or the ability to work collectively for social transformation, across different social identities (class, race, gender, and sexuality, among others). The course was part of the academic offerings of the Institute for Interdisciplinary Research under the Antonia Pantoja Program, named after educational justice advocate and ASPIRA founder Antonia Pantoja.[10] The Pantoja Program allows professors outside of Puerto Rico to serve as research mentors and professors to undergraduate students at the Cayey campus. Because of the horizontal and participatory approach of the course, the students and community collaborators from the surrounding urban hub of Cayey were co-investigators in the research project. In what follows, I present findings from this research as a case study of a course curriculum that incorporates EGP at the pedagogical, theoretical, and methodological levels. In addition, I include the perspectives and experiences of the undergraduate students who took the course, to demonstrate the impact of EGP. The findings I present in this chapter underscore the need and urgency of a feminist approach and incorporation of EGP in public education writ large in Puerto Rico.

The undergraduate interdisciplinary research course consisted of three elements: the planning, development, and implementation of participatory action research (PAR) projects, which I detail below; the incorporation of an intersectional social justice curriculum to prepare students for community-based research; and the integration of a critical dialogic methodology called intergroup dialogue (IGD).[11] The course had a duration of the entire academic year so that the PAR projects could be developed and implemented in a longer time frame and so participants could take the time to get to know one another. However, students could enroll in the course for one or two semesters.

Since the course was also part of my doctoral research, all the students met with me via phone call before enrolling so I could explain the purpose of the course and study to each of them. Because their work, class sessions, and meetings with people from the urban community would be considered empirical material, I had to obtain consent before the course began. Similarly, community partners in the PAR team also participated in the study, and their consent was also required prior to participating. Both students and community co-researchers could revoke their consent to being in the study at any time, without penalty, and could continue participating in the course and community projects. In addition to being an observer and instructor, I was also part of the research team.

I interviewed students and collaborators a total of fifty-six times to document their collaborative experience and the development of solidarity within the research team. At the beginning of the first semester, three students enrolled: Laura, Rosa, and Malena. Rosa and Malena continued the course in the second semester, when four additional students enrolled: Zoé, Cara, Sara, and Pedro. Sara and Cara were sociology majors, Laura and Zoé were biology majors, and Rosa, Malena, and Pedro were psychology majors.[12]

The interdisciplinary research course met for three hours every Friday. During the first months (August–November), the project focused on recruiting co-investigators from the community and defining the research topic.[13] We recruited Mercedes—a community leader and lifelong resident of Cayey—as part of the research team. We met in a now-closed university space located in the urban hub of Cayey. Mercedes helped us recruit Gabriel, an artisan who had also been an activist while he studied at UPR-C. Gabriel introduced us to Carlos and Carla, two agroecological activists and farmers.

In November 2019, we started meeting as a team to plan several participatory action research projects aimed at addressing the most pressing concerns of the urban hub of Cayey. The projects included an asset map and census of the resources and structures of the urban area of Cayey; a community center that went online in the context of the COVID-19 pandemic; and a digital exhibit of feminist oral histories.[14] Finally, as a result of this research partnership, a community organization emerged, named Colectivo Casco Urbano de Cayey by one of the community partners. The collective continued to be active until the end of 2022.[15]

We followed the participatory action research model developed by the

Colombian sociologist Orlando Fals Borda.[16] Participatory action research is a philosophy and an epistemological, theoretical, ethical, political, and methodological practice.[17] PAR promotes horizontal relationships in the research process and mobilizes research as a tool for political awareness and community organizing by bringing together academic and popular knowledge.[18] Participation is one of the central elements of this methodology, particularly that of "oppressed, discriminated, marginalized, and exploited" people.[19] By analyzing their own reality, those that experience oppression can transform their conditions.[20] Although PAR does not define itself as an explicitly feminist methodology, it can incorporate a decolonial feminist pedagogy by centering the experiences, knowledges, and perspectives of women and femmes. Heeding the critique of androcentrism in PAR by feminist academics and researchers such as Patricia Maguire,[21] I designed the course with this critique in mind, so that the course curriculum and research methodologies were centered around feminist perspectives, particularly decolonial feminist approaches.[22] From the conversations we had as a class and as a research team with community members from Cayey, organic analyses of the ways gender, race, class, sexuality, ability, and colonialism are imbricated emerged, allowing us all to theorize collectively. Sharing our experiences helped us to recognize both our commonalities and differences, connecting the individual to the social and collective.[23] This enhanced the group's awareness of how different forms of oppression impact people differently, fostering a sense of solidarity that was mobilized into action through our collective.

An Anti-Racist, Decolonial, Feminist Approach

Feminist, anti-racist, and decolonial methodologies and epistemologies were integral to our approach in the classroom, community meetings, and PAR projects. In the fall semester, students explored how to incorporate a gender analysis into their research. We discussed how feminist methodologies provide ethical guidelines for working across difference, identifying seemingly neutral knowledge assumptions and subverting them by acknowledging the researcher's subjectivity, positionality, and personal experience.[24] During class meetings, students dialogued about their socialization processes during elementary and secondary education. They analyzed how public education produces and reproduces sexist, racist, classist, and homophobic scripts. They reflected on the need to deconstruct these scripts through an intersectional and decolonial curriculum, which in turn better prepared them to work with the neighboring urban hub community.

The group recognized how each of us experiences the effects of colonialism differently, depending on our positions and social identities. In this way, as a collective, we built a pedagogy that made visible "the patriarchal structures that influence all dimensions of people's development as a starting point, referring to: the individual, the political, the economic, labor, family, leisure, the bodies, the sexual, the affective, the public, the media, etc."[25] For the students, the feminist oral histories project and the other PAR projects validated the role of women in society, noting how women and femmes are disadvantaged in Puerto Rican society. To understand how oppressions operate from an intersectional lens, we read decolonial feminist thinkers from Latin America and the Caribbean, including Puerto Rico, connecting these theorists to activism in the archipelago. As Cara wrote in the students' final report, the content helped her "have a deep insight into the power structures that have dominated society from its origins to the present."[26] For Malena, the course curriculum revealed "the colonial reality of Puerto Rico and its repercussions on society." The students noted the lack of EGP in their elementary and secondary education and how this absence is part of the broader context of state neglect in addressing and preventing gender violence, as was the case with its failure to declare a state of emergency to address gender violence. Since 2018, Black feminist political organization La Colectiva Feminista en Construcción has led a pressure campaign to pass the declaration. Although a state of emergency regarding gender violence and femicides passed in 2021, La Cole and other feminist groups denounced that it had no teeth.[27] Malena also mentioned that

> the lack of action on the part of the State to address gender violence and the opposition to declaring a state of emergency is due to the great religious influence exercised because it goes against the patriarchal postulates of the Church. On the other hand, we can see the oppression exerted against people who favor abortion, people who have tattoos, those who do not belong to any religion, and the LGBTTQ+ community, among others, who are not accepted because they go against the beliefs of the Church. As we can see, neither the Police nor the State intervene with these oppressive practices in religious institutions because [the] Church and State are not separate in real life.

Throughout the course, students reflected on the sociopolitical processes that impacted their participation in PAR projects and their daily lives. Decolonial feminisms and intersectionality were the theories through which they could put their own experiences and analyses into practice.

For example, the students pointed out that decolonization requires understanding racism and undoing the coloniality of gender, a concept coined by the late Argentine decolonial feminist María Lugones.[28] Expanding the work of Peruvian sociologist Anibal Quijano,[29] Lugones exposed how the modern/colonial system constituted and created a categorical schematization, in terms of race, gender, and sexuality, that did not exist prior to European colonization in the Americas. The imposition of a racialized gender system remains evident in the social, economic, and political relations in Puerto Rico and in territories that have been colonies or continue to exist under colonial rule.

Decolonial feminism recognizes the imbrication of multiple forms of oppression as an analytical framework for understanding the interrelationship and inseparability of power structures and relationships of domination and subordination. These analytical lenses resonated with the students because, according to them, they opened paths of knowledge and learning that they had not previously explored in detail. Moreover, they provided entry points for working across difference "where we can collaborate and build a project that benefits everyone," as Rosa mentioned in a written reflection.

The course held space for students to identify and analyze their experiences around oppression and privilege and connect them with the colonial reality of Puerto Rico. The students learned that neoliberal austerity policies converge with colonialism and that these policies disproportionately affect the most marginalized people in Puerto Rico, such as Black people, poor women, and queer and trans people. In their final report, Malena and Cara recognized that claims for decolonization and against austerity measures in Puerto Rico are intrinsically related to queer, trans, and feminist claims. In our conversations during the course, Malena pointed out that many manifestations and consequences of oppression, like depression, gender violence, unemployment, and LGBTQIA+ discrimination, result from our colonial system. Pedro mentioned that one of the participants in the oral history project spoke about the need to create a safe space for queer and trans people in the urban area, which for Pedro highlighted the lack of support from the government and institutions, especially outside the San Juan metropolitan area. They also highlighted the importance of reflecting, questioning, and recognizing their privileges to fully understand the needs and problems faced by a disadvantaged community but not using a colonial lens.

The Role of Elementary and Secondary Education in the Creation of Oppressive Scripts

All the students recognized in their final report that "the Puerto Rican colonial system implies that education greatly favors inequality and oppression." One of the ways coloniality and its matrix of power is manifested is through the early socialization of binary and normative gender roles in both public and private schools. For instance, Pedro wrote about how history was taught from a male-centered, Eurocentric perspective. During his primary and secondary education, the textbooks assigned represented women, including enslaved women, as domestic workers.

Cultural Christianity also imbues the public education system and curriculum. During his high school years, Pedro never received sexual health education. The few times that sex was discussed, it was with a punitive dimension, where abstinence was prescribed as the only route young people should take. Sex was seen as either taboo, avoided, or associated with shame and guilt. Cara described her school as a "heterosexual regime." Education about gender and sexuality was nonexistent, and they labeled anyone outside of the gender binary or heteronormativity as strange. Laura spoke about her upbringing in a patriarchal culture, which taught her that women were submissive and had passive roles. This led her to dream of becoming an educated and successful woman. Going to college ensured that she had a "dignified, well-paid job and did not have to depend on any man."

The topic of religious oppression came up in the students' reflections and classroom dialogues. For example, Malena noted the connections between homophobia, transphobia, and religious oppression in her schooling experience. Although she attended a private secular school, it had a strong affiliation with a Protestant church that discriminated against the LGBTQIA+ community. She observed the impact of religious oppression at the individual and social levels. She reflected on how religion intervenes in politics and how the imposition of religious practices such as prayer circles violates the rights and freedoms of non-Christians, including atheists. Likewise, she observed that both the government and the police refrain from intervening in the oppressive practices of religious groups and remain immobile and unwilling to address the crisis of gender violence effectively.

During the spring semester, students reflected on the messages they had received when they were younger regarding disadvantaged social identities. In one of her written reflections, Sara defined socialization as the naturalization process that "manifests in a society with established moral values, rules, and prejudices, resulting in the oppression of certain sectors or social groups." She pointed to self-assessment as an essential tool to understand one's privileges and use them in the pursuit of social justice. Sara was raised with strong Christian values that were then reinforced at school. In her childhood and adolescence, she perceived queer people as strange. In her house, gay men and lesbians were ridiculed. Once she got to college, she understood that her past identification as a Christian gave her privilege over non-Christians in Puerto Rico.

All the students pointed out the crucial role the University of Puerto Rico has in Puerto Rican society. Students and community co-researchers alike agreed that the university propelled their awakening to critical consciousness. Malena observed that the precarious state of UPR—in large part due to the budget cuts imposed by an unelected Fiscal Oversight and Management Board—has the effect of foreclosing access to higher education in the most vulnerable sectors of the archipelago. The austerity measures that the UPR system is currently experiencing, combined with the closing of approximately five hundred public schools, exacerbate the population's already precarious economic, social, and medical situation. According to Malena,

> they [the government] only enact budget cuts, and the various community sectors continue to be excluded from the educational sphere. This [course] gives us a chance to experience realities that will guide us during the participatory action research process, make visible the educational system's inefficiency, and promote inclusion. Bringing together the community and the university can help break with the oppressive patterns that have been instilled in us since our incorporation into school. In addition, it is important that, as individuals, we can see these schemes of oppression we take part in because of the socialization cycle in which we find ourselves. We can also work to promote actions that lessen the oppression resulting from the capitalist system in which we find ourselves.

Throughout the course, students could connect research tools and dialogical techniques with the study of social movements and theoretical frameworks that advance social justice. Cara was clear about this connection:

> Being young and working in Puerto Rico is a complete challenge. The economic crisis that we have had to live with since [Hurricane] Maria has worsened our situation. The tools and experiences [I have gained] in this course helped reaffirm me that any job I decide to have in the future must look at ways to create meaningful change, however simple it may be.

As the students mentioned, their schooling was the site where they received certain messages reinforcing patterns of domination and racial, gender, and sexual hierarchies. Consequently, the worldview that the students were socialized into during their primary and secondary education affects how they saw themselves and others who do not share their same identities. The internalization of these messages continues, often without questioning, until the students arrive at the university. An education with a gender perspective acknowledges how patriarchy and heterosexism shape our socialization. Yet we can interrupt these power dynamics by learning about our histories and the ways that coloniality and colonialism produce unequal gender, racial, and sexual relations. Undoing the coloniality of gender allows us to build "relations across difference and complex coalition-building . . . [as we fashion] new futures that do not rely on shared understandings of oppression and resistance."[30] Through a "methodology of relationality," we assumed differences as strengths and created solidary bonds across difference and mobilized that solidarity for the benefit and well-being of the surrounding community.[31]

The solidarity that developed within the PAR team took various forms. One of these was collective support, through which we shared tangible and nontangible resources to navigate the pandemic and the precariousness many of us face in the archipelago, and through the community collective that emerged from the class and the research projects. Although the pandemic disrupted the plan to open a community center that could support multiple populations, we launched two initiatives addressing the food insecurity faced by the archipelago: a solidarity pantry and a community garden.[32] The community garden continues to be active in the present and is maintained by the custodial staff of a nearby school. People from the urban hub community have been able to use the plantains and herbs from the garden.

"Where there is education and solidarity, there are struggles that succeed."

We should not underestimate the public university's role as a pillar of critical thinking, especially since it continues under constant threat of ceasing to serve its purpose and mission. Part of this mission includes training people who can contribute to the socioeconomic development of the archipelago and participation in community life outside of the university.[33] The historian Fernando Picó noted how the Cayey campus emerged as the result of community activism,[34] and Mercedes, one of the community co-investigators, echoed this history. With this in mind, we carried out a participatory action project with Cayey residents. Malena, in her final report, wrote the following reflection:

> As we can see, they are continuing to make budget cuts at the University of Puerto Rico, preventing the creation of ties between various community sectors. This happens because the Government wants people to refrain from educating themselves or forming alliances or coalitions, because, after all, [that] would imply "fostering" struggles against corruption and the ineptitude of their work. Where there is education and solidarity, there are struggles that succeed. Yes, there is a citizen interest in promoting projects that empower communities and free us from the corrupt and insufficient government that we have.

Although the course that this essay explores was focused on interdisciplinary research, the topics we covered and the way we interacted in the classroom could be adapted to almost any other forum or course, regardless of whether it has a community-engaged component. Studying oppression from the Puerto Rican lens allowed us to understand the context of the community with which we work and the context in which we live. Furthermore, we were able to establish a more just and solidary way of relating both in academic spaces and outside of them. Incorporating a decolonial feminist pedagogy that is also anti-racist reveals the historical processes (past and present) of hierarchization and racialized violence and oppression, and in turn points to other ways of being, knowing, and relating anchored in collective practices.[35] In our current juncture, in which life becomes more inaccessible every day for people who live in the archipelago, structural racism and gender violence have violent and dehumanizing consequences for Black and Afro-descendant people. A feminist, anti-racist, and decolonial pedagogy and praxis is more urgent than ever—within the classroom, in our communities and families, and in our political work.

Aurora Santiago Ortiz is assistant professor of gender and women's studies and Chicane/Latine studies at the University of Wisconsin-Madison. Her research focuses on anti-racist feminisms, decolonial perspectives, and participatory action research. Her current book manuscript, entitled *Circuits of Self-Determination: Mapping Radical Solidarities and Infrastructures of Resistance in Twenty-First Century Puerto Rico*, focuses on anti-colonial activism stemming from the student movement, particularly grassroots prefigurative political practices anchored in solidarity and spatial repurposing.

Notes

1. Roughly translates as "#phobiasoutofUPR."
2. *Primera Hora*, "UPR Cayey investiga profesor por discriminar contra comunidades LGBTQ+," September 5, 2019, https://www.primerahora.com/noticias/puerto-rico/notas/upr-cayey-investiga-profesor-por-discriminar-contra-comunidades-lgbt/.
3. I also use "curriculum with a gender perspective" interchangeably throughout this chapter. However, "curriculum" also refers to the educational content and pedagogy with a gender perspective.
4. To read Circular Letter No. 003-2008-2009 in its entirety, see https://issuu.com/ampr/docs/carta_circular_3_2008_2009_equidad_.
5. Juan Laguarta Ramírez, "Struggling to Learn, Learning to Struggle: Strategy and Structure in the 2010–11 University of Puerto Rico Student Strike" (PhD diss., Graduate Center, City University of New York, 2016), 110.
6. Transfemicides are not documented as femicides by the PRPD, resulting in an erasure of gender-based violence that trans women and trans men experience.
7. Loida Martínez Ramos, "Una historia de las políticas educativas relacionadas con género en Puerto Rico," *Pedagogía* 46, no. 1 (2013): 97.

8. See https://www.upr.edu/cayey/wp-content/uploads/sites/10/2022/02/cuestiones-de-genero-nueva-epoca-vol-5-ano-2-diciembre-enero-2022-pro-mujeres-ltm.pdf.
9. My research from this period has been published in several journals: Aurora Santiago Ortiz, "Mapping Resistance to Neoliberalism: A Case Study of Participatory Action Research in Puerto Rico," *Tracce urbane: Rivista italiana transdisciplinare di studi urbani* 8, no. 2 (2020): 270–89; Aurora Santiago Ortiz, "'Our Action Plan Was Completely Changed': Adapting, Surviving, and Collaborating Through Participatory Action Research During the Covid-19 Pandemic," *Anthropology and Education Quarterly* 55, no. 3 (2023): 309–21; and Aurora Santiago Ortiz, Antonio Navarro Pérez, Paulette Agosto Ortiz, Coralis Cruz González, and Michelle Román Oyola, "'La solidaridad no perece': Community Organizing, Political Agency, and Mutual Aid in Puerto Rico," *Curriculum Inquiry* 52, no. 3 (2022): 337–50.
10. ASPIRA was founded in 1961 by Pantoja in New York. ASPIRA is a community social justice organization aimed at fostering youth leadership, empowerment, and civic engagement within the Latine community. Pantoja later opened a chapter in Puerto Rico in 1969. For more, see https://www.aspirapr.org/conoce-aspira.
11. For more on IGD, see Ximena Zúñiga, Biren A. Naagda, and Todd D. Sevig, "Intergroup Dialogues: An Educational Model," *Equity and Excellence in Education* 35, no. 1 (2002): 7–17.
12. All names are pseudonyms. Santiago Ortiz, "Mapping Collaboration as Resistance."
13. Santiago Ortiz, "Mapping Collaboration as Resistance"; and Santiago Ortiz, "'Our Action Plan.'"
14. Santiago Ortiz, "Mapping Collaboration as Resistance"; and Santiago Ortiz, "'Our Action Plan.'"
15. Santiago Ortiz, "Mapping Collaboration as Resistance"; and Santiago Ortiz et al., "'La solidaridad no perece.'"
16. Orlando Fals Borda, "The Application of Participatory Action-Research in Latin America," *International Sociology* 2, no. 4 (1987): 329–47.
17. Orlando Fals Borda, "Orígenes universales y retos actuales de la IAP," *Análisis político*, no. 38 (1999): 73–90.
18. Joanne Rappaport, *Cowards Don't Make History: Orlando Fals Borda and the Origins of Participatory Action Research* (Duke University Press, 2020), xvii.
19. Oscar Jara Holliday, "Sistematización de experiencias, investigación y evaluación: Aproximaciones desde tres ángulos," *F(x)=Educación Global Research*, no. 1 (2012): 62.
20. Jara Holliday, "Sistematización de experiencias," 62.
21. Patricia Maguire, *Doing Participatory Research: A Feminist Approach* (Center for International Education, University of Massachusetts, 1987); and Patricia Maguire, "Uneven Ground: Feminisms and Action Research," in *Handbook of Action Research: Participative Inquiry and Practice*, ed. Peter Reason and Hilary Bradbury, 59–69 (Sage, 2001).

22. Santiago Ortiz, "Mapping Collaboration as Resistance"; and Santiago Ortiz, "'Our Action Plan.'"
23. Maguire, *Doing Participatory Research.*
24. Marjorie L. DeVault, *Liberating Method: Feminism and Social Research* (Temple University Press, 1999).
25. Irene Martínez Martín, "Pedagogías feministas: Estrategias una educación emancipadora y decolonial," *Momento-diálogos em educação* 27, no. 3 (2018): 353.
26. Quotations from students are taken from unpublished student reflection assignments and their collective final report.
27. Aurora Santiago Ortiz, "Where Is the State of Emergency?" NACLA, June 1, 2021, https://nacla.org/puerto-rico-state-emergency-femicides.
28. María Lugones, "The Coloniality of Gender," *Worlds and Knowledge Otherwise* 2, no. 2 (2008): 1–17.
29. Anibal Quijano, "Colonialidad, modernidad/racialidad," *Peru Indigema* 13 (1991): 11–29; Anibal Quijano, "Modernity, Identity, and Utopia in Latin America," in *The Postmodernism Debate in Latin America*, ed. John Beverley, Michael Aronna, and José Oviedo (Duke University Press, 1995), 201–16.
30. Yomaira Figueroa Vásquez, *Decolonizing Diasporas: Radical Mappings of Afro-Atlantic Literature* (Northwestern University Press, 2020), 14.
31. Figueroa Vásquez, *Decolonizing Diasporas*, 8.
32. Santiago Ortiz, "Mapping Collaboration as Resistance"; Santiago Ortiz, "'Our Action Plan'"; and Santiago Ortiz et al., "'La solidaridad no perece.'"
33. See https://www.uprrp.edu/misio-y-vision/.
34. Fernando Picó, *Cayeyanos: Familias y solidaridades en la historia de Cayey* (Ediciones Huracán, 2007).
35. Yuderkys Espinosa, Diana Gómez, María Lugones, and Karina Ochoa, "Reflexiones pedagógicas en torno al feminismo decolonial: Una conversa en cuatro voces," in *Pedagogías decoloniales: Prácticas insurgentes de resistir, (re) existir y (re)vivir*, ed. Catherine Walsh (Ediciones Abya Yala, 2017), 403–41.

A DiaspoRican Feminist Manifesto

JESSICA N. PABÓN-COLÓN

I want to know about Blanca.
And Lolita.
And Julia.

I want to know more about my bisabuela
and her sisters,
and their bisabuela.

I want to know how they felt,
how they dreamed,
how they fought,
how they managed.

I want to know what they wanted to know.
I want to know what they knew.

I want to know how bodyminds like mine,
bodies assigned woman,
bodies lived as queer,
bodies positioned as Other,
bodies in between and beyond colonial binaries
lived. loved. survived.

I know they survived because I am here.
Because we are here,
whether *here* is homeland or diaspora.

I want a poem,
a thought scratched on a napkin,
a spell etched into a stone,
a message sewn into a hem,
a hope beat into a drum,
a wish danced into the ether,
a memory grated into a recipe,
a story crocheted into a blanket,
a map braided into a scalp.

I want these fragments collected.
I want our Boricua feminist memories, histories, and strategies
to be tangible, accessible, visible . . .
despite the dangers of knowability.

I want us to know
that there are pathways to liberation
paved by Puerto Rican feminists.

I want us to travel those paths, and forge new ones, together.

I started writing this manifesto while facilitating a speed-writing exercise with students in my Feminist Perspectives to Decolonization course in 2023, but the sentiment of longing it espouses marks the emotion that catapulted me onto what I now understand as an educational, social, and political rematriation journey.

Jessica N. Pabón-Colón is a diasporic Puerto Rican feminist scholar of identity, community, and resistance. Her essays appear in journals including *Women & Performance: a journal of feminist theory*, *Signs: Journal of Women in Culture and Society*, and *Frontiers: A Journal of Women's Studies*. Her book *Graffiti Grrlz: Performing Feminism in the Hip Hop Diaspora* (New York University Press, 2018) is the first academic study on women's participation within hip-hop graffiti art subculture. She spends her summers as a butterfly doula helping monarchs on their migration journey and can otherwise be found baking breads, crafting, playing with her human and nonhuman children, or in a forest admiring the moss.

PART III. OUR LEGACIES

CHAPTER 10

"Were Nationalist Party Women Feminists?": Sisterhood, Solidarity, and Feminism in the Fight for Puerto Rican Independence

MARGARET POWER

A number of scholars have pointed out that feminists from the Global North have frequently developed a definition of feminism that reflects their realities and applied it to the rest of the world. This, as Chandra Mohanty famously pointed out, has led to Eurocentric and colonizing assumptions about and misreadings of women in the Global South.[1] Instead, as Amrita Basu notes, feminisms and women's movements must be understood, in large part, as products of their specific contexts. They may have transnational connections but they are, at their roots, "locally situated."[2] Puerto Rican scholar Lizabeth Paravisini-Gebert adds her own critique of the widespread problem of scholarship that ignores the specific and different realities that women throughout the Caribbean face:

> Caribbean feminism is often discussed . . . as something graspable, perceptible, complete—perhaps different from U.S. and European variables but nonetheless comprehensible, unequivocal. . . . [These discussions] infer that one could . . . seek to understand all Caribbean women through what they share with other women *as women* if we only remind our audiences that the differences allow, like political polls, for plus or minus three percentage points of error.[3]

One significant problem with US- and European-derived understandings of feminism is that they fail to consider the colonial reality and the particular and multiple forms of oppression that Puerto Rican women have lived in, adapted to, been exploited by, or struggled against for over five hundred years. Nor do they necessarily acknowledge that Puerto Rican women have developed their own meaning of feminism based on their realities. This does not mean there is one vision of feminism that all Puerto Rican women hold.

But it does recognize that Puerto Rican women have developed their own understandings of feminism, in conversation with each other, with other Latin Americans and women from across the Global South, and with feminists from Europe and the United States.

I consider Nationalist Party women feminists. To explain why I do, in this essay I explore how Nationalist Party women understood themselves as women, as political actors, and as fighters in the movement for Puerto Rican independence. Jessica Pabón-Colón points out that one way to understand feminism is to analyze how women act in the world. In other words, defining oneself or others as feminist matters, but so does how a woman performs feminism, regardless of whether she labels herself a feminist or not.[4] This insight pertains very much to how I understand the Nationalist Party women. As far as I know, Nationalist Party women did not call themselves feminists, nor have they typically been described as such either by their supporters or their detractors. I argue that their lived realities and their relationships with women reflect feminist values and practices. Further, they contributed to the liberation of Puerto Rican women (and represented positive role models for all women), for reasons I explore below. But first, I offer a brief overview of the Nationalist Party and discuss women's involvement within it.

The Puerto Rican Nationalist Party and Women's Involvement

A group of Puerto Rican men joined together to found the Partido Nacionalista de Puerto Rico (PNPR; Puerto Rican Nationalist Party) in 1922, twenty-four years after the United States invaded Puerto Rico. The men were educated urban professionals of European descent who advocated an end to US colonial rule and the establishment of an independent Puerto Rico. Although women attended PNPR events during the 1920s, it is not clear if any joined the party; they definitely did not hold any leadership positions.[5]

The party changed substantially following the election of Pedro Albizu Campos as PNPR president in 1930. It adopted a more militant stance toward the US government and called for an end to US colonial rule and for the establishment of an independent republic. In keeping with this shift, the party worked to increase its membership, both to ensure all pro-independence Puerto Ricans felt welcome within its ranks and because it understood it needed greater numbers in order to achieve independence. As a result, both the leadership and the membership expanded to include Puerto Ricans of different classes, genders, and races, including those of African descent. Women joined the party because they were encouraged to and because they sought to contribute to the end of US rule.[6]

To simultaneously incorporate more Puerto Ricans into its ranks and develop a more combative spirit among the membership, the PNPR established two gender-based organizations in the 1930s. The men's organization was the Cadetes de la República (Cadets of the Republic), which was roughly modeled after the Irish Republican movement. Its goal, according to Estanislao Lugo, a former Cadete, was to "instill discipline in members, draw them more closely into the party, and project the image of men committed to fighting to free Puerto Rico from US rule as an example for other Puerto Ricans."[7]

The corresponding women's organization had various names. In 1930, Albizu Campos announced the formation of the first Sección Femenina (Women's Section) of the Nationalist Party in Vieques.[8] Women founded similarly named groups across Puerto Rico during the next two years. Female high school students organized the Hijas de la Libertad (Daughters of Freedom) in 1932 with the mission of mobilizing other young girls to "fight for the Independence of Puerto Rico."[9] Later that same year, Nationalist Dominga de la Cruz read a petition that she and other working-class women from Mayagüez had written calling on the party to form an organization for women Nationalists, the Enfermeras de la República (Nurses of the Republic), in the Nationalist Party's National Assembly in Caguas.[10] The Assembly approved the petition, and the Enfermeras became the Nationalist Party's official women's group. According to Angelina Torresola, a former Enfermera, the group's role was "to be nurses for the [male] army. In a war there is an army and if blood is shed you need nurses."[11]

Her comment suggests that Nationalist Party women functioned as little more than a female auxiliary, helpmates to the men who were directly confronting US rule. Yet, as I have argued elsewhere, by shifting the perspective from the men to the women, a very different picture emerges.[12] Far from seeing themselves as minor figures, many of the Enfermeras perceived themselves as individuals who were making an important contribution to the liberation of their nation. They received military training, although none of them except Blanca Canales, who led the 1950 uprising in Jayuya (see below), ever used it, as far as I know. The Enfermeras never functioned as medical nurses. However, they did take on the vital task of fundraising for the party. And fundraising, as anyone who has ever belonged to an organization knows, is essential to sustain a group. They also participated in Nationalist Party marches, thus publicly identifying themselves as political actors who were both members of the party and activists in the independence movement.

In 1950 members of the Nationalist Party conducted a series of armed actions across Puerto Rico and in Washington, DC. They acted to call world attention to the efforts by then-Puerto Rican Governor Luis Muñoz Marín and the US government to convince the world that Puerto Rico's transition to a free associated state signaled the end of US colonial rule and the emergence of an independent Puerto Rico. The overwhelming majority of Nationalists who fought were men. Of the 140 combatants, only three were women.[13]

In 1954 Lolita Lebrón led three male Nationalists in an attack on the US Capitol. Once in the visitor's gallery, she unfurled the Puerto Rican flag, then shouted "¡Viva Puerto Rico Libre!" and fired shots at the cupola while the men shot at the Congressmen below. Although none of the four Nationalists expected to survive, they did and were subsequently convicted and sentenced to what amounted to life imprisonment.[14]

Very little has been written about Puerto Rican Nationalist women. According to Laura Briggs, whose pioneering study discussed Puerto Rican and US relations through the lens of reproduction, sexuality, and gender, the Nationalist Party lacked an "egalitarian vision" of gender since it "identified women with motherhood," slotting women into narrow roles of social reproduction and "reproduc[ing] both bodies and culture."[15] Per this vision, Puerto Rican women were to give birth to Puerto Rican babies in order to counter US attempts to radically decrease the archipelago's population. Unfortunately, not only did Briggs rely on a limited number of comments by two Nationalist Party male leaders, Pedro Albizu Campos and José Enamorado Cuesta, to define Nationalist Party thinking on womanhood, she also failed to include the words of Nationalist Party women or other statements made by Albizu Campos and other Nationalist Party men.

By way of contrast, Olga Jiménez de Wagenheim and José Manuel Dávila make Nationalist Party women the central focus of their studies.[16] In their writings, Nationalist Party women emerge as complex figures who saw themselves as political actors both responsible for and eminently capable of contributing to and leading the struggle for an independent homeland. Far from defining themselves primarily as mothers, they asserted their right to participate on a variety of levels, whether as members of the various women's groups the Nationalist Party set up or as armed commanders, as exemplified by Blanca Canales in the 1950 uprising and Lolita Lebrón in the 1954 attack on the US Congress.

Nationalist Party Women's Stories

One way to approach the question of whether or not the Nationalist Party women were feminists would be to discuss what they said about feminism and whether they considered themselves feminists. Unfortunately, the only woman Nationalist I have found who directly addresses this issue is Lolita Lebrón, whose thoughts I discuss below. Therefore, what I have chosen to do is to explore how other Nationalist Party women understood themselves and their social and political roles, what they did, and the impact their political involvement had on their identities. I was only able to interview four Nationalist Party women (Lydia Collazo, Lolita Lebrón, Angelina Torresola, and Isabel Rosado), since by the time I began my research, they were the only ones still alive. To supplement, I have also drawn on what other Nationalist women wrote or quotes from them.

A further consideration is that the most visible and leading female members of the party were the women who wrote about their experiences, the ones who were quoted in the media, and the ones I interviewed. These women were likely to be some of the most self-confident, bold, and independent women since they needed these qualities to attain leadership in the party. But there were hundreds of women for whom records are minimal to nonexistent and about whom, consequently, I know very little to nothing. As a result, my vision and discussion of Nationalist Party women are inevitably skewed toward and by those women who, in some cases more and in others less, challenged the gendered strictures of their time and society to become important actors in Puerto Rico's movement for independence. Because they did not address the issue of feminism directly, I paid close attention to their words and tried hard to interpret accurately what they meant. I specifically attempted to avoid externally developed criteria that ignored or distorted how these women understood themselves, their realities, and their impacts.

Blanca Canales

Blanca Canales was one of the best-known Nationalist Party women. She joined the party in 1931, but she had supported Puerto Rican independence since she was a young girl. She was born and raised in Jayuya, a town in the mountainous interior of Puerto Rico. The Canaleses were a prominent family.[17] Blanca was well educated and got her college degree from the University of Puerto Rico–Río Piedras in social work.[18] In her memoirs, she noted that the party "operated on two levels." On one hand, she was a public member who participated in fundraising efforts, was an Enfermera, and belonged to the party's women's commission. At the same time, she "never officially attended party assemblies." But she did "conspire in other aspects of the struggle that I can't talk about at this time."[19] Despite the obliqueness of her comment, her participation in the 1950 uprising indicates that she was both part of the PNPR's inner circle and that she had received military training.

In the days leading up to the 1950 uprising, Canales was in close contact with Pedro Albizu Campos, who, according to her memoirs, told her that the attacks were planned for October 30. She knew that she would play an instrumental role in them; among other things, they were being planned from her house in Jayuya, and, as noted above, she was an important figure in the party. As a result, she clearly understood that imprisonment, possibly even death, awaited her. Years later she shared that in the days leading up to the uprising, "I felt serene and determined . . . I understood that we were about to launch a life or death struggle and at the very least we would go to prison if the forces that the Yankees relied on defeated us. I understood that this was our only chance to carry out an attack that would be heard around the world so people would know that here [in Puerto Rico] there are people who want to be free."[20]

According to the plan, the revolt would consist of a series of coordinated attacks across the Island at 1:00 p.m. on October 30. After hearing the news that fighting had broken out at 10:30 a.m., Canales went to her basement, where roughly fifteen Nationalist men were assembled, and updated them on what was going on throughout Puerto Rico. She then announced, "We will march on the town." Unfurling the Puerto Rican flag, she asked the men to "defend this flag and the freedom of Puerto Rico and Don Pedro [Albizu Campos] with their lives." She told them to "swear on your knees!"[21] After they did so, the men got to their feet and then the group all went into town.[22]

Their goal was to take over Jayuya and attack institutions of US colonialism, such as the phone company, the police station, and the post office, where the US government housed young men's draft records. Canales's mission was to cut the phone lines and then go to the main hotel in Jayuya and proclaim the Republic of Puerto Rico. When she reached the hotel, she climbed to the balcony, waved the Puerto Rican flag, and shouted "¡Viva Puerto Rico Libre!" and invited the people who had gathered below to join the revolution.[23] It does not appear any did, either out of fear or because they didn't agree with her. The police arrested Blanca Canales later that day and proclaimed her one of the leaders of the uprising, a title she had not claimed for herself: "I, who had considered myself just a foot soldier heard myself called a leader by the esbirros (traitorous sellouts)."[24] She was first convicted in federal court on charges of conspiring to destroy federal property, destruction of a US post office, and "damages to other federal property." She was sentenced to ten years, of which she served five and a half.[25] She was also tried and convicted of those crimes in Puerto Rican courts and condemned to spend the rest of her life in prison.[26] However, Governor Roberto Sánchez Vilella pardoned her; in 1968 she was released after having spent seventeen years incarcerated.[27]

What struck me most about her narrative, of which I have only related a portion, was the determination and courage with which she carried out her varied activities on that day. As she said in the quote I cited above, she fully expected to either die or spend the rest of her life in prison. Neither possibility deterred her. Often acting alone, because the very limited number of other Nationalist fighters were dispersed around Jayuya, she confronted every situation with an amazing amount of sangfroid, self-confidence, and skill.

Her testimony reveals that she questioned neither her ability nor her responsibility to fully engage in the revolt. She undertook bold actions, attempting to cut the cables of the phone company, climbing to the hotel balcony, and driving a wounded comrade to the hospital in Utuado (which is where she was arrested) on her own. How can we interpret her description of herself as a foot soldier, not a leader? On one level, it echoes a sense of modesty that I found was common to many Nationalists, both women and men. At the same time, it also reveals that Canales saw herself as equal to the other (male) fighters. She never said, nor did she appear to think, that as a woman she shouldn't or couldn't be part of the armed attack on US colonial institutions in Jayuya. She was firmly convinced that she was important and had the right and the duty to fight for the independence of her nation.

Does this make her a feminist? Certainly, she never defined herself as fighting for the liberation of women in the sense that concept is typically understood. But on a different level, she saw herself as fighting for the liberation of all Puerto Ricans. Far from limiting herself to playing a secondary role or functioning in an auxiliary position to the male fighters, she put herself in the forefront of the battle for Puerto Rican independence. Indeed, as her story shows, she was comfortable telling men what to do and acting independently. Further, she manifestly rejected gendered expectations that as a woman her destiny was to marry and bear children. She never married and she bore no children. Instead, she flung herself, apparently unhesitatingly, into the struggle for her nation's freedom.

The Torresola Sisters

Angelina and Doris Torresola's stories offer further insight into how Nationalist Party women acted and saw themselves. The sisters were both born into a pro-independence family in Jayuya and were Blanca's cousins. One brother, Elio Torresola, helped to lead the October 1950 uprising in Jayuya. Another brother, Griselio, died in the failed attempt to assassinate President Harry Truman in Washington, DC, on November 1, 1950.

When I interviewed Angelina in 2013, I found her both unassuming and resolute. Unlike most of the women I discuss in this essay, she married and had children. During her long life—she died at age ninety-nine in 2015—she unequivocally maintained her commitment to a free Puerto Rico.[28] When I spoke with her, she recalled that she and other Nationalist Party women went door-to-door asking their friends and neighbors for money to support the party. And, as she recounted to me with pride some seventy years later, people gave them money: "Maybe because in the small pueblos we all knew each other, everyone liked me and the other [Nationalists], and we were honest."[29]

Her sister, Doris, was also a committed member of the party. Doris never married, nor did she have kids. She functioned as Albizu Campos's housekeeper, secretary, and trusted member of the party's inner circle. She received military training and lived and worked in the Nationalist Party headquarters in Old San Juan with Albizu Campos and other party members. She was in the headquarters, along with several other important figures in the Nationalist Party, in 1950 and again in 1954 when Puerto Rican police attacked in order to arrest Albizu Campos and the other Nationalists there. Far from surrendering or trying to escape the police, she stayed in the headquarters and attempted to repel their assault. In the fighting that followed, the police shot her in the throat. When her comrades carried her out of the building, bleeding profusely, the police arrested her and refused to give her medical treatment for six days, during which time she was in "agonizing pain."[30] She was subsequently convicted of four charges, including under the infamous Law 53, or Gag Law, and served close to three years in prison.[31] She was arrested again in 1954 and sentenced to "a minimum of nine years and a maximum of seventeen years."[32] Conditions in prison, which I discuss below, and the drugs the authorities administered to her contributed to a deterioration in her mental health, which led to her early release. She subsequently killed herself in 1972.[33]

Isabel Rosado

Isabel Rosado grew up in Ceiba, one of seven children. Her father worked in a sugar plantation and her parents had a small plot of land to supplement his meager wages.[34] Although Isabel Rosado's parents were uneducated, they made sure their daughter finished high school and college, where she got degrees in teaching and, like Blanca Canales, social work. Isabel was a determined and happy person, which is one reason she lived to age 108. She joined the Nationalist Party in 1937 after she learned about the Ponce Massacre and the imprisonment of Nationalist Party leaders, and because she "wanted to defend independence."[35]

Like many of the best-known Nationalist Party women, Isabel did not marry, nor did she have children, although she helped to raise several after their mothers, who were friends of hers, died. She was engaged to an engineer who was a Nationalist. However, she ended the relationship when he went to work in Mexico: "He wanted me to give up [the struggle for independence] and go with him. I said no."[36] Her political commitment was more important to her than marriage and the conventional family life of many Puerto Rican women.

Although Isabel had no direct connection to the 1950 uprising, she was arrested and convicted of violating Law 53, the Gag Law. She was imprisoned along with other Nationalist Party women and served one year and three months.[37] In March 1954, when the Nationalists attacked the US Congress, Isabel was in the party headquarters in Old San Juan. As had happened in 1950, the police went there to arrest Albizu Campos and other Nationalist Party leaders. The occupants responded with bullets, and a gunfight ensued. The police subdued the independentistas with massive amounts of tear gas, rendering three of them, including Rosado, unconscious. When she woke up in the hospital, she learned she had been convicted of the attempt to commit murder, a second violation of the Gag Law, and carrying arms. She was sentenced to seventeen years in prison and released in 1965.[38]

Lolita Lebrón

Lolita Lebrón is the best-known Nationalist Party woman. She led the bold attack on the US Congress in 1954 and served twenty-five years in US prisons, more than any other Nationalist woman. The prison authorities treated her particularly viciously because she was a Puerto Rican woman who had the audacity to lead an attack on the US government. They subjected her to physical, emotional, and sexual torture specifically designed to humiliate her and break her. Like political prisoners in Pinochet's Chile and other Southern Cone dictatorships, guards raped her, gave her electric shocks, isolated her.[39] They repeatedly asked her where the weapons had come from. She refused to tell them. She had no contact with the outside world for the first eighteen years of her imprisonment. The Bureau of Prisons taunted her about her young son's death by drowning and refused to let her visit her dying mother. But they were unsuccessful. She went on a hunger strike to demand her rights, which the authorities ignored, and always maintained her principles.

In 1976 Barbara Lubinski interviewed Lolita Lebrón when she was in the Federal Reformatory for Women in Alderson, West Virginia. Reflecting on her then twenty-two years of imprisonment, Lebrón commented, "I have lived and acted in the prison walls as a liberated woman and very proud to be a woman. I have remained [in] the purity of my convictions." Did Lebrón identify herself as a feminist? Yes, but based on her own understanding of feminism. For her, the women's liberation she called for was inseparably linked to the fight for Puerto Rico's liberation.[40] She valued the role of women in the anti-colonial struggle:

> In the Grito de Lares and Grito de Washington [how Lebrón referred to the 1954 attack on the US Congress] and all the liberation cries of Puerto Rico, there have been women leading. The first revolutionary woman known to us is Marianna Bracetti. She made our first flag. She gave birth to a child in prison because she was leading the revolution while pregnant. I think that is very symbolic. Even from inside prison, liberation can take birth.[41]

Not one to paper over problems, Lebrón refused to deny male supremacy existed within the National Party. As she told me, it was hard for her three male comrades to accept that she, a woman, was the leader of the attack on the US Congress: "They were from a time when men ruled supreme. They felt so much pressure, thinking they were men, they [had to be] the ones who gave the orders." At one point, they suggested postponing the attack on Congress. Lebrón rejected the suggestion and told them if they didn't want to go, "I will go alone then."[42] They followed her lead and the attack took place as planned. Her recounting of the men's attitudes and assertion of her own leadership reflected how she understood women's path to liberation: "Women must liberate ourselves from the men, as women, and then we can help them [men] liberate themselves."[43]

Whether she was leading an armed attack on the US Congress or carrying out civil disobedience in Vieques to protest the US Navy's bombing of the island, Lebrón always looked her best. She was well-coifed, made up, and dressed exquisitely. She confided to me that many on the left called her bourgeois for her attention to appearance.[44] But for Lebrón, looking her best didn't make her bourgeois or indicate she rejected feminism. For her, looking good was a public-facing manifestation of her sense of dignity. I can imagine that after twenty-five years in prison, where she was deprived of nice clothes, decent haircuts, and toiletries, and also repeatedly subjected to attacks and verbal and emotional degradation, she must have developed a keen desire to present herself to her preference, not in order to please men but to assert her identity and choice.

Life in Prison for the Nationalist Party Women

Following the 1950 uprising in Puerto Rico and the 1954 assault on the US Congress, nine Nationalist Party women and one North American supporter, Ruth Reynolds, served prison terms ranging from four to twenty-five years. For many of those years, the prison authorities severely limited the number of people who could visit the prisoners or even correspond with them, under orders from the US government. As a result, for much of the time the women were imprisoned, their primary affective community was each other. They built strong bonds of solidarity among themselves that defied the isolation, inhumane conditions, physical and emotional privations, and, in some cases, torture they experienced. They shared what little they had, comforted each other, stood up to the guards on each other's behalf, and remained strong, defiant, and committed. In their day-to-day behavior with each other, they modeled how feminists should treat each other: as sisters united in a joint struggle.

Although most of the women were imprisoned in Puerto Rico, four served varying lengths of time in Alderson, West Virginia. Blanca Canales was first sent to the federal prison for women in Alderson, where she served five and a half years of her ten-year sentence.[45] Three other Puerto Rican Nationalist women were also imprisoned there. Rosa Collazo, a member of the New York City branch of the Nationalist Party, was imprisoned in New York City and Alderson in 1950 and 1954 respectively. Lolita Lebrón spent twenty-five years in Alderson following her conviction of seditious conspiracy.[46]

Like Lolita, Nationalist women incarcerated in Puerto Rico were tortured. Doris Torresola was held in La Princesa prison in Viejo San Juan while she was on trial in 1951. In her recordings of her experiences in La Princesa, she described how she would lie down on her bed in her cell and begin "to hear the sound of a motor and vibrations." She would hear the same noises the next day. She asked her cellmate Carmen Pérez, another one of the Nationalist prisoners, to put her head on her pillow to see if she heard the same noises, which she did.[47] The sounds disappeared for a while. However, when Doris lay down to go to sleep on a subsequent night, she felt the vibrations again. "I couldn't sleep, my head hurt, and I felt dizzy," she said. "The noise and vibrations continued and grew stronger." Only after she was transferred back to jail in Arecibo did she find respite.[48]

Her experience was not an isolated one. Ruth Reynolds, a North American pacifist who worked closely with the Nationalist Party, was convicted of being a member of the Nationalist Party and imprisoned with the Nationalist women.[49] When she was in La Princesa, she, like Torresola, felt strange vibrations coming from the office below her. "I felt as if they were aimed at my head and they produced a light electric shock."[50] She also heard men talking in English about her case, the Nationalist Party, and her attorney Conrad Lynn. The men repeatedly speculated whether she had "sexual relations with [Conrad Lynn] and Albizu Campos," whom they referred to as "damned Negroes."[51] The voices and the vibrations went on and on, tormenting Ruth for weeks and weeks. She barely ate and grew progressively weaker and mentally disoriented. Finally she, like Doris Torresola, was transferred to the Arecibo prison. The psychological assaults left no physical trace on her or the other women, but they did leave emotional scars. When Reynolds arrived in Arecibo, Carmen Pérez, Isabel Rosado, and Doris Torresola noticed how nervous she seemed and how thin she had become: "When we asked her something, she often remained silent and didn't answer us. She told us she thought they—the prison authorities—were trying to drive her crazy."[52] Reynolds told Carmen, Isabel, and Doris what she had been going through and asked if she could be in the cell with them. Her comrades immediately sprang into action and made arrangements with the prison administration for her to stay in their cell. Reynolds continued to hear voices, but per her account, "they no longer bothered me as much once I was reunited with my compañeras."[53]

The exact nature of the macabre tortures that these women suffered at the hands of prison authorities has never been established. What is clear is that on top of the isolation, lack of healthy food, and unbearable heat in their small, dark cells, these women suffered physical and psychological torments that were designed to break them down and drive them insane. Equally clearly, they relied on each other and their own fortitude to get through these ordeals and retain their sanity, identities, and values. When I read these women's accounts of their frightful experiences in prison, three things struck me most forcibly. First, these women called on their inner strength to navigate through these dangerous waters. Second, they knew they could always count on each other. Instead of trying to soldier through the torment on their own, they shared their experiences and their fears with each other, and in so doing, felt comforted and enveloped in a sisterhood they knew would not fail them. Third, each one of them was always willing to do whatever she could to aid and support the others. When any of them noticed one of their own in distress, they immediately acted to alleviate the problem. They may not have called themselves feminists, but they acted in feminist solidarity with each other—because they considered their identities as women and Nationalists conjoined in the shared struggle to free Puerto Rico.

Conclusion

I began this essay by asking if the Nationalist Party women were feminists. I end by saying that it depends on how you define feminism. I am often curious how the Nationalist women would have answered if I had asked them. Of course, there is no reason to assume they would have answered in one voice. They may have shared realities and goals, but they were also individuals with a variety of experiences. Nor is there any reason to think that they would have answered the same way throughout their entire life. Because they changed over time, their perceptions of what it meant to be a feminist must have changed too, just as definitions and practices of feminism have evolved over time and varied according to place.

I suspect that if one would have asked Lolita Lebrón in 1954 if she were a feminist, she would have said no. However, if she were asked the same question in the 1970s, I believe she would have been more likely to say yes. Much happened and changed in those two decades: Lebrón's years in prison; her discovery of friendships with revolutionary white feminists like Marilyn Buck, who she discusses in her interview with Barbara Lubinski; the call from US and Puerto Rican feminists for her release from prison along with all other Nationalist prisoners, as well as those feminists' support for Puerto Rican independence. All of these factors impacted Lebrón's understanding of what feminism was and her likelihood to identify with it.

While I do not feel comfortable labeling the Nationalist Party women as feminists, primarily because they did not choose to define themselves as such, I do wholeheartedly believe that those of us who call ourselves feminists have a lot to learn from them. They dedicated themselves fully and steadfastly to the liberation of Puerto Rico from US colonialism, and they paid a heavy price for it. I have told the stories of just a few of the Nationalist Party women, only broadly sketching their multiyear imprisonment, isolation from the outside world, and torture. These women suffered for their beliefs, and yet they remained true to their principles and to each other. Far from losing their humanity or moral compass under pressure, they kept them intact. They treated each other and other people with love, kindness, and understanding. By fighting not just for themselves, but for the betterment of other Puerto Ricans, they modeled expansive, borderless sisterhood.

Fighting for liberation from colonial or patriarchal domination means confronting the oppressors. This is not an easy thing to do, in part because those in a position of power usually have a variety of weapons and resources at their disposition, and the ability and willingness to use them. Nationalist Party women went up against the most powerful empire on Earth: the United States. In doing so, they challenged multiple layers of oppression: colonialism, patriarchy, and racism. Despite torture, degradation, and sexualized abuse from their captors in prison, not only did the Nationalist women survive, they continued to struggle for an end to US colonial rule. In the process, they affirmed their dignity as Puerto Rican women, willing and able to fight for the liberation of their people, cementing themselves as lodestars for all liberation struggles to follow.

Margaret Power is professor of history emeritus at the Illinois Institute of Technology. She is the author of seven books, including *Solidarity Across the Americas: The Puerto Rican Nationalist Party and Anti-Imperialism* and *Right-Wing Women in Chile: Feminine Power and the Struggle Against Salvador Allende, 1964–1973*. She is on the board of directors of the Puerto Rican Cultural Center in Chicago and cochair of Historians for Peace and Democracy.

Notes

1. For a classic critique of Western feminists' Eurocentrism and colonialization of Third World women's lives and struggles, see Chandra Mohanty, "Under Western Eyes: Feminist Scholarship and Colonial Discourses," *Boundary 2* 12, no. 3 (1986): 333–58.
2. Amrita Basu, "Introduction," in *The Challenge of Local Feminisms: Women's Movements in Global Perspective*, ed. Amrita Basu (Westview Press, 1995), 4.
3. Lizabeth Paravisini-Gebert, "Decolonizing Feminism: The Home-Grown Roots of Caribbean Women's Movements," *Daughters of Caliban: Caribbean Women in the Twentieth Century*, ed. Consuelo López (Indiana University Press, 1997), 3.
4. Jessica Nydia Pabón-Colón, *Graffiti Grrlz: Performing Feminism in the Hip Hop Diaspora* (New York University Press, 2018).
5. For a history of the Nationalist Party, see Margaret Power, *Solidarity Across the Americas: The Puerto Rican Nationalist Party and Anti-Imperialism* (University of North Carolina Press, 2023).
6. It's important to note that the PNPR did not keep membership numbers, so I have not been able to determine how many people belonged to the party. It is not clear whether the party did not keep membership lists, perhaps for security reasons, or whether the lists were destroyed at some point.
7. Estanislao Lugo, interview with author, May 21, 2008, Carolina, Puerto Rico.
8. "Los actos nacionalistas de Vieques y Naguabo," *El Mundo*, November 15, 1930. All translations in this piece are by the author unless otherwise stated.
9. Lamia Azize Mawad learned about nationalism when she was twelve or thirteen years old. José Manuel Dávila Marichal, "'La mujer no debe, no puede permanecer inhábil': Las Hijas de la Libertad: Juventud, género, ideología y funcionamiento interno, 1932–1935," *Instituto de Cultura Puertorriqueño* 3, no. 7 (September 2017): 56.
10. Margaret Randall, *El pueblo no sólo es testigo: Historia de Dominga* (Ediciones Huracán, 1979), 41.
11. Angelina Torresola, interview with author and Janine Santiago, October 26, 2013, Guaynabo, Puerto Rico.
12. Margaret Power, "Women, Gender, and the Puerto Rican Nationalist Party," in *Gendering Nationalism: Intersections of Nation, Gender and Sexuality*, ed. Jon Mulholland, Nicola Montagna, and Erin Sanders-McDonagh (Palgrave Macmillan, 2018), 129–43.
13. Miñi Seijo Bruno, *La insurreción nacionalista en Puerto Rico—1950* (Editorial Edil, 1989), 243. Seijo Bruno combed multiple records to obtain these numbers. She also determined the race, class, and place of birth of all the combatants.
14. For a helpful discussion of the charges and sentences, see Olga Jiménez de Wagenheim, *Nationalist Heroines: Puerto Rican Women History Forgot, 1930s–1940s* (Markus Weiner Publishers, 2016), 263–69.
15. Laura Briggs, *Reproducing Empire: Race, Sex, Science, and U.S. Imperialism in Puerto Rico* (University of California Press, 2002), 75.

16. Jiménez de Wagenheim, *Nationalist Heroines*; and Dávila Marichal, "'La mujer no debe.'"
17. Her father, Rosario Canales, was the first elected mayor of Jayuya. Her brother, Nemesio Canales, was an elected representative of the Union Party. In 1909 he presented a bill in the House of Representatives, calling for women's civil rights, including their right to vote. See Nemesio Canales, "El voto femenino," *Paliques* 72 (Ediciones Isla, 1967), 175–77.
18. Blanca Canales, *La constitución es la revolución* (Congreso Nacional Hostosiano, 1997), 13.
19. Canales, *La constitución es la revolución*, 9.
20. Canales, *La constitución es la revolución*, 25, 31.
21. Canales, *La constitución es la revolución*, 36.
22. Both Canales and the Torresolas lived in Coabey, which is on the outskirts of Jayuya. To get into town, the group commandeered a bus from passersby. Canales drove alone and was the last to leave. Blanca Canales, *La constitución es la revolución* (Congreso Nacional Hostosiano, 1997), 38–39.
23. Canales, *La constitución es la revolución*, 39–41.
24. Canales, *La constitución es la revolución*, 46.
25. Jiménez de Wagenheim, *Nationalist Heroines*, 70–71.
26. Jiménez de Wagenheim, *Nationalist Heroines*, 71, 75.
27. Jiménez de Wagenheim, *Nationalist Heroines*, 85.
28. "Angelina Torresola Roura in the 1940 Census," Ancestry, https://www.ancestry.com/1940-census/usa/Puerto-Rico/Angelina-Torresola-Roura_5p2dzs, accessed August 7, 2023; and Jiménez de Wagenheim, *Nationalist Heroines*, 292.
29. Angelina Torresola, interview with author and Janine Santiago, Guaynabo, Puerto Rico, October 26, 2013.
30. Jiménez de Wagenheim, *Nationalist Heroines*, 190. For an account of Doris Torresola's life, see Jiménez de Wagenheim, *Nationalist Heroines*, 182–202.
31. Jiménez de Wagenheim, *Nationalist Heroines*, 191–92. Law 53, or the 1948 Gag Law, criminalized anyone who supported independence, and was first used against the Nationalists in 1950. Ivonne Acosta-Lespier, *La mordaza* (Editorial Edil, 1987).
32. Jiménez de Wagenheim, *Nationalist Heroines*, 199.
33. Angelina Torresola, interview with author and Janine Santiago, Guaynabo, Puerto Rico, October 26, 2013.
34. Isabel Rosado, interview with author, Ceiba, Puerto Rico, May 16, 2008.
35. Isabel Rosado, interview with author, Ceiba, Puerto Rico, May 13, 2006. On Palm Sunday, 1937, members of the Nationalist Party in Ponce staged a march to commemorate the end of slavery and to protest the imprisonment of the party leadership. Puerto Rican police, under the direction of US-appointed police chief Colonel E. Francis Riggs, opened fire on the peaceful protest, killing nineteen and wounding somewhere between 150 and 200 men, women, and children. See Arthur Garfield Hays, *Report of the Commission of Inquiry on Civil Rights in Puerto Rico* (Library of Congress Photoduplication Service, 1977).

36. Isabel Rosado, interview with author, Ceiba, Puerto Rico, May 16, 2008.
37. Jiménez de Wagenheim, *Nationalist Heroines*, 170–71.
38. For a description of this period in Rosado's life, see Jiménez de Wagenheim, *Nationalist Heroines*, 165–75; Isabel Rosado, interview with author, Ceiba, Puerto Rico, May 16, 2008.
39. Ximena Bunster-Burroto, "Surviving Beyond Fear: Women and Torture in Latin America," in *Women and Change in Latin America*, ed. June Nash and Helen Safa (Bergin and Garvey, 1986), 297–325; and Brandi Townsend, "The Body and State Violence, from the Harrowing to the Mundane: Chilean Women's Oral Histories of the Augusto Pinochet Dictatorship (1973–1990)," *Journal of Women's History* 31, no. 2 (2019): 33–56.
40. Barbara Lubinski, interview with Lolita Lebrón, Alderson, West Virginia, December 1978. To obtain a copy of the interview, contact Freedom Archives, https://freedomarchives.org.
41. Lubinski, interview with Lolita Lebrón.
42. Margaret Power, interview with Lolita Lebrón, Chicago, Illinois, September 9, 2004.
43. Lubinski, interview with Lolita Lebrón.
44. Power, interview with Lolita Lebrón.
45. Jiménez de Wagenheim, *Nationalist Heroines*, 70–71.
46. The third woman, Carmen Torresola, was a Nationalist and the partner of Griselio Torresola, who was killed in November 1950 when he and Oscar Collazo tried to assassinate President Truman. She returned to Puerto Rico after her release from Alderson and ended her participation in politics. See Jiménez de Wagenheim, *Nationalist Heroines*, 279–81.
47. Partido Nacionalista de Puerto Rico, *Tortura de los presos políticos en Puerto Rico* (Impresora Vega, 1952), 55.
48. Partido Nacionalista, *Tortura de los presos politicos*.
49. For an excellent biography of her, see Lisa Matterson, *Radical Solidarity. Ruth Reynolds, Political Allyship, and the Battle for Puerto Rico's Independence* (University of North Carolina Press, 2024).
50. Partido Nacionalista, *Tortura de los presos politicos*, 18.
51. Albizu was of mixed African and Basque ancestry, and Lynn was of African ancestry. Partido Nacionalista, *Tortura de los presos politicos*, 3.
52. Partido Nacionalista, *Tortura de los presos politicos*, 56.
53. Partido Nacionalista, *Tortura de los presos politicos*, 47.

CHAPTER 11

Clotilde Betances Jager: Puerto Rican Feminism in 1930s New York

MARÍA TERESA VERA-ROJAS

EDITOR'S NOTE: Some of the primary documents in this chapter were published in the original Spanish in María Teresa Vera-Rojas's book *El feminismo no es nuevo: las crónicas de Clotilde Betances Jaeger*, published by Arte Público Press in 2020.

Born in San Sebastián del Pepino, probably around 1894,[1] Clotilde Betances Jaeger was a firebrand feminist writer and anti-imperial intellectual. Ahead of her time, she advocated for the educational rights of children and women, racial equality, and the independence of Puerto Rico. She produced and published most of her work in New York, where she lived from the mid-1920s until she died (it is speculated) in the 1970s.

Her reputation and her work were known across island and mainland, by intellectuals, feminists, and prominent figures in artistic and literary circles in Puerto Rico as well as in the Latino colonia in New York;[2] she also had an international following throughout Latin America and Spain. Her intellectual and feminist thought can be traced through her crónicas and essays published from the 1920s to the 1950s, as well as through the dissemination of her critical studies and creative literary texts in cultural magazines, newspapers, weeklies, and periodicals—not only in New York City but also in various publications in countries including Puerto Rico, Cuba, the Dominican Republic, Mexico, and Spain.

A proud descendant of Puerto Rico's independence leader and "Father of the Nation," Ramón Emeterio Betances, she received an elite education at Cornell University and was part of the middle- and upper-class cultural Puerto Rican community in New York. This relatively privileged background was at odds with her everyday life in New York in the 1920s and 1930s, where she wrote for a living as a paid journalist, lectured at social and cultural gatherings, and participated in an articulated network of cultural and civic associations and organizations that responded both to the growing cultural demands of the colonia's residents and to their various social, political, and celebratory needs in the city. In fact, in his *Memorias* (1984)—a foundational text for the Puerto Rican migration in New York—Puerto Rican unionist, community leader, and tobacco worker Bernardo Vega mentions her as one of the members of the Asociación de Escritores y Periodistas Puertorriqueños, founded in New York at the end of the 1930s. By then, she was well known in the colonia for her publications, where she enunciated her positions on women's economic emancipation, her calls for Latina women to be aware of their potential in anti-war mobilization, and her desire for them to understand their decisive participation in national economies.

These ideas were the subject of many of her crónicas published in the New York weekly *Gráfico* (1927–31), which she began writing for in 1929 and where she published some of the most important texts of her career as a writer and feminist. It was in *Gráfico* that I first encountered her texts while working on my PhD at the University of Houston, as part of a program called "Recovering the US Hispanic Literary Heritage." I immediately admired her feminist activism and have since dedicated my research to recovering, studying, and publishing her work and about her work. Owned and edited by tobacco workers, writers, and theater actors such as Alberto O'Farrill and the abovementioned Bernardo Vega, *Gráfico*'s popularity has traditionally been attributed to its conservative position on the role of Latina women in society, as well as to its misogynistic images and sexualized representations of Anglo-American liberated women.[3] Therefore, her feminist crónicas published in this weekly can be considered as manifestos against what today would be referred to as "respectability politics," aimed at raising the awareness of Latina women in the metropolis for equality and gender consciousness. In "Charlas femeninas," a section of this weekly where she shared space with another Puerto Rican writer, María Mas Pozo,[4] they held one of the most important debates on the New (Modern) Woman in the New York Latino press regarding women's freedoms in modern society, and it is these texts by Betances Jaeger that are best known and most translated and reproduced today. These crónicas debated issues such as women's right to vote, their contribution to the economy and international economic policy, and the origins of women's oppression in society, among other polemic topics.

Clotilde Betances Jaeger was also a regular contributor to the cultural magazine *Artes y Letras* (1933–39), edited by the Puerto Rican feminist Josefina Silva de Cintrón, and she was also an active member and speaker at the meetings and cultural activities of the Círculo Cultural Cervantes.[5] Her activism was not limited to cultural activities; she was also the Puerto Rican representative of the Unión de Mujeres Americanas,[6] among other associations. She was part of the Comité Pro Huelga de Puerto Rico, whose goal was to organize activities to publicize the demands of the sugarcane cutters and dockworkers and to raise funds to support the workers' general strike in Puerto Rico (1933–34).

In addition to defending the right to vote and gender equality, Clotilde Betances's feminism was characterized by her insistence on economic equality with men, her criticism of the social impositions of the church, her historical research on the origins of matriarchy and patriarchy, and forms of direct action through the interpellation of readers to social action. Chronicles such as "El matrimonio no le trae a la mujer independencia económica nunca," published in *Gráfico*, stressed the importance of the economy and access to paid work for women's economic independence, as well as for understanding the role of their taxes in supporting wars. Clotilde Betances understood that gender inequality was perpetuated by economic and political differences, hence her criticism of social conventions that made the institution of marriage the ideal of independence and fulfillment for women.

It was also in *Gráfico* that Betances Jaeger first denounced domestic violence, the objectification of women, and inequality of civil rights and the lack of legal protections for women, through chronicles such as "La pavorosa desnutrición de la mujer puertorriqueña." In this and other texts, she also relentlessly criticized the religious and social subjugation of women, denouncing the double standards with which society legitimized women's oppression, regulated their identity, and limited their intellectual and physical autonomy. She also denounced the submissiveness and dependence that domestic work and motherhood entailed, which is why she supported free love and birth control and criticized the lack of legal protection for and social exclusion of single mothers in Puerto Rico.

Clotilde Betances Jaeger's anti-respectability feminism unified the traditions of Puerto Rican suffragists like Ana Roqué de Duprey, María Luisa Angelis, Mercedes Solá, Milagros Benet de Mewton, Librada Rodríguez Rivera, María Cadilla de Martínez, and Trinidad Padilla de Sanz who also had an undeniable presence in Puerto Rican periodicals and in the constitution of suffragist and feminist organizations in Puerto Rico since the end of the nineteenth century. Beyond that, Clotilde Betances Jaeger's feminism embraced forms of liberation advocated by socialist and anarchist feminisms, such as those led by Spanish feminists like Federica Montseny and Ángela Graupera. This confluence of ideas around her feminist position was reflected and well documented through her extensive and prolific collaborations in publications such as the aforementioned *Gráfico* and *Artes y Letras* as well as the newspaper *La Prensa* (1913–63; *El Diario La Prensa*). She was also an active contributor to the New York anarchist journal *Cultura Proletaria: Periódico de Ideas and Doctrina y Combate* (1927–53), the best-known Spanish-language anarchist newspaper in the United States.[7] These contributions are lesser-known, as are her other contributions during the 1930s to the Spanish anarchist and workers' press, such as *Al Margen*, *Brazo y Cerebro*, *Estudios*, *Iniciales*, and *Solidaridad Obrera*. In the texts published in these journals, we find another aspect of her revolutionary feminist thought, which I wanted to enshrine in this anthology through republishing "El don supremo de sí mismo" for the first time.[8] Indeed, her essays on motherhood, anarchism and communism, and the destruction caused by war expand our understanding of her feminist thought and activism. Such is the case with her article "El don supremo de sí mismo," originally published in *Cultura Proletaria*, in which she argued that sex, as a form of integral possession of consciousness, body, and desire, was one of the greatest expressions of freedom that men and women could offer each other.[9] In this sense, sex redefines the bourgeois narrative of love, family, and reproduction, by questioning the systematic oppression suffered by women not only in the conjugal sphere but also in their knowledge of themselves and their bodies. In this reflection, Clotilde Betances focused on sexual desire as a form of liberation and knowledge; her arguments were revolutionary because they framed how modes of capitalist oppression were not limited to the public sphere but also governed the private space, and because they positioned women as desiring subjects rather than objects of desire. She did this by historicizing love and sexual desire, emotions that are traditionally considered intimate and atemporal.

Clotilde Betances Jaeger's revolutionary philosophy centered a call for "complete social revolution";[10] therefore, her writings and conferences were not limited to the recognition of women's equality but also encompassed the abolition of the various forms of social slavery, including the perpetuation of racial oppression, US imperialism, and war. Thus, "complete social revolution" is the axis around which her texts of the 1920s and 1930s are oriented; this explains why topics such as the defense of the "violated rights" of women, equality of the races, and Puerto Rican independence share space in her arguments for an education free of social taboos, in dialogue with the anarchist and naturalist thought embedded throughout her texts.

For Clotilde Betances Jaeger, feminism went beyond the struggles of the suffragettes. For her, feminism was a theory and a political agenda that sought to overthrow the false morality with which the status quo legitimized women's oppression and inequality in law and society. For this reason, she demanded change and called upon women, especially her readers, to awaken from the social lethargy in which they were immersed. She called for them to understand that women's emancipation also included their economic independence, control over their bodies, greater political participation, greater intellectual development, and the transformation of the institution of marriage. Therefore, she dedicated herself to showing how feminism was a foregone revolutionary conclusion, a culmination of struggle for women's liberation from which demands for racial equality, the end of wars, and prejudice-free education were inextricable.

EDITOR'S NOTE: The following translations are of Clotilde Betances Jaeger's original writing from 1930. As a result, aspects of her critiques may not map exactly onto the norms of contemporary feminist discourse, and some of her terminology may be outdated. We encourage readers to privilege the revolutionary value of Betances Jaeger's writing in the context of her era.

The Terrible Problem of Malnutrition Among Puerto Rican Children and Single Mothers

CLOTILDE BETANCES
translated by María Teresa Vera-Rojas
Originally published in *Gráfico*, June 28, 1930

The terrible tragedy of the malnourished children of Puerto Rico leaves us with a very bitter taste in our mouths. There are many causes and multiple factors to this unfortunate situation. For now, we will focus on just one phase of this situation.

In the first place, there is the absurdity on which our Puerto Rican society is based, not facing problems that have their roots in actions, the most natural ones. This is because our society is controlled by a narrow ecclesiastical criterion that has no other purpose than to distort the natural and biological sense of certain actions.

How is it possible that the starving children of Puerto Rico can be in different conditions of well-being, when the only worthy motherhood that is conceived of is that of the married woman, even if the child is not her husband's? It is anti-vital and unnatural for an unmarried woman to become pregnant and to experience the pains of childbirth. Therefore, the unmarried mother and her offspring do not receive adequate protection, because they carry the infamous stigma that deprives an unmarried mother and legitimate child of all rights to life and happiness.

It does not take much to draw a conclusion. The single mother hides what the world calls her guilt and throws her children out on the street to be taken care of by public charity.

The Latina woman has never been taught that there is no shame in being a mother, even without the help of the parish priest or the mayor. All she has heard, in church, at home, on the street, is the eternal prudishness that procreation outside of marriage is a crime. The moral duty of motherhood has not been instilled in her; the pride of motherhood is completely unknown to her.

These fatherless children, born out of convenience, are outcasts. The mother is accepted nowhere; she receives only scorn and humiliation. If the mother cannot find forgiveness, where will she find protection for her child? These bastard children—what sarcasm! Namelessness—what sophism! Do they not have their mother's surname? Does the mother not have the right to give her child a name? Strange paradox! Legally, this woman cannot give her name to the child of her loins. However, extralegally, the illegitimate child bears the name of its mother. Actually, the mother's surname is the one that belongs most to the child. In most cases, when the father appears, he does so falsely; the mother is always present. It is always known who the mother is, but not always who impregnated her. These unfortunate disinherited children are the ones paying for the guilt of their parents. Where is this guilt? Why should it be borne only by the woman and the innocent fruit of an act in her life? Why does society insist on blaming only the woman, while the man so continues so laxly with his unconfessed or denied paternity?

Because today's prudish and hypocritical society throws the handful of mud only on the woman; because she is the weakest; because in religious countries, Mary was the only one who could have a child by magic. If children pay for the so-called faults of their mothers but not those of their fathers, it is not surprising that the average child in Puerto Rico dies of malnutrition, because they do not know their father, and their poor little mother does not have a penny to feed them unless she burns her flabby belly day and night in front of the stove.

This is a social economic problem. If this single mother had the means, her child would not go to the river to beg, would not steal, would not end up in juvenile detention, would not die of hunger.

It is true that infant mortality is universal; it is also true that ignorance about motherhood and childcare is appalling; but even in Spain, where the social conditions of women are quite neglected, attention has been given to this important matter. In Germany there is a society for the protection of children without known fathers; in Paris there are five privately run asylums for pregnant women, where no one cares about the beliefs or social status of the women shut away, and in Nanterre there is an asylum for vagrant mothers. In Puerto Rico, the charitable associations have closed their doors to the single mother, but the woman of loose morals is accepted everywhere because she has not sinned, that is, her sin has not taken shape, has not crystallized into a child sin, which, it is said, an all-loving God would always forgive.

This is not to say that the unfortunate children in Puerto Rico who suffer from anemia, tuberculosis, and other diseases caused by poor or no nutrition are all the children of single mothers. Many of these mothers are married, but so ignorant of what motherhood entails that they cannot be blamed.

The campaign that is being carried out in Puerto Rico in favor of the malnourished child must also be carried out for the mother, and not only for the single mother but also for the married mother.

To feed the children of Puerto Rico is an imperative duty, to legislate wisely to change this status quo is in order, but what is needed above all is to change the spirit of our society of cruel and refined respectability, that respectability that, as Ibsen rightly says, is frightening.

Marriage Does Not Bring a Woman Economic Independence Ever

CLOTILDE BETANCES
translated by María Teresa Vera-Rojas
Originally published in *Gráfico*, August 16, 1930

The Women's Division of the Bureau of Labor in Washington has just issued a report dealing with the many women who are leaving schools and colleges this June to scatter across the country in search of work. In one of its paragraphs, it states:

"Marriage does not mean freedom for women, but greater financial burden because of those on whom they depend, especially when husbands do not earn sufficient wages to support themselves and their families."

There is no doubt that every woman feels the desire to have a partner, a home, a family of her own. There is no doubt that if women were to stop marrying for fear of economic obstacles, the human family would be decimated and eventually disappear from the face of the earth.

In these postwar days, when values have been overturned, it is important for women to see that the economic independence they desire has never been found in marriage.

For example, many women marry when they have a good salary, which alone provides them with some economic relief. Many have substantial savings, dress well, and live comfortably. They fall in love. First of all, they have to keep working. So they make these observations that many of my readers are already familiar with: But what good did it do me to get married? Today I have a husband, I work, and what I earn is not enough. I work and I don't see the fruits of my labor. When I save, I have to spend it on one thing or another. What good would it have done me to get married? Thus begins the unhappiness of love. Economic misery hastens the crisis. Where there is not enough money, there is neither peace nor love.

With the questions come doubts: What kind of man have I married? I don't want him to support me, because I know how to support myself, but if I wasn't married, I could do whatever I want with my money, and now I can't. At the least, he could take care of himself. Does my husband have the right to live off me?

The heavy burden of economy shakes the marital edifice. It is better not to marry. And what to do when sex hurts? Get married? Think about it, women.

This is the problem of every woman today. Marriage is no longer a matter of the heart but of the head. Gone are the days of master and slave. The submissive, thin wife, worn out by housework and childbirth, is now an anachronism.

It is not that women become mercenaries and marry only millionaires. The millions disappear. The rich husband is sometimes a man poor in spirit, who, deprived of his money, is not worth a small dog. The man who is not afraid of life is the only one who is ready to fight for the economic independence of his family.

Have you not noticed, women, that many men marry with the same intention as you, that is, to seek a shield against life? Yes, they do. There are those who are so pusillanimous that instead of a backbone, they have melted butter; they are so cowardly that they do not dare to look for a job; so inferior that, if they work, they allow themselves be morally and physically kicked at work, because they do not have the courage to assert their rights as human beings and thinkers, and then they take it out on the women and children at home.

I am not telling you not to get married. But if you are looking for economic independence in marriage, you are making the wrong choice. You want more jobs, fewer outfits, more heartache? Go ahead. In the town hall, in the church, in the synagogue, get hitched for at least two duros. Then look for a way to untie this Gordian knot that the state, the church, the synagogue have tied for two dollars, and you will see. To bind you to the yoke, to the unhappiness, to the misfortune, to the tragedy of a whole life, they rush with greedy hands outstretched toward your money, your conjugal happiness, not caring less. Then ask these institutions to break the bond. You will not be able to do it as easily as you have bound yourselves.

Then you may feel compassion for the bum who was your husband; perhaps there are offspring. The situation becomes entangled, and to resolve it, hearts are broken, health is exhausted, savings are born with wings . . . bankruptcy in every sense of the word.

And there are those who are amazed that women want to vote! There are those who are amazed that women prefer to love without marrying! There are those who are astonished to see women in public life, fighting! It's forgotten that she may be supporting a slacker whom she once loved, who she no longer even respects, but for whom she feels compassion. It's forgotten that there may be many mouths to feed. They don't know that the woman's stomach is asking for bread, her brain asking for ideas, and her happiness asking for economic independence.

The Supreme Gift of Self

CLOTILDE BETANCES
translated by María Teresa Vera-Rojas
Originally published in *Cultura Proletaria,* June 13, 1931

FOR YOU

It is not my desire to glorify the flesh.

The so-called sin, I ignore the reason, the love that gives itself in a great gift, is the one I will talk about.

Sexual desire is undeniable. It exists. The doublé moralists want to cover the sky with their hand, and with such purpose, they preach that authoritarian morality that makes chaste and hysterical many women who, in the solitude of their shared beds, feel the unbearable sting of desire with more power than ever.

Two elements of utmost importance enter into the carnal attraction: a strong idealism and an inciting sentimentality.

Surrender is not easy. The man, accustomed to promiscuity, feels a certain repugnance in the sexual commerce he has bought. What will the woman, who is the preserver of the species, who is refined by instinct and sensitive, and who is thoughtful by direct reason of her feelings, the more vehement the more inhibited, not feel?

When a man and a woman forget the world, the false conventions, the hypocritical tradition, and give themselves completely, uniting their bodies, their minds, and their souls in a mystical, sensual, and intellectual delirium, they have given each other the supreme gift of themselves.

There is a soul beyond carnal love. Two lovers do not enjoy each other unless they are in sync. The caresses, the kisses, the supreme contact are companions of the love that is higher than all that.

Beyond sexual pleasure is the soul. To give oneself is to give the greatest gift to life. To give oneself is bliss.

What sleepless nights the chaste spend! The chaste are not only single women. There are also married women, legions of them, who are taken as objects by their husbands. Passively, they allow themselves to be possessed;

sufferingly, they bear children without love, simply because true and powerful love is always absent.

It is not the existence of the sexual need of man and woman to give themselves that is important, but the way in which they give themselves. To give oneself as a gift to one's husband is prostitution in every sense of the word. To give oneself to him in intellectual, ecstatic, and carnal paroxysms is love, the supreme gift of oneself.

These ideas of mine, as they seem at first sight, are not revolutionary but scientific. An intelligent person knows from reading the book of nature, which is open to all curiosity, that physiology and psychology are based on it.

Put a dam on the sexual instinct, therefore, and you will find disaster. Routinely, in thousands of cases, the woman gives herself to the man. But the time has come for her to learn to give herself. Systematic progress is the progress of love. If humanity goes from progress to progress, leaving love behind, the repressed emotional forces will explode violently and with bloodshed.

María Teresa Vera-Rojas (Caracas, Venezuela) is a professor at the Universitat de les Illes Balears and a researcher at ADHUC-Research Center for Theory, Gender and Sexuality at the Universitat de Barcelona. Her research focuses on Hispanic Caribbean studies as well as the recovery and study of feminism, literature, and cultural production of the Puerto Rican colonia in New York during the interwar period from the perspectives of cultural studies, gender and sexuality studies, and post/decolonial feminism. She is the author of *"Se conoce que usted es 'Moderna'": Lecturas de la mujer moderna en la colonia hispana de Nueva York (1920–1940)* (Iberoamericana-Vervuert, 2018), coeditor of *New Perspectives on Hispanic Caribbean Studies* (Palgrave Macmillan, 2020), and has recently edited the volume *Feminismos antirracistas: relecturas para el siglo XXI* (Icaria, 2024). She was also responsible for the compilation, introduction, and edition of *"El feminismo no es nuevo": las crónicas de Clotilde Betances Jaeger* (Arte Público Press, 2020).

Notes

1. In one of the few biographical notes dedicated to Clotilde Betances Jaeger, Josefina Rivera de Álvarez confirms that she was born in 1890. However, 1894 seems to be a more accurate year, based on some of the crónicas in which Clotilde Betances includes memories of her education and childhood. Despite these references, the information about the year of her birth becomes even more uncertain, considering that in a letter written in 1929 to the Cuban intellectual and politician Enrique José Varona, Clotilde Betances, when referring to her age, told Varona that she was twenty-eight years old at that time. There is also little information about the date of her death,

the only reference being Rivera de Álvarez, whose *Diccionario de literatura puertorriqueña* was published in 1974, and, according to the bibliographical note, Clotilde Betances was still alive when the note was included in the book. See Josefina Rivera Álvarez, "Betances Jaeger, Clotilde," in *Diccionario de literatura puertorriqueña*, Vol. 1 (Instituto de Cultura Puertorriqueña, 1974), 203–5; María Teresa Vera-Rojas, "Betances Jaeger, Clotilde," in *The Greenwood Encyclopedia of Latino Literature*, ed. Nicolás Kanellos (Greenwood Press, 2008), 126–29.

2. In the 1920s, Hispanic and Latino immigration had a significant presence in New York, mainly due to the contributions, visibility, and numerical superiority of Puerto Ricans in the city, the vast majority of whom were Black and working class—tobacco workers, needleworkers, and "unskilled" laborers. Memories and studies of Puerto Rican immigration to New York describe it as a process that dates back at least to the second half of the nineteenth century, during the period of independence struggles for the Spanish Caribbean colonies. However, it was with the United States' colonization of Puerto Rico in 1898 and the "granting" of US citizenship to its population in 1917 that migration began to be one of the experiences that would define Puerto Rican identity and, consequently, the identity of the Puerto Rican and Hispanic and Latino "colonia"—which was the common name used to refer to these settlements. See Bernardo Vega, *Memorias*, ed. César Andreu Iglesias (Ediciones Huracán, 1988); Virginia E. Sánchez Korrol, *From Colonia to Community: The History of Puerto Ricans in New York City, 1917–1948* (Greenwood Press, 1983); Lorrin Thomas, *Puerto Rican Citizen: Historical and Political Identity in Twentieth-Century New York City* (University of Chicago Press, 2010); and María Teresa Vera-Rojas, *"Se conoce que usted es 'Moderna'": lecturas de la mujer moderna en la colonia hispana de Nueva York (1920–1940)* (Iberoamericana-Vervuert, 2018).
3. Nicolás Kanellos, *Hispanic Immigrant Literature: El sueño del retorno* (University of Texas Press, 2011).
4. María Mas Pozo was a Puerto Rican writer, born in 1893 in Bayamón, where she died in 1981. She was also a member of the Asociación de Escritores y Periodistas Puertorriqueños and defended Puerto Rico's independence from the United States, along with her husband, journalist and Puerto Rican Nationalist Party militant José Enamorado Cuesta, whom she married in 1938. From the late 1920s until at least the 1940s, she was an active contributor to New York City's Spanish-language publications, such as the weekly *Gráfico*, the magazine *Artes y Letras*, and the newspaper *La Prensa*, where she was particularly active in the "De nuestros lectores" section. She also had an outstanding international projection thanks to her collaboration with publications such as Puerto Rico's *La Correspondencia and El Mundo*, the Dominican Republic's feminist magazine *Fémina*, Costa Rica's magazine *Repertorio Americano*, and *La Revista Blanca* from Barcelona, Spain. In her chronicles, her anti-imperialist position, her defense of Puerto Rican independence, her commitment to mutual support among Latin American countries, and her problematization of the freedoms that modernity brought

to both women and men are constant. She defended the moral superiority of women and their contribution to society through the conscious exercise of their roles as mothers, teachers, wives, and daughters. Her criticism of US colonialism and imperialism also defined her only known book, *El camino de la violencia* (1973), in which, from a position close to communism, she identified and criticized capitalism, consumerism, religion, and American imperialism as causes that lead to and feed violence and wars. For more information, see María Teresa Vera-Rojas, "Lecturas desde el margen: En torno a las cartas de María Mas Pozo en el diario *La Prensa* de Nueva York," *CENTRO: Journal of the Center for Puerto Rican Studies* 26, no. 1 (2014): 80–109; and María Teresa Vera-Rojas, "Mas Pozo, María," in *The Greenwood Encyclopedia of Latino Literature*, ed. Nicolás Kanellos (Greenwood Press, 2008), 748–50.

5. Círculo Cultural Cervantes was one of the most widely embraced groups among the professional and intellectual sectors of the Latino community in New York City. As explained in *Artes y Letras*, the Círculo Cultural Cervantes was founded on October 1, 1933, as a "a product of the social work of the Hispanic Episcopal Mission," although it defined itself as an association that was "neither religious nor sectarian, but simply cultural, recreational, and charitable," with the goal of promoting "the good name and prestige of our race." To achieve this goal, they sought an agenda of literary evenings led by writers from both the colonia and Latin America, conferences, poetry recitals, celebrations of patriotic dates, and tributes to Latin American feminists, writers, artists, and patriotic figures—events that sought to integrate the members of the colonia's cultural community. See María Teresa Vera-Rojas, "Alianzas transgresoras: Hispanismo, feminismo y cultura en *Artes y Letras*," *Latina/o Research Review* 8, nos. 1–2 (2011–12): 175–98.
6. Founded in 1934, the Unión de Mujeres Americanas was initially directed by the renowned Mexican feminist Margarita Robles de Mendoza. Its ranks included some of the directors and writers of *Artes y Letras*, a journal that was responsible for the Unión de Mujeres Americanas's great visibility and presence in the metropolis, precisely because it served as a spokesperson for the organization's activities not only in New York City but also in Latin America. Its creation, continental expansion, and longevity are important because its main goals (to achieve the union of Latin American women, to fight for their rights to equal citizenship, to promote peace and social improvements) were guided by the need for organization and collective awareness of women not solely as a political group but also as subjects who shared their own struggle, defined by their common origin and traditions as Latina women. See Vera-Rojas, "Alianzas transgresoras."
7. Michel Otayek, "Keepsakes of the Revolution: Transnational Networks and US Circulation of Anarchist Propaganda During the Spanish Civil War," in *Writing Revolution: Hispanic Anarchism in the United States*, ed. Christopher J. Castañeda and Montse Feu (University of Illinois Press, 2019).
8. The other two texts, "El matrimonio no le trae a la mujer independencia económica nunca" (*Gráfico* [Nueva York], August 16, 1930, p. 6, 10; see

full translation above) and "El problema pavoroso de la desnutrición de la infancia en Puerto Rico y las madres solteras" (*Gráfico*, June 28, 1930, p. 9; see full translation above), have been republished in Clotilde Betances Jaeger's anthology *"El feminismo no es nuevo": las crónicas de Clotilde Betances Jaeger* (Arte Público Press, 2020).

9. Clotilde Betances Jaeger, "El don supremo de sí mismo," *Cultura Proletaria* [New York], June 13, 1931, p. 4.
10. José Reyes Bermúdez, "Puertorriqueñas ilustres: Clotilde Betances," *Puerto Rico Ilustrado*, May 20, 1939, p. 19, 37.

CHAPTER 12

La Mujer en La Lucha Hoy

NANCY ZAYAS
TRANSLATED BY HEATHER HOUDE

EDITOR'S NOTE: Witness the magic that's made possible by building Puerto Rican feminist networks that span generations and geography—Esaí Ortiz-Rivera (author of "Unruly Bodies" in Part Five) connected me to their advisor at the University of Puerto Rico, Elizabeth Crespo-Kebler (author of "*El Tacón de la Chancleta*" in Part Three), who connected me to Nancy Zayas. The connection was magical because Zayas is one of the coeditors of a zine-like collection of essays from 1973 called *La Mujer en La Lucha Hoy*. I had spent the better part of a year searching for a way to contact the coeditors (Nancy Zayas and Juan Angel Silén) to inquire about using their publication's cover—the most fabulously '70s feminist cover art imaginable—in this anthology. The connection we made became an opportunity to amplify her work from 1970s Puerto Rico and give her a chance to write a kind of "update" to that original work. We are blessed with both, here. The original essay was published as the introduction to the collection *La Mujer en La Lucha Hoy*, published in Spanish by Ediciones Kikirikí in 1973.

2024: La Mujer en la Lucha Hoy

Throughout the twentieth century, the struggle of the feminist woman was framed within the fight for Puerto Rico's independence. First came the nationalists, then suffragists, workers, and student activists. By the 1960s we were fighting against the cult of virginity. The counterculture emerged as a result of the Vietnam War, with its slogan of "Peace and Love."

By the end of the twentieth century, women had achieved the right to vote, access to higher education, and, most importantly, *Roe v. Wade*, which recognized a woman's right to ownership over her own body. However, there was

Figure 1. Cover of *La Mujer en La Lucha Hoy*, 1973.
Image courtesy of Nancy Zayas.

still a long way to go to achieve gender equality. A married woman could not take out a loan without her husband's signature. Upon marriage, she lost her last name and was legally considered her husband's property. Women's salaries have always been significantly lower than men's, even when performing the same duties—a reality that persists today, with an estimated wage gap of 30 percent. By this time, women had begun the slow process of entering labor fields traditionally dominated by men.

Despite the significant achievements of the twentieth century that improved women's sociopolitical standing, working women remain burdened by the double shift—labor for the public good and domestic work. We continue to witness male dominance in every aspect of our lives. Take the grammar of the Spanish language, for example, where everything defaults to the masculine. While seemingly insignificant, it points to the male hegemony that began with the patriarchal revolution over three thousand years ago. We have grown accustomed to men deciding what is good or bad and determining what is necessary for economic, social, and political development. Institutions and streets, for the most part, still bear male names. There is a laughably small number of women represented in politics—nowhere near proportional to the more than half of the population that women occupy. In other words, there is no equality in the distribution of power. Male hegemony is visible to everyone—precisely because it has been normalized. Even today, in 2024, when you call the bank to inquire about a mortgage or a loan, you are still asked to speak to "the primary account holder," who is assumed to be your husband.

Excluding women from decision-making has been the gravest mistake committed by the male sector in our shared existence. As a result, our planet has been mortally wounded by what we call climate change, which is, in truth, environmental devastation caused by the reckless burning of fossil fuels. No one can truly be happy with the consequences of fossil fuel combustion, which has brought anxiety, poverty, and death to our home—the planet Earth. The year 2023 marked the highest level of fossil fuel burning on record, despite numerous meetings with UN officials. Today, there is a group of powerful interests that continues to benefit enormously from fossil fuel consumption and has no intention of reducing, much less eliminating our dependence on them. This will be the greatest challenge of our future.

The persistent problem of poverty continues to be tolerated as if inevitable. In our country, women bear the greatest burden, and 55 percent of our children live in poverty. Sociology has long shown that poverty is the breeding ground for countless other social problems, including alcoholism, drug addiction, prostitution, child abuse, and child trafficking, among others, not to mention the incalculable damage and waste of talent that results from keeping half of the population impoverished. This is why poverty must be fought relentlessly until it is eradicated. In fact, employment reaches only 46 percent of the population, meaning that 54 percent are either unemployed or working in the underground economy.

For Puerto Rican society, the greatest obstacle to socioeconomic and political progress is our colonial condition. Today, the Fiscal Control Board interferes with regulations even at the level of individual industries and has violated the very PROMESA Act that created it by ignoring its mandate to protect essential services—opting instead to privatize them. Privatization in Puerto Rico has driven up the cost of operating our archipelago. We once had a public health service called the Arbona Plan, which provided healthcare access to the entire population at a cost of $800 million a year. Today, the privatized system costs $10 billion annually and has created severe payment delays for healthcare providers. We now face the collapse of the entire hospital network, as providers wait up to a year for payment while the colonial government does nothing.

1973: La Mujer en la Lucha Hoy

Introduction to the 1973 publication by Nancy Zayas and Juan Angel Silén

The 1950s closed with the publication of *The Docile Puerto Rican* (1960) by René Marqués, one of the last ardent defenses of "Puerto Rican machismo." Starting in 1949 with Operation Bootstrap and the beginning of the island's industrialization, the groundwork was laid for the traditional and patriarchal society of Puerto Rico to be dismantled.

Women's dependence on men would eventually be transformed, along with the traditional structures of the Puerto Rican family.

However, Puerto Rican women's fight for liberation did not begin with the arrival of North American influence as some would have us believe. Throughout our history we have had many examples of women who can be considered pioneers in the fight for liberation.

Thus, we can point to members of the Creole elite such as Lola Rodríguez de Tió, who openly participated in activities deemed to be "for men," even going so far as to cut her hair, causing a scandal among her peers in San Germán. Likewise, Mariana Bracetti, who, in addition to sewing the flag of Lares, served as a liaison between secret societies—carrying messages, recruiting people, and agitating for revolution.

We can highlight the feminist work of Doña Ana Roqué de Duprey and Ángela Negrón, who fought to secure the right to vote for Puerto Rican women—a right that was finally achieved in 1932. It would be in those elections that, for the first time in Puerto Rico's history, women would go to the polls.

We cannot forget the incomparable Luisa Capetillo: member of the working class, labor organizer, tireless advocate for women's rights, and proponent of free love, free marriage, and gender equality. She was among the first to raise the issue of sexual repression in Puerto Rican society.

Along with Luisa Capetillo, there is also Juana Colón, a labor activist fighting for women's union rights, as well as Concha Torres, Valentina Carreras, and others who were pioneers in the labor struggles in Puerto Rico.

It is interesting to note that, with the exception of Pedro Albizu Campos's aristocratic stance on women, Puerto Rican independence theorists have had little or nothing to say about the exploitation of women. Thus, we find no guidance on this issue in the works of José de Diego, Gilberto Concepción de Gracia, Juan Mari Brás, or Rubén Berríos.[1]

What's worse, many independentistas believe that women's liberation is a problem imported from the United States.

Nothing could be further from the truth. Women's issues have long been addressed by various socialist theorists (Karl Marx and Friedrich Engels). Lenin himself also touched on the subject and spoke about what he understood to be the main problems facing women. It was a Marxist-trained psychiatrist, Wilhelm Reich, who first pointed out the issues related to compulsive morality and the sexual exploitation of young people and women.[2] Reich also insisted that this compulsive morality could be found in both socialist and capitalist societies, and his advocacy for a sexual education that would liberate young people—both men and women—from their neuroses led to his expulsion from the German Communist Party. Today, Reich's writings are gaining renewed relevance within historical processes such as the counterculture, the new student movement, the women's liberation movement, and the development of a new left that is moving beyond the dogmas and prejudices of previous generations.

As the old society has gradually disappeared, women in Puerto Rico have become open to new ideas. The woman who was once an object of pleasure, a possession under the omnipotent control of men, something to be admired, has now come to occupy her role as a producer within capitalist society.

The transition has not been easy. It has been hindered by deep-seated prejudices within both the family and Puerto Rican society. Yet with the breaking of confinement, the opening created by Operation Bootstrap, and the growing presence of women in the workforce, especially in the industrial sector, where they now make up 50 percent of the labor force, the old molds that once kept women in a position of subjugation are breaking.

Thus, in their struggle for liberation, women have had to confront not only men but also the institutions created by them—the family, the state, the church, and their offshoots—which uphold an entire ideology whose intention is to reduce women to the status of private property.

Within this institutional framework, the church played a crucial role in establishing the foundations of a reactionary ideology whose sole purpose is to exploit women. From Genesis to the Epistles of Saint Paul, we find a series of myths that have historically reinforced the subordination of women in society. In the creation myth, for example, the woman emerges from the rib of the man and is the one who tempts him to "sin," leading to their expulsion from "paradise." The Bible confines the role of women to bearing children, and if that were not enough, it further establishes male supremacy by designating the man as the head of the family.

The very act of the marriage ceremony "legally" establishes the man in his dominant role within the family, and the Civil Code reinforces the civil or religious ceremony by granting the man control and management of the marital assets. Faced with exploitation within the family, divorce is a woman's only solution, and this will only be possible to the extent that she has freed herself mentally and economically from the reactionary ideology that still prevails in our society.

Before the married woman is subjected to the arbitrary will of her husband, the single woman is subjected to the arbitrary will of her father, due to the paternal authority that the state has legalized in the man. The father will limit her world and her opportunities. He will establish games for boys and games for girls. From a young age, she will be socialized to assume a secondary role in our society. When the girl reaches puberty, her sexual traumas begin, as she must grapple on one hand with natural sexual urges and on the other with the restrictions imposed by the cult of virginity. Virginity becomes a social value—or, more accurately, a commodity—through which the father can "sell" his merchandise in the marketplace.

The aforementioned will no doubt shock and offend many moralists, who will see it as an attack on the sacred traditions of our culture, as well as the false revolutionaries who shed crocodile tears over the social and economic crisis our society is experiencing.

What these hypocrites fail to understand is that the dialectical process itself creates conflicts between the old agrarian society and the emerging capitalist society. As part of this process—driven by international influence (especially from North America) and by internal changes like industrialization, expanded access to credit, better educational opportunities, a growing labor force, political crises, and widespread institutional and social upheaval—the traditional structures that dominated during the 1950s and 1960s have been destabilized and are now under threat.

We are a country with a young population, eager to embrace new ideas, values, and concepts. Driven by economic growth and expanded access to credit, the media—radio, television, and the press—has played a major role in popularizing new trends that have been widely accepted, reinforcing new values and helping to dismantle the old ones. Each time the country, or parts of it, adopts and internalizes new ideas, it is a sign that the revolution is moving forward.

The growth of the Puerto Rican left (the Independence Party, the Socialist Party, the Pro-Independence Movement), the rise of the student movement (University Federation for Independence, University Independence Youth, Pro-Independence Student Federation, Student Independence Youth); and the adjustments that the traditional parties (Popular Democratic Party, New Progressive Party) have had to make—whether out of demagogy, pure opportunism, or genuine recognition of the people's pressure and the shifting direction of Puerto Rican society—all contribute to strengthening the fight for women's liberation.

The current ideological clash—marked by greater labor militancy, the extension of voting rights to eighteen-year-olds, and the growing discussion of socialism as an alternative to capitalism—along with the fact that women make up more than 50 percent of the population—points to the 1970s as a decade in which the women's liberation movement will experience greater momentum and increased militancy.

Commercial newspapers such as *El Imparcial*, *El Mundo*, *El Nuevo Día*, and *The San Juan Star* have started to print more news interviews and in-depth articles on women's liberation. The Socialist Party's biweekly *Claridad* and the Independence Party's weekly *La Hora* have done the same. However, it is important to note that over the past two years, the pro-independence press has published only about twenty-five articles on the topic. *La Hora*, aside from a special feature in its center pages for International Women's Day, has otherwise offered very limited coverage. It is also worth mentioning that we are not impressed by the fact that 12 percent of the Independence Party's candidates for elected office are women, and that there are no women among their candidates for at-large positions.

In Puerto Rican literature, the main characters—the heroes—are overwhelmingly men. This pattern is evident in the short stories of José Luis González, René Marqués, Emilio Díaz Valcárcel, Pedro Juan Soto, and many of our most celebrated writers. For example, we see it in González's stories "The Woman" and "The Coward"; in Marqués's "Two Turns of the Key and an Archangel," "There Is a Body Reclined on the Stern," "The Crucifixion of Miss Bunning," "The Living Room," and "The Knife and the Stone"; in Soto's short story collection *Spiks* and his novel *Usmaíl*; and in Díaz Valcárcel's story *The Siege*. Across these works, the authors, adopting a reactionary stance that leans toward literary pessimism, have sought to glorify the outdated ideal of Puerto Rican machismo.[3]

This generation in crisis, unable to grasp the economic transformation taking place in the country, used their female characters to glorify machismo and to attack what they called the North American matriarchy. This is why René Marqués, who seems to serve as the spokesperson for this sector of the intellectual elite, tells us:

> Puerto Rican feminism had already achieved political equality, but it had neither sought nor attempted to destroy the established social and cultural structure. It was with the wave of democratization that began in 1940 that Puerto Rican society quickly shifted toward an Anglo-Saxon-style matriarchy. The cultural and ethical patterns of a social structure based on the tradition of the *pater familias* deteriorated and collapsed so rapidly that it clearly revealed how little Puerto Rican society truly valued those traditions and ideals.[4]

The erroneous ideology guiding this statement is quite evident. First of all, women had not achieved *equality* simply by obtaining divorce rights, the right to vote, or access to certain professions or trades. At most, women had secured a few partial reforms that advanced their struggle but had not granted them "political equality" with men.

He is also wrong in claiming that Puerto Rico "quickly shifted toward an Anglo-Saxon-style matriarchy." The reality is quite different: Women were beginning to claim their rightful place in history. As our society was reshaped by the capitalist revolution, the old cultural and ethical traditions lost their relevance and became outdated. This is not a phenomenon unique to Puerto Rico; it is a reality wherever social and economic changes occur.

Later, René Marqués would reaffirm his views:

> It may seem unnecessary to clarify that when we speak of the frequency of good female characterizations in our current literature, we are referring to psychological and aesthetic achievements, not to any moral virtue. In truth, young writers seem to be taking a fierce revenge on matriarchy—a strange tradition recently imported into their culture—often portraying women in the harshest light a poor character can endure. Apparently, they—the writers—are the only ones in Puerto Rican society who have reacted aggressively and rebelliously to the disappearance of the last cultural stronghold from which collective docility could still, to some extent, be fought: machismo, a local version born from the fusion and adaptation of two centuries-old concepts, Spanish *honor* and the Roman *pater familias*.[5]

Here we see that the vision of the country's intellectual elite stands in opposition to women's liberation. The so-called "positive characterizations" of "pitiful" women lead to ethical and moral definitions of women as manipulative, scheming, cunning, castrating, hypocritical—in short, as beings who cannot be trusted (echoing the same thesis found in the Bible). All of this, coming from supposedly progressive writers, contributes to a stereotype of women that helps justify compulsive morality and sexual repression. Likewise, any change that moves toward greater liberation of women from their condition of subjugation and exploitation is dismissed as the importation of the North American matriarchal model.

The arguments put forward by our writers reinforce a reactionary ideology that only serves to hinder the struggle for women's liberation. This is why we have emphasized that behind these arguments lies a reactionary worldview—one that has not only delayed the fight for independence but also reflects a right-wing independentista ideology.[6]

This attitude toward women also manifests within political movements. It would be worth investigating how many women hold leadership positions in the various political movements in Puerto Rico. In some cases, the conversation around women's liberation has been silenced with the claim that "it's divisive." Many pro-independence, pro-commonwealth, and pro-statehood supporters have taken this stance.

We are concerned that there are still regressive currents being artificially kept alive in the new independence movement—currents that only serve to keep women removed from the struggle. This is often hidden behind the visible political participation of women in the country. The result has been an unproductive debate between liberation, feminism, and emancipation.

These empty, circular debates are part of discussions that the left has already moved beyond. A clear example is the stance Rosa Luxemburg once took toward the feminist movement, claiming that socialism would naturally bring about women's emancipation. However, it is the victories achieved by feminist movements that have not only advanced the fight for women's emancipation but have also laid the groundwork for the broader struggle for women's full liberation.

Feminism is the first stage of women's struggle—it is the awakening to the reality of their existence as second-class citizens. Emancipation is the legal process through which women have gradually gained rights that were once denied to them. And the fight for liberation is the final stage in a long journey—a decisive battle against economic, social, and political exploitation. It is a fight not only for women's rights but also to uproot an ideology that portrays women as sexual objects, that binds them to a repressive morality, that suppresses their sexuality, instills fear of their own bodies, turns them into objects of consumption, depicts them as beings of intrigue and manipulation, and denies them the right to be free—psychologically and biologically.

With the publication of *Toward a Positive Vision of the Puerto Rican* (1970), the decade we are now living through (1972) began. In that book—written even before any large-scale women's demonstrations in the United States—a Puerto Rican writer from the new generation shaped by the renewed fight for independence had already pointed out the twofold nature of women's exploitation.[7]

The chapter titled "Woman: The Double Oppression" touched—albeit superficially—on the causes of women's exploitation, the material conditions that sustain it, the emerging changes, and the crucial role of women in the broader struggle. Its greatest limitation is that it did not delve deeply enough into the fight for women's liberation in Puerto Rico. (This has been pointed out to us by many compañeras who have read it.)

As contradictions have continued to emerge, such as the numerical and ideological growth of the independence movement, the spread of socialist ideas, the rising intellectual level of broad sectors of the population, the growing involvement of women in labor and political struggles, the increasing militancy of the workers' movement, a greater concern among the people for civil and individual rights, and the influence of movements in the United States and around the world—the struggle for women's liberation has begun to find its own voice.

We want to categorically declare that we believe the struggle for women's liberation is a central part of the fight for independence and socialism. We're also not blind to the fact that not all who support women's liberation are part of the pro-independence movement.

It's important to clarify that, regardless of tone or emphasis, we are convinced that the women's liberation will *greatly* contribute to freeing Puerto Rican men from their fears, helping them break away from harmful taboos, and allowing them to live more authentically in both their family and social lives.

This is of vital importance. In the process of shaping new men and women, we pay special attention to the children, whether born of marriage or free unions, who must be raised free from the sexual prejudices that have shaped our own upbringing. We know from our lived experience that growth requires a constant struggle against old ideas, against the cultural and moral frameworks in which we were raised, against the repressive sexual morality that underpins the system's ideology, and against both dogmatism and liberal complacency.

We also believe that the struggle for women's liberation, while it must be led by women, needs and requires the *solidarity* of men. But for that solidarity to be real, men must begin to free themselves from the *authoritarian habits* in which they were raised. Authority does not stem from dogma, nor is it imposed by force. True authority emerges from democratic consensus, from a horizontal, participatory process of liberation that must take place both collectively and individually. In this sense, we affirm individuality as a positive value, and we caution against confusing it with bourgeois individualism, which is rooted in authoritarian norms, exploitation, and state supremacy.

Having established this, we want to make clear that the authors of this introduction do not necessarily endorse any of the views expressed by the contributors that may contradict the principles outlined here. We recognize that even within our own positions, contradictions may arise—contradictions that can only be resolved in practice. This is not an attempt to avoid debate. For us, revolutionary ideology is broad and ever-evolving; by its dialectical nature, it draws strength from a wide range of practical and theoretical experiences. It is in this spirit that we present to our readers the writings of several women who have dared to speak out on the subject of women's liberation.

The selection of articles was made arbitrarily, relying mostly on our own judgment. Within a selective framework, we have attempted to present a general overview of the positions various women have taken regarding the issue of women's liberation.

Finally, we dedicate these humble pages to the Puerto Rican youth in their fight for liberation.

Río Piedras, August 28, 1972

Nancy Zayas was born in Ponce, Puerto Rico, and grew up in both the United States and Puerto Rico, where she developed a sense of Puerto Rican national pride from an early age. She studied at CUNY before transferring to the University of Puerto Rico and graduated with a humanities degree and a master's in public communications and journalism. She published the anthology *La Mujer en La Lucha Hoy* in 1973, and has worked with the Movimiento Victoria Ciudadana since 2019.

Notes

1. Pedro Albizu Campos, "The Liberating Woman," *El Mundo*, May 12, 1930.
2. Karl Marx, Frederick Engels, V. I. Lenin, and Joseph Stalin, *The Woman Question* (International Publishers, 1951); Wilhelm Reich, *Dialectical Materialism and Psychoanalysis* (Siglo XXI, 1970); Wilhelm Reich, *The Invasion of Compulsory Sex-Morality* (Farrar, Straus & Giroux, 1971); Wilhelm Reich, *The Sexual Revolution* (Farrar, Straus & Giroux, 1971).
3. José Luis González, *Five Bloody Stories* (Librería Estrella Roja, 1945); René Marqués, *In a City Called San Juan*, third edition, expanded (Editorial Cultural, 1970); Pedro Juan Soto, *Spiks* (Los Presentes, 1956), Pedro Juan Soto, *Usmail* (Club del Libro, 1959); Emilio Díaz Valcárcel, *The Siege* (Ediciones Arrecife, 1958).
4. René Marqués, "The Puerto Rican Short Story in the Generation of the Forties," in *Essays (1953–1966)* (Editorial Antillana, 1967).
5. René Marqués, "The Docile Puerto Rican," in *Essays (1953–1966)* (Editorial Antillana, 1967), 170–71.

6. As part of the new movement to reassess and reinterpret Puerto Rican history, the time has come to make clear that the ideology of the new independence movement no longer has room for right-wing or reactionary beliefs. This should in no way be interpreted as an attempt to impose any kind of censorship. However, ideological struggle touches every aspect of life—and this is one of them.
7. Juan Ángel Silén, *Toward a Positive Vision of the Puerto Rican* (Edil Publishing, 1970).

CHAPTER 13

El Tacón de la Chancleta: Feminisms in 1970s Puerto Rico

ELIZABETH CRESPO-KEBLER

EDITOR'S NOTE: This essay was originally published in Spanish in the May 2022 issue (no. 6) of *Archipelagos: A Journal of Caribbean Digital Praxis*, an open access journal. *El Tacón de la Chancleta* is part of the "Documents of Feminism Collection Rivera Lassén–Crespo Kebler," which contains over four thousand documents from more than sixty feminist organizations from the period 1970 to 2010. These are documents that the authors of the collection have compiled as a result of our activism and donations from other feminist activists. The Digital Library of the Caribbean (dLOC) is an ideal space for this collection due to the visibility and permanence it offers as a digital repository. We are working to incorporate the collection in its entirety for the use of students, scholars of feminisms, and people interested in formulating public policies, as well as for the general public.

On September 30, 1974, the feminist newspaper *El Tacón de la Chancleta* circulated its inaugural issue in the weekly news magazine *Avance*.[1] By the following year, five more issues of *El Tacón de la Chancleta* were published as an independent newspaper. Looking back, we can affirm that this publication emblematized what has been called the second wave of feminisms in Latin America and the Caribbean. It was also a pioneer in what today would be called alternative feminist journalism.

An analysis of the topics that *El Tacón de la Chancleta* included, and the debates that were aired on its pages, lends itself to an examination of Puerto Rican feminisms as well as the historical continuities, ruptures, and resignifications of the issues that concern them. Topics highlighted include International Women's Year; the First World Conference on Women held in Mexico, in 1975; feminism as an intersectional political movement; abortion and women's right to control their bodies; sexual orientation; sexism in the media; sexism and racism in beauty contests; a nonsexist school curriculum; violence against women; and feminist art, among others.

Political Panorama and Historical Context of *El Tacón de la Chancleta*

To understand the contributions of *El Tacón*, we must first look at the political panorama of Puerto Rico and the so-called second wave of feminism, which took shape in many parts of the world in the decades from 1960 to 1980. The second wave emerged globally as an outpouring of demands after women gained the right to vote starting at the beginning of the twentieth century: 1920 in the United States, 1929 in Puerto Rico and Ecuador, 1932 in Brazil and the Dominican Republic, 1947 in Argentina and Venezuela, and 1964 in the Bahamas, to mention some seminal years in places throughout our geographical hemisphere.[2] Just as the suffrage movement was a global one, the feminist movements of the second wave were also global.[3] The second wave of feminism agitated for significant changes in the living conditions of women, such as increased participation in the workforce, changes in the structure of families, and reconfigurings of models of femininity.[4]

The global and transnational character of feminisms in Puerto Rico is nuanced by several factors: Puerto Rico's legal status as a nonindependent country or unincorporated territory of the United States, the constant movement of people between the United States and Puerto Rico, and the political action in different spaces within North America, Latin America, the Caribbean, and Europe. Due in large part to these complexities, early feminist development in Puerto Rico had been uniquely isolated from narratives of the second wave in both of its regional counterparts and containers—Latin America and the Caribbean on one hand, the United States on the other. Puerto Rico actually preceded many Latin American and Caribbean countries in political and social feminist advancements; for example, comparatively early, Puerto Rico established the right to abortion and created government entities such as the Commission for the Improvement of Women's Rights (1973), the Rape Victims Center (1977), as well as nongovernmental entities to provide services and shelters for women victims of domestic violence. Despite these achievements, Puerto Rico's feminist history in those early decades is largely unknown throughout Latin America and the Caribbean, in part because other countries in the region didn't replicate that trajectory until the late 1980s due to internal and external geopolitical factors that limited the possibilities of civil society to make the state responsive to women's demands.[5]

With regards to the US, Puerto Rico's legal status as an unincorporated US territory is complex, engendering both isolation and points of contact with other parts of the world. Puerto Rico does not have a seat in the United Nations and also lacks equal access to international economic resources. Adding to the alienated relationship between the archipelago and the mainland is the fact that US judicial decisions do not automatically apply to Puerto Rico. Examples of this legal disjunction include the right to vote and the right to abortion, which have a different history on the island than in the United States.[6] Because of schisms like this, as well as other historical, geographical, and linguistic reasons, the history of women's movements in Puerto Rico is not typically considered a part of United States feminist history.

Nonetheless, Puerto Rico's territorial status links Puerto Rican feminisms with those in the United States, Latin America, and the Caribbean. For Puerto Rican feminists to promote their demands, they have had to do so in the context of regional participation mechanisms, such as the world conferences promoted by the United Nations, regional forums of the Organization of American States, the Economic Commission for Latin America, and the Inter-American Commission on Human Rights, among others, drawing them into constant relation with their regional counterparts and mainland correspondents.

The transnational feminisms that course through Puerto Rico have become linked through the constant movement of people between the United States and Puerto Rico, through Boricua activism alongside other migrant groups that also moved to and from the United States and between their home countries in the region.[7] Since the history, language, and national identity of Puerto Rico are Latin American and Caribbean, in Puerto Rico feminist and women's organizations have looked to these regions for inspiration. Feminist organizations not only projected themselves within Puerto Rico but also founded and participated in feminist and human rights networks, feminist meetings, feminist and international government events, and regional and global organizations. Through this activism, Puerto Rican feminists announced themselves to the world, overcoming the limited participation of the Puerto Rican government.

The feminist movement that emerged in Latin America and the Caribbean, onward from 1970 and the advent of Puerto Rico's trailblazing, became a diverse movement. Some feminists inserted themselves in traditional political spaces such as state agencies, unions, political parties, and international organizations. It is worth noting that many countries in the region were governed by dictatorships, so the relationship between women's groups and the state was very unequal in the decades preceding the 1990s. Some feminist activists in these countries had previously been politically persecuted and even exiled at some point. In Puerto Rico, as in other parts of Latin America and the Caribbean, autonomous organizations, outside of traditional spaces, formed to influence the cultural, social, political, and economic changes needed to promote equity and women's rights. *El Tacón de la Chancleta* and the organization Mujer Intégrate Ahora (MIA) were part of this autonomous feminist movement.[8]

Mujer Intégrate Ahora and *El Tacón de la Chancleta*

Mujer Intégrate Ahora was the first autonomous feminist organization created in Puerto Rico during the decade of 1970s. The women who formed MIA first met under the name "Comité de Mujeres Puertorriqueñas" (Puerto Rican Women's Committee). They organized in response to a call made by Nilda Aponte to the attendees of the public hearings held in Puerto Rico in 1971, which discussed a report by the Puerto Rico Civil Rights Commission that documented discrimination against women in all areas of Puerto Rican society. These hearings were crucial because just a year earlier, a different report drafted by a committee appointed by the governor of Puerto Rico publicly stated that there was no discrimination against women on the Island. This lack of recognition of discrimination was characteristic of the political context of the early 1970s, in which spaces for women in the traditional realm of politics were very limited. Few women were elected to public office, and the top positions in parties, unions, and political organizations were dominated by men. One of MIA's founders recounts this systemic silencing of women: "At that time, I read everything I could find on the subject of women, and since there were practically no written stories of the struggles in Puerto Rico of the suffragists and feminists of the early century, I dedicated my free time to go and read in the Library of the University of Puerto Rico and the Library of the Ateneo."[9] (This and all translations in this essay are the author's.) MIA's founding member further narrates that her passion was echoed by five other women, three Puerto Ricans and two North Americans who shared the interest and desire to promote the feminist movement in Puerto Rico. They formally founded MIA in January of 1972 by drafting a document that described their purposes and objectives and set forth regulations for membership.

The editorial column of the inaugural issue of *El Tacón de la Chancleta* explains the origin of the publication: "A group of women within the organization 'Mujer Intégrate Ahora' (MIA), while reviewing the history of feminism in Puerto Rico, found a historical publishing tradition of promoting women's rights through dedicated magazines and newspapers."[10] Acting on its intention to make feminist history visible, the pages of *El Tacón* reviewed

Figure 1. Editors of *El Tacón de la Chancleta*. From left, Ronnie Lovler, Elizabeth Viverito Escobar, Ana Irma Rivera Lassén, Alma Méndez Ríos, Maritza Durán Alméstica, Margarita Babb, and Yvonne Torres. Photograph by Elizabeth Viverito Escobar.

the local and international periodicals published by Puerto Rican suffragists, particularly those of Ana Roqué de Duprey and her collaborators, which included *Euterpe* (1888), *La Mujer* (1894), *La Evolución* (1902), *El Álbum Puertorriqueño* (1918), *La Mujer del Siglo XX* (1917), and *El Heraldo de la Mujer* (1919).[11]

As stated in its first editorial, MIA started the feminist newspaper with the idea that it could be sold and marketed alongside commercial publications. They wanted to differentiate themselves from the women's publications of the time, which tended to reinforce women's patterns of submission and inferiority.[12] Notably, Gloria Steinem, a highly visible figure in the United States media, as well as an internationally renowned feminist and editor of *Ms.* magazine, visited Puerto Rico in June of 1974 and donated to help finance the publication of *El Tacón de la Chancleta*. In their inaugural issue, the editors describe the reasons for and the name of their publication:

> the *chancleta* (house slipper) is at the same level as the ground and its use is limited to the confines of the house. It is also an object of little value. We believe that the *chancleta* has grown a heel. . . . With the heel you can

Figure 2. Front pages of *El Tacón de la Chancleta.*

> go out into the street and you are a little above ground level. But its nature remains the same: a *chancleta*. This publication arises from the need to raise awareness among women and bring to light the situations for which we have been unfairly called and treated like *chancletas*.[13]

With this adage describing the historical moment and the social transformation that it set out to induce from its pages, *El Tacón de la Chancleta* launched.

According to its founders, although *El Tacón de la Chancleta* intended to be an independent publication, its editorials and many of its articles reflected MIA's positions. This connection is further documented in the organization's official publication, titled *MIA Informa*.[14] Puerto Rican newspapers and magazines, as well as MIA's documents, reflect the impact that the organization's activities had on local discussions regarding issues such as abortion, the image of women in the media, equality in marriage, equality in credit, and women's participation in the country's economy. MIA also brought to the spotlight the lack of local textbooks that showed women in public and private work, and discussed issues like maternity leave, childcare centers, prostitution, beauty pageants, homosexuality, and lesbianism. Further, they generated and circulated analyses of the political platforms of local parties, their proposals, and the promises they made to women, so as to influence public policy decisions.

The topics discussed in *El Tacón* and the debates that were articulated in its pages provide us a window to the past, which contributes to an analysis of the future of feminisms by allowing us to notice continuities, ruptures, and resignifications of important feminist issues.

Feminism as a Political Movement

The relationship between feminism and socialist and pro-independence organizations sparked important debates in Latin American and Caribbean feminisms. As in other countries, in Puerto Rico, the theoretical frameworks of the left established a hierarchy of priorities where the fight against capitalism had priority over the struggle against women's oppression.[15] MIA was at the center of this debate because from its beginnings, it refused to identify with any political party and did not advocate for any political status for Puerto Rico (neither independence, nor statehood, nor free association). Nonetheless, the organization was political and pronounced itself in favor of controversial issues such as abortion, free love, and nonsexist education. Its guiding principle was social justice and human rights, particularly those of women.[16]

Beginning with MIA's founding in 1972, its positions sparked controversy among many sectors. On the one hand, the mass media accused MIA of threatening the family and Puerto Rican culture. On the other hand, pro-independence and socialist sectors branded them as bourgeois and victims of foreign ideas from the United States. *Claridad*, a pro-independence newspaper of the Puerto Rican Socialist Party, published a column by Lolita Aulet, one of its prominent leaders, titled "Reformism Versus Revolution." There she argued, "Feminists, influenced by distortion and lack of information, direct their campaigns proclaiming men their enemies and seek to counteract the oppression of which they are victims with a persistent refusal to have children and other forms of vain protest." She further stated that, "while the demand for equality for women is democratic, the demand for their total liberation cannot be anything other than socialist."[17]

In response to Aulet's column, Ana Irma Rivera Lassén, leader of MIA, published an article, also in *Claridad*, arguing that ideas of women's liberation strike not only against the wall built by imperialism and underdevelopment but also against the wall of male chauvinism. She criticized those who saw women's liberation as assimilation to cultural patterns foreign to Puerto Rican culture, because, as Rivera Lassén argued, the woman problem was a problem of humanity and an essential part of the liberation of human beings, which involved both men and women. For her, the lack of equal participation of women in socialist parties pointed to complicity with sexism, something that the women themselves who were active in that party decried.[18]

In 1975, the founding of the feminist organization Federación de Mujeres Puertorriqueñas (FMP) sparked a public debate about the autonomy of feminist organizations and their organizational and ideological independence from leftist movements. In the pages of *El Tacón de la Chancleta,* editors voiced strong opposition to the FMP's belief that women's liberation could only occur after the capitalist and colonial economic and political structures collapsed. *El Tacón* also drew attention to the FMP's fear of and resistance to using the word *feminism.*[19]

The editorial column of the third issue of *El Tacón*, published in March–April of 1975, articulates the magazine's vision of feminism as a distinct political movement. In this column, the publication argued that

> the movements for the rights of the black race, ethnic groups, working class, sexual orientation and preference, student groups, national liberation, all together have enough strength to achieve changes in societies. But to achieve true change we must end not only oppression and the power of some over others but also the very idea of oppression and power. Feminist consciousness is essential if you really want to achieve real change in society, because the oppression of women is something common in all of them.[20]

Nilda Aponte Raffaele's writing published in *El Tacón* further expanded the vision of feminism as integral to social change. In her article titled "Human Liberation Women's Liberation" Aponte Raffaele argued that "women's liberation is essential to true human liberation."[21] She further argued that while some insist that women's liberation must be subordinated to other struggles and remain pending until social justice, independence, or a better world is achieved, the struggles are intertwined and do not exclude but rather complement each other, each having its reason for being even when sometimes they cannot exist together. As she saw it, "when as individuals we feel compelled to recognize more than one struggle, we can do so without having to decide whether one is compatible with the other. What we have to decide is which fight we have to give ourselves to, not because it is necessarily the most important, but because at this moment that fight best responds to our circumstances, our needs, abilities and greater personal urgency."[22] In the pages of *El Tacón*, Aponte Raffaele and Rivera Lassén, both Black women, articulated a vision that went beyond the binary of reformism or revolution and instead presented a feminism situated in their experiences and how their lives were simultaneously permeated by various forms of oppression. Evidencing its international resonance, this perspective was also expressed from another geographical space by the Combahee River Collective in their essay "A Black Feminist Statement" in 1977.[23] Placing Aponte Raffaelle and Rivera Lassén's perspective in a historical context reveals that they also advanced a vision of what in the 1980s and 1990s would come to be called "intersectionality," which, beyond adding forms of oppression, proposes to make visible the particularities of gender inequalities when they interact with race, ethnicity, social class, sexual orientation, and other categories of exclusion.[24]

International Women's Year and the First International Women's Conference

In 1974, MIA was the first autonomous feminist organization in Puerto Rico to organize a celebration of March 8, International Women's Day. This event took place even before the United Nations (UN) recognized the date as such. MIA commemorated the day at the Plaza las Américas shopping center with a two-day event that generated coverage by the media, curiosity, and support from the public. MIA continued celebrating it as part of the first issue of *El Tacón de la Chancleta* published in 1975. The celebration of International Women's Year and the convening of the First International Women's Conference, held in Mexico in 1975 under the auspices of the UN, propelled MIA and *El Tacón de la Chancleta* outside of Puerto Rico. It also brought to Puerto Rico an understanding of feminism as a global phenomenon. The coverage revealed that the debate about revolutionary and reformist feminism, bourgeois or proletarian feminism, also occurred among feminist groups at a global level. These discussions were included in the pages of *El Tacón de la Chancleta*. The July–August 1975 issue of *El Tacón de la Chancleta* was dedicated to covering this conference.

The First International Women's Conference, as organized by the UN, hosted both a government conference and a parallel meeting for nongovernmental organizations, called the International Women's Year tribune. At the government conference, member states would commit to the global plan of action for achieving the goals of International Women's Year, which presented guidelines and benchmarks for the advancement of women to be implemented through 1985. The government conference also recognized the subordinate role of women in the social, economic, and political life of all countries. However, despite having these goals, Rivera Lassén notes, a man was elected president of the government conference and many of the participants were the wives of powerful men: "This is how the International

Women's Year Conference took place and concluded in the country best known for its sexism."[25]

The parallel conference, the tribune, intended to gather the concerns of feminists from different countries, who attended as individuals or representing nongovernmental organizations. The tribune had representation from conservative women's groups, which proposed to incorporate more women in leadership positions, the police force, the army, and in other structures that promoted the status quo. It also included women who said that women's problems were the same as men's because their only enemies were imperialism, capitalism, and colonialism. Additionally, it had the representation of those who thought that the women's liberation movement divided men and women. Further, other participants argued that women's problems should be discussed without entering politics. The panels in the official program were dominated by North American, European, and African women, leaving little space to Latin American women. The excessive press coverage of North American women also contributed to the lack of visibility of Latin American women. Delegations of Indigenous Mexican women were excluded from the tribune, while their spaces were occupied by members of the Mexican government's party, the Institutional Revolutionary Party.

In a column in *El Tacón de la Chancleta*, Rivera Lassén summarized what she witnessed at the event given the exclusionary politics that transpired, and employing the paradigm of the time, where groups proposed to identify a "true" feminism: "Feminism stayed at customs," she affirmed. In summary, "what happened there was precisely that there was no feminism. If there was any triumph, it was that of those who are dedicated to discrediting the feminist movement. There are not several types of feminism, there is only one, which, well understood, is the one that fights for women's rights and a more just society."[26]

Abortion and Women's Right to Control Their Sexuality and Their Bodies

Feminist positions regarding women's health and bodies, as presented in the pages of *El Tacón de la Chancleta*, generated criticism among various groups, which either considered those stances too radical or deemed such issues secondary to worker, union, or anti-imperialist issues. In Aulet's previously cited words, the feminism she called "reformist" proclaimed men its enemies and was characterized by "a persistent refusal to have children and other forms of vain protest."

Since 1903, abortion undertaken to protect the life or health of the mother, or what is known as therapeutic abortion, has remained legal in Puerto Rico into the present. Before the United States Supreme Court's decision in *Roe v. Wade* (1973)—that is, when abortion was illegal in the United States—Puerto Rico served as a place where women went to obtain legal and safe abortions. However, beginning with its founding in 1972, MIA was a vocal advocate for the right to abortion at the request of women, meaning expanding the right beyond therapeutic abortion. In 1973, *Roe v. Wade* granted abortion on demand as part of the right to privacy. Under this legal concept, the decision to abort belonged to the women. In 1974, the United States Federal District Court in Puerto Rico (in *Montalvo v. Colón*) recognized the applicability of *Roe v. Wade* on the Island, affirming that where the Puerto Rico Penal Code recognized that abortion was legal to save the life and health of women, "health" included abortion on demand. Later in 1980, *Pueblo v. Duarte Mendoza* recognized that women's right to decide about their bodies, including abortions, was protected under the privacy clause of the Constitution of Puerto Rico. After *Roe v. Wade* was overturned, abortion has remained legal to save the life and health of women, as interpreted with the constitutional protection of Puerto Rico. Feminist activism today has been successful so far in preserving the right to abortion as the rule of law in Puerto Rico.[27]

Published in the inaugural issue of *El Tacón*, the essay titled "And Where Are The Abortionists?" exposes the dilemma presented in the 1974 Federal Court decision, a difficult situation still prevalent today.[28] The ruling held, on the one hand, that public hospitals had to open their facilities to women who requested abortions, and on the other hand, that no doctor could be forced to perform them if their consciences went against the procedure. Thus, public hospitals relied on freedom of conscience to hinder women's attempts to obtain abortions in a public facility. Hospitals also argued that their funds and personnel were insufficient. The question asked in the title of the article points to the health sector's disregard for the health and safety of women, as well as overwhelming pressure from the government to impose policies violating women's right to autonomy over their bodies and lives.

The political left saw the right to abortion as a colonial imposition. Groups of lawyers, leaders of pro-independence parties, and the president of the Puerto Rican Ateneo protested before the UN against what they described as an imposition alien to the values of Puerto Rican culture.[29] During the 1970s, women's right to control their bodies continued to conflict with nationalist discourses both within feminism and on the socialist and independent left about contraceptive methods and sterilization as genocidal policies.[30]

Contrastingly, articles in *El Tacón* advocated for women's rights over their bodies, for free contraceptives, for accessible and safe abortions in public hospitals—especially for victims of rape—and against forced sterilization. A series of essays—"Contraceptives: The Roulette of Sex" (September 1974), "Know Your Body: Vaginal Infections" (January 1975), "Know Your Body:

The Racket of Vaginal Douching" (February 1975) and "Sitting Birth" (May–June 1975)— show the publication's commitment to advocating for women's health.[31] Today, Taller Salud, a feminist organization founded in late 1979, continues this tradition of prioritizing women's health and their right to control their sexuality.

Other Topics

In the 1970s, the need for a gender-conscious school curriculum that presents girls as protagonists and dislodged stereotypical gender roles was an important issue, and it remains one today. On the cover of the inaugural issue of *El Tacón de la Chancleta*, the main heading read "The Docile Puerto Rican (Girl)," which referred to an included article that reviewed the findings of Haydeé Yordán Molini's study on the images used in the textbooks of the Department of Education. The study found that boys were presented as protagonists much more frequently than girls and that they were portrayed as active and strong beings who had great initiative and creativity; girls, by contrast, were presented as passive and submissive and were described with exaggerated emphasis on their obedience and docility.[32]

The cover of the January 1975 issue of *El Tacón* also lent room to the topic of violence against women, with the heading "In Search of Our Identity." The issue's editorial piece expressed disagreement with the idea of a natural order of things, one that justified sexual violence against women because of the identification of women as passive subjects and men as aggressors, and one that emphasized how a woman's happiness lies in attachment to a man. One of the articles in this issue tells the story of an American woman of Puerto Rican and Cuban origin, Inez García, who killed a man who'd accosted her. Her trial and conviction for the murder generated widespread protests and support from the women's liberation movement in the United States and throughout the world.[33] Throughout the 1970s, activists in Latin America and the Caribbean amplified their call for action to prevent violence against women, culminating in the first Latin American and Caribbean Feminist Meeting in Colombia in 1981—here it was decided to proclaim November 25 an international holiday commemorating the fight to resist and stem violence against women. By emblematizing Minerva, Patria, and María Teresa Mirabal—sisters murdered by the Trujillo dictatorship in the Dominican Republic—as the symbols of their movement, the activists brought attention to political violence against women as well as to domestic violence, rape, sexual harassment, and torture. In 1999, the United Nations General Assembly agreed to designate November 25 as the International Day for the Eradication of Violence Against Women.

The visual pieces and graphic material found in the pages of *El Tacón* stoke a critical appreciation of feminist art, exploring how it can redefine female sexuality and unsettle stereotypical images of girls and women. *El Tacón*'s first issue featured the image of a Taíno woman in labor, crafted by renowned graphic artist Consuelo Gotay, then known as Consuelo Claudio. The issue also includes an interview with the graphic artist Myrna Báez, conducted by Ana Irma Rivera Lassén, which presents Báez as a protagonist and outstanding practitioner of art in a profession dominated by men, in a society lacking vital spaces for the development of women artists. Today, this essay is widely cited by critics of art made by women.[34] Additionally, numerous illustrations by graphic artist Ivonne Torres grace the issues of *El Tacón de la Chancleta*; photographic essays such as Peggy Ann Bliss's, "The Face of the Puerto Rican Woman," published in the first issue (January 1975), further add to this collection. As the magazine presents, feminist art brings meaning to text and provides new dimensions to the activism that motivated this publication.

To journey across the pages of *El Tacón de la Chancleta* is to reflect on the history of Latin American and Caribbean feminisms. *El Tacón*'s installments in the 1970s are still fresh enough to challenge the present, exemplifying the importance of historical archives for activists—both to trace bygone political paths traveled and to envision futures of inclusion and equity.

Elizabeth Crespo-Kebler writes and teaches on gender, sexuality, race, ethnicity, and feminisms in Latin America and the Caribbean. Her commitment to social justice and human rights using a transdisciplinary and transnational perspective is paramount as a teacher and feminist activist. Her most recent work is centered on preserving and documenting the history of feminisms in Puerto Rico in their local and global contexts.

Notes

1. *Avance* was a political discussion magazine published from 1972 to 1975 in San Juan, Puerto Rico. It covered in its pages several articles about feminist organizations and other movements, of which the following stand out: a dossier on homosexuality with interviews from members of the Gay Pride Community, an organization created to advocate for the rights of gay and lesbian people and to repeal the article of the Penal Code of Puerto Rico that punished the "infamous crime against nature" with one to ten years in prison, *Avance*, September 2, 1974, 10–17; a dossier about beauty pageants by Ada Nivea Guerra, "Concursos de Belleza: Miss, Sí; Miss, No," *Avance*, July 20–26, 1972, 25–30; "En la silla de los acusados: La mujer se defiende de los cargos que le formulan," *Avance*, March 3, 1975, 36–39.

2. Ana María Bigegain, "La obtención del sufragio femenino en los estados latinoamericanos, avances y ambigüedades (1917–1961)," in *Mujer, nación, identidad y ciudadanía: Siglos XIX y XX* (IX Cátedra Anual de Historia Ernesto Restrepo Tirado, October 28–30, 2004) (Ministro de Cultura, 2005).
3. Robin Morgan, ed., *Sisterhood Is Global* (The Feminist Press at the City University of New York, 1996); Caroline Daley, *Suffrage and Beyond: International Feminist Perspectives* (Auckland University Press, 1994).
4. Yasmine Ergas, "El sujeto mujer: El feminismo de los años sesenta-ochenta," in *Historia de las mujeres: el siglo XX, la nueva mujer*, ed. Georges Duby and Michelle Perrot, 154–81 (Taurus, 1993).
5. Magaly Pineda, introduction to *Documentos del feminismo en Puerto Rico: facsímiles de la historia [1970–1979]*, vol. 1, ed. Ana Irma Rivera Lassén and Elizabeth Crespo-Kebler (Editorial de la Universidad de Puerto Rico, 2001), xiv; Magaly Pineda, "The Spanish-Speaking Caribbean: We Women Aren't Sheep," in Morgan, *Sisterhood Is Global*, 131–34; Marjorie Agosín, "Chile: Women of Smoke," in Morgan, *Sisterhood Is Global*, 138–41.
6. Ana Irma Rivera Lassén, "Del dicho al derecho hay un gran trecho o el derecho a tener derechos: Decisiones del Tribunal Supremo de Puerto Rico ante los derechos de las mujeres y de las comunidades LGBTTI," *Revista Jurídica UIPR* 44, no. 1 (August–May 2009): 39–68.
7. Elizabeth Crespo-Kebler, "Las Buenas Amigas," in "Revisiting Puerto Rican Queer Sexualities," special issue, *Centro Journal* 30, no. 2 (Summer 2018): 378–405.
8. Rivera Lassén and Crespo-Kebler, *Documentos del feminismo en Puerto Rico*; Norma Mogrovejo, *Un amor que se atrevió a decir su nombre* (Plaza y Valdés, 2000); Magdalena León de Leal, ed., *Mujeres y participación política: Avances y desafíos en América Latina* (Tercer Mundo Editores, 1994).
9. Ana Irma Rivera Lassén, "La Organización de las Mujeres y las organizaciones feministas en Puerto Rico: Mujer Intégrate Ahora y otras historias de la década," in Rivera Lassén and Crespo-Kebler, *Documentos del feminismo en Puerto Rico*, 106.
10. *El Tacón de la Chancleta*, suplemento especial, *Avance*, September 30, 1974, 29–41.
11. The research on Roqué de Duprey presented in the pages of *El Tacón de la Chancleta* directs the reader to other figures and organizations. Among these, the Puerto Rican Women's League, which promoted the right to vote for women, the National Woman's Party and its Puerto Rico chapter, the Social Suffragist League associated with the International Alliance of Women, the Association of Women Suffragettes, and the Insular Association of Women Voters. Likewise, the research highlights other prominent Puerto Rican suffrage figures: Ricarda López de Ramos, Dr. Marta Robert de Romeu, Muna Lee, Pilar Barbosa, Ricarda Ramos Casellas, Milagros Benet Newton, Beatriz Lassalle, and Isabel Andreu de Aguilar (first woman of the governing board of UPR and president of the League of Women Voters). Ana I. Rivera Lassén, "Doña Ana Roqué de Duprey precursora del movimiento sufragista en Puerto Rico," *El Tacón de la Chancleta*, July–August 1975, 8–9.

12. Rivera Lassén and Crespo-Kebler, *Documentos del feminismo en Puerto Rico*, 122–23; "¿Por qué?," *El Tacón de la Chancleta*, suplemento especial, *Avance*, September 30, 1974, 2.
13. "¿Por qué El Tacón de la Chancleta?," *El Tacón de la Chancleta*, September 1974, https://ufdc.ufl.edu/AA00091661/00001/pdf.
14. Rivera Lassén and Crespo-Kebler, *Documentos del feminismo en Puerto Rico*, 218–45.
15. I discuss the relationship between the left and feminisms in "Liberación de la Mujer: los feminismos, la justicia social, la nación y la autonomía en las organizaciones feministas de la década de 1970 en Puerto Rico," Rivera Lassén and Crespo-Kebler, *Documentos del feminismo en Puerto Rico*, 39–95. See also "Entrevistas a Norma Valle Ferrer y Flavia Rivera Montero," in Rivera Lassén and Crespo-Kebler, *Documentos del feminismo en Puerto Rico*, 151–78.
16. Rivera Lassén and Crespo-Kebler, *Documentos del feminismo en Puerto Rico*, 218–19.
17. Lolita Aulet, "Reformismo versus revolución," *Claridad*, April 17, 1973, 11.
18. Ana Irma Rivera Lassén, "Un debate: La liberación femenina," *Claridad*, June 3, 1973, 14.
19. "Editorial," *El Tacón de la Chancleta*, February 1975, 2, https://ufdc.ufl.edu/AA00070290/00002.
20. "Editorial," *El Tacón de la Chancleta*, March–April 1975, 2, https://ufdc.ufl.edu/AA00070290/00003.
21. Nilda Aponte Raffaele, "Liberación humana liberación femenina," *El Tacón de la Chancleta*, July–August 1975, 10, https://ufdc.ufl.edu/AA00070290/00005.
22. Aponte Raffaele, "Liberación humana liberación femenina," 10.
23. Combahee River Collective, "A Black Feminist Statement," in *The Second Wave: A Reader in Feminist Theory*, ed. Linda Nicholson, 63–70 (Routledge, 1997). Originally published in 1977.
24. Kimberlé Crenshaw, "La intersección de raza y género," in *Raza, etnicidad, género y derechos humanos en las Américas: Un nuevo paradigma para el activismo*, ed. Celina Romany, 127–39 (Publicaciones REG, 2004); and Celina Romany, "Tema de conversación sobre raza y género en el derecho internacional en materia de derechos humanos," in *Raza, etnicidad, género y derechos humanos en las Américas*, ed. Romany, 121–26.
25. Ana Irma Rivera Lassén, "Conferencia Mundial de la Mujer, el feminismo se quedó en la aduana," *El Tacón de la Chancleta*, July–August 1975, 4–5, https://ufdc.ufl.edu/AA00070290/00005.
26. Rivera Lassén, "Conferencia Mundial de la Mujer," 5.
27. *Acevedo Montalvo v. Hernández Colón*, 377 Federal Sup. 1332, 1974; *Pueblo v. Duarte Mendoza*, 109 D.P.R. 596, 1980.
28. Ronnie Lovler, "¿Y los aborteros dónde están?," *El Tacón de la Chancleta*, ejemplar preliminar, *Avance*, September 30, 1974, 12.
29. "Protestan ante ONU imposición aborto," *Claridad*, February 13, 1973, 6; Raúl González Cruz, "Una imposición colonial," *Claridad*, February 3, 1973, 11; and "Rechaza apliquen ley permite los abortos," *Claridad*, February 4, 1973, 5.

30. See Elizabeth Crespo-Kebler, "Ciudadanía y nación: Debates sobre los derechos reproductivos en Puerto Rico," *Revista de Ciencias Sociales: Nueva Época*, no. 10 (2001): 57–84; Laura Briggs, "Discourses of 'Forced Sterilization' in Puerto Rico," *Differences*, no. 10 (Summer 1998): 30–66; Rosa E. Marchand-Arias, "Clandestinaje legal: El aborto en Puerto Rico de 1937 a 1970," *Puerto Rico Health Sciences Journal* 17, no. 1 (March 1998): 15–26; Yamila Azize-Vargas and Luis A. Avilés, "Abortion in Puerto Rico: The Limits of Colonial Legality," *Reproductive Health Matters* 5, no. 9 (1997): 56–65, http://www.jstor.org/stable/3775136.
31. See also Nilda Aponte Raffaele, one of the editors of *El Tacón de la Chancleta*, "Abortos: La mujer es la que decide," *Avance*, April 16, 1973, 19–21; and "Las mujeres 'liberacionistas' y el aborto," *Avance*, April 16, 1973, 16–18.
32. "La puertorriqueña dócil," *El Tacón de la Chancleta*, ejemplar preliminar, *Avance*, September 30, 1974, 3–5.
33. *El Tacón de la Chancleta*, January 1975, 1, 2, 5, https://ufdc.ufl.edu/AA00070290/00001.
34. Ana Irma Rivera Lassén, "Myrna Báez: liberación a través del arte," *El Tacón de la Chancleta*, ejemplar preliminar, *Avance*, September 30, 1974, 8–9.

CHAPTER 14

Puerto Rican Feminism and the Young Lords Party

IRIS MORALES

> Feminism, like the ocean, is fluid, powerful, deep, and encompasses the infinite complexity of life; it moves in waves, currents, tides, and sometimes in storms. Like the ocean, feminism never stays quiet.
>
> —ISABEL ALLENDE, *THE SOUL OF A WOMAN*

Puerto Rican women have always been central to liberatory movements in Puerto Rico and in the Diaspora. In the late 1960s, Puerto Rican women joined the Young Lords Organization (YLO) to fight for the rights of Puerto Ricans in the United States and for the independence of Puerto Rico. Women also brought attention to the interconnecting oppressions of gender, race, class, nationality, and colonialism. In *Revisiting Herstories: The Young Lords Party*, I detail the rise of feminist activism in the organization from 1969 to 1972.[1] This essay introduces key ideas and several campaigns from that herstory.

Who were the women in the New York Young Lords Organization? Most of us were Nuyoricans—Puerto Ricans raised in Spanish-speaking, working-class homes. African American, Cuban, Dominican, Mexican, Panamanian, Puerto Rican–Filipino, and Puerto Rican–South Asian women also joined. We were sixteen to twenty-six years old. Among us were mothers with young children; students; workers; homemakers; survivors of domestic violence, alcohol, and drug addiction; and community organizers. English was our primary language, although most of us also spoke Spanish or Spanglish. Women were one-third to 40 percent of the members.[2] On our purple berets, we pinned a button that read "Tengo Puerto Rico en mi corazón" (I have Puerto Rico in my heart), exclaiming our love for Puerto Rico.

We didn't use the term "feminist," but we *were* feminists. At its core, feminism is the struggle for freedom. The plural, "feminisms," recognizes different experiences, theories, and movements that result from different class interests, geographical locations, and beliefs about the cause of oppression and the strategies to achieve justice. We were socialist feminists in the Black feminist tradition.

The Rise of Feminist Militancy in the YLO

As the Young Lords emerged in East Harlem in 1969, women played pivotal roles, organizing programs designed to serve the people. The needs of the community were overwhelming. Seeking to expand services, the Young Lords approached a neighborhood church to inquire about space for a free breakfast program and day care center. But the pastor, a Cuban exile, opposed the Young Lords' politics. He called the police, and thirteen people were arrested. Among them were Sonia Ivany, Elena González, Mirta González, and Denise Oliver. Ivany was the first woman to join the YLO in New York. She was Cuban, a veteran of the Young Lords' summer garbage protests in 1969,[3] and the mother of a baby girl. Mirta González, Puerto Rican, was also an early member and the mother of a young daughter. Elena González, Puerto Rican, and Denise Oliver, African American, were college students. The arrests prompted the Young Lords to take over the church and attracted hundreds of supporters. At the church steps, women members spoke passionately about dire poverty in the community. Inside, Iris Benítez, a young Afro-Boricua, explained the reasons for the church takeover to the press. The activism of young women of color inspired an exponential increase in the number of female recruits.

The Young Lords believed capitalism was a failed and declining system. Identifying as "revolutionary nationalists" and socialists, the organization's 13-Point Program called for the end of capitalism, racism, colonialism, and imperialism, but it did not mention patriarchy or sexism. Though the all-male leadership declared the Young Lords liberators of the Puerto Rican people and nation, they considered and treated women as inferior. Men assumed leadership as spokespersons and strategists and relegated women to subservient tasks. The 13-Point Program stated "we want equality for women," but what it described was an appeal to men to stop being chauvinist. It did not demand the end of the system of male domination.[4]

Naively, women in the YLO had assumed that men who identified as revolutionaries would support women's liberation. But this was not the case. As a result, the dominating machista ideas and practices led us to form a women's caucus. The original members were Iris Benítez, Lulu Carreras,

Martha Duarte, Nydia Mercado, Doleza Miah, Connie Morales, Denise Oliver, Olguie Robles, Cookie, Emma, Olgita, and myself. We sought to bring to light "a wrong, a point of view, or an urgent call for action."[5] "How can YLO leaders claim to be for the liberation of all oppressed people when they demean half of humanity?" we asked. "We joined the YLO to fight for the rights of Puerto Ricans, not to perpetuate machismo, parading under the guise of a Puerto Rican revolution." The women's caucus sought to unite all Young Lords in the struggle for women's liberation, to ensure that the future we were fighting for benefited both men and women. Otherwise, why should women remain in the YLO?

Feminism and the Revolutionary Nationalist Movement

As revolutionaries, we viewed our movement as part of a historical continuum dating back to slavery and colonialism in the Americas. Sharing knowledge and confidences, the women's caucus developed a feminist consciousness. We studied the oppression of Puerto Rican women and identified as "third world" and "women of color." The terms expressed our connection to women in Africa, Asia, and Latin America and their descendants throughout the world. Concepts such as "colonized mentality," "internalized oppression," and "nonconscious" ideology helped us analyze beliefs that promoted powerlessness, self-doubt, and negativity about our abilities, physical appearance, and skin color. We embraced the Black feminist analysis of "triple oppression," asserting that race, class, and gender were intersecting systems of oppression to be fought together. The feminism we defended was anti-racist, anti-capitalist, anti-imperialist, and anti-patriarchal.

The women's caucus of the YLO allied with women in the Black Women's Liberation Caucus, the Black Panther Party, the Third World Women's Alliance, the Brown Berets, I Wor Kuen, and other autonomous all-women groups. Through these exchanges, we became aware of the extent of sexist beliefs and practices throughout the social justice movement. Nationalist leaders pushed aside women's issues and concerns, claiming these would be addressed after the revolution. Feminists of color insisted gender justice was integral to revolutionary change, not an afterthought. In response, nationalists accused feminists of color of being saboteurs, and even traitors to the movement.

In this battle of ideas, the women's caucus submitted ten demands to the all-male central committee to transform the politics and practices of the Young Lords. The caucus demanded an end to the sexual objectification and abuse of women members. We were comrades, not walking body parts or mindless bodies. Several men ridiculed our requests as "a white woman's thing" foreign to Puerto Rican culture, as if women's liberation was solely for white women. Some men complained women were acquiring too much power, though they did not explain what they meant or feared.

The central committee declared feminist issues a detour from "real political work" and accused the women's caucus of divisiveness. Though a few leaders conceded our concerns were important, they said, "We'll address them *after* the revolution." In June 1970, the YLO became the Young Lords Party. The youngest male members, the teenagers, supported the women's caucus. With their backing, the YLP membership reached a consensus that men be held accountable for male chauvinist and sexist acts. Because of this victory, Young Lords were disciplined, suspended, or demoted for male chauvinist actions, including the central committee leaders.

Socialist feminist ideas and practices ascended. The YLP banned gender discrimination, in words if not always in deeds. *Palante*, the YLP's newspaper, published a document titled "Position Paper on Women," recognizing the integral role of Third World women in creating global social change. Women were promoted to leadership positions. A collective childcare policy enabled mothers to take part more fully in all political activities. The gender justice debate opened doors for LGBTQ people to join the organization.

Feminist Activism and YLP Campaigns for Healthcare and Prisoners' Rights

The Women's Caucus helped shape the Young Lords' organizing agenda, notably spearheading several health and criminal justice campaigns in 1970. We advocated for reproductive freedoms, including access to birth control and the right to legal and safe abortions. We mobilized to end the mass sterilization of women in Puerto Rico—where one-third of women ages twenty to forty-nine years old had been sterilized—and we declared it genocide.[6] The women's caucus organized protests, wrote articles, and engaged with the media, rallying support to end mass sterilization. Women in the YLP also united with the feminist of color movement in the United States to protest coerced and involuntary sterilization policies targeting African American, Native American, Chicana, Puerto Rican, Asian, and poor women across the country.

The push for health as a human right was central to the YLP. When administrators at Lincoln Hospital in the South Bronx announced budget and service rollbacks in 1970, the HRUM (Health Revolutionary Unity Movement) led organizing efforts. The HRUM was a network of hospital workers, primarily Puerto Rican and African American women. Closely affiliated with the YLP, leading members of HRUM were also Young Lords. Advocating for "worker-patient-community unity and control,"[7] organizers pressed for decent wages and working conditions and demanded preventive health programs in the community. Because women spent up to half their earnings for childcare, they demanded that the hospital finance "community-worker-controlled free day-care centers" in or near the hospital.[8]

On July 14, 1970, the Young Lords Party, joined by the HRUM, the Black Panther Party, the Lincoln Pediatric Collective, and others, occupied Lincoln Hospital in the Bronx to protest the budget cutbacks and demand improved healthcare. The takeover lasted twelve hours and brought national attention to the horrendous conditions in New York's public hospitals.

Five days after the takeover, Carmen Rodríguez, a mother of two, died at Lincoln Hospital from a botched abortion. An outraged public protested her death as evidence of genocide against poor women of color in the United States. Having just legalized abortion in 1970, New York was beginning to advance women's rights, but still it continued to fail poor and working-class women, as the Rodríguez case showed. Understanding the risks women of color faced in public hospitals, the YLP women's caucus advocated for the right to safe abortions, not just abortion rights. The caucus supported the right to abortion as a necessary option for women, who ultimately are expected to bear the financial, social, and emotional responsibilities of raising children.

In 1970, criminal justice also emerged as a major concern. Politicians pushing for "law and order" ushered in a get-tough-on-crime politics that fueled a zeal for imprisonment.[9] New York City's jails overflowed with poor and working-class African Americans and Puerto Ricans who could not pay bail. Prisoners fought horrific and overcrowded jail conditions and organized protests inside the jails.

During this time, a member of the Young Lords, Julio Roldan, was found hanged in a city jail. His death sparked community-wide protests. The Young Lords and other activists took over the People's Church with arms, demanding an investigation into the prison system.

During 1970, Afeni Shakur, Joan Bird, and Angela Davis were detained at the Women's House of Detention (the House of D). Thousands rallied outside the jail, demanding their release. Their imprisonment brought international publicity to political prisoners. They brought attention to the plight of poor and working-class women prisoners held primarily for crimes related to poverty, survival, and desperation. Feminists created a bail fund to secure release of detainees with low bails. The coalition included the YLP women's caucus, the Black Panther Party, Youth Against War and Fascism, I Wor Kuen, the Puerto Rican Student Union, and others. They developed relationships with women inside the prison and publicized accounts of the terrible jail conditions. They organized protests, raised funds, and produced bilingual legal information aids for detainees. The women's caucus wrote about the systemic cruelty poor women of color faced in the judicial system, such as lack of legal representation, sexual and racial violence, and other degradation. Our inside-outside organizing strategy broadened the prisoners' rights movement[10] and exposed deep-rooted racial and economic inequality, driving the growing prison industrial complex.

Today, Black, Latinx, and Indigenous women are "the fastest growing segment of the incarcerated population" and continue to be disproportionately represented and affected by mass incarceration.[11] The United States imprisons more women than any other nation, yet women in prison remain largely invisible.[12]

The Women's Union and Narrow Nationalism

By 1971, the feminist struggles in the Young Lords Party had entered a new phase. Central committee members announced that the independence of Puerto Rico was the YLP's primary mission. They opened two branches of the organization in Puerto Rico and closed the US storefront community offices.

In New York, the YLP's women's section organized a women's union, with a 12-Point Program advocating for socialist feminist ideas and the independence of Puerto Rico. The women's union grew rapidly through community activities, political education workshops, a bilingual newspaper, and collaborations with US feminists of color. Nonetheless, the central committee members dismantled the women's union, calling it a political mistake and instructing the Young Lords not to speak about sexism.[13] The central committee deprioritized gender and racial justice struggles, stating these would be addressed when Puerto Rico gained its national independence. Taking control of the women's union, the central committee members discarded the 12-Point Program and abandoned feminist organizing. By the end of 1972, the women's union no longer existed.

Present Struggles and Past Herstories

From the 1960s through the mid-1970s, the activism of African American, Chicana, Puerto Rican, Asian, and Native women created a bridge, linking past herstories and struggles to future justice movements. Feminists in the Young Lords Party pursued socialist feminist ideals and practices as part of this movement. The experiences of collective organizing and political analysis laid a theoretical and practical foundation for feminist of color activists in the United States. In 1974, Black feminist lesbian socialists formed the Combahee

River Collective and published a statement in 1977 that remains central to feminist socialist politics today. In 1974, women in the Puerto Rican Socialist Party helped form the Committee to End Sterilization Abuse. El Comité in New York formed the Latin Women's Collective in 1975. Chicana feminists produced writings that inspired interest in women of color feminism. The anthology *This Bridge Called My Back: Writings by Radical Women of Color* was published in 1981. These legacies affirm that gender and racial justice must be essential goals of *all* revolutionary movements. The socialist feminist activism of the women in the Young Lords charted new ground in the Puerto Rican diaspora. Today we continue to grapple with similar concerns still very much present.

Iris Morales is a lifelong activist and educator committed to social justice and the decolonization of Puerto Rico. She is the author of *Revisiting Herstories: The Young Lords Party* and *Through the Eyes of Rebel Women* and producer of the documentary *¡Palante, Siempre Palante!* As the founder of Red Sugarcane Press, she develops projects highlighting the Puerto Rican experience. She holds a JD from NYU Law School and an MFA in Integrated Media Arts.

Notes

1. Iris Morales, *Revisiting Herstories: The Young Lords Party* (Red Sugarcane Press, 2023).
2. Judy Klemesrud, "Young Women Find a Place in High Command of Young Lords," *New York Times*, November 11, 1970, 78.
3. For an explanation of the garbage offensive, see Johanna Fernández, "When the Young Lords Put Garbage on Display to Demand Change." *History.com* (blog), September 15, 2021, https://www.history.com/articles/young-lords-garbage-offensive.
4. The Women & The American Story website highlights the interventions made to the 13-Point Program by the women's caucus; see "Fighting Machismo," Women & The American Story, The New York Historical, accessed April 4, 2025, https://wams.nyhistory.org/growth-and-turmoil/feminism-and-the-backlash/fighting-machismo/.
5. Kathryn Blackmer Reyes and Julia E. Curry Rodríguez, "Testimonio: Origins, Terms, and Resources," *Equity and Excellence in Education* 45, no. 3 (2012): 525, https://doi.org/10.1080/10665684.2012.698571. The authors link the use of testimonio to liberation efforts and anti-imperialist movements in Third World nations.
6. Darrel Enck-Wanzer, *The Young Lords: A Reader* (New York University Press, 2010), 165. See also Iris Morales, "Sterilized Puerto Ricans," *Palante* 2, no. 2 (1970): 8. Reprinted in *Palante* 2, no. 10 (1970): 5.

7. Ritch Whyman, "How Do We Fight Racism and Capitalism?" *International Socialists*, February 1, 2012, https://www.socialist.ca/node/745.
8. Health Revolutionary Unity Movement, "Ideology," 11–12, author's personal collection.
9. Sarah Childress, "Michelle Alexander: 'A System of Racial and Social Control,'" *Frontline*, April 29, 2014, https://www.pbs.org/wgbh/frontline/article/michelle-alexander-a-system-of-racial-and-social-control/.
10. Afeni Shakur, "Women's House of Detention," *Palante 2*, no. 17 (1970): 3.
11. Emily L. Thuma, *All Our Trials: Prisons, Policing, and the Feminist Fight to End Violence* (University of Illinois Press, 2019), 4.
12. Michele Goodwin, "The New Jane Crow: Women's Mass Incarceration," *Just Security*, July 20, 2020, https://www.justsecurity.org/71509/the-new-jane-crow-womens-mass-incarceration/.
13. Young Lords Party Central Committee, "July 1971 Retreat Paper," 6, in author's personal collection. The paper summarizes activities from January 1 to June 3, 1971.

Sí Es Goya

MELINDA GONZÁLEZ

Abington Avenue, Newark, New Jersey

mi abuelita never spoke a lick of english
she would say, *¿para que? si tu me entiendes.*
in her cocina—she would boil fish heads
let me suck their eyes out
slurp guarapo, savor tamarindo
her house—it was Moca, Puerto Rico
en Newark

abuela was an operation bootstrap baby
as in pick yourself up by the bootstraps
as in save a little bit of everything
as in count your pennies and your blessings
as in bendiciones at every hour, every minute, every conversation

abuelita was a divorcee when it wasn't cool
a catholic woman who held mass in her living room
sewed her own batas, made her own tea
con azúcar que empalaga
always had food on her stove
kept our bellies full

abuelita was a mother
a mother of 8+ children
a grandmother of 30+ something
a great grandmother of many more she never got to see

abuelita was a sexile[1]
a woman left—found herself a new husband
brought sunshine in the middle of winter
always gave me un beso and then un peso para candy

abuelita was todo que tiene que ser bueno
and so many things i never understood
a pioneer, displaced
making home so far away from home

Melinda González is a poet, scholar, and sociocultural anthropologist born and raised in Newark, New Jersey, with ancestral roots in the lush mountains of Moca, Puerto Rico. Her forthcoming book examines the multi-scalar displacements Puerto Ricans face after Hurricane Maria, exploring how colonialism, systemic neglect, and environmental crises drive both internal and external migration, while highlighting emerging forms of decolonial resistance and survivance. Dr. González is an assistant professor at Georgetown University's School of Foreign Service.

Note

1 The term *sexile* refers to experiences of alienation alongside the pursuit of selfhood and freedom in a society structured by restrictive gender and sexual norms. See Vanessa Pérez Rosario, *Becoming Julia de Burgos: The Making of a Puerto Rican Icon* (University of Illinois Press, 2014).

PART IV. OUR INTIMACIES

CHAPTER 15

Manifesto for My Feminist Mother

AURORA LEVINS MORALES

Rosario Morales,
August 23, 1930–March 23, 2011

I could write a book. I can see it, see myself sitting on my bed surrounded by stacked volumes bristling with index cards, like she did during those years when she mined the feminist writings of other women, not as an intellectual exercise, not to be well read or accredited. She was looking for tools that could smash stone, break down the structures of domination, crack open the silences, free us. I could write chapters and chapters about the movement men who betrayed her and themselves, clutching their superiority and contempt as if they were precious pearls; their patrimony, their property, tearing huge rifts in the fabric of solidarity, and then blaming us, women, Black and Brown and Indigenous people, poor people, for being "divisive" when we objected.

I could write a book about her, the woman who birthed me, taught me to read and write, taught me how to fight for myself, fought for me and taught me to fight for others, taught me how to sew and bake and make ceramic pots and woodcuts, to drink tea and name all the colors of her paints. The woman who shouted, drank, smacked me, criticized me, who read aloud to us every night, who gave me books by women, took me to the Chicago Women's Liberation Union at fifteen, kicked me out of home at sixteen, made sure I had birth control, neglected me, raged about sexism in my presence, stopped drinking because she blacked out during a long phone call with me and refused to lose me that way, told me "Read this": Alice Walker, Toni Morrison, June Jordan, Jamaica Kincaid. Raged about racism, wept about genocide and war and poverty. I could write a book, but there isn't time.

There are people who say she was sweet and kind. She could be kind, but sweet was not her flavor. She was savory and picante, she was ajo con pimienta, she was hot-and-sour soup, she was bitter chocolate and smoky Lapsang souchong. Sure, she could light up with pleasure at the colors of the world. She got joy from forests and small acts of justice. She painted, made prints, knitted, embroidered, quilted, studied women's fiber arts like maps toward liberated territory. Like stars you could follow. Learned to wield every kind of needle and brush. Made beauty. Played with us. Loved the peace of her gardens. Made green mango chutney and banana bread.

But this is also true: My mother had a mind like a razor, sharp and critical, and sometimes it spread to her tongue. Whatever she was told not to read, told was incorrect, taboo, wrong, she immediately went and read. Making up her own mind. Building it from scratch.

She was a collective bullshit meter, other women turning to watch her face, to navigate by her frown. My father fell in love with her challenging questions first, then her face. She could smell mentiras, detect even microscopic quantities of crap, and she wasn't having it. She knew what she knew, and she learned to say so.

It wasn't always that way. As a child, she lived under the heavy hand of her autocratic father, in the swirling melodrama of her mother, and she was a good girl, well behaved, quiet, escaping to church for solitude, the one place she was permitted to go by herself. My fury for her begins there, in the steam and heat that simmered under the lid of her goodness.

From "I Am the Reasonable One," which she wrote for *This Bridge Called My Back*.

But now I tell you reasonably, for the last time, reasonably, that I am through. That I am not reasonable anymore, that I was always angry, that I am angry now.

That I am puertorican. That under that crisp english and extensive american vocabulary, I always say mielda. I say ai mami, ai mami giving birth. That I am not like you in a million ways that I have kept from you but that I will no more.

That I am working class and always eat at the only table, the kitchen table. That taking things is not always stealing, it's sometimes getting your own back, and walking around in my underwear is being at home.

Figure 1. Rosario Morales and Aurora Levins Morales, 1986.
Photo courtesy of Linda Haas.

I will be loud and vulgar and angry and me. So change your ways or shut your racist mouths. Use your liberal rationality to unlearn your contempt for me and my people, or shut your racist mouths.

I am not going to eat myself up inside anymore. I am not going to eat myself up inside anymore.

I am not going to eat myself up inside anymore.

I am going to eat you.

Her parents were from the foothill town of Naranjito, in long descent from early colonizers, both of them children of formerly enslaving, landowning families who had gone careening down the class ladder in the 1920s and landed in Harlem in the fall of 1929. Harlem and then the Bronx. She was born into hunger and hard work, poverty mixed with class attitude, the sense of superiority they clung to even though they had to lie, say they were Italian, to get an apartment. They were de buenas familias. At least they were not like the titeres all around them. At least they were not Black.

Africa waters my tree, she said. *I feel safe in rooms full of dark-skinned women,* she said.

She was born into a patchwork of immigrant communities, each with their boundaries, flanking the public libraries that were her other escape. The Irish and Italians beat her up on the sidewalks, so she found refuge among Eastern European Jews, some of them second- or even third-generation, some of them just off the boat, with Hitler's armies only a few steps behind them and stories of children lost along the roads.

She learned Yiddish, learned to eat and cook Ashkenazi food, and when she and Moira were stoned on the street for being Jews, she went home sobbing, saying, *no Mami, I'm not crying because they thought I was a Jew. I'm crying because they stoned us!*

She was a good student. She wanted to do physics and also theater. She was a sharp cookie. Then she was eighteen, still being spanked by her violent father for coming home late from a date where she fought off a rape attempt, but she enrolled at Hunter College, following scent trails of ideas that led her to Marx, and she said, "This makes sense of my life."

So she went to a young communists' evening of music and talk, and found my Brooklyn Ukrainian Jewish commie father, who had been raised by a feminist grandmother. Then she found the communist women, a few years older than her, who taught her to ask the millions of questions hidden inside "the Woman Question," and gave her the word *feminism*.

This is not an authorized biography. This is a manifesto by a daughter enraged on behalf of a mother she feared and adored, admired, fought, and from whom she inherited an extensive and beautiful tool kit for both survival and joy.

She was fervent in her radicalism. She said being raised Catholic made her a good communist. *Communist* with a small *c*. She had purpose, she had a lifelong comrade, she had more books to read, women to think with. Then my father graduated from studying math and genetics to being blacklisted, and the Korean war began, which no way was my father going to fight in, and they sat on a park bench in Ithaca imagining prison would part them soon, so why not go to Puerto Rico and learn her country? And because they were still blacklisted in Puerto Rico, Jane Speed, a white communist from Alabama who became my mother's best friend, said, "Buy land. That way you won't starve." So they did.

They did, and then I was born, and she felt suffocated by my infant needs, overwhelmed by night feeding and diapers and later my endless desire for her attention, for stories, for play, all while she and my father, two New York

Figure 2. Rosario Morales in Puerto Rico, 1960s.
Photo courtesy of Aurora Levins Morales.

City kids, tried to learn how to farm, and there were roundups, and machista men, and my father commuting to a lab in Río Piedras, where he could do experiments even if he couldn't get a job. That's when she began to drink. She didn't go on benders. She just sipped, all the time, and raged, a lot of the time at me.

She saw the nonsense of the Communist Party (CP) view of coffee workers, treating them as if they were Russian peasants, not laborers in an export coffee industry, more hungry for wages than land, so she and Papi wrote up a new rural organizing policy, which was accepted because nobody much cared. I didn't witness how the CP men treated her. I was too young. I was a week-old baby in her arms when the Nationalists shot up congress and the arrests began. But a decade later, I saw how the men of the 1960s Puerto Rican left came to sit at my father's feet, and she would speak, and two minutes later they would credit my father with her words. I saw that.

Here are some excerpts from her scathing short story, "Unseen,"[1] about a woman fighting to become visible in the left circles of a fictitious Latin American island nation.

She was an excellent hostess, thoughtful, self-effacing and nurturing. Pale young lawyers, mustachioed cultural gurus, callow revolutionaries, mathematical near geniuses, and multicolored social butterflies of all sexes lounged against her upholstered furniture and hand-woven pillows, among her statuettes and doilies, drinking, sneering, laughing, shouting, eating, necking, destroying reputations, puncturing egos and generally enjoying themselves. She moved softly among them, extinguishing cigarettes, replenishing drinks, re-refilling plates, extracting stilettos, applying band-aids, and restoring shoes, unseen and unheard . . .

She often tried to join in their discussions on the political future of their island home of San Felipe; did so with verve and energy. Really! The hopes these experienced young revolutionaries placed on the next election, their fresh-minted faith in that old sinvergüenza they were putting up for office. And in this country where every man with a political corpuscle in his bloodstream mentally refurnished La Casa Blanca while he shaved in the morning, and rehearsed the betrayal of his supporters in his best English while he brushed his teeth. She told them so, reminded them that while Don Alonzo was ancient history, Pedro del Campo de Fuego was just last year.

She could have saved her breath. Papo and Willie and Manolo started a shouting argument in High Left Jargon right in the middle of her second sentence and drowned out even her thoughts . . .

Occasionally they'd nod toward the corner they thought she was in (often when she was standing right in front of them). Or they'd ask Miguel how Marucha and the kids were doing (even though she was sitting at Miguel's side). Several times she was hurt rather badly when one or the other of them tried to walk right through her and knocked her down. She'd gotten very good at jumping out of the way quickly when any of them got up to use the bathroom or started to sit down on her. It kept her physically fit, but in a permanent state of mild anxiety . . .

And then jumping to the end:

Her voice became louder and fiercer, a tornado of a sound, that peppered them with truths that stung like hornets, so that they slapped at their ears and jumped about, waving newspapers at the words that buzzed at them from the air; so that they ran from them, jumped off the veranda, raced through the living room and out the door, past the slow smile that bloomed gently on Miguel's face.

In the middle of this period of her life, we were in New York, in the late '50s, and she got fired up by leftist anthropologists who first ignored and then encouraged her, and dreamt of a feminist radical anthropology in her own hands. It was an age of decolonizations, new sovereignties, repression and possibility side by side. I was about to turn five when Batista fled Cuba and all the colonized people of the world sat up straighter, and new movements sprang up everywhere like flowers after rain.

I was ten when the letter came, an invitation to my father to help the University of Havana create a revolutionary biology department. She jumped up and down and clapped her hands. She knew it was an invitation to her as well, to immerse herself in the effervescence of change, to find the Cuba of Haydee and Celia and Vilma. They parked us with friends and family for a month and came back energized, happy, lit up. So, four years later, when they asked my father back to teach, she said she wanted to spend that summer researching the conditions of Cuban women's lives, to make it part of her anthropology studies, and they said, yeah, sure, they would set up contacts, resources, make it happen.

But when we arrived in that blazing summer of 1968, all they had arranged for her was to cook and clean and care for her children while el profesor did the important work. I think it broke her heart and made her tired. We kids were busy exploring Havana, riding buses, going swimming, eating Cuban ice cream at Copelia, and she didn't talk about it very much, but I think it did break her heart and make her so weary. I want those dismissive men to rise from their graves and stand trial for her disappointment, for her grief, for the rage that had nowhere to go.

You can only glimpse it here, in her reasoned response to an anti-feminist article by a socialist woman claiming that the women's liberation movement was divisive, a distraction, self-absorbed:

We are half the world. There is not one struggle that we could not divide by asserting our rights. How many times have we fought side by side with men, only to be shuttled aside in the victory? What divides is not the fight against sexism, it is sexism itself. Sexism dooms half our fighting forces to the stove when the other half picks up the rifle, to the mimeograph machine while they lead the march. This is not the time or place to plead with women to enter into "comradely struggle" with working class men around their sexism. It is the time to plead with men to enter into revolutionary struggle with their sexism so that more and more women can also "become the real leaders of the united front against imperialism and the struggle for socialism."

Then there was anthropology, at the University of Chicago. We had moved there in 1967 because my father was denied tenure in Puerto Rico and Mami wanted to dive into anthropology, which she'd been studying in summer school in Michigan. She didn't tell me this until later, when I was grown, but she also wanted me the hell out of the Puerto Rican countryside, where my schoolmates were getting pregnant, all the women I knew had too many babies, and a bunch of them had alcoholic husbands who knocked them around. She wanted me to know women who did other things with their lives.

I know what she encountered in the university because I encountered the junior version. I was at the University High School, swimming in smug, elitist, racist liberalism, pushing back on a dress code that said I couldn't wear pants because girls don't, encouraged to become a credit to my race among the white children of wealthy suburban families, cultured academics, and finance executives, a handful of Black doctors' kids and the pale Brown offspring of Peruvian or Colombian elites. But that was small potatoes compared to what happens to a working-class radical Puerto Rican woman in her late thirties married to a professor, which in their eyes meant *faculty wife*, and why couldn't she take up flower arranging instead of bothering the big boys at their serious colonial labors? They called the people they studied "eths" and "gooks." "Gooks" was what US soldiers called the people of Vietnam they were busy killing. She drank more and more, unable to bear it.

One day when I was sixteen, I was standing in her room, watching her in profile as she got dressed for a departmental Halloween party. She was in the middle of writing about the Caduveo people of the Amazon, shredding apart the racist nonsense of Claude Lévi-Strauss, who was like God around there. She was reading about all these peoples who had been decimated, but nobody talked about murder, they just wrote papers, theorized about customs, congratulated themselves and each other. I was standing where I could see the lines of her nose, her sloping forehead, her high cheekbones. Then she took an eyebrow pencil and began drawing on her face the Caduveo designs that Lévi-Strauss said were signs of their arrogance, which, according to him, was what led to their demise. As she painted her face, I saw the Indigenous woman in her step into the stark light of day, saw her declaration of allegiance to the eths and gooks, to the Caduveo, to the Arawak in her, how she made her face into a banner, shouting that it was the arrogance and greed of European invaders, the thing no one would name, that killed people. *See me*, she said. *My ancestors were the first ones in the Americas to face you. Look at me.*

I remember her paper on the Pawnees. How she drew and colored in a medicine wheel on the cover of the folder. She knew whose side she was on.

So, she took them on. She wrote in scathing critique and ridicule about structuralism, about these European men making up stories about Indigenous peoples whose names they were always confusing with those of other people, passing their judgments on "savages," in this case, on the "uncivilized" face-painting practices of the Amazonian Caduveo. Years later, after reading a structuralist analysis of Taíno myth, I called her up and said, "Am I missing something or do they just make shit up and then quote themselves to prove it's true?" and she said "Yes!!! That's exactly what they do!"

She wrote *Tropes Tipique*, flipping the title of one of Lévi-Strauss's famous books: not *Triste Tropique*, sad tropics, but typical tropes. They held onto her thesis for a year, the sneering committee, and when they finally returned it, there was a note tucked in that said, "Let's give her the damn degree. At least we'll be rid of her." She framed it and hung it up beside her diploma.

I take a deep breath and imagine her being celebrated in a building full of feminist anthropologists, female working-class Puerto Rican scholars, Black and Brown women who read books. She is getting an award for her coraje, her chutzpah, her slicing through the self-justifying machista colonizer drivel. Rosario Morales, Decolonial Anthropology Foremother. I want a prize in her name for intellectual courage. A decade later, on her way to do research on what makes women angry, she ran into one of those nasty men, and erupted into flames on the page.

No wonder I drank. I've never written these words before in sober daylight. I'd scribble incomprehensibly, drunkenly, in large penciled letters on pads of paper or in small script on little strips which I would find in the morning. I'd write after staying up drinking, talking to myself in the mirror, shouting angrily at Yalman, Turner, Schneider, at Levi-Strauss and Malinowski. Then I would write about Pawnees dying in the thin winter sunlight, coughing up blood, or Polynesians dying on the beach in the Pacific, shot by passing whalers, or Caduveo dying of Spanish gunshot. I wrote about Wounded Knee and Canyon de Chelly, places I had names for, and all the beaches and valleys and rocky plains in Africa, in Canada, in Australia, on the Pacific Islands, on the Caribbean Islands, in tropical South America, in Arctic North America, places for which I had no names. A soundless litany of death by exploration, of death by pacification, of death by manifest destiny, of death by pioneering and frontiering and private enterprising, of death by hardworking, god-fearing farming and gold-rushing, of death by capitalist expansion in the sixteenth, seventeenth, eighteenth, nineteenth, and twentieth centuries.

Let me tell you about the . . . fish dolphin. When this fish is killed, pulled out of its life-giving water and asphyxiated in the life-denying air, it changes colors as it slowly chokes to death . . . They say as it dies it turns beautiful colors, iridescent blue to electric green to dark purple to purple red. All over its body these colors pulse while we watch.

Anthropologists watch murdered peoples die and look at the colors of their customs, the movements of the rigor mortis. And the emotional ones write vivid descriptions, the methodical ones take meticulous notes, the scientific ones make careful measurements. All the while the dolphin dies, the people writhe as their mothers die or their children or their friends, and we write and publish and get promoted, give or receive prizes and grants, and we never mention pain or sorrow or anger or death.

I tried. It's like describing the contents of an unflushed toilet at a garden party. That's what it all was: one prolonged tea party serving dying dolphin. It's no wonder I felt sick to my stomach all the while, that I was always angry, angry all the time while I smiled, while I wrote papers on Levi-Strauss and his playful toying with myths and rituals, with women's lives and women's kin, while I drank and drank and drank.

Drink deadens the pain, and now I don't drink and the pain returns undeadened, unalloyed, clear, and punishing. How can I bear it? How do you mourn endless numbers of people in endless numbers of places? . . .

I feel guilt for not shouting it out, for not screaming in their ears, not making endless scenes, burning their papers, their buildings. Bertolt Brecht said, "These are indeed terrible times when to talk of trees seems a kind of silence about injustice."

To talk about concepts of pollution is more than a kind of silence about injustice: It is a lie about murder. That's what anthropology is—your anthropology Turner and Levi-Strauss, your University of Chicago, Harvard, Yale—a lie about murder, an intellectual necrology, a crime.

But wait. We need to go back in time to the beginning of the books, to the public library, to the copy of *Hamlet* her father found on the street and brought home to her because she loved to read, and then turn around and walk hand in hand with her, forward through the alphabet, through pens with black ink and manual typewriters to where my mother writes *C-A-T* on a piece of paper, and the magic of written language floods my mind with illumination; *this*, I say to myself, *this is what I want to do forever!* And I do. I write poems in first grade, fill notebooks, devour the writings of a wild array of others, write and write and write through all the turmoils of migration, adolescence, relocation, movement politics, relationships. Meanwhile Mami fills notebooks with her ideas and feelings, writes letters to movement publications, scribbles her thoughts on legal pads, through all the years she said she was a feminist without a movement. But now it's 1970, and women are bursting into print and writing about their own lives, and we do it too. We do it in call-and-response, reinforcing each other's voices. This is feminist mothering.

Now it's 1978. I am spending the San Francisco summer as an interviewer for Diana Russell's first-ever randomized study of the prevalence of rape. *What makes women angry?* There is a cohort of women of color, each of us assigned to interview in the neighborhoods of our kin. In the evenings, we gather and tell stories of our tokenization on dozens of panels where we "represent." We dream up an agency called Dial-A-Token, share the nonsense we've been told about each other. Everything about my life explains how I

Figure 3. Rosario Morales performing. Photo courtesy of Aurora Levins Morales.

got into these rooms where I meet Cherríe Moraga, and built a writing partnership, and why, in 1981, my mother and I stand together on the dais of the Arlington Street Church in Boston with eight other women, presenting *This Bridge Called My Back* to an audience more numerous than the fire code allows. The first print run sells out in three weeks. Suddenly we are public writers. We can get paid to say what we think at colleges and universities. My mother tells everyone she is Boricua, as Boricuas come from the isle of Manhattan. She says, "I am what I am. Take it or leave me alone."

My mother, Sari, starts getting invitations to read at bookstores, at schools, at cafés in Cambridge, Boston, Vermont, sometimes New York, but she doesn't like to travel. I do, so I get around a lot more. We include each other's writing in our readings. One day Mami reads in Ithaca, and Nancy Bereano, future founder of Firebrand Books, is in the audience. Three days later, my mother calls me up to read me a letter in which Nancy invites us to write a book together. So, we do. The cover is a quilt my mother made. My father pays for the extra cost of a full-color reproduction. "Concepts of Pollution" hits the printed page. She writes true stories about her family, about trees, about love and rage, about the spaces she was pushed out of. There is room on the page. She writes her critique of Judy Chicago's famed *Dinner Party* installation, dreaming up the other dinner party, in the kitchen, with Brown women of all continents:

This is the dinner. We don't know our forebears' names with a certainty. They aren't written anywhere. We honor them because they have kept it all going. All the civilizations erected on their backs, all the dinner parties given with their labor. And they gave us life, kept us going, brought us to where we are. Come! Lay that dishcloth down. Eat, dear, eat. There will be time later, and hands enough, for the cleaning.

When did my mother begin to take charge of her health? Bring feminism and anti-capitalism and ecology home to her own body? It might have been when my friend Shannon's mother, Irene Custer, what in the 1960s people called a "health nut," gave her advice from her own experience about nutritional support to stop drinking. Irene told her to take B vitamins and read Adelle Davis. Mami did what she always did with a problem to solve, a challenge to meet. She started a notebook, read books and articles, took notes, made a plan.

She never took a medication without researching it in *Worst Pills, Best Pills*, a book and then a website run by health professionals with a conscience, full of well-documented information on side effects, interactions, scams. She gave it to me, along with a power drill, for some rite of passage into young adulthood. She and my father taught me how to read scientific papers and understand the tricks you can play with statistics. How a drug that doubles the survival rate for a terrible cancer, and actually makes you wish you were dead, might just double your chances from 1 percent to 2 percent. She taught me to say no to doctors, something my father, who could face down HUAC (the House Un-American Activities Committee) and the FBI, could not do. She said unnecessary tests led to cascades of more tests, procedures, medications. That there was no reason to get tests that were not actionable. She knew CT scans were overprescribed because hospitals had to justify the expense by plenty of use. She knew the birth control pill was dangerous, so when I needed contraception, she managed to get me the old-fashioned Lippes Loop IUD, not usually given to women who hadn't given birth, because she was suspicious of the sadistic-looking Dalkon Shield and the biochemical risks of the copper-T—a good call, since copper activates epilepsy.

It was in the late 1980s that she and a group of her kick-ass friends took on cancer as a feminist ecology and public health issue. They formed the Women's Community Cancer Project, working to expose the environmental causes of cancer and their particular impact on women. She had a crew of fierce feminist women with whom to apply her critical mind to a real woman-killing issue. In 1998–99 they collaborated with artist Be Sargent to create a mural in Harvard Square commemorating twelve female activists who had died of cancer, depicting common carcinogens and lifting up the precautionary principle that environmental contaminants are, unlike humans, guilty until proven innocent.

But in the 1950s in Puerto Rico, chemistry, including the recycled chemical weaponry of WWII, was supposed to lead to "better living" for all. It was to be an age of miracles. DDT and parathion were sprayed in the streets to eliminate the mosquito bite, and children ran laughing in the poison clouds. DDT, lindane, dieldrin, my father would come home covered with white powder and throw his farming clothes in the wash with my mother's blouses, my diapers. It had to have been in those first years on the land—her presence there a direct result of the anti-communist blacklist—that dieldrin first lit its long fuse in my mother's cells. Long, slow, deadly.

It was a colonial death, a woman's death, a death from political repression and capitalist industrial farming and reckless environmental destruction. It took fifty years. In 2002 she learned that her noncancerous blood cell condition, known as MGUS (monoclonal gammopathy of undetermined significance), had evolved into multiple myeloma, that defective plasma cells were starting to fill her bone marrow. Eventually her bones began breaking. She fired the first oncologist, who wanted to test her every month, follow every step the cancer took. She said, no, the disease would not become the center of her life. She was what the doctors call "smoldering," in a slow-burn stage that isn't treated. She found a new doctor, one who agreed to test her once a year and only tell her results that would lead to doing something. She went into remission and then came back out. The next step was a chemo that would have made her life miserable. So she called us all up and told us she was done. She had her list of people she would tell herself, and then we could spread the news while she "got on with the business of dying." Her doctor said six months, but Mami wasn't having it. She died three weeks later.

She was in her bed, no longer speaking, and anxious people were buzzing around her trying to do something, anything. Should we give her pain meds, and if so, how much? Should we turn her to prevent bedsores? The hospice nurses had made it clear she didn't have that much time. I said, STOP. I said, no one is going to do anything that she doesn't explicitly consent to even if it takes twenty minutes for her to summon up the energy to nod or shake her head no. I was standing near her head, so I got to hear the very last thing she said: "Mmm hmm." In other words, "Damn straight!"

There is so much more to say about the kind of Boricua feminist she was, about all the different women's voices she carried with her, her invisible gang of sisters, living and dead, about her practicality, her humor, her no-nonsense, her loathing for and refusal of family obligations; about all she accomplished and all she was kept from accomplishing.

About how I hold the complexity of her story, the pleasure she got from life, her friendships, her generosity, her art-making, her endless delight in language—reading *The Oxford English Dictionary* for fun, reading dictionaries of slang, looking up obscure words in old novels, calling me up to tell me she'd found a great one (the last one was *finifuge*, a person who flees endings!)—and how much she enjoyed thinking, using her mind, asking questions, probing, saying, "Yes, but . . ."

About the harshness in her, how I want to understand its roots, the criticisms with which she lashed herself as well as others. About her anxiety, about depression as anger turned in on itself, about her violence and our entanglement.

About the clarity and enduring value of her political thought, her passion for an all-inclusive liberation, the words she set to paper. Her illustrated article on the "Origins of Racism," with tiny figures decorating the margins of the pages. Her commitment to whatever democratized life.

About the haunting silences where she was shut down, after the doors shut in her face, and what she might have told us as a working-class Harlem Boricua about Cuban women in the ninth year of the revolution. About what kind of anthropologist she might have become, what other lies and distortions she might have broken open to reveal new insights, the unpredictable discoveries in her unfinished book on the bromeliads of Puerto Rico. Who she could have grown into if feminism had been stronger and more radical, enough to successfully face down the men who despised us, if it had grown into the better, stronger, richer movement where she could have thrived. I am crying as I write this, infinitely proud of her, loving her and wanting so much more for her, for myself, for us all.

I will not have her disappear. I will not have it. As I am writing this, thunder is growling in the Caribbean sky. Rain is roaring on the roof. I feel the heat of her story burning in my belly. I want to grind my teeth, but I know it's not good for them. Mami always said it was important to take care of your teeth, how tooth decay could make you sick, how early malnutrition had left hers weak, and I have inherited her easily damaged ivories. Instead, I grind out words. *How dare you. Civilizations on our backs. I will eat you. She was what she was. Take it AND leave her alone.*

I could write a book. Maybe I will.

Aurora Levins Morales (b. 1954) is a prominent Puerto Rican Jewish writer, independent scholar, and lifelong liberationist, with a doctorate from the Union Institute in women's studies and history. She is the author of nine books, including two collaborations with her mother Rosario Morales, the subject of this essay. Her book *Remedios* is a feminist retelling of the history of the Atlantic world, centered on Puerto Rican women's lives, and written in prose poetry. Her book *Kindling* is an important disability justice text. Her work has been widely anthologized and has been translated into seven languages. She writes and farms in Maricao, Puerto Rico.

Note

1. Rosario Morales and Aurora Levins Morales, *Cosecha and Other Stories* (Palabrera Press, 2014).

CHAPTER 16

"M'ija te quiero dejar saber": A Testimonio of Gratitude to Young Moms

MELISSA COLÓN

Esto es un testimonio de amor, un momento de agradecimiento, a thank-you, a todas las mamas Boricua jóvenes. I dedicate this to Amaya,[1] Bianca, Crystal, Isa, Jahlys, Karelys, Kayla, Luz, Mia, and Nancy, ten young moms who shared their testimonios with me[2] and taught me so much about mothering and resistance. This, too, is dedicated to my primas, tias, amigas, compañeras, de ahora y de mis antepasadasas, who were young mothers themselves and whose stories echo those of the testimoniolistas. In the spirit of testimonios, cuentos, aguinaldos, plenas, bombas, and all truth-sharing ancestral epistemologies and critical knowledge movements, I begin by sharing my own testimonio and the origins of this project. I then discuss foundational sabidurías, wisdoms, that emerged from the testimonios, mapping what I learned to the complexities and beauties of Boricua feminisms. My work is guided by gratitude, as I know that there is so much to share and learn, and that the testimoniolistas themselves are always better equipped to tell their own stories.

I did not know it then, but I grew up surrounded by the warmth and love of a thriving Puerto Rican community. My childhood was spent in the rural community of San Diego, Coamo (Puerto Rico), whose residents were, largely, landless agricultural workers—this a legacy of genocide, slavery, and settler colonialism. Many children of these workers, including my father, Miguel Colón Espada, ultimately migrated together, to the Boston area to work in factories. It was there that I was born—but like so many Boricua children, I lived aquí y allá, allá y aquí. No matter where we were, we gathered almost every Sunday in celebration. Church, quinceañeros, parandas, bodas, barbeques, baby showers, cumpleaños, funerals, and what felt like hundreds of no-reason hangouts in people's crowded living rooms, just because we wanted to be together. In almost every single one of those gatherings, there was a mamá joven with her child or the child of a young mom. Despite their everyday and ordinary presence in our lives, there persisted a resounding silence about their existence because a young pregnant body is subversive.

Puerto Rican women have long resisted colonial ideologies that center on chastity, submission, suffering, protecting one's reputation, and desiring above all else to be a mother in a patriarchal home. However, these ideals continue to play a role in conceptions of gender roles and behaviors in Puerto Rican communities.[3] This is particularly salient when we consider que es una nena buena. Isis, a friend who had her first child at seventeen, described how others viewed her as follows: "Eres un puta if you become pregnant. Eres una irresponsible y una mala if you have an abortion, but if you have the baby, sigues siendo una puta, una irresponsible, y una mala."[4] Isis's experience speaks to the convolutions of being a young Boricua mother. As these mothers strive to make decisions about their own bodies, colonial ideologies at the nexus of gender, class, and religion press upon those decisions, producing a "conventional wisdom" that there is no winning for young women who stray from expected norms regarding sex, sexuality, age, and motherhood.

Isis's experience and that of other young mothers I came to learn from is also consistent with hegemonic narratives that have long positioned young Black, Indigenous, and Puerto Rican mothers as deviant and hypersexualized, their choices and children deemed irreparable.[5] Young Boricua mothers have particularly been constructed as responsible for the erosion of "traditional" American family values and as perpetual drainers of public coffers.[6] They have long been subjects of policy debates and punitive social interventions whose primary focus has been to control their bodies and reproductive choices, because having a child "out of order" presents a violation of what is socially acceptable and "developmentally appropriate."[7] Yet, at the co-construction of heteropatriarchy, racism, nativism, classism, and colonialism stands the young Boricua mother—a subject who has failed to assimilate to colonial rules that govern women's bodies.[8] A robust body of feminist scholarship maps how the state and its conspiring colonial institutions in Puerto Rico and the diaspora are mechanized against the autonomy and self-determination of Boricua mothers.[9] This literature stands against dominant public discourses that vilify Puerto Rican motherhood, particularly young Boricua mothers.

Yet despite majoritarian constructions of pregnancy and parenting during adolescence as deviant, teen parenting is quite ordinary. Historical, longitudinal, and cross-cultural analyses suggest that adolescent "sexual activity and pregnancy in the past, as well as presently, have been considered normative, expected, and almost universal occurrences."[10] While rapidly changing, across cultures and contexts, for most of human history, having a child before the age of twenty-one has been the norm rather than the exception, including in Puerto Rican communities. As documented in the research of esteemed Boricua scholar Cynthia T. García Coll, Puerto Rican communities, particularly Boricua women, do not adhere to a dominant framework of "incompetence" or "deviance" if a woman has a child before the age of twenty.[11] To be clear, the existing research does not suggest that Puerto Rican families encourage or want their adolescents to become parents at an early age. Rather, there appears to be a cultural orientation among Puerto Rican families that with the right supports in place, motherhood during adolescence does not signal a permanent crisis.[12] Having the support of one's loved ones, however, does not protect young mothers from the punitive gaze and material consequences of colonial, gendered, racialized, classed, and anti-teen-mother attitudes writ large.[13] As the testimoniolistas taught me, mothering under these conditions is not for the faint of heart; resistance in the shape of Boricua feminisms lives there.

I came to better understand this form of resistance after I had the opportunity to work on a research project focused on teen moms. In many ways, I am the "opposite" of a young mom. I arrived at motherhood reluctantly, filled with fear, pain, and grief. The words *geriatric pregnancy* and *high risk* are splattered across my medical records. This was especially apparent when I started my doctoral studies while pregnant, with a four-year-old son, and as a "nontraditional doctoral student" for many reasons, including the fact that I was "older." I still remember the looks of awe and shock I received as I waddled around campus with mi pansa y mi nene holding my hands. I was treated gingerly and with contempt, with tenderness and disappointment. I was described as courageous, always with a strong hint of condescension. It was a very lonely time in my life, as I spent most of my waking hours with people who knew and cared very little about Boricua children and families, the center of my life and scholarly interests.

But then something shifted. As part of my program requirements, I was placed in a lab that was conducting a randomized longitudinal mixed-methods evaluation[14] of a statewide home-visiting program designed for first-time adolescent parents in Massachusetts. The project included thousands of qualitative and quantitative data points spanning seven to eight years, including interviews of program participants. I discovered that almost one in five of the program participants were Boricua young women, and their words quickly became part of my thinking. I was hungry to learn more about their lives; in the loneliness that is academe, I was inspired by their words, their stories—how they persisted through schooling while parenting, facing challenges much more difficult than those I was encountering. Their communities, families, and lives felt deeply familiar. I knew that they had so much more to say than what was included in the interviews, and I had much more to learn. To do so, I developed a testimonios project that focused on the schooling experiences of young Boricua mothers. When I met the testimoniolistas, they were now in their twenties. While our project focused on schooling, their narratives and teachings provided me with important insights into Puerto Rican feminist praxis.

"Standing Up to the Man"

> I kept telling them over and over during the meeting, Don't you hear yourself? Every time you guys keep talking, you guys keep saying, "we think." Well, guess what? That whole "we think" can go in the trash because you don't think the way that I do. I'm not going. I'm staying in this school, and I'm going to graduate from this school.
>
> —KAYLA

All the testimoniolistas involved in our project were teenagers enrolled in high school when they each gave birth to their first child. Yet to protect their lives and those of their children, they had the formidable task of having to stand up against the heteropatriarchal power of the state[15] while still being minors. As young women, with young children, who were all economically precarious, they were expected to navigate complex public systems, including the healthcare system, public housing, school districts, employer relations, and the nonprofit industrial complex. These "systems of care" colluded to weaponize benevolence, saw the young mothers as failures, and pushed them to give up, to disappear.[16] Without much of a choice, the young women had to learn to advocate for themselves.

Kayla, one of the testimoniolistas, shared how she gradually built the courage to stand up to government officials and advocate for herself. Personal experience had taught her how deceptive and sophisticated these governmental systems could be. When she was sixteen, the Department of Families and Children (DCF), working in conjunction with the criminal "justice" system, decided to "lock her up" because Kayla had a violent altercation with her father—after she stepped in to protect her mother from him. Kayla spent years being afraid of DCF and tried to do everything right so she would not be taken away from her mother again. When she found out she was pregnant in her senior year of high school, she was terrified that DCF would want to control and surveil their lives, so she came to believe that the only path forward was to take them and their conspirators head-on. Though she earned good grades at school, when administrators learned of her pregnancy their first response was to transfer her to a special program for pregnant mothers. They wanted to get rid of her, but Kayla refused. With the support of her mother, Kayla wrote letters, made phone calls, and attended meetings where she continuously questioned the school agents' intentions and refused to accept their decision. Eventually, they "let" her stay—a win for Kayla.

All the testimoniolistas shared countless stories of how they had to "stand up to the man" to subvert the power of various authorities. Karelys, for example, found herself trapped in a perpetual policy limbo. Because she was a minor at sixteen years old, she often needed her legal custodial parent—whom she did not live with and who was largely absent from her life—to grant her permission to access services she needed for herself and her baby, including housing. With the support of friends, she eventually found a loophole in the legal custodianship policy and was able to secure housing. Later she worked for a nonprofit organization helping other first-time parents "beat the system." Crystal, another testimoniolista, had to file a complaint against her local public school system when they failed to enroll her in school, time and time again, despite her having completed all the necessary steps. Nancy had to check in with a truant officer and the principal when she was labeled as "missing" school due to being ill, and was eventually threatened with police arrest. Bianca became an expert on the rights and services for special needs children when her premature baby began demonstrating worrisome symptoms, which everyone but her was ignoring. They were all just teenagers at the time of these confrontations.

While the control of sexual reproduction is often used as the most apparent colonial intrusion into Puerto Rican women's bodily autonomy, this control must also be understood within the context of other state institutions.[17] Dangerous intrusions from schools, healthcare systems, and other state apparatuses into Puerto Rican women's lives are not a past phenomenon; they are ongoing and present in our ordinary lives, and our resistance to them is an "urgent, daily, embodied struggle."[18] Further, Boricua feminists have taught us that the exploitation and racism that Puerto Rican women endure is directly connected to how colonialism is mechanized in Borikén, first by Spain and now the United States, and that these violent entanglements affect the lives of women on multiple levels both in Puerto Rico and the diaspora.[19] As such, the testimoniolistas' efforts to advocate for themselves exemplify these embodied struggles that help to destabilize colonial powers.[20] Important to underscore, while none of the testimoniolistas in this project called themselves organizers, activists, or even feminists, they nonetheless stood up to the state, just like hundreds of thousands of Puerto Rican mothers before them, including other mamás jóvenes, serving as living examples of el espíritu de la lucha.[21] They are living proof that the work to destabilize coloniality is life work, community work, which seldom happens alone—most often including a praxis of helping others.

M'ija Te Quiero Dejar Saber: Community Care, Mutual Aid, and Reciprocity

> Our people are set up to help. You come across somebody and that person's like, m'ija te quiero dejar saber que esto es bueno; they are familiar with it, and they tell you, listen I'm familiar with this, go and get it.
>
> —KARELYS

Our work together began in January 2017, nine months before the catastrophic climate, political, and humanitarian crises of Hurricanes Maria and Irma. In the aftermath of those disasters, the world witnessed what we have always known, that "community is our best chance of survival."[22] At this juncture, the Boricua feminist practice of solidarity and mutual aid was pivotal in the lives of young moms. Aid took many shapes, including collaborative economics through the provisions of shared housing, transportation, food, and childcare, as well as encouragement and advocacy. In their first year after having a baby, the testimoniolistas were most likely to receive critical support from their mothers, who in large part showed up to help their daughters. They provided food, shelter, and childcare so that their daughters could attend school; most importantly, they provided a sense of home and belonging. As their children grew, the testimoniolistas' roles shifted; rather than primarily receiving aid, they began to provide aid to others. They served as caregivers for siblings and other children so that family or friends could attend school and/or go to work. They also contributed to the functioning of the family home by cooking, cleaning, serving as translators and navigators, and, when possible, contributing financially. The testimoniolistas also reported that they found out about education and social programs from family or friends, who either had participated in the programs themselves or knew someone who had. Once they determined a particular program was a worthwhile opportunity, they told others about it and did so with cariño. As Karelys further explained, "Everything I've learned, I've learned from people who have gone through it. Those are the people who have helped me. I don't need someone who's read a book. I could sit down and read a book myself."

Karely's skepticism of people who claimed expertise with little to no lived experience was shared by other testimoniolistas. The young women did not perceive the social workers, school administrators, program staff, and other state actors they encountered as naturally altruistic. Rather, the testimoniolistas told me that it was precisely these individuals who were often responsible for creating roadblocks that impeded the testimoniolistas from accessing critical resources and services. Amaya, who had her first child only a year after migrating to Boston from Puerto Rico, theorized that the challenges placed before her by schools, housing authorities, and even her own family were like a "mountain" that no one expected her to overcome. She said,

> I am a person that finds it really tough to give up. You tell me I can't do it, and I'm like, just to mess with you, I will do it. You don't know how to climb that mountain. I will be scared to death, but I will be on top of that mountain. When I'll get down, I'll be like, shoot. Scoot down, but I'll do it.

When I asked what helped her to persevere against the "mountains" in her life, she said,

> I went through a lot of things, but it was like every time it felt like I was going to be done, there was always be [*sic*] somebody that said "Hey Amaya, we got this, what do you think?" Yeah, that's exactly what I needed! Never give up.

Certainly, we can argue that the mountains should not have been there—but there they were, and there they are. In their struggles to overcome them, the testimoniolistas recognized the importance of both receiving and offering help "to our people." Their recognition and embodiment of practices of solidarity reminded me of the stories I learned about my grandmother Juana Espada Espada and other women like her. She was a go-to person in our barrio, known for helping others, especially those who had just given birth. My father recalls that despite their family's dire poverty, his mother, mi abuela, continuously found space in her life to help others. And she was not the only one who manifested an ethic of community care. He also recalls other women from the barrio, who showed up to help when his mother needed it most. Mi abuela did her best to live a joyful life and was a fierce cantante de música jíbara. My father wrote this short aguildado in her honor:

> Mi vecina a mí me dijo
> Que su finca quería sembrar.
> Y yo rapido le dije
> Pues yo le voy a ayudar.
> Estuvimos todo un día
> Sembrando sin descansar.
> Solamente nos sentamos
> A la hora de almorzar.
> Mi vecina muy contenta, hasta me quería pagar.
> Le di un abrazo y le dije
> Yo vine para ayudar.

The testimoniolistas were helpers and also open to receiving help. Their commitments to community care, mutual aid, and reciprocity reminded me of the importance of these Boricua feminist practices in our everyday ordinary lives. Decolonial Boricua feminist practices demand that we continue to reimagine labor and care, particularly when it pertains to the responsibilities of family life. Mutual aid and reciprocity are not only important forms of solidarity; they are also central to decolonial efforts and resistance movements in the face of government inaction and violence, unconditionally necessary for our survival and futures.[23]

Open Secrets and Joyful Resistance

There's nothing that's going to stop us.
—MIA

Primarily, I worked with the testimoniolistas in their homes. They lived in different communities across Massachusetts, so, naturally, their homes were all different. Some were extremely tidy, where everything shined and was perfectly placed. Others looked very lived-in, with books and peluches on the floor, blankets on the couches, or piles of laundry waiting to be put away. Some had yards with trees and holiday decor on their doorways; some had balconies looking out into the busy city streets, and some had none. Whether they lived in a house, a triple-decker, or an industrial city apartment, the homes shared one thing in common: an abundance of sweetness and joy poured into celebrating Boricua childhoods.

The testimoniolistas filled their homes with photos of their children. There were pictures of children in sports teams, with family members, and of course, impeccably dressed and smiling for school pictures. The photos were hung neatly on the walls, stuck to fridges and propped on tables, tucked in the testimoniolistas' wallets, and glowing as their phone backgrounds. Many of the mothers had made impromptu altars for their children, including flowers, pictures of family, school calendars with important dates, souvenirs from family trips, magnets with their faces, and countless certificates and ribbons their children had received. There were baskets full of toys and tiny shoes by doorways. Sometimes, during our interviews, the testimoniolistas would pull out photo albums, digital and print alike, to show me important events in their lives, like their baby showers, high school or college graduations, baptisms, and weddings. Several participants showed me tattoos of their kids' names or birthdays on their bodies. I never asked to see any of this, but they always wanted to show me their children and families, and they also asked to see mine. One photograph permanently etched into my mind is that of Kayla on the day before she gave birth to her baby. A teacher had taken her picture by a classroom's doorway. She was wearing denim overalls and a striped yellow shirt. Most importantly, Kayla was holding and pointing to her belly, smiling ear to ear, while also staring deeply and directly into the camera: proud, happy, and filled with grace.

The testimoniolistas spoke to me about how proud they were to be Boricua and how they wanted their children to feel the same way. Flags, coquis, and other Puerto Rican paraphernalia were in almost all the salas and cocinas I visited. Spanish, Spanglish, salsa, hip-hop, and reggaeton almost always found their way into our visits. In one kitchen, a mom had perfectly laminated labels of everything, in English and Spanish: Puerta/Door, Ventana/Window, Horno/Oven. She wanted her kids to be bilingual, even though she "didn't speak Spanish well." Another mother shared that she and her husband saved for three long years so that they could take their two kids to Borikén. In addition to the everyday labor of being a mother, they also saw themselves as keepers and transmitters of culture; this was important work and a source of joy.

Much has been written about how shame is animated in the lives and identities of Boricuas, especially women and cuir folk. Negrón-Muntaner traces the archeology of shame, despair, and unworthiness to colonial domination and its afterlife in the Boricua experience.[24] And while shaming is a form of social control that has, in part, been used to pathologize Puerto Rican communities, there has always been resistance to it—particularly in how we choose to let go of shame and reclaim our identities.[25] The young mothers whose lives shaped mine resisted shame. Their pregnancies were open secrets that drew state actors and others to aggressively stigmatize them and take away their opportunities for advancement, including the right to pursue an education while pregnant or parenting. The testimoniolistas were aware that others wanted to wound and shame them, which at times did make them feel embarrassed about having to tell people that they were pregnant, that they were "another Puerto Rican teen mom." However, they did not allow these feelings to overpower how they felt about their children, themselves, and motherhood.

Mia was the youngest of all the testimoniolistas I met. She had just turned fifteen when she found out she was pregnant. Her strict religious parents had not known she had ever kissed a boy, let alone that she had a fourteen-year-old boyfriend. While Mia and her boyfriend were incredibly worried about both of their parents' responses, after some initial shock, their parents came together and told the young mother and father that they would help them with their baby so that they could finish school. Mia and her boyfriend promised each other that nothing would stop them from finishing their education. With the support of their families, they both graduated and continued their education, both receiving vocational training that later helped them earn stable incomes. Nine years later, they were still together and had another child. During our last meeting, Mia was in the middle of cooking a huge calderón of arroz con gandules, several perniles, and guineos verdes. As this was the first week of January, later that evening, she and her family were going to celebrate el Día de los Reyes. Under her Christmas tree were gifts for her kids.

When master narratives about Puerto Rican children, youth, and families are largely about what is wrong with them—what is wrong with us—the testimoniolistas vigorously choose to celebrate their children, to find joy, to live love. The commitment and careful attention to celebration and joy is a reminder of Boricua feminist praxis, which teaches us that part of resistance is our ability to continue to exist, to create, and to find joy even while experiencing the grips of colonialism. This "embodied persistence and pressing-on" is a form of decolonization, as our endurance destabilizes "every facet of colonial power" and allows us to reimagine our futures.[26]

Conclusion

In my work on teen mothers, I always find it maddeningly necessary to remind people that:

Teen
Mothers
Are
Human.

So, forgive me, mamás jóvenes, for having to say this again for the people in the back.

In sharing the testimoniolistas' stories and what they taught me, I do not aim to idolize or romanticize teen motherhood. First, motherhood is intensely and unjustly laborious. Being a Boricua mother under the imperialist white supremacist capitalist heteropatriarchal state[27] can at times feel impossible to do well, especially for Black, Indigenous, and Boricua young women, who are particularly vulnerable to state intrusions. And while motherhood was at the center of our project, "mother" is not all that the testimoniolistas each are, nor all they want to be, nor all they will be. Neither is "mother" all that we, those of us who are committed to liberation, aspire to be or need to be. Motherhood, under colonial regimes, is a tenuous experience. For those of us who can choose this path, it can complete us, limit us, heal us, hurt us, and liberate us at the same time. Young mothers are also, like all of us, complex human beings who dream, who love, who have regrets, who meet goals, who disappoint, who impress, who succeed, and who also fail. As such, mothering while young is further complicated by enduring constructs of gendered notions of what is appropriate, alongside the structural and social supports, or lack thereof, that sustain communal and intergenerational well-being, joy, and freedom.

In this work, my goal is to contribute un granito arena toward depathologizing, complicating, and, most importantly, decolonizing our understandings of Puerto Rican adolescent bodies, sexualities, and motherhood. Within all these complications, the testimoniolistas' lives offer us critical standpoints of a liberatory Puerto Rican feminist praxis. Their ability to stand up against colonial systems that aim to harm us, their willingness to contribute to ongoing solidarity efforts that center mutuality and reciprocity, and their commitments to honoring themselves and their children, to seek and claim joy wherever it lives, all amplify feminist practices. Their testimonios, their lives, and, yes, their children, provide living examples of resistance; together they cocreate a canon of sabidurías and anti-colonial liberation strategies that are foundational to Boricua feminist futures.

To all young Boricua mothers, whose love exudes, explodes, and reimagines our futures—a love so rebellious that it stands against colonial ideologies and their regulations of acceptability and respectability; against a state that wishes them, and therefore us, harm—I say gracias. Gracias mamá, mami, mom.

Melissa Colón is a former schoolteacher and organizer, now an assistant professor of urban education, leadership, and policy studies at the University of Massachusetts Boston. Her work largely espouses critical community-based participatory approaches to learn about the schooling lives of Black and Latine urban public school students. Her latest project takes on disasters, racism, and abolition in urban schooling. She is coeditor of the anthology *Critical Perspectives on Latino Education in Massachusetts*, forthcoming with University of Massachusetts Press.

Notes

1. Pseudonyms have been used.
2. The testimonios were collected as part of a mixed-method longitudinal study on the schooling experiences of young Boricua mothers. As such, some sections of testimonios shared here have been previously published. See Melissa Colón, *"We Are Beautiful People": The Schooling Experiences of Puerto Rican School-Aged Mothers* (Tufts University Press, 2019).
3. Norma I. Cofresí, "Gender Roles in Transition Among Professional Puerto Rican Women," *Frontiers: A Journal of Women Studies* 20, no. 1 (1999): 161–78, https://doi.org/10.2307/3346999.
4. Other teen moms have also shared with me that the term *puta* has been used to injure them.
5. Laura Briggs, *Reproducing Empire: Race, Sex, Science, and US Imperialism in Puerto Rico* (University of California Press, 2003); Patricia Hill Collins, "Black

Women and Motherhood," in *Motherhood and Space*, ed. Sarah Hardy and Caroline Wiedmer, 149–59 (Springer, 2005); Wendy Luttrell, *Pregnant Bodies, Fertile Minds: Race, Gender, and the Schooling of Pregnant Teens* (Routledge, 2003); and Wanda Pillow, "Teen Pregnancy and Education: Politics of Knowledge, Research, and Practice," *Educational Policy* 20, no. 1 (2006): 59–84.

6. Nathalie A. Augustin, "Learnfare and Black Motherhood: The Social Construction of Deviance," in *Critical Race Feminism: A Reader*, ed. Adrien Katherine Wing, 144–50 (New York University Press, 1997); Chris A. Barcelos and Aline C. Gubrium, "Reproducing Stories: Strategic Narratives of Teen Pregnancy and Motherhood," *Social Problems* 61, no. 3 (2014): 466–81; Laura Briggs, "La Vida, Moynihan, and Other Libels: Migration, Social Science, and the Making of the Puerto Rican Welfare Queen," *Centro Journal* 14, no. 1 (2002): http://www.redalyc.org/resumen.oa?id=37711290004; Briggs, *Reproducing Empire*; Luttrell, *Pregnant Bodies*.
7. Nancy Lesko, *Act Your Age! A Cultural Construction of Adolescence* (New York: Routledge, 2012), 135–45.
8. Melissa Colón and Sabrina Vaught, "Testimonialistas' Self-Determination: Boricua Mothers and Colonial Schooling," *Feminist Anthropology* 3, no. 1 (2022): 75–91.
9. See, for example, Briggs, "La Vida"; Briggs, *Reproducing Empire*; Elena R. Gutiérrez and Liza Fuentes, "Population Control by Sterilization: The Cases of Puerto Rican and Mexican-Origin Women in the United States," *Latino(a) Research Review* 7, no. 3 (2009): 85–100; and Iris Ofelia López, *Matters of Choice: Puerto Rican Women's Struggle for Reproductive Freedom* (Rutgers University Press, 2008).
10. Cynthia T. García Coll and H. A. Vázquez Garcia, "Definitions of Competence During Adolescence: Lessons from Puerto Rican Adolescent Mothers," in *Adolescence: Opportunities and Challenges*, ed. Dante Cicchetti and Sheree L. Toth (University of Rochester Press, 1997), 294.
11. García Coll and Vázquez García, "Definitions of Competence"; and Cynthia T. García Coll, "The Consequences of Teenage Childbearing in Traditional Puerto Rican Culture," in *The Cultural Context of Infancy*, ed. J. Kevin Nugent, Barry M. Lester, and T. Berry Brazelton, 11–132 (Ablex, 1989).
12. Barcelos and Gubrium, "Reproducing Stories"; García Coll and Vázquez García, "Definitions of Competence"; Melissa Colón, "'We Are Beautiful People': The Schooling Experiences of Puerto Rican School-Aged Mothers" (PhD thesis, Tufts University, 2019); and Lillian Comas-Diaz, "Mainland Puerto Rican Women: A Sociocultural Approach," *Journal of Community Psychology* 16, no. 1 (1988): 21–31.
13. Colón and Vaught, "Testimonialistas' Self-Determination."
14. The critiques of this approach for minoritized communities, which I did not know at the time, are well documented.
15. Audra Simpson, "The State Is a Man: Theresa Spence, Loretta Saunders and the Gender of Settler Sovereignty," *Theory and Event* 19, no. 4 (2016),

https://muse.jhu.edu/article/633280?casa_token=Qhimp6ULx7IAAAAA:v38vxDwcUHb7bNSeHr9z32N-qLCsrRGtPvUrR46_4QsTKzvoZqRS8-6Vljh_WWZO3oeMy1pWzyw.
16. Colón, "'We Are Beautiful People.'"
17. Briggs, *Reproducing Empire*; Gutiérrez and Fuentes, "Population Control by Sterilization"; and López, *Matters of Choice.*
18. Heather Montes Ireland, "Decolonization Is Imminent: Notes on Boricua Feminism," *Feminist Formations* 35, no. 1 (2023): 20.
19. El Comite de Mujeres Puertorriqueñas, "In the Belly of the Beast: Puertorriqueñas Challenging Colonialism," in *Sing, Whisper, Shout, Pray! Feminist Visions for a Just World*, ed. M. Jacqui Alexander (EdgeWork Books, 2003).
20. Montes Ireland, "Decolonization Is Imminent."
21. El Comite de Mujeres Puertorriqueñas, "In the Belly of the Beast."
22. Christine Nieves, "Why Community Is Our Best Chance for Survival: A Lesson Post-Hurricane Maria," TEDMED Talk, 2018, https://www.tedmed.com/talks/show?id=731041.
23. Aurora Santiago Ortiz, Antonio Navarro Pérez, Paulette Agosto Ortiz, Coralis Cruz González, and Michelle Román Oyola, "'La solidaridad no perece': Community Organizing, Political Agency, and Mutual Aid in Puerto Rico," *Curriculum Inquiry* 52, no. 3 (2022): 337–50, https://doi.org/10.1080/03626784.2022.2072669; and Karrieann Soto Vega, "Puerto Rico Weathers the Storm: Autogestión as a Coalitional Counter-Praxis of Survival," *Feral Feminisms*, no. 9 (2019): 39–55.
24. Frances Negrón-Muntaner, *Boricua Pop: Puerto Ricans and the Latinization of American Culture* (New York University Press, 2004).
25. Negrón-Muntaner, *Boricua Pop*; Clara Rodriguez, Irma M. Olmedo, and Mariolga Reyes-Cruz, "Deconstructing and Contextualizing the Historical and Social Science Literature on Puerto Ricans," in *Handbook of Research on Multicultural Education*, ed. James A. Bank and Cherry A. McGee Banks (Jossey-Bass, 2004), 288–313; and Clara E. Rodriguez, Virginia Sanchez Korrol, and José Oscar Alers, eds., *The Puerto Rican Struggle: Essays on Survival in the US* (Waterfront Press, 1984).
26. Montes Ireland, "Decolonization Is Imminent," 21.
27. bell hooks, *Outlaw Culture: Resisting Representations* (Routledge, 2006).

CHAPTER 17

Tlazocamati y Bendición: For the Chicana and Boricua Women Who Paved the Way

BEATRIZ HERRERA

> But the identity of being a mixed person is really hard.
> Being a Caribbean person is really hard.
> Being a magical person is really hard.
> —DESTINY FRASQUERI, AKA PRINCESS NOKIA,
> IN CONVERSATION WITH BROWN UNIVERSITY

"Mexican and Puerto Rican? Diache, que combinación."[1] I heard this phrase countless times as a child in NYC. Growing up, I didn't know a single other Mexican *or* Puerto Rican family, let alone one like mine, and often felt culturally distinct from my neighbors in Harlem and elsewhere on the Upper West Side of Manhattan. My parents' strict parenting style didn't help my sense of belonging either. I wasn't allowed to just chill on the stoop with my friends or sleep over at anyone's house. Unlike my neighbors, we didn't throw large family parties, blast salsa or bachata from our windows, or spend entire summers in PR or DR with grandparents or extended family. As a young girl, I felt confined, restricted, and caged. I dreamt of freedom, friendship, and adventure away from their watchful, worried eyes.

I do remember visiting both Mexico and Puerto Rico as a child with my family on separate occasions. I was only five when I visited Mexico, so the memories are vaguely marked by the smell of charcoal and tortillas, water bugs, and eating pan del pueblo at my Tío's house, a red sugar-coated bread that makes me salivate even thinking about it now. Puerto Rico, on the other hand, was not dry but wet, and smelled like fresh cut grass and my Tío's lechón rotating on a spit. Even at eight years old, I remember admiring my beautiful blonde-haired and green-eyed cousin, who moved confidently through land and sea. She lent me her two-piece bathing suit—a revealing suit my Mami would never let me wear at home. Not to mention, I couldn't swim. I covered my midsection with one arm. I used my other hand as a Band-Aid to protect my leg against the gnats feasting on a scratch I got from a piece of driftwood. I curled into a ball and sat miserably on a rock by the water while my cousins splished and splashed. This Diasporican was no match for Island life. When I finally got my full-piece bathing suit back a day later from the clothesline, my mom made sure I wore panties underneath "por si acaso." Just in case what? I wondered.

Mami only went to school until the third grade. Once, and only once, she told me about how teachers would make fun of her for showing up to school in a muddy uniform and dirty feet—a testament to her miles-long trek to school from her home in the campo fleeing barking dogs and crossing barbed wire. Mami didn't like talking about those things, however. From her, I learned a true Puerto Rican woman was vivacious, playful, bubbly, strong-willed, energetic, and rarely tired, in a bad mood, or focused on negative things. When I was growing up, Mami liked to tell me punny jokes, and would even write them down on little scraps of paper and leave them for me around the house. Every once in a while, she still sends me little chistes via text. Recently, Mami sent me this one, that she got from my Titi in Puerto Rico:

> Mami: ¿Que hacía una ratita en una esquinita?
> Me: No sé Mami
> Mami: Esperando un ratito jaja get it?
> Me: Jaja sí Mami that's a good one

One night when I was young, my dad came home with a request from a coworker—could we videotape *West Side Story* when it played on PBS? I became enchanted by this televised Nuyorican rite of passage. I hit rewind and play over and over again, watching Rita Moreno's purple dress whirl and spin like the reels of the tape. She shook her skirt like a Boricua matador, and I knew that Rita was no juanaboba. I wanted to be just like her. I learned to put on a brave face during times of struggle, editing diary entries with footnote happy faces and explanatory redactions for anything that sounded too negative—just in case my parents would read it. I felt consistently surveilled by both my helicopter parents and my Catholic all-knowing God. The smiling mask I wore, as big as a vejigante, hid the sense of fear and anxiety that wracked me from childhood.

My perpetual worry intensified when my dad started to suffer from a debilitating illness with no diagnosis. My only escape from the household stress was school. I never missed an assignment or day of school from kindergarten through high school and excelled in every subject, winning spelling bees and art, poetry, and writing contests. When my dad went into his fourth brain surgery my junior year of high school, my anxiety turned into a full-blown panic disorder. I didn't feel safe anywhere. Despite my mental health issues, I got into college on a full ride, and never really looked back.

I went to a private liberal arts college in upstate NY, my first time entering a space of enormous wealth and privilege. I felt like Dorothy in *The Wizard of Oz* when the film turns from black-and-white to color. She wasn't in Kansas anymore, nor was I in Harlem. Tom Hanks walked into my dorm on moving day and asked for a light bulb. Three weeks later, 9/11 happened; along with a few of my peers who had family in the city, I desperately attempted to call home, but all lines were down for hours. I was terrified but also felt guilty because I was glad to be away from the city at the time of the attacks. I searched for other Latino students like me, to survive not just that moment but my new environment. I joined on-campus student of color organizations. For the first time in my life, I met Chicanos from Los Angeles who were politically conscious and demanded an ethnic studies curriculum at our college. I wondered, who taught them to be so bold or imagine such a possibility? Through them I built relationships with not just other Chicanos but also other self-described half-a-Ricans. Being with them felt like my true home. We struggled, laughed, cried, drank, had breakdowns, survived, and even excelled in college *together.* I felt politically and almost spiritually connected to these Chicanos and half-a-Ricans in a way that I had never felt with any community before. Tlazocamati[2] to my first-generation-college family.

A year later, at a conference at Yale, I was sitting in the back of an auditorium when I saw a presentation about the artwork of Chicana artist Yolanda López. Her painted series, *Guadalupe*, where an elderly seamstress sews the Virgen's blue-starred cape, struck something inside of me, and I felt tears well up in my eyes. My own paternal grandmother was named Guadalupe and for so many of us, the Virgen represented our maternal Indigenous ancestry mixed with our colonized Catholic side. Everyone began to file out of the auditorium, but I wouldn't leave. I couldn't take my eyes off the images. I knew I wanted to be near and around this type of work—this art, our history, my people—forever.

After lunch, I remember a few of the Chicanos from other campuses made fun of me for not knowing what horchata[3] was. They laughed dramatically, and although I was somewhat embarrassed, as a half Nuyorican, their opinion of me felt off. In my head I thought of listing food and drinks that would be foreign to them. Would they know the difference between a morir soñando[4] or a Malta?[5] Their critique was bizarre within the larger Afro-Caribbean diaspora in the Northeast that I was used to. I knew they likely would feel othered themselves, outside of the West Coast, so I did my best to let it go. Suerte raza.

In moments where I didn't feel like I belonged, I turned to my Puerto Rican side to steady me. Mariposa Fernandez's "Ode to the Diasporican" poem became a prayer, a mantra, and a song that played on repeat in my mind whenever my Boricua identity was under some type of contestation or scrutiny. I imagined this was true for many Nuyoricans familiar with her work. I still hear her voice and thick Bronx accent whenever I recall her words:

Mira mi cara Puertorriqueña
A mi pelo vivo
A mis manos morenas
Mira mi corazón
que se llena de orgullo
Y dime que no soy Boricua.[6]

Some people say I'm not bonafide
Cuz my playground was a concrete jungle
My Río Grande de Loíza
Was the Bronx River
Cuz my Fajardo was city island
My Luquillo, Orchard Beach
And summer nights were filled with city noises
Instead of coquis . . .

What does it mean to live in between?
What does it take to realize
that being Boricua
is a state of
mind a state of
heart
a state of soul . . .

"Sooooouuuuullll," she lingered, over the last word. I feel a familiar tingle in my heart whenever I hear her draw out those vowels, the same feeling my mom implanted in me as a child when she made sure I knew that I was Boricua. I have learned to recognize that feeling as love and pride wrought from pain and struggle. It's the fight my mom instilled in me, her voice sometimes trembling, as she described que "somos Puertorriqueños," and that no one could take that away from her, me, us, even in our mixed family. With every tiny and large flag that decorated her bedroom, with every enthusiastic scream for her favorite Yankee, Puerto Rican Bernie Williams, with every sip of her coffee and buttered crackers, Mami taught me to love myself as part of her bloodline. She established in me a deep sense of belonging with our extended family on the Island while living on an island of our own, Manhattan. What a gift. Bendición,[7] Mami.

After I graduated, I moved to El Barrio because I wanted to be in close proximity to both Mexican and Puerto Rican communities. I began volunteering at an organization working with street vendors, most of whom were undocumented Mexican immigrants. I found joy in working with this community in the heart of Spanish Harlem. I visited the music stores filled with salsa records, ate pastelillos from the cuchifrito spot, and walked down Tito Puente Way to my tiny apartment. Me persignaba regularly whenever I left or came back home, because El Barrio was dangerous, and I suddenly felt newly Catholic. I witnessed robberies and police car chases with guns drawn, and I heard about neighbors being shot nearby. I passed large groups of men at night who eyed me up and down, and it was the only time in my life I was called a spic. Aren't we all spics in Spanish Harlem? I thought to myself. Still, I preferred to live there than to go back home. In El Barrio, I was free.

One day while volunteering a staff member told me he was going to spend an evening at an event for a local artist known as La Bruja, aka Caridad De La Luz.[8] La Bruja was powerful and also beautiful, and when I discovered her album *Brujalicious*, I became obsessed. I must have listened to her album over a hundred times. I would play it for anyone who would listen. I even burned it into the iTunes libraries of all my friends' laptops. They must have thought I was crazy. I thought it would change *their* lives too, but I didn't realize that she wouldn't mean as much to them as she did to me, for reasons that had so much to do with my own positionality in the world.

La Bruja's music made me feel seen, centered, like I belonged, like I was included as a young, vulnerable, scared Diasporican woman with no real political mentors to look up to in NYC. La Bruja mixed salsa and hip-hop with spoken word poetry in Spanglish to narrate a survival guide to Boricua womanhood in NYC. In the manic "Olvidate," a group of men boast and threaten each other with violence, and La Bruja interrupts them with the following bars:

Si tu llegaste aqui pa' pelear
yo no yo llegue pa' bailar,
pa' vacilar yo se, yo se que
tienes razón pa' pelear pero
yo te haré olvidar,
disfrutar, olvidar.[9]

the only thing I clap is my hand
I wanna see peace throughout the land
To make you comprender
el amor es algo espiritual
nada puede comparar
con un día lleno de alegría
esta cultura es la mía
La Brujita armada con una sonrisa un placer, nice to meet ya
maybe I could teach ya
how to relax, sit back and forget that we under attack.[10]

La Bruja's spells had alchemical powers; she could somehow transform energy from negative to positive. Bruja's masculine vocal timbre and delivery conveyed a seriousness and strength of character distinct from her more feminine and warm lyrics. Her message revealed a role Boricua women have played for decades in the face of urban violence, patriarchy, and colonialism: mediators, handlers, life-force conveyors, bewitchers, and mess cleaner-uppers. Garnered through oppression, Bruja's positive message was not Pollyanna-ish, it was strategic: Let's try to have a good time before someone gets hurt (and we women are left to pick up the pieces). We knew the fates of Maria and Anita in *West Side Story* all too well.

I decided I would try to see if I could meet La Bruja at her documentary film screening in Brooklyn a few months later. I arrived at the venue early and sat at the bar awkward and alone, the place nearly empty. After about a half hour, from the corner of my eye I could see someone who looked like Bruja near the projector screen. I hid behind my drink and when I looked up again, she seemed to be peeking out from behind a pillar, playing hide-and-seek with me. I couldn't believe what was happening. Was she really playing a game? Finally, she inched her way over and sat next to me at the bar. We spoke for a little bit, and while I don't remember our conversation, I remember feeling like she was looking out for me, as an older sister would. We took a picture together on my little disposable camera that I had brought just in case the occasion arose. I kept that picture for many years. I'll never forget what that encounter meant to me. I learned that support could be sweet, playful, and fun, existing even between strangers and fangirls. Bendición, Bruja. In my heart, you will always be a good witch from the Bronx.

I was offered a job in California, and I left Afro-Caribbean New York for Aztlán. Some of the Chicanas and Central American Latinas I encountered demanded I display my street cred. "Who are you? Where are you from?" they asked immediately and often. "Why? Is there a problem?" I would ask, my tone bemused. I asserted my cultural and geographic credentials easily;

I had been questioned about my identities, in both curious and aggressive ways, since childhood. I had also learned over time that just claiming New York and Puerto Rico carried weight, especially to people who had never left their neighborhoods. An older Salvadoran woman, who should have known better, told me that I was not a real Puerto Rican and that, in fact, she was more Puerto Rican than me because I was nothing like the Puerto Ricans she knew from when she lived in El Barrio in the 1980s. My blood boiled as I patiently explained that no, despite her protestations, I was Boricua, actually. Because she was an elder, I tried to display some grace, while in my mind, Mariposa whispered, *Some people say I'm not bonafide . . .*

I was often told by Latino men that my skin was dark, so I "must be Caribbean." I looked at the backs of my hands with new eyes. I was never called or considered morena, trigueña, or negra like my sister, yet I reflected on the fact that my brown skin tone came from my Oaxaca-Poblano father and his possibly Indigenous roots, and not my lighter-skinned Boricua Mami. Unable to place my Chicana-Rican Spanish, many West Coast Latinx also often guessed I was Peruvian. I wondered what about my look and lexicon placed me, geographically, in South America. Had I been psychologically teleported there for a reason or was Peru simply the equivalent of carajoland?[11] The questions I was constantly asked about my identity persisted from childhood to adulthood: "Which half do you side with more, Mexican or Puerto Rican?" Tired of the implications of perceived bastardization, as if self-love required pedigree, I grew to say at times, "I'm not half anything, I am 200 percent." Pa' que tu lo sepas.

In graduate school, Chicana professor Laura Perez provided me with a new and healing path toward navigating my bicultural identity, drawing largely from the Chicana feminist canon. Her classes felt more like sermons (in a good way!) than academic spaces. Professor Perez taught me that Latina scholarship and artivism were not only worthy of intellectual pursuit but often essential and rooted in our ancestry and survival. In her work, she stated, "Indigenous, African-diasporic, and decolonizing hybrid spiritualities in our own time have nourished, strengthened, and given social courage to our peoples, assuring us in the face of racist discourses of our intrinsic worth."[12]

Professor Perez invited my class to journal, draw, perform, and present our own art and writing during class assignments and final presentations, creating spaces of healing and community building. She invited us to deeply reflect on Chicana feminist scholar Gloria Anzaldúa's work, and in turn, Anzaldúa taught me a new way to interpret my hybrid identity. She applied the philosophical and Mexica philosophical concept of nepantla[13] to her reality as a Spanish-Indigenous, queer, Chicana Texan:

> Nepantla is the site of transformation. The place where different perspectives come into conflict and where you question the basic ideas, tenets, and identities inherited from your family, your education, and your different cultures. Nepantla is the zone between changes where you struggle to find equilibrium between the outer expression of change and your inner relationship to it.[14]

To Anzaldúa, nepantla was a site of reconstruction, providing those who navigated it with an almost psychic ability to experience deeper realities and see things that others could not fully perceive. Anzaldúa gave me the words to understand the chaos of living and representing two culturally distinct identities within one physical body across distinct geographies. I wanted to share what I had learned with other Latinas, who I was sure were navigating similar struggles. I had the opportunity to do so when I was invited to teach a class for Latina women at a city college. Inspired by Professor Perez, I did my best to incorporate Latina feminist writing and cultural production into my classroom teachings. I relied on Bay Area Chicana artivists such as Melanie Cervantes and Ester Hernandez to engage both the political and creative sides of my students' minds and hearts. I wanted my girls to consider their own oppression as first-generation Latinas through writing and art that inspired play, fun, joy, and, when appropriate, righteous rage. Our classes became spaces of knowledge transfer and healing, for my girls as well as for me. Tlazocamati to the Chicana artivists and scholars who illuminated this path for us.

While searching for content for my class, I discovered a mural that had been painted in El Barrio in the style of Frida Kahlo's *Las Dos Fridas* by Boricua artist Yasmín Hernández. My jaw dropped because it was the first, and only, time I've seen an artist directly connect the histories of my people in this way. Hernández's *Soldaderas* mural drew connections between the legacies of oppression, colonization, and feminist resistance through Mexico's Frida Kahlo and Puerto Rico's (and El Barrio's) Julia de Burgos. In the mural, these icons were seated, holding hands with their respective flags painted directly behind them. In an interview, she spoke about the process of creating this mural shortly before rematriating to Puerto Rico from NYC. She reflected:

> I learned from [Borikén]. This land cracked me open. It was brutal. It expanded me and expanded my consciousness. To understand that my role in wanting liberation for Puerto Rico and all people on this planet . . . is not about having a relationship with the oppressor and the colonizer, where they strike and we strike back. . . . Liberation takes hold from your heart space, and that is the place where it develops from, and all of our strategy has to be informed by our spirit and heart and not by the tactics of the colonizer.[15]

Hernandez's "heart space" liberation moved me. The realization she came to was wrought through a painful growth process, as she deepened her roots into herself and Borikén. She reinforced the notion, much like Anzaldúa described, that the path toward self-revelation and healing was often only possible after psychological and somatic disorganization.

Afro-Indigenous Nuyorican artist Princess Nokia shared an important insight in an interview with Brown University. A former foster child, and daughter of a Boricua mother who died of AIDS, Princess Nokia's life story is one of unbelievable resilience, like many girls forced to raise themselves under impossible odds. She discussed coining the term "urban feminism" and starting the Smart Girl Club podcast. When pressed on why she shied away from using the term "political" to describe the themes explored in her music and art, Princess Nokia stated defensively, "Because I am undereducated in politics and don't want to fake the funk. . . . And that may be a poor answer, but it's an honest answer. I don't involve myself in politics, because they are extremely intricate and complicated and they are always demised to oppress."[16]

Princess Nokia rejected providing an overly polished or intellectual response as would typically be required of media or academic interviews. She refused to evaluate herself, her work, and her thoughts through the oppressive and myopic lenses of white supremacist forms of elitism—perhaps because she had grown up excluded from them. To her, the word "political" was simply too restrictive a term to capture what she was doing and saying, and held negative connotations she did not wish to be associated with. She reclaimed her right to her voice genre-bending music, on her own terms, as a young, queer woman of mixed ancestry. Bendición for your raw rebellion, Princess Nokia. I know your Mami is looking over you, her Destiny.

To end, I want to share my experience of wrestling with an increasingly controversial piece of art as a Chicana-Rican. In 2019, a friend of mine invited me to a $50 performance of *Hamilton*. I had missed the original obsession when it came out in 2015, so I sobbed uncontrollably as I watched and listened to this '90s-hip-hop-and-rap-infused musical tell the problematic and inspirational story of Black and Latinx founding fathers who breakdanced their way toward American independence. I watched the few young women of color in the theater sing along to every single lyric of the verbose musical and was awestruck by their allegiance, which I quickly grew to share. And just like I did with the album *Brujalicious*, I asked anyone and everyone to see the play with me or listen to the soundtrack. However, people whose politics I trusted deeply, for the most part, rejected my request.

The world had changed, and in a political and literal climate, post–Hurricane Maria, marked by a collective reckoning against police brutality, anti-Blackness, and disaster capitalism, *Hamilton* was no longer judged solely from a removed, theatrical, and white artistic lens but from a political one. Lin-Manuel Miranda's politics were put under the microscope as the son of Jose Miranda, a corporate Democrat and Party fundraiser who actively supported the creation of the PROMESA oversight board—an arm of US colonialism—among other political offenses. Suddenly, to support and enjoy this play meant being complicit in the exploitation and colonization of Puerto Rican people, including efforts to undermine Puerto Rican independence and sovereignty. I cried again and again, this time out of despair, as members of my own activist and artist community, Boricua, Chicanx, and non-, told me I was very, very wrong to enjoy this work. Still, however, my heart could not let go of its obsession with this production. To help me process, I journaled and took long walks, engaged in conversations with a trusted few, wrote long-winded Facebook posts, and tried to understand what it was that I was so desperately holding on to. I tried to reflect on my own biases, ignorance, and stubbornness and what had made me so resistant to the valid critiques of this piece of theater. Why was I so wounded by their rejection of a play about a great white American male colonizer?

I thought about Princess Nokia's words, how she described politics as "demised to oppress." I mulled over Yasmin's heart-centered description of liberation. I thought about my hybrid identity and the ways I navigated not just Chicana- and Puerto Ricanness but also my equal commitment to political activism and Latinx art. I thought about how both of these worlds had saved my life over and over again but also about how rejection from either of these worlds often cut me to my absolute core. I thought about the intense scrutiny that both Latinx artists and activists were often forced to endure, and my fierce desire to protect them. I wondered to myself as a Chicana-Rican, if there was room for complexity in questions of art and Puerto Rican sovereignty. Could I want to see my family in Puerto Rico free of LUMA's electrical stranglehold, while also singing every word to "My Shot"? Was I free to question what true Puerto Rican nationalism could look like in a twenty-first-century context? Could I share unpopular and undeveloped opinions without fear of being rejected from communities I so desperately sought to belong to? Could I be accepted as my whole, bifurcated self?

Perhaps a heart-centered Chicana-Rican understanding of national liberation would allow for this political and sacred form of nepantla to exist. Perhaps a heart-centered Chicana-Rican understanding of freedom could provide me and others with the grace and space for self-reflection and growth without fear of abandonment. Perhaps a heart-centered Chicana-Rican understanding of love could hold questions of Puerto Rican national sovereignty and statehood with patience and care. Perhaps a heart-centered Chicana-Rican understanding of self would find ways to balance sharp and valid critiques with spaciousness garnered through joy and creativity. Perhaps a heart-centered Chicana-Rican feminism would welcome public mistake-making, redactions, and recalibrations without collapsing under the weight of shame. Perhaps a heart-centered Chicana-Rican feminism would help me finally realize that navigating the rocky terrain between binaries, polarities, and contradictions was the most sacred gift of all; that this was the path of knowledge, growth, healing, and wholeness. That this was the path of the decolonized heart space, stretching a Chicana-Rican wider every time, to the point of almost snapping. Perhaps a Chicana-Rican body could expand and hold this, developing flexibility instead of tension, easing to hold love, fear, and pain like a heavy sob, only to be released and cleansed through sacred tears and deep breaths. Tlazocamati y bendición to the mujeres who paved the rocky terrain for a Chicana-Rican like me to traverse. With every trembling step, I see a clearing.

Beatriz Herrera is a Chicana-Rican community organizer, educator, interpreter, and trainer from New York City who calls the San Francisco Bay Area home. She obtained her BA in English from Vassar College and MA in Latin American studies from UC Berkeley.

Notes

1. "Damn, what a combination."
2. "Tlazocamati" means "thank you" in Nahuatl, an Indigenous language spoken in Central Mexico. It is often used within Chicanx healing, spiritual, and politicized spaces.
3. Horchata is a Mexican drink made of rice, milk, sugar, and cinnamon.
4. A "die-dreaming," a Dominican drink made of orange juice, evaporated milk, and sugar.
5. A Puerto Rican soda.
6. "Look at my Puerto Rican face / at my lively hair / and my brown hands / Look at my heart / that fills with pride / and tell me I'm not Boricua."
7. In Puerto Rico and among the PR diaspora, "bendición" is both a request for a blessing and the granting of a blessing to others.
8. Her name means Charity of Light.
9. "If you came here to fight not me, / I came to dance, to have fun I know / I know you have a reason to fight / but I'll make you forget that / have fun, forget."
10. La Bruja, "Olvidate," track 3 on *Brujalicious*, De La Luz Records, 2006, compact disc. Recorded April 17, 2006. Lyrics are reprinted by permission of

Caridad De La Luz. Find out more about La Bruja at CaridadDeLaLuz.com or @LaBrujaNYC on Instagram, Twitter, and TikTok.

11. A word Mami often used meaning "some damned place over there."
12. Laura Perez, "Decolonizing Spiritualities: Spiritualities That Are Decolonizing and the Work of Decolonizing Our Understanding of These," *Latino/as in the World-System* (Routledge, 2015), 163–68.
13. In Mexica philosophy, "nepantla" described the concept of energy transfer, a sense of motion change that existed in nature that helped maintain the sacred energetic balance of the universe.
14. Gloria Anzaldúa, B*orderlands / La Frontera: The New Mestiza* (Aunt Lute, 1987).
15. Yasmín Hernández, "Yasmin Hernandez Art," https://www.yasminhernandezart.com/soldaderas.
16. Princess Nokia, "Princess Nokia in Conversation at Brown University," public conversation, April 27, 2017, posted May 16, 2017, by Brown University, YouTube, https://www.youtube.com/watch?v=JWQlj10xwXI.

CHAPTER 18

Summers con Wela: Notes on Catholicism, Queerness, and Love

JESSICA N. PABÓN-COLÓN

EDITOR'S NOTE: Originally published as a blog on jessicapabon.com, February 27, 2019; revised in 2024 for this anthology.

Summers con wela taste *like the everyday meals of perfectly made cream of wheat with warm milk for breakfast, like Chef Boyardee Beefaronis with Tang for lunch, like arroz con habichuelas, pollo, y tostones for dinner, like tiny cups of coconut limber purchased from the woman next door, like the wafer that dissolves on my tongue as I return to my pew during mass on Sundays, like giant Fla-Vor-Ice popsicles bought with the quarter I got for being a "good girl," and like the freedom of walking to the bodega alone to buy it.*

Summers con wela sound *like the barking of all her little dogs (mostly chihuahuas) tied to the bathroom door as alarm systems ready to rat my cousins and I out if we weren't napping (we were never napping), like the hacking away at the carcass of a whole pig on the floor of her tiny kitchen, like the nonstop music (salsa, bachata, merengue, hip-hop) blasting into her windows from cars passing by and creeping in through the crevices between apartments, like the sobbing of mujeres brokenhearted by machismo men in the novelas on her television, and like her praying in Spanish—the whispered rehearsals of the rosary before bed every night.*

Summers con wela smell *like that church incense, like asapoa on the stove for hours, like dollar-store perfumes in tiny ultrafeminine bottles, like bleach and Fabuloso because everything has to be CLEAN, and like piss and spilled beer because we were in poorly maintained projects and, as clean as the apartments were kept on the inside by determined and pious abuelitas, people were drunk and disrespectful in the hallway.*

Summers con wela feel *like damp clean laundry being hung in the communal space outside the door of her building, like a skinned knee from the concrete ground or a bumped head from the metal playground, like the sting on my red skin from the too-hot bath water to make sure que no esta sucia (that I was not dirty—in all the ways a little girl could get dirty), the joy of a tiny apartment packed to the brim with people singing and dancing, the thwack of a coco-taso (a hit on the head) for transgressing my subordinate place in the domestic hierarchy as girl child, and the excitement when dad would pick me up for a weekend with family in New Hampshire or when tití would pick me up after work and take me to the mall with my cousins.*

Summers con wela look *like perfectly pressed church clothes (even socks and underwear), like already too-hard Black and Brown teenage boys wearing Adidas sweat suits and gold chains on street corners, like little girls with hair pulled back and braided into trenzas so tight they will one day have bald spots, and like young straight couples making out in hallway corners away from the punitive and pious gaze of mami, papi, and priest.*

Wela Nydia was born in Coamo, Puerto Rico, in 1938; she married (too) young, divorced her adulterous husband, and moved to South Boston in the mid '60s, where she raised five children (two boys, three girls) with some help from her mother-in-law, my bisabuela Paula Marrero. I imagine that, much like the experiences of my mother, father, aunts, and uncles, the racism and sexism wela survived as a Spanish-speaking single mother living in the predominantly Irish Catholic community of South Boston contributed a great deal to her tough, rigid, and strict disposition—personality traits that she wears like armor to this day.

I share a name with this abuela and I love her something fierce. Whereas I consider my Spanish comprehension lacking in conversation with everyone else, with her it is easier because it is familiar. As I continued my academic career and moved from farther and farther away from her, the long stretches of time between seeing her made communication more difficult. We tried writing letters, but I discovered that sort of stressed her out because, although she is fluent in Spanish, she is not confident about her writing. She calls me "mija" (my daughter) and is the only one (including me!) who routinely uses my full name—Jessica—without anglicizing it.

When I was three and a half years old, my mother packed the two of us up and we moved away from the Spanish-speaking Caribbean community of Jamaica Plain in Boston, Massachusetts—where most of both sides of

Figure 1. Author and her abuela, 1981. Photo courtesy of Jessica N. Pabón-Colón.

my family live—to *UP*state New York (Plattsburgh), where my grasp of my native language faded in a community as white as the snow that often covered it. Every summer for the next six or so years, my mother would allow my father to come pick me up and drive me back home to Boston. And though dad picked me up, the fact that he was a semifunctioning alcoholic meant that he was not allowed to keep me. I lived con wela and her husband (*not* my abuelo) in her Archdale apartment, a public housing complex in Roslindale, Massachusetts. During those 1980s summers, she cared for four of her grandchildren—Gabino, Janette, me, and Krystina.

Summers were my reprieve from the familial and cultural isolation I experienced in rural white upstate New York. Summers meant spending time con familia, and familia always included family friends who became cousins, titis, tíos, whether they were blood-related or not. Summers meant stoop hangs. Block parties. Cookouts. Puerto Rican Day parades. Cuchifritos. Summers also meant church. Summers were spent reaching for the pleasures of youth whilst being tethered to the strictures of a rigid, unforgiving Catholicism as a young person assigned female at birth.

Summers con wela came to an end when we moved back to Boston in 1989–1990. While not as devout as wela, my mother made sure we had new Easter dresses, attended midnight mass on Christmas Eve, and received confirmation. I left the Catholic church *right after* confirmation, though the printed programs I brought home every Sunday communicated otherwise to my unknowing mother. I knew the teachings of the church were not for me, but it wasn't until I started studying feminism that I would be able to articulate why—the Catholic church I knew was not a safe space for women who used their voice, who had questions about their place, or who expressed a desire for sexual pleasure beyond reproduction. And as a young woman coming into a queer feminist consciousness, there was no place for me to be me there.

Eventually, I left Boston too. I left seeking more education. More experiences. More opportunity. More feminism. More freedom. I would realize, much later, that moving away for "more" of some things—especially as an academic—meant having access to less of other things, specifically Puerto Rican culture and geographic closeness to family. I try to bridge these gaps for myself and for my child whenever we visit Boston.

One Sunday in February of 2019, my husband, child, and I visited wela after she got home from church. I was standing in her kitchen contemplating the mouse that was chillin' in her apartment, stressing about the mostly empty fridge and wondering how she always found a way to feed us despite living on a meager fixed income provided by the state, when my four-year-old gender-fluid child—M—came to me upset and confused: "Mami, bisabuela said I can't paint my nails because I am a boy?!"

For some reason, I was surprised. Taken off guard by the urgency in and wounded tone of M's voice, I was hailed into a position of reconciling my beliefs about the power dynamics between adult and child, about gender and self-expression, with hers. I had developed my queer feminist beliefs and sensibilities at a safe distance, thousands of miles away from wela and her religiosity. I hadn't yet had the experience of coming to this reconciliation work from the position of adult and parent, from the position of being nieta y madre at the same time. If I had spent any time thinking about how my grandmother would interact with my assigned-male-at-birth child—who was at that time regularly asserting their desires beyond a gender binary—I would have expected her resistance to M's freedom and sense of bodily autonomy. My first instinct was to fix it, to repair this rupture between two people I love. "Let's go talk to bisabuela," I said. "She didn't let me wear nail polish until I was like fourteen!" I fixed a smile on my face and carried M into her bedroom with the hopeful pretense that her "no" to the nail polish was about age.

She was in her bedroom quietly rearranging the nail polish M had clearly thumbed through. Her dresser was a wonderland of objects, an altar, an ode to femininity and religiosity all at once: perfumes, candles, nail polish, statuettes, knickknacks, tiny jewelry boxes, rosary beads. As soon as we walked into the room, M asked her (again): "Bisabuela, can you paint my nails?" Pointing to the shade, M asked, "Can I have red? Pink? . . . No?!" Wela responded assertively, but not aggressively: "NO! I told you, baby: You're a boy!" M looked at me in disbelief, clearly hurt and utterly confused by her refusal. M must have been thinking, since when am I a "boy" and what does being a boy have to do with not wearing nail polish? M was not taught these lessons at home. M had learned that abuelas say "yes" to makeup and nail polish and all things sparkly, from the books we read (Leslie Newman's *Sparkle Boy* was a favorite at that time) and my mother, M's wela. I intervened: "We let him accessorize however he wants. Come on wela, what harm can it do?" Again, holding on to the hope that her refusal was about the colors M wanted—red or pink—I tried to compromise: "Maybe blue or green?" Still, she shook her head no. She looked down at M and said, "Mami can do clear polish, pero no puedo." And then she left the room.

I was struck by her choice of words. She didn't say "I won't," she said "I can't." She said it with the kind of resolve I know to be unshakable. M didn't want clear nail polish, so her gesture solved nothing from my child's perspective. The clear nail polish and the permission she gave for "mamí to do it" created an opportunity for me to become a bridge between these two. I tried to take my child's hand in one of mine and hers in the other, but they would not budge. Perhaps M was the teacher in that moment; in refusing the clear nail polish, there was also a refusal of the queer invisibility seemingly required to receive bisabuela's approval.

Earlier in our visit, wela took an opportunity to tell me my toddler was "like this" (hyper) because M was not baptized (reader, my child is neurodivergent). I shrugged it off and reminded her that when M was almost a year old, we held an interfaith blessing and welcoming ceremony where we lived in Kingston, New York. M was welcomed to this life in community, in love, and in protection, but from her perspective, it didn't count, because this "baptism" was not performed by a priest in a Catholic church.

I looked around and let the familiar atmosphere wash over me: rosaries of all sizes overlapping images of baby Jesus becoming tapestries on the walls, statuettes of Mary Mother of God and a variety of saints, innumerable prayer cards—you get the picture. Taking this all in, the full weight of her "I can't" comes into my understanding. I remembered how closely she holds her faith and why. She had always been the most devout Catholic, but after she was diagnosed with breast cancer in 1993, her piety was unmatched. As she prepared to have the cancer removed, she prayed and promised God that if he took her cancer away forever, she would never cut her hair. She has been cancer-free since. We both believe that the power of her prayer played a major role in her remission (albeit from different belief systems). The aspects of her Catholicism that I view as oppressive and experience as barriers to my liberation are for her pathways to the promise of heaven.

I walked over to my child, kneeled so our eyes met, and said, "I know that you don't want clear polish, but that means we can't paint your nails right now. Bisabuela has different ideas about gender than we do. Since we are in her house, and this is her nail polish, we have to be respectful of her decision. But when we get home, you can have whatever color you want." I was fine on the outside, empathizing with him but not wanting him to have a negative association with someone who was so important to me. That said, my heart was hurting—feeling into that pain transports me back to a time when I was the child having my bodily autonomy surveilled and my deviance punished. My flight response activated, and I wanted to leave almost immediately. My cisgender, straight-passing self was safe there, but my child was not. Not safe enough to be free with gender expression, not safe enough to exercise bodily agency without reprimand. I wrote and rewrote those last two sentences about seven times, because "safety" is such a loaded term, and I would never want to suggest she would purposefully harm my child. What I mean to say is that M's gender-binary transgressions were not welcomed, and because I married a cis man, my queerness was out of sight, out of mind. Hell, even when I brought my ex-wife into her home years before and my queerness was very much *in* sight, she pretended we were just friends. She willfully ignored that I shared a home and a life with another person assigned female at birth and that we had a spiritual but not religious (or state-sanctioned) wedding in a renovated Texas chapel.

I texted my friend, who is also my PhD wyfey and sister-in-law: "Do y'all have red nail polish? My grandmother just told [my son] that boys don't wear nail polish. I need to fix it. . . . I think it's less important to paint his nails and more important for someone else in his life to reinforce that it's ok. . . . She wasn't mean about it. Just very Catholic about it."

For a time after that visit, at least once a day, I stressed about how I handled it. Did I acquiesce? What did I model for him in that moment? Was I avoiding conflict with my abuela at his expense? Was I performing revolutionary motherhood in that instance? How else could I have handled it? What did he make of the fact that she—Latina, elder—said no and his aunt—white, young, queer—said yes? What stereotypes did this affirm? What sense of belonging did it trigger? What ideas about gender, queerness, and Puerto Ricanness were set in motion?

I know these are *my* concerns, concerns that stem from other memories associated with wela; for as much freedom as she gave me to go buy my own sweet treats at the bodega, there were many more things I could not do (wear anything too "revealing"), things I had to do (serve my older cousin Gabino and her husband their meals first), and things I was severely punished for ("being fresh") *because* I was a girl. She didn't intervene when her husband yelled and threatened to hit me for not wearing tights under my church dress (too provocative at eight years old, I guess).

None of the difficulties or relational ruptures I've shared in this essay have been resolved or repaired. When we left her apartment, we let it go. Today, wela still sends M gifts for every holiday. Smiles when she is near us. Refers to M as "my baby" when she calls, even though he is ten now.

She has also cared for and protected me when others couldn't; she has loved me deeply and sincerely. And I her. She is the only family member who did not scoff or fuss at me for wanting a home birth. She shared that some of her children were born under trees, or was it that she was born under a tree? Either way, my (unfulfilled) desire to avoid a hospital birthing experience was totally fine in her view, beautiful even. I didn't have to explain why I chose to work with a midwife. I call her and ask her to pray for me and my friends when we are in need; she in turn prays for things I do not ask for and do not want. For example, praying for my divine forgiveness when I got my first pixie haircut. When I told her over the phone, she told me that cutting my hair was like cutting my femininity out, cutting my womanhood away, which in her eyes, was a sin.

Years ago, I wrote about being a queer feminist mamí trying to parent from a place of radical decolonial love. I wrote about the difficulties of practicing my politics in my parenting—as too white for some Boricuas, too Boricua for some whites, I noticed the disgust at the options for bodily autonomy and nonnormativity we gave our child acting as the place of overlap between these groups. I wrote about how folks on social media demanded that I "'straighten' his gender presentation and 'fix' his body" onto a heteropatriarchal gender binary violently imposed by centuries of colonization. It's not just folks on social media, obviously. And it's not so easy to resist their demands. To accept their rejections. To fight against their convictions. To accept the tension between the joy of family and the rigid gender roles and sexual normativity demanded by the kind of Catholicism governing that same family.

Spiritually, I find home in what some call a "radical dharma." I find solace and strength in Buddhist teachings, meditation, and letting go of attachments. I have no love for, or attachment to, the Catholic church. And yet, I believe in her belief.

The difference between us—Nydia and Jessica Nydia—is difficult but not irreconcilable; it does not sever the bond that we made every summer that she was my primary caretaker. She has never sent me away or cut me off from her love and she has never compromised her beliefs or changed her personal practices. Perhaps it was she who modeled for me how to have unshakable resolve in my beliefs, no matter the cost or circumstance.

M moved toward public identification with "he/him" and "boy," began refusing to wear his dresses and denying he ever loved pink, precisely when the teasing in pre-K started. It would be disingenuous for me to pretend these shifts in M's self-fashioning did not affect me. It is hard to watch your child "shrink" themselves to fit a gender binary you reject with every fiber of your being. For a while, I grieved the loss of what I perceived as the "more" I had earned for both of us with my feminist struggles as a queer woman, a queer parent, a queer Puerto Rican.

M now uses "he/him" pronouns on some days and "he/they" pronouns on others. Some days he is a boy, and others, tells me: "I am not a boy or a girl, mom, duh." I know it changes because I make a practice to ask how M identifies rather than assume or police. Perhaps that is where the "more" comes in—in the options he's given and the ones he takes, the autonomy to have long hair or short hair, painted nails or plain, and the freedom to be whoever he needs to be, knowing that he is safe and loved no matter what.

Jessica N. Pabón-Colón is a diasporic Puerto Rican feminist scholar of identity, community, and resistance. Her essays appear in journals including *Women & Performance: a journal of feminist theory*, *Signs: Journal of Women in Culture and Society*, and *Frontiers: A Journal of Women's Studies*. Her book *Graffiti Grrlz: Performing Feminism in the Hip Hop Diaspora* (New York University Press, 2018) is the first academic study on women's participation within hip-hop graffiti art subculture. She spends her summers as a butterfly doula helping monarchs on their migration journey and can otherwise be found baking breads, crafting, playing with her human and nonhuman children, or in a forest admiring the moss.

CHAPTER 19

Daughter of Operation Bootstrap: Feminist Awakenings, Commitments, and Tensions

MAURA I. TORO-MORN

Introduction

In the opening pages of her essay "The Feminist Evolution of an Artist, Survivor, Conjurer from the Tropics," Panamanian feminist writer Marta Sanchez declared, "I became a feminist at creation, not at birth, but between conception and the light." She adds, "Feminism named me, while my grandfather strung binding words together beneath a tree. My father nurtured me a feminist."[1]

I cannot tell you precisely the day I uttered the words, "I am a feminist." Feminism's central ideas about women's rights, empowerment, liberation, dismantling patriarchy, and its constitution as a social movement were not available to me—but I deployed them intuitively as a young woman while growing up in the west side of Puerto Rico. I can state with certainty that, in contrast to Marta Sanchez, the one person responsible for my feminism was not my father, nor my grandfather, but my mother, Rita Segarra Ramos (1929–2011). She was a working-class woman who throughout her life defied a society that pushed her to the margins because she did not marry a man. She asserted her agency by not allowing herself to be defined by an institution—marriage—and by not allowing a man's desires, presence, and dictums to shape her life or her children's. She was a single working woman—"una madre soltera," as she frequently described herself. She embodied, lived, and articulated feminism for me long before I learned the meaning of the word as a college student at Interamerican University in San Germán in the late 1970s.

Her pride and dedication to her identity as a factory worker in an export-processing zone in Mayagüez, Puerto Rico, allowed me to understand and always be attentive to the social class struggles of working women. Her life as a working woman anchored my budding consciousness in the intersections (or tensions) of social class and gender. True to a commitment to work that marked the women of her generation, she used to say, "Le di mi vida a la fábrica" ("I gave my life to the factory"). My mother constructed a community of support with other women in la fábrica, her comunidad, and her non-blood-related family, exemplifying for me several tenets of feminism: an ethic of care, solidarity with other women, and respect and pride for the work women do. I begin this essay with my memories of growing up in Cabo Rojo; to borrow a term used by the Latina Feminist Group to describe memories and events that are difficult, contradictory, and painful to relive, these memories constitute my "papelitos guardados."[2] Offering a brief description of my mother's work experiences, and my own, allows me to "reinhabit not only [my] own past, but also [my] own body."[3]

In high school, my inquietudes had me making observations about the world around me based on what happened to the women in my barrio. At some point, I wanted to study law and become a lawyer, because men needed to be jailed for hitting women and women needed to be defended before the eyes of the law. It was at Interamerican University where my feminist college professors encouraged me to follow my inquietudes and questions, to engage in research about Puerto Rican women. They also encouraged me to make connections between women's experiences in other countries in Latin America. One of my college professors, Dr. Yamila Azize, a well-known Puerto Rican feminist, taught me about Luisa Capetillo and the struggles of working-class women in the aftermath of the US occupation of the archipelago. She recruited me as her research assistant to help her delve deeper into Capetillo's life and work through archival research. She encouraged me to attend the meetings and events organized by a group of women in San Juan, La Comisión de Asuntos de la Mujer. They eventually became the official governmental agency charged with advocacy and policymaking to address women's issues; in the early 1980s, they represented the feminist movement in Puerto Rico. I went to San Juan, compelled to represent the experiences of women living in the west side, like my mother, whom I knew could not travel to those conferences to speak about their own problems with domestic violence, unfair wages, and bad working conditions. In retrospect, this was my introduction to the social class divisions that have characterized feminist movements around the globe. Many of the women who helped organized La Comisión de los Asuntos de la Mujer[4] were highly educated professional women, children of the elite, who were there to represent themselves and their social class interests of upward mobility. I learned very early that women are not a monolithic category and that our task as feminists is to recognize, understand, and confront the differences that exist between us.

Figure 1. My mother, Rita, walking toward our house from the main road, late 1970s. She probably dropped something at a neighbor's house and was walking back to the house. Photo courtesy of the author.

Like many women of my generation, I left Puerto Rico in the early 1980s to pursue graduate studies in Illinois—a change that, unbeknownst to me, strengthened and expanded the "political grammar"[5] of my feminism.[6] This was also the time of profoundly important—very public and difficult—conversations in the US among women of color and white women about racism, difference, and solidarity.[7]

In the early 1980s and '90s, I could not keep up with the flood of new books and articles, the explosion of academic and scholarly work produced by feminist scholars. In one book that stands out for me, Robin Morgan's *Sisterhood Is Global*, I opened the table of contents to find representation from every country in the world—yet not Puerto Rico. Why? Why were Puerto Rican women left out? This magnified the fact that here, too—in a book about feminist solidarity and sisterhood around the globe—Puerto Rican women's experiences were missing. I was already committed to writing about and studying Puerto Rican women, but in this context it became my life's work.

Sara Ahmed writes that "feminism is often memory work. . . . We work to remember what sometimes we wish we would or could just recede."[8] For me, putting the pieces that hold this essay together is an excavation of memories, letters, conversations, and events that refuse to be forgotten. As Ahmed proposes, "body is memory." This is when the past becomes heavily marked by a "biography of violence." The violence of colonialism, industrialization, modernization, and migration are marks we carry in our bodies and over time. Committing my memories to words in this essay has not been easy. It is the work of looking back, tracing a genealogy through a terrain that is vast and complicated, one that admittedly cannot be captured in one essay.

Perhaps a more fitting way to describe the work I offer here is that of a "feminist testimonio," a term that the Latina Feminist Group used to call the process that allowed them to capture in writing the complexity of their lives. They note that the practice of testimonio has been used in Latin America and the Caribbean by women to tell the story of the collective violence inflicted upon them and their communities. The Latina Feminist Group used testimonio as a tool to "theorize oppression, resistance and subjectivity,"[9] to capture our pain, our secrets, and our complicated lives. I have used this method before to write about my experiences providing care for my mother in a transnational context.[10] Thus, this essay is part testimonio, part memory, and part conversation with the written work of feminist scholars that I have encountered, studied, and come to admire. Citing their work, their testimonios in particular, is itself a feminist practice to make sure our scholars' work remains visible.

Daughters of Operation Bootstrap: Las Mujeres de la Fábrica

In the groundbreaking volume *Telling to Live: Latina Feminist Testimonios* (2001), Luz del Alba Acevedo coined the concept that forms part of the title of this essay. Acevedo writes, "I did not realize that I was a daughter of Bootstrap until I looked back on my life from the perspective of a migrant."[11] She adds, "My parents, willingly or not, participated in the process of producing conditions of modernity espoused in the political project of Operation Bootstrap. I participated more as a consumer of modernity than a producer of it, and I had to endure the trials of living with new values, rules, norms, and social expectations regarding modern life."[12] Acevedo felt she embodied the contradictions of the socioeconomic and cultural transformation of the archipelago. There is a whole generation of us who are still living with these contradictions, the daughters of Operation Bootstrap—a modernization project that was implemented in Puerto Rico in the 1950s. The violence of that project marked us all in complex ways that have yet to be conceptualized. Much has been written about it that is beyond the scope of this essay, but its foundation was itself the creation myth of a modern Puerto Rican nation.[13] And yet the labor of these women—both productive and reproductive—was foundational to the modernization program.

My mother became a factory worker in the export-processing zone of Mayagüez in the 1960s, shortly after I was born. As a single mother, she needed two jobs to provide for my brother and me. On weekends and holidays, she worked retail at various stores in Mayagüez and Cabo Rojo, and during the week, she worked en la fábrica of Propper International. The third factory to the right as one entered the industrial park in Mayagüez, Propper was a manufacturing company for uniforms for various branches of the US military. It still thrives in Puerto Rico today, though they closed the plant in Mayagüez and consolidated its assembly line into one massive industrial park in Cabo Rojo. I have lots of memories—"papelitos guardados," some good, some bad—of my mother's work experiences in the factory. On one level, she loved her work. She derived her identity as a woman from her work, and it gave her control of her money, which she could then determine how to use. Of course, her meager wages barely left enough money for us to eat, but we always had a line of credit in the local tienda. Poverty for us did not include absence of food, because there was always rice and beans. What defined our poverty was living paycheck to paycheck, meaning we always had to look for other ways to buscarse el peso. She didn't drive a car and we could not afford one until I was in college. We lived in a modest wooden house, with one bedroom that I shared with my mother and my brother. Not until my mother won money in the illegal lottery, la bolita, was she able to build a cement house—a mark of progress in Puerto Rico.

At work, my mother hated the repressive management techniques, the fear tactics to keep people working under the most horrific conditions, and the grueling quotas imposed on them. She had to work even when she was sick. She got up incredibly early to make herself breakfast, café con pan. We got up with her and walked down the street to Chispa's house. Chispa (Heremita Martinez) was mi mamá de crianza, my other mother. She lived down the road from us with her husband, Pablo Aguilar, who was a police officer. Chispa's three children, Marlyn, Miriam, and Pablo, became my siblings. I don't know how my mother first secured Chispa's help with childcare, but her family became part of my extended chosen family. Did Chispa embody idealized notions of 1940s and 1950s Puerto Rican domesticity? Perhaps. Chispa's world was her home, but she hardly met the criteria of the stereotypical

Puerto Rican mother: the imagined "Marianas" that were said to be ruled by marianismo, the problematic construct that was offered to explain the lives of Puerto Rican women bound to the home.[14] Chispa had a wicked sense of humor and had total control of her home. She had a network of friends in the barrio and was very efficient with her housework. She cooked, cleaned, and cared for her own children and my mom's—and even another girl, Tita, for a short period of time. My brother was born prematurely, and Chispa cared for him beginning when he was just days old so that my mom could go back to work. My brother called her "mami" too. Before leaving the hospital, my mother agreed to having "la operación," which is how women referred to the controversial contraceptive method imposed by most doctors on poor, Black, and working-class women in Puerto Rico—sterilization.[15]

In the early rainy mornings during hurricane season, it was an ordeal for us to reach Chispa's house. With her umbrella in one hand and her other arm laden with my baby brother, her purse, and the bag of stuff she took to sell at the factory, my mother had no hand left for me to hold. But there was the rim of her blouse, which I gripped like I now hold onto these memories. Chispa was already awake and waiting for us. My mother stood by the side of the road, in front of Chispa's house, for her "pon," a colloquial word used in Puerto Rico for a free car ride. Who gave her a ride? This was the time of carros públicos, public paying cars. Road 103 was the main road to go from Cabo Rojo to Mayagüez. Sometimes, if she missed her ride, she had to wait for a carro público, which meant she would be late to work. Most of the time she rode to work in a car packed with other women workers. Today this practice is known as "carpooling," but this was (and still is) a common practice among women working in these export-processing zones. A woman in the neighborhood who owned a car picked up the other women on her way to work. My mom was the last person to be picked up because we lived between both towns. I remember the chatter and laughter as she was getting in the car. At the end of the week, the driver would get a few dollars as payment for the transportation services she provided. Chispa got a weekly payment for our care, too. When my mother could not pay, it was okay, because she would pay with clothing or other things that Chispa may have needed for herself or her home. My mother took clothing, sheets, shoes, and other items on credit at the retail stores she worked at on weekends as extra money-earning strategies. What I am describing here is an ethic of care and obligation to one another that women developed in the context of their work and family lives. I am also describing informal income-generating strategies used by working-class women to deal with the new expectations of a modern consumer nation. I was raised by a community of hardworking women, mujeres luchadoras, who made the best of what the modernization program handed them. The women of my neighborhood and family took pride in their work, laughed, cried, got angry, put their hair up, painted their nails, and let go of it all in a day's worth of work.

The modernization program placed my mother and me at odds with each other. She tried to hold onto her job in the factory while raising us according to a gender order that no longer held any currency. The traditional gender order had been fractured, shattered to pieces, although many families held onto it as tradition. After my high school graduation, the idea of going to college was acceptable as long as I didn't go far away. At the time I wanted to pursue studies in Ponce because they had a law school, and as I mentioned earlier, I wanted to study law. But she refused to let me go. Instead, I had to go to Interamerican University, which was located a mere fifteen-minute drive from my house. That meant I could live at home and still go to college, which I did because that was my only option.

There is a phrase that captures the lived contradictions of the modernization project for a whole generation of us: "Tienes que estudiar por si acaso tu marido te sale malo," or, "You must get an education in the event that your husband turns out to be a bum."[16] Like my mother, I countered that my worth was not defined in relation to a man. Further, I wanted my freedoms—to study, travel, have sex, discover myself first—before I had to confront those gendered expectations. At the time, my feminist commitments entailed a rejection of all the traditional gendered roles imposed upon me as a Puerto Rican woman. My struggle in Puerto Rico was to wrest more agency and freedom for myself. Today, looking back, I don't think I meant a complete rejection of those ideals, since I ended up getting married and having a son, though I did so later in life and under different conditions. My ideas and actions were an outright challenge to the traditional gender order that was expected of me, and as a result, the fights between me and my mother were epic. She always won, until the day I left Puerto Rico.

I belong to a generation of Puerto Rican scholars that have studied and analyzed the contradictions of the modernization program and migration.[17] I have also worked to add an understanding of migration as a strategy to escape gender conditions that are limiting and oppressive.[18] The decision to leave Puerto Rico for Illinois was hard, but my departure was made possible because, ironically, my mom had agreed to it and orchestrated it: A neighbor's daughter and her husband were there, and so I was not going to a place where I had no one. In retrospect, letting me go was one of the most courageous and modern things—maybe one of the most feminist things—she did as my mother. But my migration fractured our family in ways that I am still trying to comprehend. I left, but I didn't really leave my gendered obligations to her as the eldest daughter. I left and realized that my gendered obligations followed me everywhere.[19] I flew to Puerto Rico every year and talked to my mother on the phone every day. Puerto Rican anthropologist Jorge Duany describes the migration of Puerto Ricans as a "vaivén." The vaivén is a deeply gendered process as we try to keep our families from fracturing even more due to migration. It is hard work that is frequently invisible because it is primarily done by women, women who also bear the emotional work of sustaining families across time and space.[20]

The moment I left the island, we became a transnational family, and the emotional work of caring for each other took place between Illinois and Puerto Rico. We stayed in touch with each other through letters and phone calls. When I left in the 1980s, she was still working, so the stories of the abuses and pocas vergüenzas continued until they forced her out. After so many years of work in the factory, she had nothing: no pension, nothing. She had social security that barely paid her expenses. We called each other every day without fail, and sometimes we would call each other more than once. We provided emotional care for each other as my "temporary" departure to study became a permanent move. In the early 1990s, when I took a job as an assistant professor at Illinois State University, I became part of the army of Latin American mothers and daughters who reconstitute care in the context of our transnational existence between two worlds. The trips home in December were nonnegotiable for me. We flew to Puerto Rico in December like clockwork, no matter the conditions.

Even in her old age, my mother was fiercely independent—until she suffered a debilitating stroke that robbed her of her freedom. We moved her to a private nursing home in San Germán. I reconnected with las mujeres de la fábrica—my mom's former coworkers—in the last years of her life. They visited frequently just to be with her, to make her laugh, and to remember "los revolus de la fábrica." They were also with me, by my side, paying testimonio to my mother's life, when we buried her one sad afternoon in September.

Concluding Thoughts

Centering the lives of Puerto Rican women was (and still is) the underlying foundation of my consciousness as a feminist. These inquietudes started in my childhood and grew into full-blown questions and areas of inquiry as I matured into a feminist scholar. Gloria Anzaldúa calls it "the silence that hollows us."[21] She adds that "for silence to transform into speech, sounds, and words, it must first traverse through our female bodies." I belong to a generation of Puerto Rican women who, while searching for a language—or a multiplicity of languages—declared ourselves feminist by our actions and our scholarly work. In graduate school, the absence of work about Puerto Rican women was jarring, fueling my determination to place the stories of

Puerto Rican women in the growing body of work that developed in studies of migration, in sociology, women's studies, and eventually landing in Latina/o/x/e studies. We have built a corpus of work that is impressive and necessary. As Puerto Rican feminist Carmen Lugo-Lugo states, through our work we have exposed the specific struggles of gendered colonial domination.[22] Yet there is still something missing. Like in the 1980s when I opened Robin Morgan's book, I still feel that our work has been absent in the academic feminist canon. Why? Heather Montes Ireland writes, "If the subaltern is speaking, yet no one is listening, how might the condition of coloniality reify a silence around, and the abjection of, Puerto Rican feminist theories and subjectivities?"[23]

The analysis I have shared in this essay was made possible and generated through many years of psychological therapy to excavate, name, and analyze our complex gendered worlds. I had always perceived my mom as a victim; a victim of my father, a victim of patriarchy, a victim of the modernization program, and a victim of a deeply sexist and classist society that robbed her of her choices and exploited her. Some of that analysis is true, and it fueled my feminist understanding. After many years in therapy, a female therapist turned all of that around for me. She suggested that maybe my mother had some choices; that in spite of the significant constraints in her life and, yes, her exploitation, there were some areas of her life she had control over.

I want to believe that for her, loving my father—on her own terms—was a choice. My father was a married man when they got involved. I do know this was a topic of conversation with many people in my family and neighborhood over the years. She was often asked, Why don't you find a good man? My mother's response was fiercely unequivocally: "Para que? Yo no necesito un hombre que me mande" (For what? I do not need a man to rule over me!). Not getting attached to a man was one choice she exercised fiercely.

Ironically, as I write these notes, I cannot contain the tears, because this is one truth, her truth, that I cannot confirm in the wake of her passing. My mother was a mystery to me, una cajita de sorpresas, until the day she died. And still long after, she continues to animate my feminist consciousness.

Maura I. Toro-Morn is the director of the Latin American and Latino Studies Program at Illinois State University. She helped launch the Latino Oral History Project in the McLean County Museum of History, a project that records the culture and experience of Latinos who live and work in McLean County, Illinois. She cowrote, with Ivis Garcia, *Puerto Ricans in Illinois* (Southern Illinois Press, 2024), the first book about Puerto Ricans in Illinois. She has published essays in the *Latino Studies Journal, Centro: Journal of the Center for Puerto Rican Studies,* and the *Journal of Latino/Latin American Studies.*

Notes

1. Marta Sanchez, "The Feminist Evolution of an Artist, Survivor, Conjurer from the Tropics," in *Click: When We Knew We Were Feminists*, ed. Courtney E. Martin and J. Courtney Sullivan (Seal Press, 2010), 145.
2. The Latina Feminist Group, *Telling to Live: Latina Feminist Testimonios* (Duke University Press, 2001), 2.
3. Sara Ahmed, *Living a Feminist Life* (Duke University Press, 2017), 30.
4. For a time La Comisión's ascendancy to official government agency was a measure of success for the feminist movement in Puerto Rico. But then the agency became mired in the typical problems of government agencies: budget, corruption, and lack of leadership. There is widespread agreement that today they are ineffective in moving Puerto Rico toward greater gender equality.
5. Clare Hemmings, *Why Stories Matter: The Political Grammar of Feminist Theory* (Duke University Press, 2011).
6. "Sex roles" was the phrase feminists used until the density of critiques about the biological determinism embedded in that language made it possible to replace it with "gender roles."
7. In a recent interview, Chandra Mohanty and Angela Davis described that time as "productive and generative." These difficult conversations took place through discussions and confrontations in classrooms, in universities, and at various conferences; for example, the National Women's Studies Association. Collaboration as a form of solidarity was evident between Angela Davis, Gloria Anzaldúa, Cherríe Moraga, bell hooks, and others. These conversations need to be seen in the long history of community activism that preceded the formation of women's studies programs.
8. Ahmed, *Living a Feminist Life*, 22.
9. The Latina Feminist Group, *Telling to Live*, 2.
10. Maura I. Toro-Morn, "Migration and Gendered Webs of Obligation: Caring for My Elderly Puerto Rican Mother in a Transnational Context," in *Critical Gerontology Comes of Age*, ed. C. Wellin (Routledge, 2018), 225–42.
11. Luz del Alba Acevedo, "Daughter of Bootstrap," in *Telling to Live: Latina Feminist Testimonios*, ed. Latina Feminist Group (Duke University Press, 2001), 147.
12. Acevedo, "Daughter of Bootstrap," 147.
13. Hilda Lloréns, *Imagining the Great Puerto Rican Family: Framing Nation, Race, and Gender During the American Century* (Lexington Books, 2014).
14. In the 1960s, local high schools offered literacy programs in the evenings. Chispa tried to attend school in the evenings to learn to read and write, but her domestic life won over the work (and dangers) of walking to the local high school. She was a full-time mom. Her family lived in a relatively comfortable wooden house, much bigger than ours, down the street from where we lived. They, too, eventually reconstructed their house in cement. Her household included her husband, her children, and her father-in-law, whom she cared for until he died.

15. I don't know if this was her choice, but it seemed as though for the women of her generation this was the enforced method of contraception.
16. Acevedo, "Daughter of Bootstrap," 144.
17. Elizabeth Aranda, *Emotional Bridges to Puerto Rico: Migration, Return Migration, and the Struggles of Incorporation* (Rowman and Littlefield, 2006); G. M. Pérez, *The Near Northwest Side Story: Migration, Displacement, and Puerto Rican Families* (University of California Press, 2004); Maura. I. Toro-Morn, "Yo era muy arriesgada: A Historical Overview of the Work Experiences of Puerto Rican Women in Chicago," *Centro Journal* 13, no. 2 (2001): 24–43; and Marisa Alicea, "'A Chambered Nautilus': The Contradictory Nature of Puerto Rican Women's Roles in the Social Construction of a Transnational Community," *Gender and Society* 11, no. 5 (1997): 597–626.
18. Maura I. Toro-Morn, Ivis García-Zambrana, and Marisa Alicea, "De bandera a bandera (From flag to flag): New Scholarship About the Puerto Rican Diaspora in Chicago," *Centro Journal* 18, no. 2 (2016): 4–35; and Maura Toro-Morn and Ivis García, "Gendered Fault Lines: A Demographic Profile of Puerto Rican Women in the United States," *Centro Journal* 29, no. 3 (2017): 10–35.
19. Maura I. Toro-Morn, "Migration and Gendered Webs of Obligation," 225–42.
20. Alicea, "A Chambered Nautilus"; Aranda, *Emotional Bridges to Puerto Rico*; and Toro-Morn, "Migration and Gendered Webs of Obligation."
21. Gloria Anzaldúa, *Making Face, Making Soul, Haciendo Caras: Creative and Critical Perspectives of Feminists of Color* (Aunt Lute Books, 1990).
22. Carmen R. Lugo-Lugo, "Writers of the Colony: Feminism via PuertoRicanness in the Literature of Contemporary Women Authors on the Island," *Latino(a) Research Review* 7, no. 3 (2010): 101–20.
23. Heather Montes Ireland, "Decolonization Is Imminent: Notes on Boricua Feminism," *Feminist Formations* 35, no. 1 (Spring 2023): 18–29, 22.

Cucubano

TAÍNA ASILI

Cucubano is a type of lightning bug native to Puerto Rico

Cucubano, cucubano,
cucubano, ilumina el mundo (illuminate the world)
con tus sueños, con tus sueños, (with your dreams, with your dreams)
sueña todo lo imposible (dream all the impossible)

Aquellos que fueron esclavizados (Those that were enslaved)
alguna vez soñaron (once dreamed)
con la posibilidad de nuestra libertad (of the possibility of freedom)

Cucubanos, cucubanos,
Cucubanos nacieron para enseñar a brillar (you were born to teach us how to shine)
con amor, con amor, (with love, with love)
nos convertimos en una brújula (we become a compass)

Somos un reflejo de las estrellas (We are a reflection of the stars)
Bioluminiscencia (Bioluminescence)
Con el poder de iluminar la oscuridad (With the power to illuminate the darkness)

De los sueños, de los sueños (Of dreams, of dreams)
de los sueños un nuevo mundo se está creando (of dreams a new world is being created)
con justicia, con perdón, con amor (with justice, with forgiveness, with love)
y con paz (and with peace)

Taína Asili is a dynamic singer, composer, interdisciplinary artist, and activist who carries on the traditions of her Puerto Rican ancestors, fusing past and present struggles into a soulful and defiant voice. For thirty years, she has delivered energetic performances inspiring audiences to dance to the rhythm of rebellion. As a songwriter, she has released numerous anthems to amplify our social justice movements, using music as a powerful force for liberation.

PART V. OUR STRATEGIES

CHAPTER 20

Colectivo Moriviví Statement: Muralism, Artivism, and Community

RAYSA RAQUEL RODRÍGUEZ GARCÍA
AND SHARON NICHOLE GONZÁLEZ COLÓN

We formed as a group of eight students at the Central High School of Visual Arts in Santurce, Puerto Rico. We wanted to paint a mural together for the Santurce Es Ley (SEL) Urban Art Festival, which at that time was in its fourth year (SEL4). Our desire arose after we met Alexis Bousquet, curator of the festival, who was talking about his career as an artist and cultural manager in the discussion "The Curator and His Function / The Artist and His Proposal" at the Art Museum of Puerto Rico in 2013. We approached Alexis and pleaded for a mural spot as students of La Central, to which he agreed.

Being an all-women collective was not a premeditated decision. A fairly large group of students wanted to make this mural, but the only ones who continued with the project were eight young women. Everyone was impressed with our mural work and how young we were, so much so that they called us "the girls from La Central" because we did not yet have a name as a collective. As the days went by, Alexis proposed we name ourselves so people could identify us. After discarding many ideas for possible names, we ended up playing the Puerto Rican version of "I Spy" (Veo, Veo) in front of our wall. The site was full of morivivís, a common weed in Puerto Rico—so one of our companions exclaimed, "Moriviví!" *Moriviví* is a word composed of *morí* and *viví*, which translates exactly to English as "I died" and "I lived." Over time, we unearthed deeper connections to our name, realizing the relationship it has with our work. Today, we see moriviví as a symbol of our Puerto Rican roots, a mythologically feminine flower of the Taíno culture, a sensitive plant.

As our work became more popular through our participation in different urban art festivals in Puerto Rico, organizations and community leaders

Figure 1. *Una Bocanada de Mariposas*, Santurce es Ley 4, 2013, San Juan, Puerto Rico. Photo courtesy of the authors.

began to contact us. From the beginning, we knew that public art has great potential to connect with people. Therefore, we felt the responsibility to visibilize, transgress, and question important issues about our society—always taking into account the community where the project is located. Once we began to collaborate with different organizations, we allowed ourselves to integrate the community directly into our projects, from the conceptualization phase to the creation of the design and its elaboration. We have had ten years to grow and evolve. Now our organizing model has changed, as we have two co-directors and other collaborators who participate according to the location and scale of each project.

Urban Art, Muralism, Protest Art, and Community

Colectivo Moriviví was formed in an urban art festival, but we consider ourselves muralists. Urban art and muralism are distinct concepts. Muralism is a medium, while urban art is an artistic movement. As an artistic movement, urban art in Puerto Rico predates the founding of the collective by more than ten years. Before us, there was a persecution of the graffiti artists who led the movement in Puerto Rico; without their struggle to have their work considered art, we would not have had the forum in which to be born as an artistic collective. The foundational work that the urban artists did paved the way for the muralists to become part of the public space again, with a greater boom in urban spaces.

The urban art movement, as its name denotes, is born from the culture of cities. Cities are spaces where the individual is easily isolated and lost in the crowds. The population density and the amount of work that is generated in cities create a level of hustle and bustle in which people tend to ignore others and individualize themselves. This quality is evident in urban art. The visual language of urban artists consists of creating their own quickly identifiable style, bordering on a "trademark." Many of them travel the world leaving their mark. It is the individual trying to say, "I was here," to leave their mark in a world that ignores their presence. This is something we noticed quickly, in our first debut in SEL4.

Although our collective was born in the context of urban art, as muralists we differ from urban artists. Muralism as a medium has a great historical legacy since ancient times. Before the Industrial Revolution, muralism was used primarily as political propaganda. More recently, and within the Latin American context, there was the school of Mexican muralism, a political propaganda movement tied to the government but focused on narratives that spoke to the people. Mexican muralists produced rich narrative images that we find relatable to our own Latin American identities, making it one of the historical art movements that we most identify with.

After a short time in the world of urban art as muralists, we realized that when artists paint the walls in neighborhoods and communities, these can become cultural destinations with touristic value. Unfortunately, if we, the artists, are not careful, we may end up attracting outsiders to the communities our work impacts, and not all of them have the community's best interests at heart. Art and culture can become double-edged razors: art attracts capital, and capital displaces lower social classes. In this manner, public art and urban art have the potential to aid gentrification. Such has been the case in neighborhoods like Wynwood in Miami, Florida, and Williamsburg in Brooklyn, New York.

Gentrification has been a stubborn threat to Puerto Rico, looming larger after recent years of fiscal crisis and the economic disaster unleashed over the past decade. As artists, we must recognize that threat and know that we can facilitate its fruition. That is why it is our duty to turn urban art into a tool for our communities instead of a weapon against them. At Colectivo Morivivi, we believe that if we paint the walls of a community, that art must reflect the realities and identities of the people who live there. Furthermore, it is our responsibility to involve the community to the greatest extent possible, since at the end of the day, those walls belong to them. These beliefs led us to focus on community art and to seek new ways of working together with communities, from the conceptualization stage of the artwork.

It is important to mention the influence community mural practices in the US have had on us. Our first debut outside of Puerto Rico was in 2016

Figure 2. *Trenzando legados: Homenaje a nuestras mujeres*, 2022, Tocones, Loíza, Puerto Rico. Photo courtesy of the authors.

through a small collaboration with El Puente Academy for Peace and Justice in Williamsburg, Brooklyn, New York. It was an enlightening experience, through which we got to see how much organizing happens in diasporic communities, how openly political they were. We observed that being Puerto Rican in the US draws our communities to confront their political reality much more directly than in the archipelago. Although Puerto Rico is a US territory, and Puerto Ricans are US citizens, we are not equal to those born in the states; Puerto Ricans in the archipelago do not have the same rights as those who live in the mainland. However, Puerto Ricans that live in the mainland are not seen as equals by their fellow US citizens, facing much of the same discrimination the Latinx community in the US faces as a whole. This situation instigates them to organize and express themselves about Puerto Rico's unfair and colonial treatment more bluntly and openly than many of those who reside in the archipelago. Our eyes were also opened from witnessing how community organizing can be taught in schools in the US. By virtue of being in New York, we were also able to meet fellow muralists and get in touch for the first time with artists who received training in actual schools of community muralism, like the Philadelphia Mural Project.

After these experiences, we began to position ourselves as community organizers and art educators. Through our work, we fight for the accessibility of art and to maintain our communities as ours.

Community and Community Arts Strategies

Every space, every wall, belongs to the community where it is located. We are invited into other people's home environments, their parks and streets, and it is our responsibility to genuinely contribute to the health of those spaces. We feel lucky to have always been invited by organized leadership into the communities where we have worked. When we enter communities, it is important to know about them and contribute to the work that is already being done—as opposed to carrying out unrelated independent projects. Communities do not need saviors or extractors, those who take cultural capital from them, benefit from their circumstances, and profit off them. In saying this, we don't mean to invalidate independent project-building, but we have to stress the importance of contributing to the organizing that's already being done from the ground up. We consider ourselves facilitators of our skills, in the organization and leadership processes that are already happening in each community.

Our community arts strategies have taken time to develop. Our first attempts at community participation were limited to consulting and community painting sessions. Now we offer several community workshops to inform the ideas that are going to be portrayed, as well as opportunities for locals to critique the design and agree on changes.

In our workshops, we begin with exercises that spark people's creativity, nurture language around the concepts we are working with, and offer some insights for analyzing art. Then we brainstorm. For this, we bring a series of questions to be answered in writing or drawing. Some questions are concept-oriented and others are image-oriented. The goal is to create a list of concepts for the idea of the mural, and a list of visual ways to touch on those concepts. Then we design; sometimes we work with just one option, other times we have up to three designs to choose from. We present them to the community we're working with, and participants can critique them and vote on their favorite. During the last interaction before we start painting, we present a final design that incorporates suggestions from the group critique.

The community painting sessions have evolved over the years. In our early years, we used a paint-by-number system and worked directly on the wall. Then we developed color mapping, where we outline sections with colors and numbers, which made it less confusing and less prone to mistakes when working with younger kids. Since 2021, we have introduced the polytab technique to our practice. It's a technique where you grid out the mural and paint it on five-foot square pieces of very thin fabric. Then, you install those pieces on the wall, adhering them with gel medium. Not every project is done with this technique—we still paint directly onto walls—and the decision to use it is made on a case-by-case basis. Generally, it's meant for larger-sized projects where community participation would be limited by painting directly onto the wall because of a location that would require people to be on lifts or scaffoldings. However, sometimes there are time frames or budget limitations, as this technique is more expensive and labor-intensive than painting directly on the wall.

In addition to painting community murals, we also simply facilitate art

Figure 3. *Libre y Peligrosa*, Humacao Grita, 2019, Humacao, Puerto Rico. Photo courtesy of the authors.

workshops for the community that vary according to their interests and necessities. We have given drawing and painting workshops and even sign-making workshops. The most popular events are our workshops on art as therapy, which are filled with creative mindfulness exercises that help with anxiety and inducing relaxation. We produce public art, but also collective art experiences that nurture healing processes and replicate the therapeutic benefits that can be obtained from art practices.

Connecting with Our Diaspora

Over the years, we have organized many community projects with the Puerto Rican diaspora in the United States. Connecting with our diaspora is very important because as of today, the majority of Puerto Ricans live in the US. Puerto Ricans of the diaspora face the reality of our political relationship with the US every day, mainly because of discrimination, language barriers, and violence against their communities. Because of this, they need to organize and politicize in order to defend themselves and our motherland. On the flip side, many Puerto Ricans living in the archipelago think of diaspora Puerto Ricans as foreign and removed from their culture. This is a hurtful idea, which we think should be eradicated. We believe that we need to nurture a relationship with our diaspora and create meaningful exchanges in which both parties benefit. We hope that in nurturing this relationship, Puerto Ricans from the diaspora will be inspired to use their political power but also to connect with their culture, maybe even return to Puerto Rico one day. We also believe that for Morivivi, these interactions impact our work and views. We grow immensely through engaging with how our community loves us from an ocean away, how they fight for us every day.

Artivism

As a collective, our artistic production consists of muralism, community muralism, and "performance" protest actions. "Artivism" is the combination of art and activism. We produce artivist experiences and practices both in collectivity and in collective spaces. The term *artivism* applies to protesting in the streets, but it is not limited to that one action. We believe that through artivism we can promote awareness of social problems and nurture the strategies and behaviors that will help solve them.

Activism, as a word, implies activation. In our practice, public art allows us to activate spaces. This is another facet of what we call "artivism." Through muralism, we activate walls that often structure unused and even deteriorated spaces. A mural transforms the space into a cultural place of significance, thus *activating* its potential to bring the community together. In our experience, when we are stimulating these spaces, the people of the community want to get involved in the improvements to their neighborhoods. In this way, through muralism, spaces are enlivened through collective action.

Artivism manifests in another way that occurs in the early stages of our community projects. When we offer workshops to community groups to develop concepts for murals, this practice allows us to create spaces to stimulate people's collective memory. They can even become spaces for relief and collective healing, nurturing community bonds.

Collective Imaginary

Through public art, we produce and contribute to what we call the collective "imaginary"—a set of images that become representative of our culture and our reality as a people. Colectivo Morivivi contributes to this imaginary through the images that we construct in our body of artistic work. We compose images that challenge traditional societal notions and amplify Puerto Rican narratives from the ground up, to strengthen our collective memory. Our intention is to build community and make sure that our histories of resistance as Puerto Rican peoples are not erased; that is why we use public art.

The collective imaginary is the great visual compendium of each community. Some images become traditions, symbols, and even clichés of culture. We try to articulate a visual narrative that transcends their two-dimensionality. We create images that convey the idiosyncrasy of our people with the complexity of their sociopolitical backgrounds. Our images provoke and invoke. By working in the public space, our images become part of a compendium that we identify as our own. We give visual language to those who do not have it or have very little, through images that have layers of meaning and visual signifiers that we have to face, confront, expose, and transgress. Our goal is to expand the collective imagination and review the collective memory, offering new interpretations of our identity, our historical legacy, and our sociopolitical baggage.

The Collective as Model

Being a collective of artists, our internal process is different than that of a single artist who may choose what they're going to do without input from another. Decisions at Moriviví are made in consultation and through group discussion. The ideas and images that we work on go through a process of criticism constantly, to transform each into something new that we have created together.

We replicate the collective model in every community project we carry out. Teamwork is a very necessary skill in society, as the capitalist model has made us very individualistic and has stunted our ability to work together. When we do community projects, we teach strategies that help us organize to achieve a common goal. A space for social interaction is created that strengthens community bonds. This is crucial because the environmental and political challenges of the twenty-first century demand our collective attention and the organization of our communities more than ever.

We aspire to continue replicating this model on other scales. Little by little, we are changing from being a group of artists to a social enterprise, affirming the meaning of the word *collective* that is part of our name. We want to become a space for collective organization. We would like to cover more areas of public art. Finally, we aspire to become an alternative school of artistic practice for those interested in immersing themselves in art and their community. We hope that our work doesn't skip future generations.

Themes and Transgressions

Over the years, after our visual discourse expanded, we realized that our name, Moriviví, reflects the narrative of our images. The duality reflected in our name is presented as a theme over and over again in our work: either

Figure 4. 2015 mural *Paz Para La Mujer*, restored in 2021, Santurce, Puerto Rico. Photo by Kelvin Rodríguez Soto.

feminine/masculine (e.g., the mural we created for SEL5), creation/destruction (e.g., our murals in The Miracle Project, China), going/coming (e.g., our Fresh Paint Springfield murals), life/death (e.g., *Peace for Women* mural). When looking back, we observe a duality in the human condition, with the body as the protagonist and main element.

The body is the great constant in our works of art. All transgressions end up being on our bodies. The body is a universal reality in which we all live. It appeals to the viewer's empathy. The body can look at, confront, and even call to the viewer. That is why it has always been an element in our pieces.

Who is represented in the work of art? This question applies to the body but also to the reality that each artistic piece appeals to. In our visual discourse, we will see the predominance of women, Black bodies, nature, the earth itself as an element that is revisited, and the integration of landscapes.

The body of the woman has been subjected to many, many transgressions. "Women, like the earth, are a territory of conquest" is a common protest slogan that transmits our vision and the discourse toward which we lean in our work. Transgressions permeate the representation of our bodies. Representing a body, as it is, can become an act of protest, as it was with the mural *Peace for Women* in 2015 (fig. 4).

The mural *Peace for Women* has been one of our most important projects because of what it represents and its history. This project arose from a collaboration with the organization Coordinadora Paz Para La Mujer, a coalition that provides services, assistance, and education to women victims and survivors of domestic violence, gender violence, and sexual abuse. This and other entities organize to commemorate the International Day for the Eradication of Violence Against Women, every year on November 25. A call to establish that day of remembrance and resistance was initiated by the Latin American feminist movement in 1981, commemorating the day of the assassination of the Mirabal sisters—activists who fought against the dictatorship of Rafael Trujillo in the Dominican Republic, whose collective code name was "The

Three Butterflies." As part of the organization's campaign to prevent and educate about violence against women, we were invited to create a mural. This was one of our first projects directly linked to feminism.

From the beginning, we were aware that we did not want to represent a classic image of domestic violence, since it would reproduce subjugating and victimizing visual language, totally contrary to our aim, which was to empower. We understand that violence against women lies in how women have been and are seen in the eyes of society. That is why part of eradicating violence against women involves eradicating the image of women typically consumed through media. Our mural had to transgress the distorted image of the woman that we consume without sufficient questioning, in which unreal, unattainable, hypersexualized, and objectified bodies are shown. Nudity in and of itself is not offensive. This is why we decided to present the body of a Latin and Black woman just as she is, with her asymmetrical breasts, wide hips, and full thighs. That is the woman that exists, that is the woman that must be accepted and protected. We wanted to question which bodies offend us. The conclusion we reached is that if we cannot view the natural image of women with appreciation and respect, how are we going to see such women in our lives?

For this reason, we decided to represent a woman who reflected our Black heritage and made visible the Santurcina-Dominican woman, a woman who is part of the community where the mural is located. In turn, we represent nudity as something linked to nature. Two female figures, like trees in a forest full of monarch butterflies, travel on their long journey, where the cycle of life and death is depicted. Such a journey can be associated with the same cycle faced by victims and survivors of gender-based violence.

After a few months of having finished and installed said mural, one of several people (who remain unidentified) painted bras and panties on the painted bodies, attempting to clothe them. With this action, the woman's body in the mural became the subject of public discussion. Thousands of Puerto Ricans crowded the media and social networks to denounce, question, and comment on what had happened. The discussions were about defending the mural as a work of art and denouncing the act as one of violence against women and even as an act of anti-Blackness. Nursing mothers and women stood firm in protest, exposing their half-naked bodies, with their breasts exposed in the same pose in which the two women in the mural were painted. For us, it was a beautiful and surprising experience, because we had not foreseen that the simple image that we built would stimulate something so powerful and emancipatory. The anonymous intervention that many interpreted as censorship or vandalism in fact validated the decision to portray that image in the first place.

Several months after the two female figures in the mural were defaced with underwear, we responded with another intervention. Instead of completely restoring the mural, we decided to somehow immortalize what had happened. We opted to make a photo installation over the painted bra: a pixelated image, alluding to censorship, of the breasts of the main figure. Inside each pixel, we included the images of the women who protested half-nude in front of the mural, as well as some of the demonstrations that took place on social media. This was intended to document and immortalize what happened. We felt that if we restored the mural in its entirety, we would be erasing an event that is still important to remember, still part of the story.

In 2021, six years after the last intervention, signs of fading on the mural were severe. The photo installation was also completely blacked out because of UV exposure. The artists, knowing the cultural and political importance of the mural, worked with the support of fellow organizations Coordinadora Paz para la Mujer (Peace for Women Coordinator, CPM) and FRIDA Young Feminist Fund in an effort to revitalize the mural. This third intervention brought a couple of changes. The background, the butterflies, and the second figure remained faithful to the original design, infused with a fresh layer of color. It is the first figure that carries the evolution of the artwork. Instead of a new installation, the pixellation was painted directly onto the mural, with minor changes to the imagery. The other significant change is the incorporation of the names of victims of femicides occurring from the start of 2021 until November 25 of that year, written on the dead butterflies that lay over the main figure.

Our experience with creating the mural *Peace for Women* shows that when we question the representation of women, we question the prejudices of our society, and we ask ourselves which women need representation. It provided more justification than ever for our focus on representing our Black roots and our Black women. We find it more than necessary to transgress our internalized racism and insist on painting Black bodies as beautiful, strong, and free.

In our figural work, we approach the body in comparisons and contrasts with nature. Our archipelago is a paradise that has experienced trauma on different scales, like a body "keeping the score." This trauma seeps into and continues to transcend the centuries of our coloniality. For this reason, we visually articulate our interactions with and our experiences in our environment, by including diverse landscapes in the scenes we construct. For example, in the two murals we completed for The Miracle Project in China—*Cacibajagua* and *Island-Man*—we see the human figure entwined in the landscape. *Cacibajagua* illustrates Mother Earth giving birth to a colony of ants that blooms in precious phases like the flower known as "Lady of the Night." The figure lies in the layers of the earth, in a composition that presents a cut in the earth itself to show us the scene. On the other hand, *Island-Man* presents a man adrift, made of a colony of ants that try to keep him afloat in

Figure 5. *Las mujeres hacen matria*, El Grito del Arte Festival, 2021, Lares, Puerto Rico. Photo courtesy of the authors.

the middle of the sea. We cannot determine whether the island-man sinks or will be able to rise. These are examples of the visual narratives that we build by combining the human figure with landscape. These two murals illustrate our gaze toward coloniality. We know that our history is one of conquest, time and time again, and we denounce it as a patriarchal ideal. This is how we transgress that coloniality in our works of art.

Not only do we represent ourselves as Puerto Ricans, but we represent the places where we have created community, the landscapes that resonate in our memory, and our evolution. Some of these ideas can be seen in the murals we made for Fresh Paint Springfield in 2019: *Ellos se van con el éxodo* (They Are Leaving with the Exodus) and *Brincar el charco* (Jump the Puddle). *Ellos se van con el éxodo* shows an imposing landscape of the coast of Puerto Rico that includes the elements we see when we take a plane to the US: the mountains, the neighborhoods like La Perla and Loíza, the forts like El Morro, the coast, and the blue ocean. Four girls are on the coast. Three look to the sky, while one confronts the viewer. A phrase is intertwined with the foam of the sea: "They are leaving with the exodus even though they do not want to go." At the far left of the mural, a woman standing in the water holds a mirror in front of her face. In it, you can see the image of the confrontation between the protesters and the police on May 1, 2018. The mural presents the panorama that Puerto Ricans and the youth of the Island face.

Meanwhile, when crossing the street, you will find *Brincar el charco*. This mural presents an urban landscape of brick buildings, iconic of cities in the US. In its point of emphasis, we look into a window where a Puerto Rican family of a young woman and her daughter live. The daughter waters the plants, providing sustenance to her roots. The mother reads a letter in front of the window. Then our eyes travel over some laundry lines where newspapers hang, showing the news about Puerto Rico and headlines that appeal to the scene. Our gaze stops on a pole with signs identifying the address. One points to the first mural and reads: "Pedacito de tierra" (Little Piece of Earth—as in, home), while the other redirects us to the scene and reads: "Brincar el charco" (Jump the Puddle). "Jumping the puddle" is a commonly used phrase by Puerto Ricans. It encompasses the feeling of having to move to the US. Our baggage travels with us and we look back. However, we have to look ahead as well. We underline this with the girl who cares for new growth while she waters the seedlings.

In our work, we confront the erasures of our history. We make sense of our experience. We claim our representation. We connect with our diaspora. Our work threads together elements that we know, underlining their meaning or their impact on our identity. We provide new interpretations of our history and our environment. All this to awaken a collective memory of resistance, of a people that has always been hardworking and has always sought to move forward.

Transgressions: Feminist Realities

Being a group of women led us to position ourselves as feminists. We cannot say that Morivivi organized to be a feminist group explicitly. First, because our feminism arose organically. Second, because we started at a crucial stage in our youth. It was through Morivivi that we transitioned into our adult life. Our lived experiences as women led us to create work based on our survival within a still-patriarchal society. So much so that, since we were all women, automatically other groups and sectors identified us as feminists before we could articulate ourselves as such. Now, we embrace feminism and are continuously learning to do better. Intersectionality is an important quality and principle that we must continuously keep in mind and put into practice. Besides, there is no "correct" way of navigating it. Our systems and structures are not designed to be intersectional, so we make mistakes constantly. With as much conscientiousness as we can muster, we make a huge effort to stay critical of ourselves and do better. We strive to continuously better our practices and policies.

Looking back, those of us who remain in Morivivi after ten years wonder why we have never abandoned the project. The answer is that we created a

Figure 6. *Cimiento de sus venas*, Springfield, MA, 2024. Photo courtesy of the authors.

space by ourselves, for ourselves, and we know that we are not the only such case. The creation of spaces by women for women is our way of transgressing and claiming something that was denied us for too long. Still, claiming our place and our space is a challenge. We still need more women in positions of power. We claim our power through art.

Colectivo Moriviví is a group of women artists based in Puerto Rico who have been producing public, community, and social art since 2013.

Raysa Raquel Rodríguez García is an interdisciplinary artist with formation in drawing and painting. From an early age, she showed interest in the visual arts, for which she had the opportunity to take her first courses at the School of Arts and Design of Puerto Rico and at the Art League of San Juan. From 2008 to 2009 she studied visual arts at the Carolina School of Fine Arts. After her preparation at the School of Fine Arts, in 2009 she entered Puerto Rico's Central High School of Visual Arts and graduated in 2013 with a certification in drawing and painting. From 2017 to 2018, she was part of the Program of Independent Studies (PEI) at Puerto Rico's Museum of Contemporary Art (MAC). In 2019, Raquel earned her BFA in painting from the School of Art and Design of Puerto Rico. From 2017 to 2022 she worked as an educator and exhibition assistant at the San Juan Museum.

Sharon Nichole González Colón is cofounder of Colectivo Moriviví, a muralist, and a community arts educator. In 2013, she graduated from Puerto Rico's Central High School of Visual Arts, earning a Drawing and Painting Certification. In 2017, she took courses at the University of Puerto Rico, Río Piedras campus. During the spring of 2018, she was a Climate Refugee Scholar at Hampshire College in Amherst, MA. From 2017 to 2019, she was part of the Program of Independent Studies (PEI) at Puerto Rico's Contemporary Art Museum (MAC). In 2023, she earned her BFA in sculpture with a minor in printmaking from the School of Fine Arts and Design of Puerto Rico (EAPD). She had her first solo exhibition, *De la tierra y el Recuerdo*, at Espacio Emergente in Bayamón, Puerto Rico, in 2024.

CHAPTER 21

Léeme La Cuerpa: Queer Laziness and the Body Politics of El Perreo Combativo

ISABEL PADILLA CARLO
INTERVIEWS WITH DJ PERRA MÍSTICA (KARINA IVETTE GONZÁLEZ PLATA) AND KARLA CLAUDIO-BETANCOURT

On July 24, 2019, at the intersection of anger, uncertainty, and hope, an archipelago and its diaspora held their breath, lungs expanding with anticipation of the news that Ricardo Rosselló may resign. Tension took hold of everyone's bodies; spirits were on alert. Television sets across the Island were tuned in to the same channel. The words on the corner of the screen read "Gobierno en jaque." All the while, bodies sporting "RENUNCIA" bandanas, sparkly balaclavas, retro sunglasses, "NASTY WOMAN" T-shirts, chunky jewelry, and Puerto Rican flag-print bikinis exceeded the visual field of the camera. Viewers were witnessing an unrestricted flesh, part celebration and part protest. Thereafter, a news reporter appeared on the main stage, introducing the final act for the evening: "El perreo intenso acaba de comenzar."

And what an extravagant coda it was! A pleasurable climax to mark the end of the summer of 2019 Island-wide protests. Atop the steps of a historic cathedral, dancers of all shades, ages, sizes, identities, and orientations converged. Bodies upon bodies danced as if they had just witnessed the end of the world and the birth of a resplendent future. They gyrated their hips, making flesh bounce, and contested violent age-old hegemonic structures. They arched their backs, supporting themselves on the cathedral walls, and made visible the bodies that had been historically erased from conversation. They threw their pelvises against each other, staring keenly at their partners, and transformed the gendered roles ascribed to reggaetón's social dance form. They danced, and danced, and danced, and collectively enacted a tremendous feat of collective resistance and joy. Sin perreo no hay revolución.

The #RickyRenuncia movement was what brought these disquieted bodies together in solidarity through dance. Leaked Telegram group chat messages between former governor Ricardo Rosselló and members of his cabinet, containing apathetic remarks about Hurricane Maria victims and derogatory jokes concerning female journalists, queer celebrities, and rival politicians, among many other offenses, became la gota que colmo el vaso, the drop that spilled the glass. More so, what fueled fifteen days of collective action that paralyzed many of the urban centers of the Island were years of state-inflicted violence in the form of budget cuts, neglected infrastructure, and federal bribery schemes. This is the context in which el perreo combativo emerges as a public display of defiance.

As seen in many recordings of this event, some dancers held Puerto Rican flags, while others held beer cans; nonetheless, all participants danced in unison to the boom-ch-boom-chick rhythm of reggaetón. The image of gyrating bodies amid the summer 2019 call to arms reminds us that el perreo combativo was simultaneously a party and a protest. It was a spontaneous yet strategic performance of what Rocío Zambrana describes as "queer laziness." As Zambrana helps us understand in her book *Colonial Debts*, Puerto Rico's colonial structure reduces people's bodies to their economic potential as they are instigated, through traditional gender roles, to serve the state through means of reproduction and labor. Queer laziness arises as a means to "defy not only [their] own proper place but also the very project of moving the country forward. . . . Refusal to work is here understood as a refusal of the ethic of work in a neoliberal key. It is to imagine life beyond the binary."[1] In other words, leisure in response to a colonial structure can be quite revolutionary, as it materially and symbolically interrupts the gears that keep the capitalist machine turning. The objective of this protest was made clear in the use of the cathedral as its stage, the transgender flag as its backdrop, and the protesters as its performers. Queer, gender-nonconforming dancers appropriated a gendered dance form to undermine the function of the gender binary in modern coloniality. Moreover, by organizing a massive block party, dancers of all backgrounds reclaimed their erotic autonomy and "interrupt[ed] the construction of the body-territory, of the body-colony: the racialized/gendered body as something to contain, bound, control, extract, [and] police."[2] In this impromptu carne vale, these bodies enacted the radical politics of solidarity, collective care, self-love, and refusal that lie at the heart of Black, queer, and feminist praxis. El perreo combativo was a party turned protest, resistance put into motion.

What is widely known as el perreo combativo began as an accidental yet fortunate encounter between three separate initiatives that convened in different sectors of Old San Juan. The first of these was a Guayoteo block party in Calle Fortaleza that was prompted by a national call for un perreo intenso. Another, subsequent to this one, was set in Plaza de Armas by DJ Kevin el Sacamostro, prompted by a desire to gather more people for this call to action. The most contentious party was held in front of a historic cathedral in Calle

Cristo. Unlike the others, this party was organized as una grajeada combativa, a militant make-out session titled "Léeme los labios" (Read My Lips). El Grupo de Trabajo de Género (GTG) occupied the steps of the Metropolitan Cathedral Basilica of Saint John the Baptist and engaged in an unapologetic make-out session with queer, gender-nonconforming bodies at the forefront. The convergence of el Guayoteo and Léeme los labios was all but premediated . . . Perhaps fate, kismet, luck, or simply mere confusion led to what would become what DJ Perra Mística (co-headliner of la grajeada combativa) accurately describes as a cathartic happening. Sensing the energy of the crowd, la grajeada combativa inadvertently responded to this national call as DJ Perra Mística and DJ Kaya Té played reggaetón, utilized the church's steps as a dance floor, and laid the foundations for the radical manifestation that would ensue.

Perreo as a social dance form is a product of cross-cultural exchange between European social dance practices and African communal symbolic dance.[3] These African dance forms were misinterpreted by the European settlers and perceived as sexually charged movement. In time, these ceremonial dance practices were adopted and distorted, separating them from the community space, and brought into the close quarters of heterosexual partner-dancing. Despite the miscegenation between these European and African dance forms, it induced in white society a moral panic because of its associations with Black sexuality. The stigma toward these racialized movements perdured well into the twenty-first century, as merely two decades ago, the Anti-Pornography Campaign was initiated in 2002 by Puerto Rican Senator Velda González, seeking to eliminate perceived vulgar and pornographic content from all media, particularly focusing on reggaetón due to its provocative music videos. Of specific concern was the dance style accompanying the music genre, perreo, where a cisgender man bumps or grinds his pelvis against a cisgender woman's hips in a "doggy-style" position. Delineating the origins of perreo makes evident that movements that have historically brought Black communities together have constantly been persecuted because of how they are perceived through the colonial gaze. Not only are bodies racialized, but movement itself is prescribed a gender binary that restricts masculine- and feminine-presenting bodies to certain codes of conduct. For this reason, el perreo combativo that was performed on the steps of the cathedral was so important, as bodies rearticulated the gendered movements ascribed to perreo and symbolically contested colonial structures through their bodies, the movement, and the space they occupied.

In spite of reggaetón's emergence into mainstream popular culture, el perreo combativo was met with much backlash, specifically the party held in front of the church. When videos of this protest went viral on social media, the movement was reprimanded by conservative and liberal groups alike; in their view, protesters had allegedly gone too far by desecrating the church with their explicit music and graphic sexual acts. Perreo can be seen in quotidian spaces from local nightclubs, small gatherings, and beaches to global or virtual stages like music videos, concerts, and international award shows. On that premise, if such movements are so prominent in the environments of our everyday, why was el perreo combativo received with such apprehension? Precisely because this perreo did not look like the one that is usually showcased on television and social media. El perreo combativo represented a diverse swath of Puerto Ricans. Mabel Rodríguez Centeno perfectly describes the impact of this performance: "When the street is the political territory and the language is that of women's bodies, racialized bodies, feminist bodies or queer bodies, the alteration of the symbolic space of normative culture is such that it unleashes terror."[4] It unleashed such terror precisely because these protesters broke unwritten rules of social order through their ways of moving and being in the world. By dancing in front of the church, protesters seized a historic space of oppression to transform it, even if momentarily, into a utopian realm where freedom and joy were paramount.

The aspects of el perreo combativo that were sensationalized were based on the limited perspective of the video that went viral.[5] In the aforementioned YouTube video, the camera captures two subjects: a large crowd squeezed together in a small space, and a dancer sporting a bikini with Puerto Rican flag print. Throughout the video, the camera mostly remains on the bikini-clad dancer, then it pans to the crowd for a few seconds before returning to its main subject. Although many others stood next to the bikini-clad dancer, news coverage of the event centered its narrative on this singular subject and placed the other bodies that were involved in the protest on the sidelines. In this skewed narrative, perhaps prompted by gender bias and respectability politics, the conglomerate of individuals was dismissed as unruly youth and the image of the bikini-clad dancer was utilized as evidence that reggaetón corrupted society. Although the hypersexualized image of the female body is prevalent in all forms of media, it is when the femme-presenting person has autonomy over their own erotic power that it signals a threat to normative culture.[6] The bikini-clad body is empowered, refusing to serve the purposes of the state through reproduction or capital interest: to be consumed or exploited. Their performance, literally combining politics (in their choice of the flag) and bodily expression, implies a connection between the colonized subject and the sieged territory. Hence, the dancer was performing in proclamation of not only their own corporal freedom but the nation's political autonomy, as "freedom starts in the body."[7]

Another video of the event, produced by activist Karla Claudio-Betancourt and titled "El boom del pueblo," or "The Boom of the People,"[8] showcases

Figure 1. "El perreo combativo." Film still. Karla Claudio-Betancourt, Vimeo, 2019.

the plurality of perreo and how queer dancers have rewritten reggaetón's gendered script to create new possibilities within its social dance form. Hence, the distinct performances shown in this video are choreographies of resistance, an example of the "embodied practices through which minoritarian subjects claim their space in social and cultural realms."[9] Instead of focusing on the huge crowd with the dancer sporting the bikini as the subject of the video, Claudio-Betancourt chooses to showcase a more intimate view of these dancers. This perspective transports spectators a un jangueo de marquesina, to a block party where dancers dismantle oppressive structures one song at a time. The pair shown in the opening of the video is dancing perreo the conventional doggy-style way; however, the femme dancer is dancing in the male "dominant" position and the masc dancer in the female "submissive" position. This reversal of traditional gender roles is very significant, as it defies the idea that men must abide by reggaetón's hypermasculine aesthetic and that women have no power in perreo's dynamic. The second pair shown in the video is dancing perreo in a nontraditional but not uncommon way, with both people facing each other and moving their hips toward each other. Though this move is popular, it negates the idea that perreo can only be danced in its doggy-style form and affirms that dance, much like language, is a dynamic, ever-evolving artform. The third pair is a same-sex pair dancing in the doggy-style position. Through this act, these dancers actively disrupt normative culture by bringing an eerie queerness to the doorsteps of religiosity and openly celebrating queer pleasure in defiance of an institution that rejects their ways of being. Although perreo is usually danced in pairs, the video also showcases individuals dancing by themselves, alone but not partnered. These dancers wearing glitter, jewelry, and sequins were combative in their own way as they developed distinct choreographies of resistance while staying on-beat and maintaining unity with others.

Much like the improvisational elements that characterize perreo as a social dance form, this block party was a spontaneous political demonstration that infringed upon the behavioral norms of regulated space. The playfulness and el puro vasilón of el perreo combativo prove that collective joy can be just as powerful as indignation and, as Rodríguez-Centeno suggests, even more "terrifying." El perreo combativo was a jayaera, that is, a collective act of self-acceptance, happiness, and liberation, where femme and queer bodies felt safe to be entirely themselves.[10] These minority groups created a utopian realm where people could celebrate their identities and find goce, enjoyment through music and dance. Music was especially a crucial component in creating a protective barrier between the dancers and the police violence taking place a few streets away. Collective care was at the heart of "Léeme los labios," and that did not falter when it became a much larger event. Everyone looked after each other, often reiterating the rule of consent: "Busquen a su pareja y con cien porciento consentimiento pónganse a perrear," "look for your partner and with one hundred percent consent go dance."[11] It is unfortunate that we don't live in a world that looks like the one created amid this event. Through their movement, the participants of el perreo combativo give us a glimpse of what a future without gender hierarchies would look like. Perhaps the absence of these scripted roles in the male/female binary allows us to be liberated, androgynous in a way, to exist in our bodies and with other bodies without marginalization or violence. This is precisely how these dancers created new possibilities within perreo's gendered choreography: pushing it and pulling it toward their needs, experiences, and future aspirations. By encouraging fluidity and play, dancers are not constricted by perreo's heterosexual pairing and can rewrite the narrative to place freedom, joy, and, most importantly, consent at the forefront of this practice.

As the coda reached its natural conclusion, Puerto Ricans stayed glued to their television screens and protesters kept dancing. Sweat marked their devotion to this collective movement. Tears marked their sacrifice. Body rolls, dips, sways, and thrusts became part of everyone's shared vocabulary. Dancing became an outlet to shake off tension and exhaustion after fifteen consecutive days of protest. It was nearing midnight as Rosselló's message began. Suddenly, everything went quiet. All that could be heard were the muffled noises of television sets atop the protesters on Calle Cristo's colorful verandas. It was a sight to behold from below, as Rosselló's message played on all the television screens. Some protesters kept staring upward, while others huddled around a few phones. When Rosselló finally announced his

Figure 2. "El perreo combativo." Film still. Karla Claudio-Betancourt, Vimeo, 2019.

resignation, roars could be heard throughout the Island. The people of Puerto Rico had succeeded.

In the aftermath of Rosselló's resignation, music artists like Residente and Bad Bunny were portrayed as the forefront leaders of the #RickyRenuncia movement. The media overlooked the contributions of women, people of color, and the queer community, who spoke out against these politicians long before the Telegram chats were leaked. Trans femme trap artist Villano Antillano used her platform to shed light on this erasure, asserting, "The people who led this movement, taking rubber bullets and pepper spray, were Black women and queer people. We're the ones who always show up."[12] That said, it is important to recognize that introspection regarding el perreo combativo doesn't end here, as this event wouldn't have been possible without the dancers, the accompanying soundtrack, or those who witnessed it. Following this essay are interviews I conducted with two of the many artivists[13] who played pivotal roles in shaping what we now refer to as el perreo combativo. Whether it be constructing a makeshift table for DJ turntables or devising a system for the camera to document the protests on the go, DJ Perra Mística's and Karla Claudio-Betancourt's practical improvised movement enabled them to produce a cultural phenomenon that began in the ephemeral space of the party and kept transforming within the virtual landscape. These artivists are, in the words of Villano Antillano, "the ones who always show up." Without them, there is no revolution.

"The Ones Who Always Show Up": Interviews with Queer Ricans on the Front Lines

EDITOR'S NOTE: Both interviews were originally conducted in Spanish, translated by the author, and modified for clarity's sake with consent from and revision by the interviewees.

The artivist (artist + activist) uses [their] artistic talents to fight and struggle against injustice and oppression—by any medium necessary. The artivist merges commitment to freedom and justice with the pen, the lens, the brush, the voice, the body, and the imagination. The artivist knows that to make an observation is to have an obligation.

—**MOLEFI KETE ASANTE JR.**, *IT'S BIGGER THAN HIP HOP*

INTERVIEW WITH DJ PERRA MÍSTICA (KARINA IVETTE GONZÁLEZ PLATA)

ISABEL PADILLA CARLO: During the summer of 2019, one of the most striking ways in which Puerto Ricans protested state-inflicted violence was el perreo combativo. As one of the DJs that was headlining this massive event, could you tell me how this party-made-celebration, this jayaera, came to be? What were your expectations for this event?

DJ PERRA MÍSTICA (KARINA IVETTE GONZÁLES PLATA): El perreo combativo occurred during the context of El Verano Combativo, days of protest to remove Ricky Rosselló, our then-governor, from his position of power due to the comments he had made that were leaked through Telegram. The Center for Investigative Journalism was a major player in making these messages public, which later evolved into these protests, which in my opinion were very diverse. It wasn't just el perreo combativo, it was the way that the summer was already being established; it had a cuir (queer) energy, associated with the arts, moving away from traditional forms of protest.

The most important information for me is that the original call was not for el perreo combativo but what was called la grajeada combativa. On other occasions this type of protest has been made in the context of the university and was usually called simply grajeada or besada. In this case, it was a combative initiative for queer and gender-nonconforming individuals to kiss or make out and bore the name "Léeme los labios" (Read My Lips). El Grupo de Trabajo de Género (GTG) invited me to participate as a DJ in this grajeada within the context of the protests. I was a coagent of the organization when the GTG was founded in 2015 at the University of Puerto Rico–Río Piedras

Campus during a time when there were many important political changes occurring around cuirness (queerness). Although it was not formalized in what are the bureaucratic processes of the university, we as a group radicalized this type of academic space and made many calls to action.

El perreo combativo was a sporadic and contingent manifestation. Contingent in reference to what could or could not have been. I wasn't anticipating it either. Much of what happened there, for el perreo combativo, was rhizomatic, a combination or interaction of all the events that were taking place at that time. I did not have expectations. Instead, I was motivated and focused because the space was very precarious. We managed to create a music space where a DJ could manifest themselves, but it was not an easy task, considering the fact that this event occurred amidst the protests, police presence, and cobblestone streets in front of the church. Structurally, Old San Juan is not the most comfortable place. Our presence was a challenge to the space itself.

The grajeadas in essence have political power precisely because they expose bodies that do not comply with certain regulations. The grajeada also has a sexual and erotic essence, placing the bodies, their internal processes, their feelings, and their subjectivities, at the forefront to fulfill a certain political purpose that is almost always one that stems from antagonism (as named by Chantal Mouffe and Ernesto Laclau), nuestra otredad. "Grajeada" is also a very Puerto Rican word. We are using that to our advantage since grajeadas in this cultural context are not so intimate, breaking away from traditional ideas of sexuality and relating with each other. The clear point of the grajeada was that we were going to do this in front of the church. We wanted to put the paterías, the energies, the cuir lives there at the forefront. Music helps the crowd feel comfortable in la grajeada. I felt prepared to do this job because my experiences with performance have precisely prepared me to be able to reach out, feel the energy of others and myself in order to play a good set. My collaboration with Piso Proyecto, founded by Noemí Segarra—to mention a particular performance intervention that we coined as DJ Móvil—in addition to having been able to cofound Colectivo Entrecejo, helped me trabajar con lo que hay, work with what you've got. You have to work with the present moment, public spaces, body movement, authentic actions, and even precariousness. My participation in la grajeada combativa during the protests was conditional since at the time I didn't even have a place to connect my equipment in front of the church; I needed electricity and at one point we couldn't find a place to connect it. Where we managed to attain electricity was within the structures of the church. I know it sounds a bit bizarre, but even the same divine and universal energy (usually associated with the spiritual, and consequently, the church) was protecting us in that moment. That was the condition of possibility for there to be music. As you know, the archbishop and many other people from the religious community made very harsh comments. It was intense because there were collective intentions to protect the space for the dancers and others involved, but by the time the movement was recognized, there were so many people who despised what we were doing. In the aftermath, there existed these two opposite energies, one positive and one negative. Luckily, the positive energy drowned out the negative, as many people recognized that this political moment was important.

What preceded el perreo combativo has different levels, or different layers let's say, since it arose from a national call for a perreo intenso, at the same time that la grajeada combativa was going to happen. The grajeada began earlier, so it had the energy of la grajeada for two or three hours; however, when the night fell, another sort of electric energy was felt. People were arriving, asking, "Donde esta el perreo?" Later, there was a particular moment where we decided to participate in the national call, and we put on reggaetón. We even asked the GTG for permission.

Because of the invitation to la grajeada combativa that was extended to me, I also invited other DJs. I had a premonition that something was going to happen, and I thought, "I won't/can't do this alone." I did provide the equipment and some of the conditions of possibility for it to happen, but it cannot be denied that it was an extremely collective effort. I am also very grateful for the trust that the GTG had in me. El perreo combativo happened because there were different energies at different moments in time that were instigating the catharsis that was el perreo combativo. Sometimes we think that things are very planned out, and I know it is because of our political preconceptions, but it was so mystical!

IPC: How would you describe your creative practice? Do you freestyle your mix based on the dancers?

PM: My way of working as a DJ is valga la redundancia, based on energy. Specifically, what comes to mind is how I feel in that particular moment, and what intention I would like to propose in the space I am manifesting myself in. I had the responsibility of visiting the space beforehand to conduct a type of scouting since we needed electricity. We had tremendous music equipment at our disposal. Starting with the table, for example, a relative of mine made a DIY table with a skinny wooden body and a piano stand as its base. The table was made precisely to be able to be easily transported and it manifested that purpose unintentionally, too, when transporting all of the equipment to Calle Cristo, a somewhat uncomfortable space during the protests. It seems like a nonimportant detail, but it is as if everything was aligned for the experience of el perreo combativo to happen.

My practice as a DJ focuses on house music that originates in Chicago and is associated with techno, from Detroit. That is my energy, but since I'm also an "open-format" DJ, it gives me an ability to interact with different genres, which was facilitated by my experiences with performance and improvisation. I really had no plan with the mix, necessarily. It reminds me of the meme making fun of DJs: "What do DJs do? Do they just press a button?" As a DJ, I believe that we should be creating the mix at the moment, not bringing the mixes already made, because, for me, the creative power and the communication between you and your audience is lost. As Perra Mística—my DJing persona—my energy is very varied. I don't follow a recipe. I am always aware of the people around me and the space. I use music to my advantage to create a protected environment. There is quite an open dynamic when I'm DJing—an openness to and channeling of performance, love, trust, mystery, and, of course, the mystical. With el perreo combativo, my mix had un poco más de sazón, a bit more spice. Although my practice is more focused on house music, I played reggaetón, and I love reggaetón, I've always had it in my heart ever since I was little and I play it in my mixes because I am, primarily, an open-format DJ. Nonetheless, after el perreo combativo, the people who invited me to play expected me to always play reggaetón. Even in el perreo combativo, I played a little bit of house and, at a certain moment, people asked me for more reggaetón or "¿dónde está el perreo?" but I stayed true to my craft.

What you say in your writing about the protests is very spot on; it is very true that there was an internal niche, like a capsule. The bodies were scattered on the center platform of the stairs, and among them the energies were more concentrated from people of the cuir community, easily recognizable in the bodies, the outlines, and how they were dancing. Further back was a large group of people that were very squished because of the dimensions of Old San Juan, but they were also participating in the event. There were people who didn't know where the main perreo combativo event was taking place. Instead of resuming their search, they joined us. Others even thought that we were the main perreo event. I favor the view that the concept of el perreo combativo itself arose after this massive event occurred. For me, its development began when the news anchor Jorge Rivera Nieves had announced that "el perreo intenso acaba de comenzar." Even then, there was another person who coined or, more accurately, popularized the term "el perreo combativo" per se.

IPC: Yes, I believe that it was Tommy Torres who wrote that tweet.[14] But it is very interesting how it is almost as if la grajeada combativa joined in with el perreo intenso by chance, many intentions of resistance existing at the same time in the same space, which merged to form something bigger, something historic.

PM: I agree, it was a symbiosis of different elements. Through social media, el perreo combativo was already being cocreated at the same time that it was happening. We were even being broadcast on national television! The fact that there was the call for el perreo at a national level, lumped together with the confusion, everything somehow managed to settle into what is known today as el perreo combativo. It makes sense. It is logical and necessary even, as if el perreo combativo needed to happen (even though it was contingent). There was an intention that could not be controlled. El perreo combativo took on a life of its own, it had that kind of energy.

IPC: Although the GTG didn't make the call for el perreo combativo, the dancers that were on the stairs ended up being the faces of this historic event. These bodies were used as political ammo for critics that argued that this form of protest was unnecessary and that reggaetón corrupted the youth. What do you think of the scapegoating, the harassment they had to endure?

PM: For me, the distinction between people is a bit problematic, since it is important to protect the fact that the space was for everyone and that includes these people who could maybe "identify" as cis or straight. To be clear, I don't like those particular categories. There is a misconception that cuir folks were in the middle, separated from all, and the rest was just not cuir energy; indeed there was a concentration on the stairs, but that's that. Visually there was a particular spatial form, therefore many beings were violentadxs, stigmatized, and even outed for being there. In various social media, many people commented on how they felt and how they handled the immediate shock. I felt affected in a certain way because those are bodies that belong in or relate to my communities, and because, as a DJ, I felt a certain responsibility for the space and what occurred there.

There was also constant negotiation in this space. Once a group of people encapuchadxs (those in hoods) came to me and said, "Look, the police are going to bring a strike force, we have to move away from here." Although it was protection that those people wanted to provide, there was another element of responsibility and power at that time and space. I'm paraphrasing Foucault here: "We all have power, there are many points of resistance. Power does not exist only in the center but in all places."[15] Hence, I didn't move (me or my equipment), although they told me to, because I felt responsible for the people there. Thinking about music strategically, combatively, like in a war in the trenches, music is a powerful tool because it distracts you, it calms you down, it diminishes your anxiety. I think that if I had turned off the music when the party was that intense, with so many people participating,

I would have overexposed those bodies in the space. The music was protecting all of those energies.

IPC: I am very curious to learn more about the psychophysical energy waves that you talk about in your personal biography. How do these energy waves create community? Do you think that a sense of community was created within Calle Cristo, the site of protest?

PM: The psychophysical has a lot to do with feeling. In early schooling and academia, we are taught that we must separate mind and body. In retrospect, how much body awareness are we really taught in school? When we say "mind-body," it already implies a division. The dichotomy is set in the language. In contrast, for example, performance manifests an all-encompassing and preexistent integrity between mind, body, and spirit. To see the world that we want to see, there are certain things internally that have to happen first, things that have to do with the self, self-conceptualization, and self-love. El perreo combativo was one of the best examples of the psychophysical for me, as bodies were behaving and moving with a great deal of authenticity and freedom. The bodies that were there had their own agency, without forcing it or resorting to a formal organization of protest. The bodies began to create the political, new worlds. I believe that a community was created, but it is not a community of a group, a nucleus, or attached to the cuir specifically, but one of intention that counteracts the current colonial and neoliberal political systems. I think that a feeling of recognizing somos más y no tenemos miedo, "we are more, and we are not afraid," was formed. From el perreo combativo, an acknowledgment was generated that we had a collective and personal power that could not be denied.

IPC: It was precisely that. Could you tell me what happened in that space of jayaera when Rosselló finally renounced?

PM: Ricky announced his renunciation just as we were packing up in the car to leave. To be frank, we ended the perreo combativo around 11:00 p.m., as again, I felt responsible for the bodies in this space, and my equipment was fragile. I would also add that the space had cleared out and there were no people left, as in, massive concentration, or as seen in the video archives. However, within ten minutes of packing all our things, everything went still. From all the balconies of Old San Juan, you could see inside the houses all the televisions turned on with Ricky's broadcast. We all heard that historic news at the same time, and that party of protest did indeed turn into a celebration, energetically. The celebratory energy carried on to the aftermath as well. At least, I celebrated at La Perla con corilla, with my friends.

IPC: Many could argue that the reggaetón music genre was, and still is, very hostile toward women and queer people. Therefore, it is very significant that these communities are taking space within this genre and are able find pleasure in something that was once very unwelcoming. Since perreo was, in its origin, a very gendered dance form, what do you think about the transformation that it has undergone these last few years?

PM: For me, reggaetón has always been cuir. Now, it is recognized that there is something different from what circulated before but that has always been present. I am not in favor of history, of how things are judged in the dichotomous categories that are related to language. I like to protect the idea that cuir people have always existed. It is such a fragile thing to say, "This was the first person who did this." Language is a tool, but it also has its complications, which is why I love performance, as it has to do with theory/praxis (as a unit) and the psychophysical. For me reggaetón has always been cuir, and I say that, even so, because my own devenir (forthcoming energy) is cuir. There has always been a certain and important type of intersectionality in reggaetón. Now, what we see is a revindication of the desire that comes from different bodies and in different ways. And as you mention in your writing, reggaetón itself is not bad but, rather, a reflection of society.[16]

IPC: As an activist, do you see el perreo combativo becoming a staple in Puerto Rican protests, much like the cacerolazos and la plena combativa?

PM: I think that el perreo combativo as it happened in the summer of 2019, will never be replicated exactly tal cual. The focus should not be in "re-creating" it. Let's take, for example, the cacerolazos, the besadas, the plenas; those are movements that are looser and less particular in their characteristics, in my opinion. The elements of el perreo combativo are less reusable as a format: the sound of the DJ, how it would be organized, the protection of the public in that place in time, et cetera. If another perreo combativo happens in some other context of political protest, that would be great! But I don't think its specific energies could be reproduced; like you said, el perreo combativo can be an inspiration, but for me it should not be a format, a strict format. To recreate it exactly as it happened (in every aspect), is a little bit problematic for me. We also have to take into consideration the bodies that were there and how to protect them, as we are not objects to fulfill a political aesthetic. This was something so particular—within a political context that was also very particular—so different, and it was effective. I understand people that ask, "Could we adapt it as a political tool?" I want to take care of this; it's a meneito. In essence, though, we have to be careful not to over-define and over-hold things too much politically. I'm very protective of that thought. What I can assure is that art is a pillar in what I feel are these new porvenires of protesta, these new becomings of political protests, and that is not limited to el perreo combativo. My question would be, why do it and for what? For me it was very difficult to separate the event, as it happened in space and time, from the onlookers, or "spectators," after the fact. There were already comments circulating that what we did was a spectacle and that we wanted to show off, when in truth, everything was the complete opposite of that, much more genuine than mere spectacle. Political movements should be anchored in the genuine, in authenticity. Those were cuerpas bellas y perras, beautiful and stunning bodies in self-expression, people moved by and for genuine feelings. That is why I do not deny the performance part of el perreo combativo as you and I recognize it—but I want to take care that it was not fetishistic, stereotyped, or a show with costumes. Although it was sporadic, this event was something protected and mystical; it took a lot of work and heart and soul.

INTERVIEW WITH KARLA CLAUDIO-BETANCOURT

ISABEL PADILLA CARLO: Please share a little bit about yourself and your work.

KARLA CLAUDIO-BETANCOURT: My name is Karla Claudio-Betancourt and I'm a multidisciplinary artist and educator. My pronouns are she/they. I work in various disciplines such as illustration, zines-making, and experimental documentary. I have also been working with ceramics and natural dyes and pigments—both mineral and botanicals—for almost five years. I run an itinerant art and ecology lab called La Recolecta, which started as an editorial project in 2015 that centered on food and material sovereignty through the study of wild plants and resources of the immediate landscape.

IPC: What brought you to el perreo combativo? What was your first impression of this protest turned celebration?

KCB: When the protests began, I was going almost every day. It was during that time that I was writing my article "Boricua Women Fight Misogyny with Art." For this reason and many more, I felt that I had to be present for what was happening. Especially after the second day of the protests, when people started camping out in the streets of Old San Juan. I thought, "This is going to be long. We will get Ricky out of office." Esto va para largo. Vamos a sacar a esta persona. When I talk about my experience in the summer of 2019, I always mention the fact that I was going through a tough time, as I had recently separated from my partner. Hence, I channeled all the energy of that rupture into documenting the protests. I created a lot of short videos for social media to spread the word about what was going on. Precisely the day of el perreo combativo, I felt depressed and was inclined not to go, but then I thought, "He is going to quit today. Rosselló will resign and I will be present to record." When I arrived, I met up with my sibling and their partner, and we felt such wild energy. There were so many people in Old San Juan. It was so strategic, meeting there in such a confined space, right next to tourists, protesters paralyzing the economy. Not only did I feel the need to record, but I also went because I wanted to dance. For me, perreo is enjoyment and healing. I dance reggaetón like it's burlesque. Es un vacilón. Almost as if we were making fun of hypersexuality while simultaneously enjoying it. I think a lot of people dance reggaetón that way too: not taking the act or themselves very seriously.

IPC: In your video "El boom del pueblo," you demonstrated that people can enjoy reggaetón in many different ways, not just in its traditional, rather gendered, form. Can you tell me a little about your documentation process? Instead of including videos of the massive crowd like many others did, you decided to capture small, intimate scenes between individuals, exposing a variety of different movements and subjects. How was that video documentation process for you, and why did you decide to include those types of shots?

KCB: Although I did not have a concrete vision for how this video would turn out, I was indeed looking for a variety of pairings, not just the traditional heterosexual one. I was also looking for people who, through nonverbal language and cues, consented to being recorded. Although some dancers were people my sibling and their partner knew, while recording I sometimes felt a pang of conscience. Luckily, some dancers have randomly come up to me, smiling and shouting out, "I'm from your video!" Reconnecting by chance with many of them has been a very gratifying experience.

IPC: Although the el perreo combativo was a massive event, in your video, it felt like a block party, como un jangueo de marquesina. Not only did you display the playful intimacy between many individual pairings, but also the slow-motion edit in your video captured the energy of that fast-paced ephemeral moment for us all to look back upon. The intensity of this celebration can be felt through the screen. Could you describe the editing process for this video?

KCB: Slow motion was something that I had recently discovered. Hence, during the protests, I recorded an unbelievable number of videos in slow motion. I think that, yes, slow motion does capture the surreal aspect of the summer of 2019. We couldn't believe that it was happening. It was unconceivable. We were ousting the governor of Puerto Rico.

IPC: Rosselló announced his resignation during the event of el perreo combativo. Were you able to record before and after the announcement went live?

KCB: Yes, I was there on Calle Cristo, near Calle Fortaleza, when Rosselló announced his resignation. It was an incredibly beautiful moment. Imagine crowds of people watching Rosselló's resignation clustered around a few cell phones. When he finally resigned, I cried, my sibling did as well. We hugged, hollered, and danced with strangers. I had never experienced something like that. It was collective glee.

IPC: Did you have any challenges capturing this ephemeral moment?

KCB: I had a system; where to put the camera, the lenses, so that they could be accessible at all times. When I saw banners or events that caught my attention, I would pull out my camera and take a quick photo or video. I also carried the same bag every day, which contained not just my equipment but also tools to protect me against police violence. I carried antacid mixture, luckily, as it was the first protest where I was pepper-sprayed. Luckily, there was a lot of cooperation when brutality like that occurred; people washed each other's faces. Protesters peacefully coexisted, even those that did not usually get along.

IPC: When I read your article "Boricua Women Fight Misogyny with Art," some words that caught my attention were "freedom starts in the body." The dancer with the flag-print bikini was claiming not only their own bodily autonomy but that of the Island as well; they heralded the flag over the most suggestive parts of their body, empowering themself and the island they call home. Can you tell me about your thoughts on this prominent visual figure of el perreo combativo and the backlash it suffered after videos of the event went viral on social media?

KCB: I had never thought of it that way, as you describe it, but I love that interpretation. I laughed a lot when I saw that bikini and that beautiful jeve perreando in front of the church. Well, to talk a little bit about the reaction

. . . My family did not understand why this protest was carried out in front of the church. They asked why it couldn't be held somewhere else. They disregarded the church's colonial history and the significance of the event taking place in its steps. Pero en la iglesia no, they remarked.

IPC: I ask you about the dancer with the bikini, because other videos position this figure as the protagonist of the event, against a backdrop of a conglomerate of people—but in your video, there is no such protagonist. In your rendition, I see a more inclusive and collective documentation.

KCB: Yes, I wondered why some bodies are allowed to be at the forefront and others aren't. The media simplified the entire movement. They did not show the Black and queer bodies that led the protest.

IPC: Nor did they include the messages those Black and queer protesters wanted to carry out, as well. Some media networks even cropped the trans flag that hung in front of the church out of pictures and videos of the event.

KCB: Exactly.

IPC: This claim to autonomy was not simply a decolonial performance but also a radical act of love and acceptance. Could you feel that sense of jayaera, of "we are here, accepting ourselves as we are"?

KCB: Yes, absolutely. I grew up listening to reggaetón and lived through that gender-based violence. Macharranes would approach you from behind without asking your consent or force themselves on you. So, to witness a space where consent, relaxation, and joy was of utmost importance was incredible . . . a total jayaera.

IPC: Do you think that el perreo combativo can become a "staple" of Puerto Rican protests?

KCB: Yes, because it is a collective vibration, a collective joy. I think that it offers a space where one can feel empowered and comfortable in one's body, precisely because it is danced with consent. In addition, el perreo combativo is carried out in a space that is rightfully ours. These streets are ours, and we pay taxes fairly to maintain them, despite corruption. It all reminds me of Audre Lorde's ideas in "Uses of the Erotic: The Erotic as Power"[17] and adrienne maree brown's *Pleasure Activism*.[18]

IPC: Of course, and that subversive way of enjoying reggaetón breaks with reggaetón's more violent past. What do you think of the genre's trajectory these past few years?

KCB: The trajectory of reggaetón is wild. To see how we have transformed a form of expression that has been dominated by the violence of the patriarchy for so long. Now, we use it for our own joy. Before, I would play songs and listen to the lyrics and think, "Wow, the words are so terrible, but the beat is so sharp!" trying to navigate the rocky terrain. I like to see people like me inserting themselves in the industry, exposing themselves to possible violence, and singing regardless.

IPC: Can you tell me a little about what you're doing now or some of your upcoming projects?

KCB: Currently, I am teaching natural pigments, a class in collaboration with the Museum of Puerto Rican Contemporary Art at Miramar Housing for the Elderly; my workshop is called "Imaginación y sinestesia desde la botánica." In this workshop, we work with natural dyes, botanical dyes, mostly with plants that are present in the home area. We explore and engage with botanical dyes using all of our senses. I have also been working on some interactive ceramic sculptures that have watercolor mixing. These are community ritualistic objects that can also be used for play in galleries or cultural spaces. These sculptures here represent Boinayel and Márohu, who are the Indigenous cemies that control the weather, drought, and rain. In terms of upcoming projects, I'm producing a movie called *Matininó*. It is a docu-fiction film about the Villanueva Rodríguez family of Villa Calma in Toa Baja and how they transform their experience with gender violence through a science fiction film that they imagine and write. It has been very nice to collaborate with them. Now, we are going to film the science fiction component in the Dominican Republic. I'm super excited to be doing work like this because it combines a lot of my research interests such as mythology, storytelling, gender violence, and material sovereignty.

IPC: What connection do you see between art, as well as other self-sufficient practices, to the liberation of our own bodies and the island we live on?

KCB: I feel that creativity and imagination cultivate joy in the struggle. Shining with pleasure, humor, and beauty in the face of state violence arms us with courage, releasing our anger, stress, and pain in the psyche and body. It gives us the power to rewrite internal and collective narratives. Art can also be that north star that adapts us to new circumstances and challenges, finding creative solutions to new problems. Relating to the landscape and other nonhuman species through crafts and other creative disciplines cultivates love and the will to defend the territory. As activist Vandana Shiva affirms in her book *Monocultures of the Mind*, "Living diversity in nature corresponds to a living diversity of cultures."[19]

This state's contempt for education and the arts makes me think of the secondary metabolites of plants. They are the chemicals produced by a plant that do not necessarily contribute to its development, growth, and reproduction. They are the products of metabolic processes that constitute the color, taste, and smell in a plant. For a long time, it was unknown what they contributed, and today it is known that they support the attraction of polarizers and repel harmful insects. Her job is desire and beauty as a weapon of defense. What I am getting at is that the state wants one to be happy surviving, with the minimum, and does not value the way in which art enriches our lives. Art is not a secondary metabolite, it is a catalyst for change, a balm against pain, and a regenerative force to continue defending life.

Isabel Padilla Carlo is a PhD student in the Department of Performing and Media Arts at Cornell University. At the intersection of memory and body studies, Isabel's research examines how dance and performance play a role in challenging or reinforcing particular social imaginaries in Puerto Rico, helping shape collective identity on the archipelago and the diaspora.

DJ Perra Mística (Karina Ivette González Plata, he/him/they/them) is a DJ, contemporary dancer, and performance artist whose creative practice is primarily concerned with corporality and authentic movement. Through their mix sets, they aim to inspire psychophysical energy waves, with the purpose of cocreating a community with love and jayaera at its core. DJ Perra Mística co-headlined el perreo combativo, provided the soundtrack for the choreographies of protest that occurred before the governor's resignation, and set the mood for the celebration that ensued.

Karla Claudio-Betancourt (she/her/they/them) is an artist, filmmaker, and educator based in Hato Rey, Puerto Rico. Their creative practice is guided by ethnobotanical research, Caribbean oral histories, and land-based knowledge in support of material sovereignty. Through their video "El boom del pueblo," Claudio-Betancourt documented el perreo combativo from the point of view of the activists that organized the event and the dancers who performed choreographies of resistance. Through her video, those who participated in el perreo combativo were able to reclaim their own narrative after it had been taken out of context and criticized by many conservative and liberal groups in social media, news stations, and television networks.

Notes

1. Rocío Zambrana, "Subversive Interruption," in *Colonial Debts: The Case of Puerto Rico*, 110–38 (Duke University Press, 2021), 129.
2. Zambrana, "Subversive Interruption," 137.
3. Wayne Marshall, "From Música Negra to Reggaeton Latino," in *Reggaeton*, ed. Raquel Z. Rivera, Wayne Marshall, and Deborah Pacini Hernandez (Duke University Press, 2009), 19–76.
4. Mabel Rodríguez Centeno, "Pe-pe-perreito o ponerle el cuerpo cuir a lo político en Puerto Rico," in *Actas VIII Coloquio ¿Del otro lao? Perspectivas y debates sobre lo cuir: Arte y activismo cuir en el Puerto Rico contemporáneo*, ed. Beatriz Llenín Figueroa (Editora Educación Emergente, 2021), 271.
5. MujerSatanica, "El Perreo Combativo," July 27, 2019, YouTube, video, 8:39, https://youtu.be/Gx-G0txXEdA?si=XJLX0AENB-e6620y.
6. Petra R. Rivera-Rideau, "The Perils of Perreo," *Remixing Reggaetón: The Cultural Politics of Race in Puerto Rico* (Duke University Press, 2015), 55.
7. Phrase adopted from Karla Claudio-Betancourt's article "Ni Una Más: Boricua Women Fight Misogyny with Art," *ArtsEverywhere* (blog), accessed April 9, 2025, https://www.artseverywhere.ca/boricua-women/.
8. Karla Claudio-Betancourt, "Perreo Combativo," July 25, 2019, Vimeo, video, 10:09, https://vimeo.com/350139441.
9. Ramon Rivera-Servera, "Quotidian Utopias: Latina/o Queer Choreographies," in *Performing Queer Latinidad: Dance, Sexuality, Politics* (University of Michigan Press, 2012), 161.
10. "Jayaera" derives from the word "hallarse" in Spanish, which means to "find oneself." The term was popularized after Macha Colón y los Okapi released the song "Jayá."
11. MujerSatanica, "El Perreo Combativo."
12. Richard Villegas, "Meet the Women Fanning the Flames of Protest in Latin American Rap," KEXP, October 5, 2021, https://www.kexp.org/read/2021/10/5/meet-women-fanning-flames-protest-latin-american-rap/.
13. "Artivists" is a term that comes from the word "artists" plus the word "activists."
14. Tommy Torres (@ Tommy_Torres), "¿Perreo Combativo??????? Wtf," Twitter (now X), July 23, 2019, https://x.com/Tommy_Torres/status/1153853484778840066.
15. Michel Foucault, *The History of Sexuality*, vol. 1 (Pantheon Books, 1978), 95–97.
16. Referencing a longer version of the author's paper, titled "Decolonization Through Artivism in Puerto Rico's 2019 Summer Protests: Examining Reggaetón's Queer Choreographies of Resistance," presented at the Puerto Rican Studies Association conference "Moriviví: Activating Puerto Rican Futures" (2022).

17. Audre Lorde, "Uses of the Erotic: The Erotic as Power," in *Sister Outsider: Essays and Speeches* (Crossing Press, 1984).
18. adrienne maree brown, *Pleasure Activism: The Politics of Feeling Good* (AK Press, 2019).
19. Vandana Shiva, *Monocultures of the Mind: Perspectives on Biodiversity and Biotechnology* (Zed Books, 1993), 7.

CHAPTER 22

Not in Our Name: A Puerto Rican White Supremacist in Charlottesville

ROSA ALICIA CLEMENTE

EDITOR'S NOTE: An earlier version of this essay was published on Clemente's blog on August 17, 2017.

I am a Black Puerto Rican woman.
Alex Ramos is a Puerto Rican white supremacist.

Two days ago, while watching the *Vice News* report on what happened in Charlottesville, I noticed a man getting into a van with David Duke, and I saw the Puerto Rican flag folded in his hands.

All day, I kept watching that clip, and then when my husband came home, I asked him. He said, "Yeah, babe, that is the Boricua flag." I got up and went outside and screamed. **I was physically sick, hot all over my body, and infuriated.**

Alex Ramos was a participant in the assault against teacher and artist DeAndre Harris during the Charlottesville terror attack.

As I sat down and gathered my thoughts, **I reminded myself that this is not just white supremacy; this is anti-Blackness. This is self-hate.** Ramos's is the colonized mindset that the Martinique-born psychiatrist, philosopher, and revolutionary Frantz Fanon wrote about in *Black Skin, White Masks.*

The sad truth is that although Alex Ramos expressed and enacted the most vile and violent form of white supremacy, his thinking is not uncommon among a minority of Puerto Ricans.

The current governor of Puerto Rico, Ricky Rosselló, is working at the behest of white supremacy as he slowly sells our homeland piece by piece to Wall Street. At the same time, he is enacting policies through a militarized police force that are economically oppressing the majority of Puerto Ricans or outright pushing them off their land.

Unfortunately, some in the broader population of Latinx/a/o people in the United States practice anti-Blackness on a daily basis. **Anti-Blackness is taught and reinforced in homes, in church, at school, and via TV networks like Univision and Telemundo.**

In this moment of national crisis, Latinx/a/o people in the United States are going to have to come to terms with who we are. We need to force discussions that break the media binary that often marginalizes, disappears us, or tells us that Ana Navarro or Jorge Ramos speak for or represent us.

They do not.

Many of us, no matter how much we try to hide it or refuse to claim it, are people of African and Indigenous descent. Puerto Ricans and other Latinx people in America must be as forceful about speaking out against white supremacy and anti-Blackness as we are about wanting to see Puerto Rico decolonized and become an independent nation.

For those of us who have studied our history and understand our connection to the African-American struggle here in the United States, we must align ourselves unapologetically with our Blackness.

What does this mean? First and foremost, we are going to have to stand up and reject the race to whiteness. We are going to have to see Blackness outside of phenotype. In a country obsessed with skin privilege, what we look like outwardly matters, **but Blackness is a political identity as well.**

When we say we are African-descendant, or Afro-Latinx/a/o, what does that actually mean? Do you wake up every day and say, I love Black people? Do you wake up every day and place yourself within the Black radical tradition in this country? Do you know the history of struggle between African Americans and Puerto Ricans in this country? Do you fight anti-Blackness?

I've had to tell family members who are anti-Black and refuse to change that I will no longer sit at a table with them.

Every day I wake up with the freedom of my people on my mind. Since the day she was born, I have purposely racialized my daughter and taught her that she is a Black Puerto Rican young woman.

Alex Ramos or any other blanquito/a neo-Nazi-minded Puerto Rican, or any Latinx person that chooses white supremacy as their ethos, cannot go unchallenged.

I must speak out and say NO! NOT IN MY NAME, NOT IN MY PEOPLE'S NAME, NOT IN PUERTO RICO'S NAME.

Alex Ramos assaulted DeAndre Harris and almost killed him. He not only brought shame to my people, he is a disgrace to humanity.

I try to practice the politics of prison abolition, but my anger against him has me hoping he is arrested, thrown in jail, and that his pain is worse than the pain he inflicted on Deandre Harris. I can't lie about how I feel.

To my fellow Latinx/a/o gente, it is no longer enough to wave flags, to have cultural pride, to be proud of your ethnicity—but to not have racial pride.

It is not enough to call yourself Afro-Latinx/o/a and then just talk about hair, skin color, or the clothes you wear. **In America, when you are devoid of racial consciousness, you essentially give up your political power.** Not everyone will call themselves a Black Puerto Rican woman like I do, but everyone who identifies as a Latina, a Latino, or Latinx should be fighting white supremacy and be aligned with Blackness.

In the 1960s, the Young Lords Party taught us to root out the idea of pelo malo y pelo bueno. They also instructed us to embrace our Africanness and root out white supremacy. As Dr. Neely Fuller said, "If you don't understand the system of white supremacy, everything else that you think you understand will only confuse you."

White supremacy is not only carried out by white people, it can be carried out by our own people, whether they be African American like Clarence Thomas or Puerto Rican like Alex Ramos. My hope is that we can begin to eliminate the white supremacist ideology that often permeates our consciousness.

Now is the time for us as a people to understand that **as long as anti-Blackness exists within our communities, we have a responsibility to fight anti-Blackness and the system of white supremacy by any means necessary.** It is up to all of us to halt the race to whiteness.

Because when all Black people are free, we will all be free.

Rosa Alicia Clemente is an award-winning organizer, speaker, political commentator, producer, independent journalist, scholar-activist, and former vice presidential candidate. A leading voice of her generation, the Bronx-born Black Puerto Rican is frequently sought out for her insight and commentary on Afro-Latinx identity, Black and Latinx liberation movements, police violence, colonialism in Puerto Rico, hip-hop feminism, third-party politics, and more. She is the creator of Know Thy Self Productions, under which she has organized multiple national tours; PR on the Map, an independent, unapologetic, Afro-Latinx-centered media collective founded in the aftermath of Hurricane Maria; and the Black Diasporic Organizing Project, a nonprofit dedicated to combating anti-Blackness within the wider Latinx community. She was associate producer on the 2021 Oscar-winning biographical drama film *Judas and the Black Messiah*. She is currently completing her PhD at the W. E. B. Du Bois Center at the University of Massachusetts Amherst.

CHAPTER 23

Flora of the Valley

ADRIANNA RÍOS

EDITOR'S NOTE: Author Adrianna Ríos has created an interactive Google Map of the feminicides in Puerto Rico from January 2021 to April 26, 2023. Readers are encouraged to visit this map at https://bit.ly/FloraoftheValleyProject.

It was 9:00 a.m. in Puerto Rico on January 1, 2023. I was scrolling through Facebook looking at pictures from everyone's New Year's parties when I read *Primera Hora*'s latest news report. Carmen M. Torruella Santiago, sixty years old, was murdered by her husband at a New Year's Eve gathering. I thought to myself: otra más, another one. I felt a surge of emotions, but more than anything I was in **shock**. He committed feminicide on a holiday, in front of family members. Her life didn't mean anything to him. *When did this become the new norm in Puerto Rico?*

My shock rolled into more questions: How are people not taking to the streets after this? When will it be enough for the government to step in and do something? When will we start investing in our resources, particularly in our school system, and equip ourselves?

Those questions, their lack of answers, led me to clarity in the form of **anger**: Puerto Rico's school system needs to promote awareness of gender-based violence. Puerto Rico needs more resources that empower individuals to recognize and report abuse. The government should run self-defense training to ensure that people have adequate tools to protect themselves.

I could have gone on, barreling toward the country I wanted in my mind; the **anger** stayed with me and settled inside, brewing into fuel.

Later that January, I read Audre Lorde's 1981 "The Uses of Anger," where she writes about the importance of alliances, listening, unlearning, and how there's power within our anger.[1] Lorde's teachings have stayed with me. I remembered her words as I read Catherine D'Ignazio's and Lauren F. Klein's *Data Feminism* (2020) a week later. Similar to Lorde, they are angry. In their book, they question who has access to power, "who benefits from data science and who is overlooked."[2] In the context of feminicides, they argue that a more comprehensive collection of data could expose the government's indifference and, in turn, could become a tool for reform.

I'm grateful to have read *Data Feminism* because it introduced me to the work of María Salguero. Salguero has been mapping feminicides in Mexico since 2015 to counteract the government's lack of response and poor law enforcement. She gathered information about the women's lives and organized her data in Google Maps depending on the location of each feminicide.[3] Salguero records specific details about each person, humanizing the victims and going beyond a call for reform. Her map serves as vessel for remembrance, a commemoration of the individuality of each life lost, and a reparative tool for the families left behind. When I saw her map, I immediately thought about how a tool like this could help inform Puerto Ricans about our current state of emergency, especially considering that until 2022—despite years of advocacy efforts from feminist organizations—the government refused to acknowledge the rampant feminicides. A map is a way of remembering the lives of those we have lost, as people instead of statistics. Salguero, Lorde, D'Ignazio, and Klein gave me **hope**.

Upon beginning my research, I found out that most of the data about feminicides in PR is collected by the Observatorio de Equidad de Género (OEG).[4] They've done an excellent job at gathering information about feminicides according to the Latin American model, which counts direct feminicides and indirect feminicides. Direct feminicides are defined as the killing of women through purposeful subjection to gender-based violence. These are subcategorized as follows: as intimate, transfeminicidios, under investigation, familiar, and non-intimate. Indirect feminicides, by contrast, are defined as the killing of women due to the vulnerability rooted in their gender, rather than as a result of intentional violence. These are subcategorized as organized crime, overdose, and deaths of young girls or older women due to negligence. In addition to the OEG data, Todas PR created a map of direct feminicides that happened between 2018 and 2019 in the archipelago, plus seven feminicides from 2020. Their map was similar to the one I intended to make, with precise locations for each feminicide, and highlighted differences in age groups.[5]

How could I contribute? How could I make the information that we already have better? I thought about these questions alongside Judith Butler's essay, "Violence, Mourning, Politics," from *Precarious Life* (2004).[6] Butler's essay comes from a different context, but their question of who counts as "grievable" can be applied to how Puerto Rican authorities overlook feminicides whenever they don't fit the criteria of domestic violence between partners. For Butler, there is no life that is not grievable. Instead of looking away, they ask us to look through our eyes and the eyes of others. I knew that I had to include the wide range of feminicides gathered by the OEG. Limiting the project to feminicides that result solely from domestic violence between intimate partners would erase other forms of feminicide. These include the feminicides of drug users, trans individuals, queer persons, and young girls—many of whom may also experience gender-based violence within their relationships or households. Salguero, Lorde, D'Ignazio and Klein, and Butler led me to my map.

My research made me **restless**. I spent weeks collecting data, and countless hours looking at old news stories, trying to gather details to narrate the stories of these women, and yet I didn't feel I could act quickly enough. I felt this task was urgent.

All the information I put together was possible thanks to the OEG's diligent monitoring of feminicides. However, gathering external information to personalize each story was challenging. I spent hours navigating through inaccurate narratives from different media outlets. I did my best to decipher the truth and tried to get as close to accurate as possible. When local journalists narrated feminicides, many of the general elements overlapped, but the details—such as location and age—varied depending on the news outlet. I found *Primera Hora* to be the most reliable and accessible source, whereas other newspapers like *El Nuevo Día* were privatized by paywalls. How is inaccuracy and gatekeeping useful? How can we educate and inform if citizens from poorer communities are not able to access these stories? These paywalls create a cycle of disinformation and ignorance, which is part of what perpetuates gender-based violence. Free access to information is crucial because it can generate accountability, promote advocacy, and stop the silencing of marginalized voices. I paid for *El Nuevo Día*'s subscription and used it to supplement the OEG's data. I credited all my sources by placing links at the end of each entry so anyone can have access to the reports, the images, and the videos from the day the news broke. Now, because of my map, those details are open to the public.

Amidst my research, I started studying the life of Ana Roqué and reading her short novel *Sara la obrera* (1895).[7] The novel is about domestic violence and sexual abuse. It's a testament to Roqué's fury against nineteenth-century patriarchal customs. When I finished reading, it was **upsetting** to realize that after all this time things haven't changed. As I studied Roqué's life, I learned that she sought education for everyone, regardless of gender, race, or social standing. Although Roqué's time is long gone, today, when we consider accessibility, we are still seeing echoes of the issues she wrote about. Who has access to the best education? Who has access to resources that teach about abuse? Is the information presented by the OEG easy to understand? This is why I crafted my map with inclusivity in mind. I used Google Maps, which is more user-friendly than a set of tables and graphs: Most people can access the map with their smartphones. I chose to write my entries in both English and Spanish so that the map and its contents can reach people in the archipelago and throughout the diaspora. I wrote the entries using accessible terms so that people with different educational backgrounds can engage with the stories.

Thinking alongside Roqué's tragic novel made me feel upset. But it also motivated me to continue. This is why I decided to pay tribute to Roqué with the project's title and flower icons. They're both inspired by her pseudonym, Flora del Valle (Flora of the Valley).[8] The flowers have three shades of purple, each color symbolizing a specific year of lives lost to violence: 2021, 2022, 2023. Even though the first elements one notices when they look at my map are the flower icons, the names of those we've lost are also on the map—a kind of caption under the flower. Instead of referring to them as victims like the OEG does, I used first names to identify each life lost. I was purposefully repetitive in my writing so that the names stay in your memory after reading each entry. Also, I made sure to try and write something about each person at the end of their story. You'll notice that many of them have a final sentence with details about them such as their profession and their relations, if they were mothers, sisters, friends, et cetera. I did my best to mention the time of the crime and to place the icon at the precise kilometer where events happened, instead of just the town. The intention behind all of my decisions when designing my map was to help people establish some sort of connection with these women, a kind of familiarity. I want readers to see that something like this could happen to them or to their loved ones. I want readers to remember their lives instead of their deaths.

Each day, the map grew. Every week, I saw it slowly getting covered by purple flowers. As I navigated news outlets, I felt accomplished whenever I was able to find accurate information on a given woman. It felt as if her story was complete and her life honored. However, I felt an immense sense of guilt because I was not able to do that for all of them. Even worse, some of them never made news reports and all I had of them were their initials, or I had to write the entry as "mujer no identificada" (unidentified woman). These cases made me think about the police and how they have the power to fill in these gaps if they'd share records publicly. The lives of women linked to local celebrities, or those of young girls, capture the most media attention.

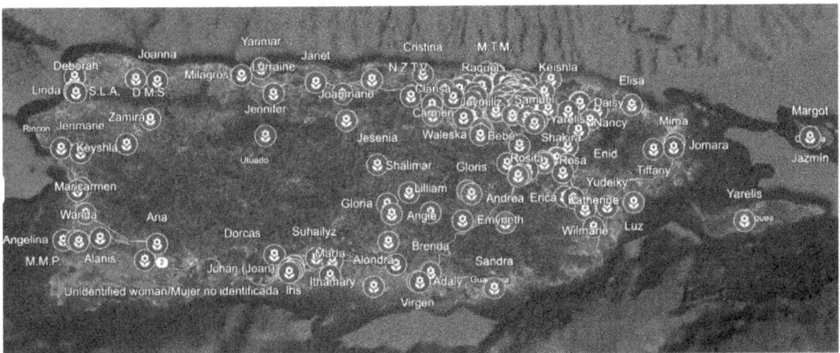

Figure 1. The "Flora of the Valley" Google Map. Image courtesy of Adrianna Ríos.

Meanwhile, feminicides where the victims are drug-using women, houseless women, and elderly women are underreported. Why are their lives worth less for reporters? I felt **guilty** and impotent because I couldn't do them justice.

I use my emotions to relate this narrative because they're an intrinsic part of my research project. All of these emotions—shocked, hopeful, restless, upset, guilty—were **anger** manifesting in different ways. I've been angry about the feminicides in Puerto Rico for so long and I've internalized it to the point where I couldn't recognize it. Today, I understand that I was **shocked** because I was angry. Anger made me **restless**; anger made me think I was **guilty** and **upset** when it wasn't me but rather the lack of information available. I was **hopeful** because I learned how to transform anger, from the feminist thinkers who transformed theirs. They led me to channel my anger into this map. This work is my way of taking power back and trying to produce something of value for those marginalized in society. It serves to expose governmental indifference and flaws within media outlets, and questions societal oversight. The Flora of the Valley Project is for everyone. Anyone that is interested in learning about these women, anyone that wants to remember them, and anyone that wants to educate themselves and their families about the infuriating reality in Puerto Rico.

Every time I attempted to finish the mapping project, the OEG would update their page, reflecting that the feminicides continue. I chose to stop on April 26, 2023, because I wanted to spend time analyzing the data, drawing comparisons, and looking into each individual case. Doing this, I was able to conclude that feminicides have occurred mostly in the metropolitan parts of the archipelago, which includes the towns of San Juan, Bayamón, Carolina, Cataño, Guaynabo, Trujillo Alto, and Toa Baja. I was expecting this to be the case given that these are the most densely populated areas in Puerto Rico. The city where the most feminicides occurred was the archipelago's capital, San Juan. While feminicides happened to women living in both poor and wealthy neighborhoods, unsurprisingly, the majority took place in areas where poverty was prevalent—like in the public housing complexes and barrios.

After spending some time looking into cases in barrios, and public housing complexes in particular, I noticed that some cases shared similarities with others. For example, the cases of Carmen Lydia (1958–2022) and Carmen Milagros (1952–2022)—they shared the same name, were close in age, and were both found dead at Urb. Santa Juanita in Bayamón. Also in 2022, there was three-year-old Yamileth Aymar and her neighbor, an unidentified woman, who both lived in the same public housing complex. Did Yamileth Aymar's mother know the unidentified woman? They lived so close to each other, and both seem to have died due to domestic violence. How might the people that live in this complex feel after reading these stories? Lastly, there's Daisy (1976–2022) and Nancy (1979–2022). Both were mothers. They were killed by their husbands and lived at Bo. San Isidro in Canóvanas. All these similarities led me to question if they were due to poor data-sourcing. At first, I fixated on these patterns because they seemed too striking to be coincidental—names, locations, and circumstances aligning in unsettling ways. I wondered if data errors were at play, but as I found more cases, I realized these were just coincidences. As I searched for connections, I was hoping to trace a cause—and, perhaps, a way to address it.

Out of all the coincidences I found, the similarity of the stories behind Myreliss (2004–2022) and Angelina Jolie (2004–2022) was the most shocking. The cases resembled each other like mirror images. Both girls were high school seniors, killed days before their graduations and birthdays. I was shaken not only because of their youth but because I was able to learn numerous details about their lives, friends, and families thanks to the outpouring of media attention they received.

The map revealed other patterns as well. For instance, the feminicide weapons of choice were guns. Sometimes feminicides happened during holidays, often in front of family members, and most in the person's residence (others took place in cars). Most feminicides in 2023 happened to women in their forties or older; perhaps younger men are changing their ways, or it indicates that the older generation of women upholds conventions like practicing submission and enduring abuse for the sake of financial support or their children. Another factor to consider is the increase in women's advocacy organizations, which can reach younger generations more easily due to their significant presence on social media. Although there's no clear answer, the age contrast in 2023 suggests that, however unevenly, current advocacy efforts are working.

Through protests, activities, and social media, many activists and feminist organizations are teaching the importance of speaking up against abuse. Still, the Flora of the Valley map demonstrates that speaking up is not enough. There are women, like Andrea Cristina (1986–2021), that continuously pleaded for help. Andrea Cristina did everything she could, but the system failed her. Her family took her case to the Supreme Court, and her story is widely known, thanks to extensive media coverage.

If that same attention had been paid to each of the 148 persons logged in my map, we'd have so much more information available. I say this with the map's many unidentified women in mind—justice would necessitate their stories be told. All the individuals in my map deserve justice and recognition. We cannot remain indifferent to their lives, as their stories will start the conversations we urgently need. Puerto Rico yearns for change, and it can only happen if we acknowledge and share the stories of those who have been silenced by violence.

The law enforcement system fails every time it doesn't catalogue cases as feminicides. Back in 2020, the government approved Law 157-2020 to improve protocols around the first-degree murders of women. However, the term *feminicidio* wasn't recognized. Moreover, the law didn't protect transgender gender-based murders, also known as transfeminicidios. Puerto Ricans had to wait until 2021 to get this law amended with the senate's Proyecto 130.[9]

The first woman to receive the limited kind of justice offered by the carceral system was Damaris Ortíz Rosario (1972–2021); her case was the archipelago's first feminicide where the murderer was charged with feminicide. Hers was the first, but the vast majority are still incorrectly cataloged. Some perpetrators seek ways to negotiate themselves into lesser sentences and others are sentenced for murder instead of feminicide. Feminicide specifically addresses the killing of women. When judges categorize feminicide simply as murder, they fail to recognize the gender-based violence behind the attack. As a result, victims receive a misaligned form of justice, and perpetrators are not held accountable for their true intents.

Another indicator of system failure is the lengthy amount of time these cases take to be solved. Take Keishla (1993–2021), whose feminicide was highly publicized because her murderer was the famous boxer Félix Verdejo. Despite the mound of evidence that authorities had against Verdejo, his trial was postponed (until June 2023) due to his lawyer's conflicting schedules. After the trial, Keishla finally received justice and Verdejo was imprisoned, though it is unclear if the same justice would have been served if not for the pressure of Verdejo's notoriety and name. If only that same attention had been paid to each of the 148 persons in my map.

Although my findings seem discouraging, I feel hopeful. I hope that there will be no need to continue mapping these cases as we move forward. I hope it's a wake-up call for those that see it. But above all, I hope that my map will make Puerto Ricans question the government like they did back in the summer of 2019. Back then, a leaked Telegram chat revealed homophobic and misogynistic comments from the governor, Ricardo Roselló. Enraged, half a million Puerto Ricans mobilized in the streets, successfully demanding his resignation.

Puerto Rico's previous and current governments have not done enough. They need to allocate more funding to programs that fight feminicide, improve the judicial system, and fix issues of accessibility in terms of information and documentation. Most importantly, there needs to be a change in the archipelago's public education system. As Ana Roqué, one of our earliest educators, once said, "Soy el eco del pasado que viene a despertar a la mujer del porvenir."[10] She implies that in order to have a better future, we must reexamine our present by looking into our past. Schools on the archipelago urgently need to implement more gender perspective into their curriculums, so that we can break with the patriarchal mindset still omnipresent in many Puerto Rican households. We must interrupt the cycle so that our tíxs, hijxs, hermanxs, vecinxs and amigxs can be safe.

To all those who engage with this map: feel the feelings that mask your anger. Instead of mourning in silence, talk about it with others. Yell and scream if you must. Use your voice. Say their names, remember them.

Since April 26, 2023, we've lost twenty-six more women. Their names were Nellie, Eliza, Janybel, Anais Marie, Betzaida, Adriana, Zulmary, Jesmarie, Mary Lynne, Carmen, Maribel, Judy Enith, Nashaly, Jaimy, Margarita, April, Carolyn, Yahaira, Nitza Marie, Channel, María del Carmen, Gloria, Tanaisha, and Nahia Paola, and two women remain unidentified.

Ni una menos.

Adrianna Ríos is a PhD candidate in English at the Graduate Center, CUNY, where she specializes in nineteenth- and twentieth-century Puerto Rican women's literature. Her research explores the intersections of gender, race, and class in these works. She holds an MA in English from Brooklyn College, CUNY. Adrianna's work has been supported by fellowships from the Mellon Foundation, the Women Writing Women's Lives Seminar, and others. Currently, she is investigating early Puerto Rican feminist thought.

Notes

1. Audre Lorde, "The Uses of Anger," *Women's Studies Quarterly* 25, nos. 1–2 (1997): 278–85, http://www.jstor.org/stable/40005441.
2. Catherine D'Ignazio and Lauren F. Klein, *Data Feminism* (MIT Press, 2020), 17.
3. For more information, see María Salguero's "Feminicidios en México," https://www.google.com/maps/d/viewer?mid=174IjBzP-fl_6wpRHg5pkGSj2egE&ll=23.94298335987288%2C-101.9008685&z=5.
4. The Observatorio de Equidad de Género was my main source. For details about their charts, see https://observatoriopr.org/.
5. See https://www.todaspr.com/nos-arropa-la-violencia-de-genero/.
6. Judith Butler, "Violence, Mourning, Politics," in *Precarious Life* (New York: Verso, 2004).
7. Ana Roqué, *Sara la obrera* (Imprenta de Manuel López, 1895).
8. Ana Roqué's pseudonym is commonly mistaken as Flor del Valle (Flower of the Valley). Her correct pseudonym is Flora del Valle (Flora of the Valley). This is evidenced in a copy of her magazine, *La Mujer*, dated June 25, 1896.
9. The Microjuris website offers more details on Law 157-2020 and Project 130. See, for example, https://aldia.microjuris.com/wp-content/uploads/2021/01/proyecto-del-senado-130.pdf.
10. Ana Roqué, "A mis Compatriotras," *Revista de la Asociación de Mujeres Graduadas de la Universidad de Puerto Rico* 4, no. 1 (1941): 19–20.

CHAPTER 24

Unruly Bodies: Excess and the Performance of Jayaera in La Vampy's "Ustedes Me Hacen Fuerte"

ESAÍ ORTIZ-RIVERA

It must have been somewhen in 2013 when I first watched La Vampy's "Ustedes Me Hacen Fuerte" on YouTube.[1] That was the era of the vlogging boom, when creators built the platform into a space of sharing—and performing—daily life itself. Somehow, La Vampy's Facebook Live transmissions and videos gained traction and popularity in Puerto Rico, as she would often dance while cleaning her house or as a spectacle wearing lingerie. What I remember from the discourse during that time is that many used Facebook to denounce her extreme exhibitionism, resorting to ridiculing and dehumanizing her by way of insults and jokes directed at her body, looks, and fatness. The discourse on her online acts moved rapidly through the web and more so when she decided to contest the insults by releasing a music video responding to critics by singing, dancing, and performing to the beat and rhythm of Miley Cyrus's "Wrecking Ball."

La Vampy, a fat, middle-aged, working-class woman, just "wanted to have a laugh," to enjoy her body, as she used her social media platforms to express herself. The parody is dedicated to all her critics who mocked and offended her with their comments. The starting scene reveals a close-up of her face, wearing vibrant red lipstick, light makeup, and her distinctive golden blonde hair. She stares directly at the lens with determination, and a faint grin appears as the opening verse begins. Her lyrics begin by narrating all the things she has done in her videos and how she has only received attacks. Yet, the verse takes a turn to highlight her perseverance in her pursuit of self-expression, to slowly enter the chorus that underscores the idea that "ustedes me hacen fuerte / y siempre me dan ganas de seguir." In doing so, she reworks the discourse weaponized against her and repurposes the actions to reaffirm her aesthetic. As such, she continues by declaring that "jamás me van a ver caer," which responds to the collective demands for her erasure and silencing for her excess. The chorus ends with "ustedes me hacen re-re-reir" which flips the existing narratives exploiting her videos and aesthetics for the purpose of mockery, to a self-determined resignification and reappropriation of her online identity. As such, the video meant to be a parody reflects and reconfigures normative discourses on her performances and challenges the collective desire to punish, silence, discipline, and contain her body.

Her video gained traction on various platforms, and once shared by popular platforms like *Comedy Central* and *BuzzFeed*, it reached other countries.[2] Today, the video remains in its original format on YouTube with the opening title "Así no se puede pedir la estadidad," a popular phrase used to dismiss or mock anything that would be categorized as excessive, shameful, or disgusting. However, it goes beyond this simple definition of something being out of touch or deviating from normative expectations for "how things should work." This phrasing is used to refer to objects, people, occurrences, or performances of everyday life that have gained attention in the media and even more so outside of the Island, with the intention of communicating that in order to seek statehood, we must behave and represent ourselves as respectable, honorable, and worthy of being accepted and admitted to the union. The excessive and unruly performance of La Vampy is framed here as a portrayal of everything that is wrong with Puerto Ricans as per a rubric shaped and framed by cis-heteronormative colonial ideals that serve to police Rican bodies. This policing emerges largely from the dominant class's investment in appealing to whiteness as both a means to seek admission into the US nationalistic discourses and to become more desirable in turn, measuring La Vampy's worth against the grain of this mythical ideal and desirable Puerto Rican citizen.

In this essay, I begin by looking at La Vampy's performance in the music video, through the lens of jayaera as a performance tactic against coloniality, white supremacy, cisheteronormativity, patriarchy, and ableist practices within Puerto Rico. Through my theorization of jayaera, and a theoretical expansion of Macha Colón's definition of jayaera in her song "Jayá,"[3] emerges a theory of how everyday performances in Puerto Rico contest the logics of colonial and imperial violence and the subjection to white supremacist aesthetics within the Island. La Vampy's performance challenges notions of what it means to represent Puerto Rico as a nation and reveal the uncovered aesthetic discourses that frame representational politics within the archipelago. Who gets to represent Puerto Ricans, and what bodies are permitted that honor without reservations? Furthermore, the popular discourses in reaction to her video shine light on what is deemed excessive and how the white gaze comes to limit our capacities to represent ourselves. What does that white supremacist gaze demand of our bodies? And as such, how does anti-fatness come to the forefront of these discursive practices that discipline and punish bodies that deviate from this imagined norm? La Vampy's intervention disrupts this politics of representation, and the colonial, white supremacist gaze that severs and limits the performance of Puerto Rican identity, by asserting her jayaera and using spaces that were not meant for her, to enjoy herself, her sexuality, and her body.

Setting the Scene: Everyday Life in Puerto Rico

Navigating the difficulties and precarities emerging from the colonial context of US imperial domination in Puerto Rico is a constant struggle for us Puerto Ricans. The colonial context constrains the possibilities for living a dignified life in the archipelago. Life in Puerto Rico is saturated with austerity and overdetermined by colonialism, as has been evidenced in the past few years after the imposition of PROMESA and its fiscal control board, the political disaster following the landfall of Hurricane Maria, and, consequently, the Ricky Renuncia protests. Yet, the relationship between colonizer and colonized remains untouched. As Sandra Ruiz argues in *Ricanness*, "at the apex of the Rican colonizer/colonized dialectic exists a subject that is continually hunted and unwanted, and is equal parts needed and inessential."[4] In this sense, our bodies are classified as a racialized and ostracized *other* and unimportant to the United States. But, in order to reproduce its empire, we are made to (re)produce and live for imperial rule. As a result, most Puerto Ricans are constantly drowning, gasping for air where there is none, and attempting to claim life in a death-ridden space. Our anti-colonial resistance is not merely an act of performing life but rather, as Jill Casid puts it, "doing things with being undone."[5]

Performances such as La Vampy's serve to disrupt the logics that hold us hostage within the toxic fumes of the constant appeals toward whiteness. In a sense, "ustedes me hacen fuerte" signals so much more than a response to La Vampy's public; I read the phrase and can't help but feel moved from its performative lure. This is not to reproduce clichéd discourses on colonial resilience but rather, to attest the many ways we confront the colonial logics of dominion, asserting our right to stand, to dream, to live in the "scene of our undoing."[6] Allow me this brief diversion to contextualize the sociopolitical scene that marks our lives as colonial subjects, with the promise to return to La Vampy later on.

In the colonial landscape of Puerto Rico, even time works differently. Ruiz contends that Ricans exist in what she calls "colonial time," wherein linear notions of time are defied.[7] Time bends itself under colonialism and through the violence that colonial subjects are forced to endure. We exist under a temporality that defies narratives of modern progress and instead generates precarity. In doing so, any fantasy of reaching the "good life"[8] remains constrained by this temporal loop. As such, the Puerto Rican body walks in the present, oriented toward a nonfuture that constantly forces it to contend with its past.[9] In other words, the past is never-ending, as it continuously haunts our present. We're not just living our lives in the moment, or the here and now, guided by our fantasies and desires for a "good life"; rather, we live our present constantly having to endure the violence of our present past.

The current landscape of the political status of Puerto Rico under colonial rule generates the social conditions for what Achille Mbembe calls "death-worlds," which refers to geopolitical spaces in which the population is subjected or made to live under conditions that expose them to a near-death or death time and again.[10] In this sense, Mbembe is pointing toward the many forms through which the state becomes disinterested in the well-being of its citizens and instead, through its policies, distributes death by abandonment, precarity, maiming, and exposure to violence. As Puerto Ricans, we have seen this with the political disaster during the aftermath of Hurricane Maria and, more recently, the state's neglectful stance during the COVID-19 pandemic. As such, it becomes evident that Puerto Rico is itself a necrozone formed by its relation to colonialism and coloniality. Coloniality, according to Maldonado-Torres, refers to "the longstanding patterns of power that emerge as a result of colonialism, but that define culture, labor, intersubjective relations, and knowledge production well beyond the limits of colonial administrations."[11] Part of coloniality relies on the normalization of the distribution of violence, similar to the one that occurs within war zones (e.g., murders, rape, violence, dispossession).[12] This gestures toward our lived experience within the archipelago, as we constantly face the crude reality of incessant violence and the asphyxiation resulting from politics of austerity and precarity.

While I do argue that Puerto Rico is a necrozone, there are spaces of exception that are less exposed to death as a result of their socioeconomic status. Hence the reason behind the disproportionate representation of queer, trans, feminized, Black, poor, disabled Puerto Ricans in the death tolls, and their exposure to precarious contexts. Judith Butler contends that "precarity designates the politically induced condition in which certain populations suffer from failing social and economic networks of support, more than others, and become differentially exposed to injury, violence, and death . . . [it is] the differential distribution of precariousness."[13] This uneven distribution of precariousness underscores the effects of coloniality as it provides evidence of how certain sociopolitical positions will grant people distance from exposure to death and the state's neglect. However, distance doesn't equal immunity. Their existence within coloniality still subjects them to its logics, and yet their access to resources grants them other possibilities to work through or, at times, move away from precarity.

Performing Jayaera

While in my first semester of graduate school in the Midwest, I found it hard to navigate the academic landscape and the city of Madison. The predominantly white social sphere felt intimidating as a colonized, fat, queer, racialized person. I would walk down the street and feel some stares, side-eyes, and at times, a constant discomfort that made me feel as if I wasn't welcome. While many friends, colleagues, professors, and staff embraced me with open arms, I missed home. My longing for the Island led me to jayaera as a praxis and performance tactic to mentally survive graduate school, while it also became my academic project. I came in contact with Macha Colón y los Okapi's song "Jayá" during that first semester, and the wheels began turning until it became clear that it was time to theorize jayaera as performance.

Listening to music is an act that occurs repeatedly, yet each reproduction of the song requires that we listen *as if* for the first time.[14] In doing so, details emerge and become clearer as we approach the material with humility. In *Listening in Detail: Performances of Cuban Music*, Alexandra Vázquez proposes an ethos for listening in detail to analyze and rehearse music.[15] As such, her proposal invites one to approach the object of study through intellectual humility, as each listening encounter provides one with the opportunity to learn more; thus, it refuses grand claims and proclamations of knowledge or comprehension of the performance.[16] My reading of "Jayá" is grounded in the details of the performance while recognizing my position in relation to the object. The aim of my theorization is not to reproduce extractivist practices or academic domination over the performance and the artist's work. The analysis I present here is in part mine, but not in its entirety, as the term *jayaera* has been deployed, used, and reworked by many along the way. In the end, I don't seek to possess jayaera as a concept, but rather, I attempt to uplift the political uses of the term. This analysis will never be complete, as jayaera will continue its transformation as it is performed in different contexts and spaces by different people. Thus, jayaera is an invitation to always arrive *as if* for the first time.

The song begins with the rich sound of the bass, adding depth to the rising beat of the drums that joins the arrangement. After a few measures of the accompaniment, the cuatro introduces a melody that generates a queer resonance, as you wouldn't expect its rich sound to be part of such ensemble. Macha Colón's voice follows as she begins to sing the words that serve as the prelude to this sonic performance. In the first lines, she begins by narrating different scenarios of feeling jayao'—such as feeling love for the first time, going shoe shopping, and listening to music for the first time. These verses gesture toward feeling jayá as something one embodies for self-enjoyment and excitement, a presentation or performance of the self to the public. After the second chorus, the song shifts to a solo wherein Macha takes a moment to explain what *estar jayao'* means, for anyone who still doesn't know. She begins by mentioning how Obi-Wan Albita (the cuatro player) thinks that "estar jayao' es estar en orden con el universo." To this, she then offers her own interpretation as "estar contento con uno mismo y donde uno está parao'." Here marks another shift as being jayao' becomes more than just embodying a state of mind or performing identity. Being jayao' goes beyond the individual, referring to the set of relational and affective attachments with space and others. In other words, jayaera is about feeling good with oneself and performing that feeling. Yet it is also about relationships: jayaera as potential for collective enjoyment and for its political deployment as a tactic against oppression.

In many senses, *estar jayao'*, or the embodiment of jayaera, serves as a way to contest the logics of colonial time, the necrozone, coloniality, and precarity that we face as the colonized. Performing jayaera as anti-colonial resistance signals to a reconfiguration of what Ruiz calls the "looping sensation"[17] that hinders our capacity for imagining an otherwise.[18] It becomes a tactic that defies the death mandate and disarticulates the logics of the distribution of precarity. This becomes evident through the examples Macha Colón y los Okapi name throughout the song and La Vampy's daring video response. As they dare to explore desires beyond the rubrics and metrics that constrain our bodies, centering collective enjoyment and empowerment, the deployment of jayaera disrupts the reproduction of colonial logic. If we are meant to be living-dead and in a state of exception guided by the normalization of violence, then experiencing love for the first time, listening to music, and gathering in collective assemblies that center queer joy and relationality subverts the discourses, practices, and technologies that bind us to a set of possibilities and colonial frames of recognition.

Jayaera as a concept has moved around political groups in Puerto Rico for a while now, revealing that not only did Macha Colón's own explanation gain fame and exposure but also that people started to perform *and use* jayaera in their daily lives. From these performances, it could be said that jayaera moves beyond performing life or reclaiming that which has been taken by colonial structures. It is a radical reconfiguration and reworking of the rubrics that make colonized bodies recognizable within normative, hegemonic, and dominant frames. It becomes a queering pursuit insofar as it reworks and deconstructs narratives that constrain the Puerto Rican body by imposing standards that generate normative forms of performing Puerto Ricanness. In a sense, jayaera is the process of becoming unrecognizable to the colonizer, becoming that which resists definition and discipline, the abject. It is a performance of life that engenders new frames[19] that recognize life outside the margins: the lives of queer, feminized, disabled, fat, trans, and other minoritarian subjects as not in proximity to death but, rather, against the conditions set in the necrozone.

Mapping the Idealized Body: La Vampy's Excess

Staring into the camera, singing a comeback response to critics, La Vampy dared to perform to defend her right to enjoy and express herself. In so doing, she flipped the narratives and discourses that hold her to a set of standards that have been historically and culturally reproduced. Her performance and her embodiment served as a container for the projection of aesthetic ideals, representation politics, and the disciplinary and punitive actions taken in order to control the image of Puerto Ricans around the globe. As the song continues, the scenes shift to her wearing a white tank top with white shorts and pitch-black construction boots. The playground where she performs contains a pile of sand, and other elements of construction are seen throughout the video. In some scenes, she licks the pickaxe, and in others, she sits on a swing on top of an exercise ball. Her performance not only gestures to Miley Cyrus's usage of industrial and construction site materials in her music video, but it also sends a message about building an artistic practice, what she does and how she does it. "Ustedes me hacen fuerte" as a phrase portrays her conviction to perform strength, resolution, and determination to continue embodying herself. In this sense, La Vampy becomes an example of jayaera insofar as she centers her enjoyment and pleasure through her dancing, singing, and comedy videos.

As a result of the massive distribution of La Vampy's videos, people constructed narratives around her intentions and the ideals of representation of Puerto Ricans in media both nationally and internationally. The shame surrounding the narrative of the virality of her videos became a form of enacted collective violence toward La Vampy and her aesthetic. Suddenly, she wasn't just a fat, middle-aged, working-class woman who wanted to enjoy herself. She was a disgrace, a totally shameful character that represented everything wrong with the Island, and a setback to years of progress in the attempts to represent Puerto Rico as a civilized, progressive, cultured society. Thus, her performance intervened in the public sphere by disrupting the politics of representation and the normative idealized body. Along with this, she interrupted the imposition of an affective normalcy that discursively constrains the performance of Puerto Rican identity to a set of practices and specific embodiments that are recognized as acceptable by the public. La Vampy's performance in "Ustedes Me Hacen Fuerte," and the narratives constructed around it, provoke a reflection on the marginalization of certain Puerto Rican subjectivities; those made to live in the peripheries for not measuring up to the idealization of the Puerto Rican body and the tyranny of its standards.

Within the context of Puerto Rico, certain performances of identity fail to comply with the covert mandate for decorum and respectability. La Vampy's peripheral performances evidenced the existence of discursive practices that crystallize into what I call the *idealized-normative affective embodiment of the nation*. This embodiment regulates and disciplines bodies, affects, and identitarian performances while also enforcing a set of rules, rubrics, mandates, and standards imposed in order to be able to "represent" Puerto Ricans with supposed dignity and decorum. Discourses and narratives that hold an idealized standard in terms of identity serve as the underpinnings for the weaponization and public reprimand of those who perform an otherwise. Similar to José Esteban Muñoz's "burden of liveness,"[20] majoritarian subjects demand that all Puerto Ricans perform their cultural and national identity in ways that are palatable to elite, hegemonic, dominant narratives seeking to maintain the colonial status quo. In order to understand how this idealization process works, it becomes important to show how the racial, white supremacist, and colonial discourses form this body, ground the normalization of certain affective states, and demonstrate the national negotiations that shape this body.

The end of the nineteenth century brought changes to the racial categories used to describe Puerto Ricans on the Island. The creole elite generated a new racial category that condensed both race and class: raza de color.[21] In the late period of Spanish colonization, Puerto Ricans who were descendants of enslaved people were not identified as Black but instead compounded with other nonwhite Puerto Ricans. When the US invaded the Island in 1898, the creole elite contended with the racialization that came with colonialism. As historian Ileana M. Rodríguez-Silva suggests, during this time, racial discourses were split in two: those who saw the US as a vehicle toward the whitening of Puerto Rico through eugenicist practices and those who argued that race wasn't a problem in Puerto Rico. The latter generated a cultural narrative that located anti-Blackness as part of the United States and therefore foreign to Puerto Rico, causing many to argue that the Island was morally superior. Rodríguez-Silva considers that the construction of a racial harmony narrative paved the way for the silencing of race and the erasure of Blackness on the Island. This silence later shaped the Puerto Rican social imaginary of race, generating narratives that gave ground for the emergence of what anthropologist Isar P. Godreau calls "scripts of blackness," or the institutionalized narratives around and about Blackness.[22]

The scripts of Blackness sustain a narrative of racial harmony in the Island, crystallized in the words of Luis Muñoz Marín: "la gran familia puertorriqueña." Racial harmony contends that Puerto Ricans are a product of the mixture of three races: Indigenous from the Taíno heritage, Black from the enslaved African, and white from the Spanish colonizer. What emerges from this formulation are different things that bear importance to this analysis: (1) the myth of racial democracy, which holds that there was an equal contribution of each race to the ancestry of all Puerto Ricans; (2) the emergence of a phenotypically white, racially mixed body in the cultural imaginary of the nation; and (3) the notion that Blackness is inherited from a distant past. The narrative of racial harmony was adopted and fostered within the Instituto de Cultura Puertorriqueña (Institute of Puerto Rican Culture) and other governmental institutions under the Muñoz Marín administration in the 1950s. The rise of these narratives furthered the progress narratives of the populist government and the development of the Island under US colonial rule.[23] As such, these served as a tool for the erasure of Black bodies, generating a social imaginary that only recognizes Blackness in folkloric representations and within marginalized spaces in the Island. Thus, Blackness is deemed foreign and an excess to the nation.[24]

Consequently, it is worth underscoring that the negotiations with the racialization processes to which Puerto Ricans were subjected are still present today. US-based conceptualizations of race that determine "belonging" to the nation are projected onto the Island through cultural imperialism. Iris Marion Young defines *cultural imperialism* as a vehicle to disseminate the hegemonic ideology that centers the dominant groups' values as normative and universal.[25] This is the case with the idealized Puerto Rican body and how US hegemonic and dominant ideologies of values and respectability impact its formation. This is not to say that Puerto Ricans remain passive and adopt the demands from the cultural-imperialist project, but rather, in the negotiation with the terms and conditions through which Puerto Ricans become recognized as subjects (humans), some of these values are incorporated into the cultural construction of the idealized body. To elaborate further, it is helpful to think with José Esteban Muñoz, who argues that in the context of the US, there is a normative affect that responds to whiteness while other racial identitarian performances are seen as excessive to the nation itself.[26] As such, performances of Puerto Rican identity are heavily influenced by US discourses and the pursuit of whiteness as the vehicle to gain recognition. Turning to the public reaction to La Vampy's performance, we can glean how these discourses operate. The demands directed at her for not representing Puerto Ricans in a dignified manner, and the reduction of her body to an abjected position reminiscent of a nonhuman, shows how this idealized body gains centrality in identitarian formations and negotiations. As such, Puerto Ricans that enact a performance of their identity that distances from this normative affect and idealized body receive a form of violence that devalues and question their worthiness to belong. In a sense, Puerto Ricans disidentify with this white ideal, as they "desire it but desire it with difference."[27]

Of course, not all identity formations in Puerto Rico follow a simple dominant logic whereby Puerto Ricans desire to assimilate into US culture. Undoubtedly, this desire can exist in the many performances of Puerto Ricanness, but to reduce the complexity of this cultural context to this simple formulation fails to comprehend other forms through which the US reproduces its colonial logics within the territory. The notion of a normative affective embodiment assumes Muñoz's assertion of a normative affect in the US that responds to whiteness, while also recognizing that the creole elite and the discursive practices from Spanish colonization that continue to circulate in the political sphere also generate normative discourses around bodies, affects, and Puerto Rican identities. Such is the case of hispanophilia, or the desire to construct the nation by tracing roots to Spain, which we can see in certain social groups.[28] Thus, Puerto Ricans contend with a plurality of discourses around identity formation that come by way of political processes (coloniality), while also catering to the desires of the dominant class. Through this process of negotiation, the construction of the normative Puerto Rican body becomes hegemonic, as it constrains the possibilities of performing Puerto Rican identity in the public sphere.

Culturally sanctioned performances of Puerto Rican identity are constructed by these notions of the normative body. Performances such as the quiet, subordinate Rican who doesn't dare question anything, complies with every demand (cultural, political, social, and even religious), and whose body is considered to be desirable in terms of their aesthetic are part of the many iterations of this normative body. These hegemonic cultural narratives in Puerto Rico regulate affects and other bodies to preserve notions of respectability and of the appeal of Puerto Ricans as a nation. Therefore, all performances of Puerto Rican identity are measured against internalized ideals of how Puerto Ricans *should* be represented. La Vampy's performance and her presumed representation of Puerto Ricans serves as evidence of this process. One of the words used to describe her was *cafre*, a term with a racist history used to describe embodiments, behaviors, affects, and actions that are associated with poor, uneducated, disrespectful, racialized, and Black communities. *Cafre* is often used as a tool for class segregation since those who say it want to distance themselves from this othered social class. La Vampy's performance of her identity and its reception reveal a project to contain, discipline, and civilize bodies while also revealing the many ways Puerto Ricans enact tactics that contest these logics, such as jayaera. These practices gather from the narratives of the normative body that serve to uphold the dominant notions of respectable behavior. The national discourse constructs Puerto Ricans as loud, joyous, and always desiring to celebrate almost anything. If Puerto Ricans are "excessive," then why the commotion with her performance? Why does an individual whose only desire was to celebrate her body and enjoy it by way of inhabiting cyberspace suddenly become subsumed under these exigencies to represent an entire nation? This paradox reveals that there's a differential access to the embodiment of this loudness, the affects of joy, and the display of self-enjoyment. In this context, La Vampy's performance disrupts notions of respectability and desirability required to represent Puerto Ricans, and in doing so, she and her art become heavily discredited. As such, it is not Puerto Rican identity that is in question but, instead, who is able to embody it and how and when it is embodied.

The normative body ideals that constrain the performances of Puerto Rican identity are not foreign to anti-fat motivations. Historically, anti-fatness has been at the center of class marginalization,[29] white supremacy,[30] and other moral discourses that aim to classify fatness as inferior and a product of a lack of rationality.[31] As such, the fat body is "uncivilized," as it is believed that a fat body is a body that cannot control or contain itself; it is an excessive, unruly body. What causes La Vampy's body and performance to be discredited, shamed, and othered is a combination of her feminine aesthetic, the expressions of sensuality and pleasure, fatness, her status as a working-class woman, and the racialized aspects of her body as deviating from the white ideal. As I mentioned before, Ricans disidentify with this white ideal. Through this endeavor, they continue to reproduce frames of recognition[32] that hold bodies to a set of standards in order to appeal to the white, colonizing gaze. La Vampy's body becomes a territory for the deployment of violent discourses seeking to punish her for daring to exhibit her body, for performing her pleasure, and disrupting the status quo and the appeal of Puerto Ricans as a nation. Of course, this deployment occurs both unconsciously and consciously as these ideologies are reproduced in the sociocultural sphere. She embodies jayaera for herself but unknowingly deploys it as a tactic against discourses that seek to contain her excess and unruliness. Moreover, her performance interrogates the existence of the normative body and reveals the classist, racializing, sexist, and heteronormative narratives that undergird it.

La Vampy's performance of jayaera underscores the possibilities for performing life and national identities from marginalized spaces, the peripheries of the nation, the ugly that the colonial project has sought to eradicate, the unruly bodies whose excess is always in detriment to the respectability politics that center the colonizer's recognition. La Vampy represents the abjected subjects of the nation and, through her performances, unmasks the colonizing, disciplinary tactics that affect Puerto Rican bodies—by submitting them to a scale that measures their appeal and ability to represent (or fail to represent) Puerto Rican culture.

Coda

The performances of jayaera show us the possibilities for existing outside of the colonial constraints that limit life itself within the Island. What we can imagine collectively through jayaera is a future that works for us; a future that replaces the nonethics of war with a feminist ethics that centers relationality and our capacity to exist in difference. In a sense, jayaera serves as a tool for imagining an otherwise that moves us in the present toward new horizons that defy death itself. I can only hope that more people dare to embody jayaera and embrace its powers to mobilize and reclaim their agency as political subjects. The post-lockdown world has left us relationally and collectively scarred, alienated through the neoliberal politics of isolation, scarcity, and hyperindividualism. With the rise of fascism internationally, jayaera becomes an option to defy oppressive politics.

Quiero finalizar con una invitación a estar jayao', a jayarse contra la opresión de los sistemas y a rebelarnos desde una política de amor radical que nos permita generar coaliciones y sostener la vida misma en el terreno baldío y árido de la necrozona. Ese es el legado de la jayaera y lo que Macha Colón y La Vampy me han provocado pensar. En las palabras de Macha: Gracias por ayudarme a jayarme.

Esaí Ortiz-Rivera (they/he/elle/el) is a cultural theorist and critic, professor, and currently a PhD candidate in clinical psychology at the University of Puerto Rico. They completed a master's in gender and women's studies from the University of Wisconsin–Madison, where they focused on the intersection of performance studies, decolonial theory, and visual cultures. As a post-disciplinary scholar, they constantly seek to disrupt boundaries within academia to generate knowledges that transcend disciplinary constraints.

Notes

1. The video on YouTube is titled "Wrecking Ball," but on her Facebook page, La Vampy captioned the same video as "Ustedes Me Hacen Fuerte." Carne Frita TV, "Wrecking Ball—Featuring La Vampy," YouTube, November 13, 2013, video, https://youtu.be/apOiBgqGdN8?si=wmHsTZbkrb2F9-gn.
2. More about this on *El Nuevo Día*, "Video de boricua imitando a Miley Cyrus llega a medios estadounidenses," *El Nuevo Día* (San Juan, PR), November 14, 2013, https://www.elnuevodia.com/entretenimiento/farandula/notas/video-de-boricua-imitando-a-miley-cyrus-llega-a-medios-estadounidenses/.
3. Macha Colón, "Jayá—Macha Colón y los Okapi," YouTube, November 22, 2012, video, https://www.youtube.com/watch?v=i2K__dfInfY.
4. Sandra Ruiz, *Ricanness: Enduring Time in Anticolonial Performance* (New York University Press, 2019), 1.
5. Jill H. Casid, "Doing Things with Being Undone," *Journal of Visual Culture* 18, no. 1 (2019): 30–52, https://doi.org/10.1177/1470412919825817.
6. Casid, "Doing Things with Being Undone," 30.
7. For more on this, see Ruiz, *Ricanness*, 4–34.
8. The notion of the fantasy of the good life derives from Lauren Berlant's theorization of cruel optimism. Lauren Berlant, *Cruel Optimism* (Duke University Press, 2011), 23–50.
9. Ruiz, *Ricanness*.
10. Achille Mbembe, "Necropolitics," in *Necropolitics*, trans. Steven Corcoran (Duke University Press, 2019), 92.
11. Nelson Maldonado-Torres, "On the Coloniality of Being," *Cultural Studies* 21, nos. 2–3 (2007): 243.
12. Maldonado-Torres, "On the Coloniality of Being," 255.
13. Judith Butler, "Gender Politics and the Right to Appear," in *Notes Toward a Performative Theory of Assembly* (Harvard University Press, 2015), 33.
14. Alexandra T. Vázquez, *Listening in Detail: Performances of Cuban Music* (Duke University Press, 2013).
15. Vázquez, *Listening in Detail*, 7.
16. Vázquez, *Listening in Detail*, 7.
17. Ruiz, *Ricanness*.
18. José Esteban Muñoz, *Disidentifications: Queers of Color and the Performance of Politics* (University of Minnesota Press, 1999), 181–200.
19. Judith Butler, *Frames of War: When Is Life Grievable* (Verso Books, 2016), 2–12.
20. Muñoz, *Disidentifications*, 181–200.
21. Ileana M. Rodríguez-Silva, *Silencing Race: Disentangling Blackness, Colonialism, and National Identities in Puerto Rico* (Palgrave McMillan, 2012), 6.
22. Isar P. Godreau, *Scripts of Blackness: Race, Cultural Nationalism, and U.S. Colonialism in Puerto Rico* (University of Illinois Press, 2015), 20–21.
23. Godreau, *Scripts of Blackness*, 178–79.

24. Godreau, *Scripts of Blackness*, 183–90.
25. Iris Marion Young, "The Scaling of Bodies and the Politics of Identity," in *Justice and the Politics of Difference* (Princeton University Press, 1990), 122.
26. José Esteban Muñoz, *The Sense of Brown*, ed. Joshua Chambers-Letson and Tavia Nyong'o (Duke University Press, 2020).
27. Muñoz, *Disidentifications*, 15.
28. Godreau, *Scripts of Blackness*, 163–64.
29. Amy Erdman Farrell, *Fat Shame: Stigma and the Fat Body in American Culture* (New York University Press, 2011).
30. Sabrina Strings, *Fearing the Black Body: The Racial Origins of Fat Phobia* (New York University Press, 2019).
31. See Farrell, *Fat Shame*, 59–81. More in Susan Bordo, *Unbearable Weight: Feminism, Western Culture, and the Body*, 10th anniv. ed. (University of California Press, 2003).
32. Butler, *Frames of War*, 5–12.

Afterword

MARISOL LEBRÓN

As I write this, there is no doubt that many of us find ourselves in a moment of danger—in Puerto Rico, in the US, and globally. For over a year, we have been forced to watch a genocide unfold in Gaza in real time on our smartphones, a contemporary nakba that is still ongoing. We are living through the rise of brazenly fascist regimes across the globe that promote the "traditional values" of white supremacy, religious nationalism, and gender oppression with a populist gloss. In Northern California, where I live and work, an anti-democratic movement that has taken hold of the techno-elite preaches of a coming Dark Enlightenment that will provide a "hard reset" and restore the hierarchies of the past. Freedom of the press and academic freedom erode with each passing day. The wealthy are orchestrating a massive upward redistribution of money and resources, further immiserating most of the world's population. The planet is burning and climate activism seeking to address it is increasingly criminalized. There is no question things are dire, but we've also been here before. If we pay attention, we have routes of resistance that illuminate a way out. This collection, grounded in Puerto Rican feminist praxis, helps to provide maps rooted in both the past and present that can lead us to a more just future.

White Feminism Will Not Save Us

In the introduction to the volume, Jessica Pabón-Colón traces her own trajectory of coming into Rican feminism. She notes that the white feminism that is at the forefront of the popular consciousness often stands on the necks of women of color, downplaying their contributions in order to manufacture a cohesive political identity held together only by gender. In contrast, Rican feminism understands that gender is a node through which various forms of economic, racial, colonial, spiritual, and embodied subjugation operate and cannot be disentangled from larger structural forces, even as they shape the deeply intimate and everyday.

As Zoán Tanís Dávila Roldán, a member of the feminist collective La Colectiva Feminista en Construcción (La Cole), notes, Black feminism functions as a spine for Puerto Rican liberation: "There is no possible independence, no possible liberation, no possible anti-capitalism, and no possible feminism without us. There is no revolution possible without us." Rican feminism as it articulates with Black feminist praxis reminds us that we must struggle in solidarity with those occupying the most marginalized positions within society, eschewing respectability politics and superficial forms of normative inclusion.

Building from the insights of the Combahee River Collective, La Cole writes in an "Anti-Racist Manifesto," penned in solidarity with the Black Lives Matter uprisings sparked by the police murder of George Floyd in 2020, "We reaffirm, together with the Black feminists who have gone before us, that the liberation of Black women will be the end of all oppressions, the end of the racial state in all its manifestations and all its articulations with different structures of power. The end of the racial state will be the end of the colonial state and the post-colonial criollo state, it will be the end of capitalism, it will be the end of patriarchy, and it will be the end of systemic and epistemological racism and its identitarian reproductions."

Rather than appealing for rights based on hierarchical markers of privilege, Rican feminism requires the dismantling of white supremacy and colonial capitalism and a centering of those who have been historically marginalized based on race, class, gender, and sexuality. Rosa Clemente, in her reflection on white supremacist violence perpetrated by Puerto Rican men like Alex Ramos in Charlottesville and the former Puerto Rican governor Ricardo Rosselló, notes that Puerto Ricans must commit themselves to Blackness as a political identity rather than a folkloric tradition that foregrounds combatting anti-Blackness as key to opening new worlds. Echoing La Cole, Clemente urges: "Now is the time for us as a people to understand that as long as anti-Blackness exists within our communities, we have a responsibility to fight anti-Blackness and the system of white supremacy by any means necessary. It is up to all of us to push back against the race to whiteness. Because when all Black people are free, we will all be free."

Rican feminism, then, is not about facile categories of identity (i.e., Puerto Rican, woman) but rather real political commitment and solidarity. Rican feminism is rooted in a belief that none are free until all are free. Rican feminism is unwilling to sacrifice anyone for the crumbs of inclusion in an oppressive social order. In this way, the volume provides a crucial ethical blueprint for navigating the moment of danger that we find ourselves in.

Diasporic Longings and Connections

One of the beautiful things that struck me as I read this volume was the way that Pabón-Colón labored to bridge the gulfs that exist between Puerto Rican feminists in the archipelago and the diaspora. As she eloquently puts it, "What would it take for Puerto Rican feminists, wherever and whenever we are, to see each other? To remember each other?" In many ways, Pabón-Colón's questions are rooted in her own experiences of diasporic longing, a feeling that many of us who grew up primarily in the diaspora can recognize, and one that a number of the pieces in the volume address, such as Melissa Rosario's reflections on rematriation and Wanda Raimundi-Ortiz's piece on el monte. These longings for connection speak to the colonial realities faced by Puerto Ricans and how colonialism has been entrenched though forced migration and separation.

At the core of colonial subjugation is an effort to estrange Puerto Ricans from one another and from themselves. This is done through physical distance and through efforts to present the needs, concerns, and experiences of those in diaspora and archipelago as incommensurable. This is not to deny the very real differences that exist in communities in the archipelago and the diaspora, but to say that they confront (albeit in different ways and degrees) similar issues of racial discrimination and white supremacy, economic exploitation, climate degradation, housing insecurity and displacement, cisheteropatriarchy, and state violence and repression. In bringing together feminists from the diaspora and archipelago, this volume facilitates connections and allows for conversations across difference that are rooted in solidarity and mutual recognition. In the movement between archipelago and diaspora across the volume, we see the points of connection necessary to challenge the structures of oppression that Puerto Rican feminists see as shaping the life chances and opportunities of women, femmes, queers, trans folks, Black and dark-skinned folks, and other marginalized populations.

Throughout the volume, we see example upon example of solidarity between Puerto Ricans and between Puerto Ricans and other groups. From the Puerto Rican nationalists discussed by Margaret Power to the Young Lords discussed by former member Iris Morales to the embodied performance in Alicia Díaz and Patricia Herrera's *Entre Puerto Rico y Richmond*, we see the importance of shared struggle and recognition as essential for not only identifying but ultimately working to dismantle oppressive power structures. These examples help to ground us in an ethos of solidarity as we confront this moment of danger, and they remind us that the liberatory project of Puerto Rican feminism not only needs all of us but is also *for* all of us.

Pleasure Against the End of the World

As much as Rican feminism is about struggle, this volume reminds us that there is pleasure in struggle. Culture, play, music, and dance provide venues for connection and solidarity. Protests become sites of joy as sweaty bodies blow up the world and make it anew in dark corners and to pulsing beats, as we saw during the perreo combativo that punctuated the #RickyRenuncia protests of 2019. Queer, trans, and femme Ricans are lodestars—providing us visions of alternative ways of being and being with one another that are rooted in pleasure as a framework for liberation.

As Esaí Ortiz-Rivera puts it, "With the rise of fascism internationally, jayaera becomes an option to defy oppressive politics." A feeling of freedom rooted in queer joy and engagement, jayaera emerges as a mode of resistance that seeks to combat the everyday violence of colonialism, displacement, extraction, racism, and cisheteropatriarchy. Far from frivolous, these forms of pleasure are central to maintaining and restoring the humanity that colonial capitalism seeks to erase. They are also about claiming space in a society structured to engineer the death of vulnerable and marginalized populations. Ultimately, Rican feminism takes pleasure in life. As fascism creeps deeper and deeper into our lives, Rican feminism reminds us to fight like hell for the living because we're all that we've got.

—Marisol LeBrón
Santa Cruz, California
March 2025

Marisol LeBrón is an associate professor of feminist studies and critical race and ethnic studies at the University of California, Santa Cruz. She is the author of *Policing Life and Death: Race, Violence, and Resistance in Puerto Rico* (University of California Press, 2019) and *Against Muerto Rico: Lessons from the Verano Boricua* (Editora Educación Emergente, 2021). Along with Yarimar Bonilla, she is the coeditor of *Aftershocks of Disaster: Puerto Rico Before and After the Storm* (Haymarket Books, 2019). She is also one of the cocreators and project leaders for the Puerto Rico Syllabus, a digital resource for understanding the Puerto Rican debt crisis.

DR. JESSICA N. PABÓN-COLÓN is a diasporic Puerto Rican feminist scholar of identity, community, and resistance. Her essays appear in journals including *Women & Performance: a Journal of Feminist Theory*, *Signs: Journal of Women in Culture and Society*, and *Frontiers: A Journal of Women's Studies*. Her book *Graffiti Grrlz: Performing Feminism in the Hip Hop Diaspora* (New York University Press, 2018) is the first academic study on women's participation within hip-hop graffiti art subculture. She spends her summers as a butterfly doula helping monarchs on their migration journey and can otherwise be found baking breads, crafting, playing with her human and nonhuman children, or in a forest admiring the moss.

The Feminist Press publishes books that ignite movements and social transformation. Celebrating our legacy, we lift up insurgent and marginalized voices from around the world to build a more just future.

See our complete list of books at **feministpress.org**